CIRCLE OF LIFE

CIRCLE OF LIFE

Traditional Teachings of
Native American Elders

JAMES DAVID AUDLIN (DISTANT EAGLE)

Illustrated by Jody Abbott

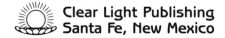

Clear Light Publishing
Santa Fe, New Mexico

Dedicated...

To all the Grandfathers and Grandmothers; to my traditional teachers, the spirit teachers, and all my ancestors, especially the two of my great-grandparents whom I knew in this life, May Snell Soper Vock and Mary Arquette Marshall Audlin; my grandparents, James Clifton Vock and Lillie Erickson Vock, and Louise Kirschner Audlin and Leland John Audlin; and my parents, Eleanor May Vock Audlin and David John Audlin, Sr.; and to my brother, David John Audlin, Jr.; my sisters-by-honor, Karen Stortz, Brightstar, and Two Wolves; my brothers-by-honor, James L. T. Bowier, Jr., Bear, and Otter; Manx, first of friends and wisest of spiritual companions; and all who have danced, sung, drummed, laughed, wept, prayed, and sweated with me as we have walked together along the Red Road. And to all my descendants to the seventh generation and beyond, especially my children, Katharine and John; my daughters-by-honor, Shammara and Odessa; and any descendants yet to come into my life; may your eyes be clear and your hearts be loving. And to all those who know my heart is always open to them. And most especially my Beloved One.

Nia:wen skenno ko:wa.
Inon Thi À:kweks.

Clear Light Publishers
823 Don Diego, Santa Fe, New Mexico 87505
www.clearlightbooks.com

First Edition
10 9 8 7 6 5 4 3 2

Library of Congress Cataloging-in-Publication Data

Audlin, James D.
  Circle of life : traditional teachings of Native American elders / James David Audlin (Distant Eagle) ; illustrated by Jody Abbott.
    p. cm.
  Includes bibliographical references and index.
  ISBN 1-57416-082-6
  1. Indians of North America—Religion. 2. Indians of North America—Rites and ceremonies. 3. Indian philosophy—North America. I. Title.
  E98.R3A83 2004
  299.7—dc22

                                                                    2004012317

Earlier versions of several short portions of this book were first published in *The New Phoenix* and *The Eagle*. The poem "Ode to an Astronaut in Winter", by James David Audlin, is excerpted on page 39. The story told on pages 270–71 is "Moths that Seek the Moon," by James David Audlin, copyright © 1983 by James David Audlin. A brief passage from the novel *A Mirror Filled With Light*, by James David Audlin, is excerpted on page 320.

  Grateful acknowledgement is made to the following: Saba Ali, for excerpts from personal correspondence to the author; Tim Giago (Nanwica Kciji), formerly editor and publisher of the *Lakota Journal* and *Pueblo Journal*, for excerpts from one of his newspaper columns; N. Scott Momaday, for an excerpt from his book, *The Names: A Memoir*; Duncan Sings-Alone, for an excerpt from one of his essays published in *The New Phoenix*; Manx Starfire, for excerpts from her book, *Wild Ways: The Path to Wild Magick*; The University of Nebraska Press, for excerpts from *Black Elk Speaks*, by Black Elk, as told through John G. Neihardt (Flaming Rainbow); *Lakota Belief and Ritual*, by James R. Walker, edited by Raymond J. DeMallie and Elaine A. Jahner; *My People the Sioux*, by Luther Standing Bear; and *The Soul of the Indian*, by Charles A. Eastman (Ohiyesa). All other material quoted, translated, or paraphrased in brief excerpts for illustrative purposes, under the fair use doctrine of American and international copyright law, is hereby respectfully and gratefully acknowledged. All translations are by James David Audlin (Distant Eagle).

Table of Contents

Introduction

Since I was young, it has been my great fortune to have studied with elders from several nations. These elders taught me well—they were far better at teaching than I was at learning—and a great deal more has found its way into written form than I had first estimated. As I continue to reflect on what they said to me many years ago, I find it reveals more unexpected meaning—often beyond my ability, at least yet, to put into words. And, of course, elders are still teaching me today. I realize that their wisdom has sunk deep like rain into the thirsty soil of my memory such that, like a tree growing from a tiny seed, this work has slowly grown greater and stronger over many years, sending roots deep down and reaching out with many branches and leaves.

What I offer you has been this entire lifetime (and perhaps others too) in the learning, and yet it is by no means now or ever fully learned. This book was twenty years in the drafting and another two years in the final composition and editing. I could continue writing for the rest of my life and never finish it, or editing forever and never make it perfect. For most of those years I resisted the frequent suggestion that my written summaries of oral teachings, circulated only among friends and students, be published. But I have finally been persuaded to do so by the fact that most of the elders who taught me have since "dropped their robe" (died) and that there are not many people alive who remember much of what these elders taught. Fewer yet have the ability to translate an essentially oral tradition and conversational-experiential teaching method into written format, into a conversation frozen in form.

This book, therefore, is not my book; let there be no confusion about that. My name goes on the cover because I put the words on paper, but what you hold reflects the teachings of the elders whom I have been most fortunate to know. These teachings belong to no one person or group of people. They are sacred, and sacred things are beyond ownership. They belong to the Creator; they belong to the world. The elders carried them to me; I carry them to you.

This book is not an instruction manual. You cannot read it and become wise in the ways of the Red Road. Would that it were that easy!, but nothing so sublime as spiritual enlightenment comes that conveniently. This is not an intellectual philosophy, as is found among the children of the classical Greek thinkers, but a practical philosophy: apply it and you will live better. If as you read you feel drawn to the Red Road, please understand that you cannot learn it by reading a book, any more than you can learn to swim by reading a book. You can only "jump in the water" by humbly sitting at the feet of a traditionally taught elder and by joining in the sacred ceremonies. If you are meant to walk the Red Road, your teacher will find you; you shouldn't go looking for one.

Reading this book will not make your path through life any easier. In fact, it would be much easier for you to stay with the path that is ordained by the present-day dominant culture than to try to live in accordance with these traditional teachings.

This book is also not meant to be an exhaustive, scholarly compendium of the broad spectrum of Native American spirituality. At most, I have only heard scattered pieces of a few nations' traditions—some of them so smashed by the dominant culture that all there is to gather is pieces—but I don't know the first thing about the traditions of most of the nations of this continent.

Rather, this book is meant to help in its own small way in the accomplishment of two goals: to restore the Sacred Hoop of All the Nations—the circle of all life—lest the broken pieces destroy each other and this Earth, and to pass on to the seventh generation the teachings shared with me by the elders I had the great fortune to know, so that what little I carry will not be lost.

Native Americans now constitute a minuscule proportion of the population of North America; even fewer actually honor that ancestry by keeping their family heritage and culture alive. Some communities and individuals do still keep the old ways alive, while some continue them only in outward display at pow-wows or on stage. But many people of Native ancestry—most, perhaps—don't even do that much to maintain the old ways.

As a result of these factors, a significant possibility exists that the traditional ways will die out entirely. Already, in this continent and worldwide, many nations have been extinguished, and others continue in name only. This is especially a matter of concern since there are abundant signs that there will be cataclysmic changes in the future, and that this wisdom will yet prove essential, as the White Buffalo Calf Woman said, for the salvation of the people—*all* people.

There are individuals who nevertheless maintain that no one has any right to be involved with the Red Road unless that person is full-blooded Native American, even though such exclusivism drives this wisdom even faster toward extinction. They carry this attitude to all sorts of extremes, such as by insisting that only members of their own particular nation have any right to know the first thing about what its elders have taught. Yet, when someone from their own nation chooses otherwise, they amend their dictum, saying in effect that only those individuals within their nations whose views and practice they approve of may learn or teach. What it basically boils down to is that these individuals have set themselves up as judges, reserving to themselves the right to decide who gets to learn or teach. They have forgotten the essence of this sacred path, which the Beautiful One said is to pray with and for all life so the Sacred Hoop is restored; the essence of this path is *Respect.*

I show respect for those who have been taught different ways to walk the traditional Red Road, and I expect the same of them in return. What I share here is only what I have been taught. As one Grandmother often said to me, "Stand in your truth!" Here in this book I stand in my truth and ask you to stand with me in yours.

In 1986 I had a vivid dream of building a Sacred Stone People's Lodge on the quadrangle in the middle of the campus where I attended seminary. As I prepared to sweat, people of all religions and ancestries—hundreds, perhaps thousands—were coming into the lodge. Ten years later, I dreamed that I was in Great Britain talking about Native American spirituality, and a British woman approached me saying she had Native American ancestry dating back to the 1600s, when several Indians were brought over and "put on display." These dreams assure me that these teachings are not for a certain people but *all* people who want to live their lives in harmony with the rest of creation.

The Sacred Hoop of All the Nations has been broken not only through war, enslavement and greed, but through overly pious codification that turns the traditional ways into museum pieces lacking the free flow of spirit. Responsibility lies not only with the European invaders; the fracturing of the Sacred Hoop had begun in some ways before they first arrived. The bloody ways of Tadodaho were vanquished by Skennenrahawi, Jikonshaseh and Aionwantha (Hiawatha), but ever thereafter the Hodenasaunee (Iroquois Confederacy) have often failed to obey the Peacemaker's teachings. There was an ancient history among many nations of revenge killings, vicious tortures, kidnappings and betrayals long before the Long White Bones Man arrived.

Native American culture, before and after the European invasion, has never been the perfect mystical ideal the foolish have often proclaimed it to be. I am equally aware that Western culture—European-American culture—is not the rampaging monster depicted by some. Both have committed heinous wrongs and both have much goodness and wisdom to contribute to the entire world. I am no historian or sociologist; I do not attempt to analyze or justify the good or evil done by either Native Americans or European Americans. Nor do I excuse or apologize for ostensibly negative, even possibly stereotypical, comments about either, whether the comments be mine or an elder's. The purpose of this book is to heal wounds and try to prevent or minimize future catastrophe. But to do that we must first seek to understand the roots and nature of the *sicha* (imbalance) in the world today.

In the face of all the horror of past and present, and before humanity commits the ultimate horror of its own annihilation, the Sacred Hoop must be restored. This ought to be the first goal of every individual who walks or wants to walk the Red Road. Exclusivism, divisiveness and the continued raping of the Earth will never restore the Sacred Hoop. As a certain Grandfather said to me, "There is only one race—the human race—and this race we win, or lose, *together.*"

Blood quantum was never an issue until the United States government established the Bureau of Indian Affairs in the United States and the Department of Indian Affairs in Canada, and it wasn't for my teachers, either. Full-blood are you? The elders weren't impressed. Mixed-blood? Unimportant. No Native blood? Not an issue. What they asked for, rather, was sincerity and commitment, trust and honesty, honor and respect. One medicine man said many times, in several variations, "I don't care about the contents of your pedigree, but the contents of your heart." Another elder, despite growing up poor in the rural Ozarks, educated himself magnificently and became an expert on the religions of the world, studies that convinced him that Native American spirituality is but one expression of the true faith of all the Original Peoples. Another one frequently emphasized to me that ancestry never makes anyone a better person, but that humility, honesty and commitment do. Yet another told me of a powerful vision of people of all races walking up different sides of the same hill, gradually coming close enough to form a circle as they neared the peak.

While ancestry should not be an issue and while these traditions should not be turned into a mimicry of a "traditional way" that never was, these traditions should not be arrogated or ripped out of their proper context. To those individuals who feel a call to the Red Road I say, as the elders said to me, that this is not an easy path. But it is a good path; it is the path of this sacred land on which we live, Turtle Island (North America); and it is good to learn the spiritual "language" of this land and her children. I strongly believe learning something of these ways will help you become a better Jew or Christian or

Muslim or Buddhist; at the least, it will help you to be less of a "stranger in a strange land" (to quote the Torah) as you walk this continent.

How, then, should you read this book? I suggest that you read it the same way I wrote it—slowly. Rather than scanning it quickly and putting it back on the shelf, try reading it at speaking speed. Try reading it aloud, or even have a friend read it aloud to you; this book, after all, represents *oral* teachings, and it would be better absorbed that way. Pause from time to time as you read to let the old teachings sink in through silence. Reread portions of the book that are hard to understand, that are difficult to accept, or that move you strongly for reasons you can't quite ascertain. Think of us as having a conversation; you might ask questions aloud as we go along together, and I suspect they will be answered in due course.

It is primarily the sacred teachings these wise ones carried that are reflected in the text that follows and are the focus of this book. The wisdom shared by the elders is what's important, not the nation or the person who carries it and shares it. The person is only the robe (body) for the wisdom. Just as different people tell the same traditional story in different ways and embody it with different words and embellishments, so the teachings that follow are shaped by the teller. While they are not my teachings, you will find on many occasions that the words in which the teachings are embodied record my own way of orally explaining them, and my own views regarding their interpretation and application. That, too, is traditional; the elders I knew frequently intermixed the personal with the age-less—that, in fact, is how, in each generation, the teachings that can be passed on grow greater and reach out farther, just as a sapling branches into a tree.

Yet, to borrow an analogy made by Gautama Buddha, what they gave me to carry is but a single leaf amid the great forest of sacred wisdom. Even though that single leaf can be a very heavy burden at times for this frail, humble soul to carry, it is yet essential that I, and every one of us who carries no matter how small a scrap of the old wisdom, save it and share it, lest it be lost entirely. For, as one elder taught me, even a single leaf is enough to reconstruct the entire forest; it *is* the forest in microcosm, and—even if it's a single word, say, the word *Respect*, it might be enough to help people listen to the natural world around them and find the rest taught by the other leaves, the other living beings.

When speaking of the traditional ways, I customarily use the present tense. I realize, of course, that, unfortunately, much of what I am saying is traditional is rarely followed these days. Often have I seen on reservations the painful reality of traditional ways largely lost to the ugly specter of poverty, unemployment, drugs, alcohol, sickness, depression and suicide—or to the poisons that come with high-stakes casino gambling, manipulative developers and sudden vast amounts of money. Off the rez, even full-bloods have lost their connection with the traditional ways as they struggle to survive according to the rules of the dominant culture. Still, I use the present tense because these ways, whether they are common today or not, still *are*, in a sacred realm outside of Western linear time, a realm where time is cyclic. They are still there, for those who wish to remember them and even perhaps live by them. I will not let them slip quietly into the past. I hope and pray they will continue to live—and so, even if there are those who may object to my use of the present tense, I use it anyway as a sign of hope that the Circle of Life will come around again after the chaotic and difficult times that lie ahead for this Earth.

The preponderance of teachings in this book come from elders of the Hodenasaunee (Iroquois Confederacy) of the Northeast, the Tsalagi (Cherokee) of the Southeast, and the Lakota of the Great Plains. While these nations have vast differences, they also have much in common, and there is as well a lot of shared history. I also see a strong connection between the Northeast and West-Southwest of Turtle Island. A number of nations with languages and cultures similar to the Lakota—the Saponi, Tutelo, Catawba, Monacan, Winnebago (Ho Chunk) and others—can still be found in the East. In early post-invasion times they had a complex history with such Eastern peoples as the Hodenasaunee, including adoption, and they still have a presence in the East, especially in place names.

Likewise, anthropology and oral history agree that the Hodenasaunee—whose sacred teachings I refer to very often, and who know why I love them with all my heart—originated in the desert regions of the American Southwest, moving by stages to the confluence of the Missouri and Mississippi rivers, into the Ohio lands (where the Huron, Erie, Cherokee and other nations split off), into the Trois-Rivières region of Québec where they were enslaved by the Algonquians, and eventually into the Saint Lawrence-Adirondack region. There in the Northeast they were taught by the Peacemaker, Aionwantha, Jikonshaseh and Handsome Lake. And now a book about the traditional ways written in the Northeast has been released by a publisher in the Southwest—there is an amazing balance and a oneness here.

Ultimately, the philosophy I describe is in large part universal to all the Native peoples of Turtle Island—and, in fact, so my personal experiences tell me, to traditional peoples the world over. You will, therefore, not be surprised to find references to the wisdom of other heritages herein. I do this because I am sure that among my readers will be faithful adherents of the world's great religions; I hope to give them some points of familiarity as stepping stones to help them understand the tradition I seek to describe. I have also done this because I have always been taught that the traditional peoples worldwide—from whom most of the world's religions have sprung—are part of the same heritage. We are *all* a part of the Sacred Hoop.

When I use the common English word for the Creator, I have written it with a hyphen replacing the vowel: "G-d." This is to honor a good and wise tradition of the Jewish people, who teach that the name of G-d should not be written out in full, out of respect. I hope I do not need to add that this English word and its equivalents in Arabic, French, Chinese, Hebrew, Lakota, Kanien'kéha:ka and every other human language, are just words, terms for *the same Eternal Being.* While the Christian understanding (for instance) of G-d is vastly different from the Native American, I still emphatically reject the notion that the Christian G-d and the Native American G-d are different deities. There is, in my view, only one G-d, though different cultures and faiths may vary widely in their understandings of deity—including seeing G-d as singular or plural or even nonexistent, as masculine or feminine, as a transcendent creator beyond the universe or as immanent, very present in and through the universe (panentheism).

I am an ordained clergyperson in the United Church of Christ, a denomination in the Protestant branch of the Christian religion, and I have served local churches all my adult life. I have taken precepts in the Chogye Zen Buddhist tradition, have publicly avowed the Shema and many times participated in Shabbat worship and led the Seder of Judaism, have publicly avowed the Shahadah and accepted the Five Pillars of Islam, and have had the incredible blessing and fortune of learning from elders of other world religions—Bahá'í, Hindu, Native African (Grebo-Ashanti), Pagan and Taoist in particular. These connections, I believe, have put me in a unique position to say, with conviction, that we are all one—and that we should cease from pretending otherwise. "For after all the great religions have been preached and expounded, or have been revealed by brilliant scholars, or have been written in fine books and embellished in fine language with finer covers," said Grandfather Luther Standing Bear, "man—all man—is still confronted with the Great Mystery."

If this book serves any purpose, let it be to help us bring the Sacred Hoop of All the Nations back together again so we and all who live may stand as one in silent awe before that Great Mystery.

A Note on Elders & Language

After much thought and prayer, I decided not to name in this text which elder taught me or said to me which particular thing. The reason for this is simple—this book is not a *potpourri* of the teachings of several individuals from several nations, but a unified practical philosophy that they all shared in teaching me. Ethnologists stress differences and speak of the traditional religions—plural—of this continent; the elders I learned from invariably insisted there is one traditional spiritual way shared, with only relatively unimportant differences in language and practice, by all the original peoples of this continent. Not only have I found that the elders taught me the same essential philosophy, notwithstanding their nations of origin, but, in several cases, they knew each other, and I heard them agree with each other that, despite their different tribal origins, they held a synoptic view on the traditional ways. Moreover, these teachers all said to me that the sacred wisdom is the point, not the individuals who voice it. One elder emphasized that the spirits don't speak Lakota or Tsalagi or Kanien'kéha:ka—or English, or any other language, for that matter—but the language of Spirit: in other words, he said, they are *one*; it is we, we still in the flesh, who do the dividing, not they. I have not exhaustively studied the traditional ways of one nation, but, as is typical especially in the East, where so much has been lost, I have studied with the elders of several nations. And I have found, to my delighted astonishment, that what has been shared with me, even though it comes from several nations, coheres harmoniously into a perfect whole—and one that makes sense, one that helps me live a better life.

I owe these elders everything, and, though my mistakes have been more than many, I pray I have not utterly failed in carrying what they shared with me, that I have not been entirely unworthy of their trust, and that I am still learning from them, even if their physical voices are now stilled. It's pathetically inadequate to say, but it's true; I love and honor all these wise ones so much. Truly, as Benjamin Franklin—a friend to the Native American peoples—said, I stand upon the shoulders of giants. Any wisdom in this book reflects their teachings. Any mistakes in it, and I am sure there are plenty, are my own. Though I am sure not everyone will be entirely pleased with what they read herein, I assure them that the mistakes reflect not only my fallible humanity but also my willingness to try to learn the traditional ways of these elders. I believe that they, along with all wise ones worldwide, create part of a spiderweb of wisdom that I pray will yet save this Earth from destruction if only it is heeded.

I will, however, name here as a group certain elders (some living and some who have since "dropped their robe") whose teachings I describe or whom I quote, in some cases many times and in other cases only once or twice, in the approximate order in which I encountered them: Running Deer (Steve Williams, Cherokee); Yehwenode (Twylah Nitsch, Seneca); Sings-Alone (C. W. Duncan, Lakota-taught Cherokee); Eli and Alloday Gatoga (Cherokee); Longman (Joe Norris, Lakota-taught Cherokee); Red Bear Smith (Cherokee); Grey Horse (Six Nations Seneca); George White Wolf (Lakota-taught Monacan); Rolling Thunder (Paiute-, Lakota- and Tuscarora-taught Cherokee); Thundercloud (James Hawkins, Tutelo-Saponi); Slow Turtle (John Peters, Wampanoag); Big Eagle (Golden Hill Paugussett); Gladys Tantaquidgeon (Mohegan); Mourning Dove (Doris Minckler, Abenaki); Hollis Littlecreek (Anishinabe); Roger Foisy (Algonquian); Blue Eagle (Luc Bourgault, Algonquian); Red Thundercloud (Catawba); Margaret Cromartie (Cree); Grey Eagle (Frederic Van Allen, Mohawk-Mohegan); Big Bear (Oneida); Wassaja (William Gibson, Onondaga); Airy Dixon (Tutelo-Saponi); Henrietta Wise (of an unknown Native American ancestry); Jody Abbott (Munsee); the Rev. Nickolas M. Miles (Powhatan); Gary Kitzman (Menominee); He Who Hunts Underground (Erwin Gordon, Seneca); Donna Coane (Mohawk-Blackfoot); Gloria Fogden Tarbell (Mohawk); and Rudolph Mendoza (Aztec).

There also were others I learned from many years ago whose names are not recorded—an old Lakota medicine man, a young Tsalagi (Cherokee) woman, and a Kanien'kéha:ka (Mohawk) Grandmother being preeminent among them, as well as other elders who have come to me in powerful, vivid dreams and visions. And there have been numerous wise people who I knew only briefly, but whose wisdom impressed me deeply and permanently, even if hardly a word was spoken. And there have been many dear friends—people who have been in the Sacred Stone People's Lodge with me, friends I've made at pow-wows, Native American socials, among the Red Feather Council (formerly the Snake Band—especially its Red Feather Council Singers), the Good Medicine Society, the Association of Native Americans of the Hudson Valley (and especially its Cloudbreakers' Society and Moon Lodge Society) and others I've known of many different traditions who sometimes have themselves mediated the wisdom of the *wakan* or, with powerful questions, evoked it.

There have also been wise wild creatures I have encountered in the woods and fields, skies and waters, the four-legged friends and teachers who have shared their lives with me and who have taught me much about the true nature of love, as well as other nonhuman entities, such as spirits, who have taught me well through dreams and visions.

And there have been teachers of many of the traditional tribal cultures of other continents who have taught me well, whose ways are ultimately no spiritually different from the Red Road—my unbounded gratitude especially (again, in the order in which I met them) to Sri Ramamurti of Hinduism; the Rev. Kenneth Cohen of Taoism; Zen Master Seung Sahn;, Lama Norlha and several rinpoches and lamas of the Vajrayana lineage; the Rev. James Levi Tobias Bowier, Jr., of the Grebo and Ashanti Nations; and Manx Starfire, a High Priestess in the Wild Witch tradition.

In this text I have named the *non*-Native American teachers from whom I have had the honor to learn of a people's oral traditions, and have only named specific Native American elders as sources when the teaching came to me indirectly (when it comes from Grandfather Hehaka Sapa [Black Elk], for instance, as recorded by Neihardt or Brown), so you can go to the original published source and read the teaching in its context. I do, however, name Native American teachers I know or knew personally when the teachings they gave me orally can also be found in published works—Sings-Alone, Rolling Thunder, and Aigle Bleu (Blue Eagle, Luc Bourgault), for example. Published works which are prominently cited in the text are included in a bibliography.

To all of these teachers, of every kind and heritage, named or unnamed, I owe infinite appreciation and love for what they shared with me.

There are no English words for many of the concepts I try to explain in this book. It would be cumbersome in a work of this sort to try to give all, or even a few, of the words in Native American languages for these concepts. Therefore, through much of this work, I have chosen primarily to use the Lakota terms, even though I am not at all related by blood to that great and noble people and have no standing among them, and even though the preponderance of the traditional ways discussed in this book accords not with the traditions of the Plains Nations but with those of the Northeastern Nations, particularly the Hodenasaunee (Iroquois Confederacy). I understand that to do so risks perpetuating the stereotype that depicts all Native Americans in the "leather and feather" of the Plains Nations. But I do so for three good reasons. The first is that it was from a Lakota medicine man that I first learned about these ways—beginning at the formative age of twelve—and the first way one learns something remains lifelong the strongest. The second is that, thanks to the recorded teachings of such wise men as Lame Deer and Black Elk and the work of sensitive, dedicated scholars like James R. Walker, Dennis and Barbara Tedlock and Raymond J. DeMallie, the Lakota perspective on these traditions is more widely known and better understood than any other. (The Lakota long ago "let the horse out of the barn.") The third, and historical, reason is that nations linguistically and culturally affiliated with the Lakota, Dakota and Nakota lived and still live in the East, so the roots of their traditions are nourished by both the great forests of the East and the great tallgrass plains of the West.

I want to be very clear that I sometimes use Lakota terms (or their equivalents in the closely related languages of Nakota and Dakota) in ways that may be at variance with common use among the Great Sioux people, including their medicine men and women, or with ethnologists and other non-Native scholars. None of these should be held in the least responsible or accountable for these non-standard usages; I take full responsibility for them, and intend no offense to anyone by using them. To the elders of the Lakota, Dakota and Nakota people I offer my humble gratitude and respect.

Three words bear particular explanation.

Washichu (sometimes spelled *wašichu*) is commonly understood as referring to people of European ancestry. Given its root meaning ("takers of the fat"), I use it rather to refer to people, of whatever ancestry, who arrogate to themselves without giving fairly in return. Several elders have insisted to me that this is more correct, since, of course, many people of European ancestry aren't at all greedy, and people of other ancestries (including Native American) can be extremely greedy.

Washte (sometimes spelled *wašte*) usually carries the same connotations as the English words "good" and "pleasant," or even "attractive," such as in reference to a person's appearance. I use the word exactly in this way, however I limit it to what is good, pleasant or attractive about things or persons in human society—the kind of goodness that is gathered and maintained by human endeavor.

Wakan is generally used to refer to the sacred, to the clear presence of Spirit. I use it in exactly this way; what is perhaps unusual is that I present in this book a dialectic between *washte* and *wakan* that was shared with me by one elder, and I believe is supported by early ethnographers' notes on the teachings of such medicine men as George Sword and Napa (Finger).

Hau, mitaquye oyashin!

I

Time & Place

Many of the original North American peoples refer to this continent as Turtle Island. One reason is the continent's shape. The North American continent has the ovoid shape of a turtle's shell with a spiny ridge, the Rocky Mountains. Protruding from the shell are the tail of Mesoamerica, the limbs of Florida, Baja California, Alaska and Québec-Labrador, and the head pointing toward the North Pole. This continent also has thirteen discrete cultural and geographical regions that correspond to the thirteen plates on a turtle's shell. Since the traditional year also has thirteen moons in it, the circle of the turtle's shell represents the Circle of Life both in time and in place: the circle of the year and all the nations on thirteen-plated Turtle Island.

Another reason for calling this continent Turtle Island is that traditional elders say the natural, sacred way for the people to govern themselves was taught to them by the very nature of the turtle. The seven vital points of the turtle represent the holy person, who is always looking to the needs of the people and the land. These points, associated with the seven Sacred Directions, are the four legs for the cardinal directions, the head for zenith, the tail for nadir and the heart for the seventh direction, the one in which we go in dreams and visions and when we die.

Some of the old medicine men and women still know how to talk with the turtle and other living beings in their own language and are no doubt aware of the turtle's primacy in this land. The turtle, a survivor of the cataclysm that destroyed the great dinosaurs, carries a survival wisdom that may enable us to survive the coming cataclysm.

This ancient history may indeed be reflected in stories that are told about the turtle, such as this one of the Maya:

In the earliest days, when the Earth was covered with water, the animals tried, one by one, to create land, so they could stop swimming and rest. After all the other animals tried and failed, it was Turtle who—despite suffering some derision from the others, even though they themselves had failed—dove down many, many times to the bottom of the primeval sea, holding her breath far longer than any other creature can, and, bringing up a small mouthful of dirt each time, eventually created this continent.

The Kanien'kéha:ka (Mohawk) tell a slightly different version of this story, describing the time following the advent in this world of the first woman, Iotsitsisen (Mature Flower), about whom I will tell you more a little later.

In this telling of the creation story, Turtle is willing to let the animals put mud on his great shell to make a land for Iotsitsisen to live on. Beaver and Otter try to bring mud up from the bottom of the endless, primeval sea, but drown. At last, Muskrat tries as well, and also dies, but in his lifeless mouth is enough mud to create land. The woman lives in this land, and gives birth to a daughter who makes love with the West Wind and gives birth in turn to twins.

Right-Hand Twin, maker of hills and lakes and flowers, and Left-Hand Twin, maker of cliffs and swamps and whirlpools, are rivals much like Cain and Abel or Jacob and Esau. Right-Hand Twin eventually kills his brother with a deer antler and throws him over the edge of the Earth. As a result, Right-Hand Twin rules the Day and the Earth, and Left-Hand Twin rules the Night and the Underworld. His Grandmother, Iotsitsisen, condemns Left-Hand Twin, and he, out of anger, kills her. He cuts off her head and throws it up in the Sky, where it becomes the Moon. He throws her body into the water, where it becomes all the fish nations. Out of her womb grows the corn, and from her breasts the beans and the squash—the Three Sisters. And, from her heart, the tobacco grows.

This is shapeshifting. And it's beyond good and evil: she dies but she lives in a new robe. There is no death; only a change of robes (bodies), a change of worlds. And to this day, Right-Hand Twin is associated with the goodness of daytime and social life (the *washte*), and Left-Hand Twin is associated with the sacredness of nighttime and the wilderness (the *wakan*).

The Kanien'kéha:ka also tell a story that parallels the Western myth of continental drift:

In the beginning, all the families of the world lived together on the shell of a turtle (Turtle Island). However, as time went by, they began to argue and even fight with each other. Seeing this, the Creator pulled the shell's thirteen sections apart, separating them by impassable, undrinkable gulfs of salt water, to prevent them from continuing to bicker with each other.

And so we see from the beginning that stories create the world around us, and the world around us gives us her stories in return. The scientists say this is not so, but it *is* so—in a spiritual sense.

Turtle Island is sacred because it is the land of our ancestors. As Plenty Coups, Chief Sealth (Seattle) and Luther Standing Bear said, every step we take is taken upon the dust of our ancestors. All the traditions we have came from them. All the stories we tell came from them. They are always around us, guiding and protecting us, and we must honor them in keeping the sacred ways.

Turtle Island is also sacred because it is the land of our descendants. Faithkeeper Oren Lyons expresses it in this way: With every step we take, there are faces looking up at us from the Earth, and these are the faces of our descendants. So we must remember to care for the Earth, and to pass on the sacred stories and ways to the seventh generation.

Turtle Island is also sacred because the Creator made it. Because the Creator made it, everything in it is sacred, and every being (plant, animal, spirit and "inanimate") teaches us something of the wisdom of the Creator.

One of the most sacred of traditional ceremonies is the Sacred Stone People's Lodge (often called the sweat lodge). The structure in which it is kept is sometimes called "Turtle." This is first because of its carapace-like shape, with the small entrance like the head hole of a turtle, the spirit trail extending from it like a neck, and the Sacred Mound like a head. It is also so called because during the ceremony we sit right on the Earth, Turtle Island. Sitting inside the structure, we are like the turtle inside her or his shell. As suggested in the Mayan version of the Turtle Island story, we can no more be separated from the Earth than can the turtle from its hard breastplate, and no more separated from the Sky than can the turtle from its dorsal battlements. So, when we keep this ceremony, we honor and remember our sacred land, Turtle Island.

Every religion in the world looks to certain places as its holy centers. Christian churches were often situated so that the altar is oriented toward Jerusalem; for this reason, their entrances are called the westwork. Muslim *masjids* (mosques) include a *mihrab*, a niche that points out the *qiblah*, the direction toward

Makkah (Mecca). Houses of worship, worldwide, are often built on spots that have long been considered sacred, at the intersections of ley lines. In Europe, many great cathedrals, such as Chartres, are above locations that had been venerated in the Pagan tradition, the pre-Christian tribal ways of that continent. The reason for this is that such places serve as dynamos of spiritual energy, revitalizing the land and living things.

Hodenasaunee (Iroquois Confederacy) leaders warned early European immigrants not to "sever the spirit from the body." But, in establishing the religions they brought with them, they inadvertently broke the connection between sacred land and sacred spirit. These days, most people look to holy places so distant that they will never see them in this life. In fact, most houses of worship are built wherever the worshippers can afford to purchase land, and they are pointed toward the street, for ease of ingress, with little thought to their larger orientation in place and time.

Turtle Island was and still is, as a whole, sacred to the peoples native to it. It had and still has places that are especially sacred to those people. But the people who came to this continent saw here only unfamiliar forests, lakes, mountains, deserts and plains. So the spiritual centers of the native peoples such as the Black Hills, Big Horn Medicine Wheel, Mount Shasta, Onondaga Lake and the Black Mesa, became, in the eyes of most members of the dominant culture, just land like any other, to be used, occupied or plundered at will.

With the power of the holy places of Turtle Island raped by greed and foreign law, the Native people are not being cleansed of their spiritual poisons, as regular pilgrimages or the great ritual ceremonies otherwise would do. Without a sacred center to draw the spirit, the integrity of the community is weakened and it becomes easier to slide into dehumanizing extremes.

What, then, is the solution? To reclaim the holy places of the traditional cultures of this continent and reclaim them as holy, not to be owned, regulated or exploited. Christians, Jews, Muslims, Hindus or Buddhists can benefit by attuning themselves to these sacred sites and letting their spiritual energies cleanse and revitalize their souls. As the Creator instructed Moses: Take off your shoes. Literally, maintain a contact with the Earth, our mother, who nourishes us, and metaphorically root yourself in this land—for this land is holy. If we do this and pray regularly, with and for all living things, we will cease exploiting this sacred land and its children, both human and nonhuman.

I've heard there is a traditional nation in the desert lands, I think in Mexico, that every day gathers before dawn at the edge of an eastward-facing cliff. There in the darkness the people join together in an ancient song-prayer that, they say, "raises the Sun." They maintain that, if some morning they were not to do this, the Sun would not come up. And who can say that they're wrong? I hope we never have to test their conviction. Each of us, according to whatever our spiritual tradition may be, ought to greet the dawn and perform our other spiritual activities with equal seriousness. Yes, perhaps the Sun will come up anyway, whether we do this or not; but it is certain that, if we do not attend to our spiritual responsibilities, our souls will eventually rise no more, but go dark and die.

The sacredness of these lands is rooted not only in place, but in time. The new peoples in this continent think of the formative Sacred Events in their own religious traditions as having happened long ago. For the original peoples, the Sacred Events, being sacred, happen outside of time altogether; not really in the past, present or future, but in one transcendent infinite moment that cannot be located on the time line of linear events. In science-fiction terms, they are present in another dimension of time. These Sacred Events are very close at hand in every moment, if only we know in what temporal direction to look. They don't take place in the kind of time the Greek philosophers called χρονος (*chronos*), ordinary "clock time," but in καιρος (*kairos*) — what Mircea Eliade and Paul Tillich called the Eternal Now, what Plato and Jesus called the ἀεον (*æon*), what in Arabic is called *waqt* and in Farsi *dam*. Whenever the Sacred Pipe is passed, it is again the White Buffalo Calf Woman who places it in our hands so that we may remember our connectedness to the Earth and Sky and all living things. Whenever we enter the Sacred Stone People's Lodge, we are not sweating alone, but with all our Grandfathers and Grandmothers, with all life now about us in the Medicine Circle, and all our descendants as well, to the seventh generation.

Therefore, when we enter into the sacred place of this or any religious tradition, we properly travel not so much in ordinary as in sacred place and time, to the center of the holy story itself. On many occasions when people have been in ceremony with me, they come out again to be stunned at how much or how little "clock time" has gone by. Going into the Sacred Stone People's Lodge in broad daylight, we come out again, after what seems at most an hour or so, to darkness and a full Moon; or we are in the lodge for what seems to be many hours, and come out to see the Sun has hardly moved at all. Emerging, we realize dimly that we are coming back to ordinary place and time, τοπος (*topos*) and χρονος (*chronos*), from a sojourn in sacred place and time, γαια (*gaia*) and καιρος *(kairos)*. When celestial time and place are entered into in a worshipful manner, one can step out of ordinary existence for a while and participate in the Story. We step out of the *washte* (the ordinary) into the *wakan* (the sacred). Just as Jews tell Haggadah or Christians tell the story of the Eucharist—so too the traditional peoples join in the retelling of their sacred story, actually living it in the moment of its being told.

How, then, do the original peoples understand the universe around us? I will answer this question according to the way I was taught. You have to remember that, although the core understanding is the same, its expression varies from nation to nation, and even from individual to individual within the same nation. That is because the spirituality of the original peoples is handed down by elders, not by a religious hierarchy, and it is not based on a required set of tenets that one is expected to believe in. Thus there will be variations on a common theme—how the desert nations or the nations of the far North or the fishing people of the Northwest understand the universe will not be identical to how the Great Plains people or the Eastern Woodlands people do.

I was taught that, wherever we are, we are at the center of the universe. The horizon around us reminds us of this fact. No matter how far we go, we still see the edge of the visible Earth equidistant around us in all directions; no matter how far we go, the Sky still stretches itself over us. This constant presence reminds us of the Sacred Hoop of All the Nations, *Changleshka Wakan*, and the Circle of Life, *Womime Wichoni*. These two are essentially the same circle, one in space and one in time, like warp and weft, weaving all reality into a family relationship. The first is the great circle of all living things, the sum of all the circles of all the various nations of animals, plants, spirits and rocks, in which every nation and every individual is a vital part. The second is the great circle that encompasses all the smaller circles of the seasons, of day and night, of infancy-growth-maturity-old age, of the Moon, and so on. Joseph Epes Brown recorded Hehaka Sapa (Black Elk) as saying in *The Sacred Pipe* that peace enters the human soul when it recognizes its oneness with the universe and that the Creator dwells in the Seventh Direction, at the center of the universe, which is everywhere and within each person. This is the same compassionate peace known to most other spiritual people, such as the Hindus in the phrase *tat tvam asi* ("that thou art"), in the oneness of *atman*, the individual soul, with Brahman (G-d). "In them [the Great

Powers] all things are one," Mari Sandoz quotes Bad Arm as saying: "the rock, the cloud, the tree, the buffalo, the man." He ended his statement by giving the sign for the All—the right hand, palm downward, moving in a horizontal arc, at the height of the heart.

A naturalist friend of mine has shared with me his recollection of first visiting the Santo Domingo Pueblo. "As I drove onto the reservation, I felt a comfortable transformation that I can only liken to the time I visited a prison as a part of a county grand jury. We left the prison after a three-hour 'tour.' As I walked out the front gate into the sunshine and fresh air, I felt a tremendous weight lift off me. I had that same feeling that day as I departed the non-Indian world and entered Santo Domingo. Dan Lavato's Trading Post was so homey, the people so lacking in pretense, that I didn't want to leave. The Squash and Turquoise Clans' dances, adorned in evergreen, seemed so familiar. The world of McDonald's golden arches has never seemed so far away."

One Grandmother told me of her own first visit to Santo Domingo, and feeling for the first time a sense of home other than with her immediate family. "It was what was *not*—not money, position, exploiting each other, development or expansion, not overlooking everything to get somewhere else, not seeing everything as something to use for personal gain. The People were talking about the world from inside the world. The whole world a sacred kiva, church, synagogue, masjid, temple. The whole world where there is no outside or inside because the world is infinite—full of air and light, fire, earth, water, rock, stars, and all, and understanding we being made up of all this."

No matter how far we travel, we are always on *Maka Ina*, our Mother Earth, and beneath *Atë Makpiyah*, our Father Sky. No one has ever gone so far as the edge, where Father Sky comes down and meets Mother Earth—except, of course, in some of the primordial stories. We can no longer do this, the old ones tell us, because so much has changed, so much spiritual wakefulness has been lost. That place is very sacred, *lela wakan*, and only sometimes do we glimpse it in our dreams and visions. Besides, we have no need to find it— Mother Earth provides us with shelter, water and food, and Father Sky arches over us, providing us with air, light and water.

I was taught to know Grandmother as a transcendent presence beyond the immanent presence of Mother Earth, and to know Grandfather as a transcendent presence beyond the immanent presence of Father Sky. And yet they are very close to us—to quote from Saint Augustine, they are "closer to me than I am to myself"—and they guide, protect, admonish and teach us constantly.

The Earth and the Sky are, ultimately, robes (bodies) for the transcendent presence of the Creator as Grandmother and Grandfather.

No matter how far we go, we are always at the crossroads of the Red Road and the Blue Road. The Red Road circles sunwise from East, birth and childhood, to South, adulthood, to West, old age and death, to North, the between-lives (what the Vajrayana call the *Bardō*). The Red Road, as represented by the course of the Sun through the day, images for us the traditional ways of the ancestors, and also the course of life—the life of each individual and the life of all things, the Earth and Universe, collectively. The Blue Road, which goes from West to South to East to North, and is represented by the course of the Moon through the month, images for us the pathless path beyond life and everything familiar, in the Spirit World or Dream World (the *Bardō*, where we go in dreams, visions, and when we die). (I will tell you later about two other roads, the White Road and the Yellow Road.) The fact that we are always at the crossing of these two sacred roads teaches us that they are properly found together, and we deny one or the other at our peril.

The Red Road is commonly understood as a path from East to West, but it is really a circle. The sunwise path is, as the name implies, associated with the day. Activities, living beings and things that are *washte* (ordinary, predictable) are associated with the sunwise path. The coming of the day and the seasons occurs in a sunwise manner. Sunwise is also the way the other Stars take: they revolve sunwise around the North Star.

The Blue Road follows the course of the Moon, which appears first in the West as a new crescent, moving to full phase in the South at its zenith, then rising as a waning crescent in the East before dawn, and finally "appearing" as an invisible new Moon to the North thereafter. The darkness of the Moon travels moonwise across her face—from right to left. The Blue Road is commonly understood as a path from North to South, but it too is really a circle. The moonwise path is—as the name implies, associated with the night. Activities, living beings, and things that are *lela wakan* (particularly powerful, sacred, dangerous and mysterious) are associated with the moonwise path—it is most often during the night that we see or hear the supremely wild creatures, the owls and wolves, for instance, and when the medicine men and women most often gather the rare, powerful herbs that are predominantly *wakan*. In the dark of night, we see shapeshifting presences that we might not so readily see in the daytime. And storms, at least in this continent, usually come from the West or North, not the place of beginnings, the East.

Sunwise and moonwise have their parallels in other traditions; the Pagans, for instance, speak respectively of deocil and widdershins.

The sunwise circle and the moonwise circle are different manifestations of the same circle: the Sacred Hoop that binds all the nations. These two great ways interpenetrate to bring about life: male and female, beings of the day and beings of the night, *washte* and *wakan*. Indeed, if you are observant, you will realize that sunwise and moonwise reflect each other. If you walk sunwise around a tree, observe the tree and you will see it is, relative to you, like a reflection in a mirror, "moving" moonwise around its axis. If you trace your finger sunwise around the rim of a bowl, it is the same as if the bowl were rotating moonwise beneath your finger. If an eagle flies from West to North to East to South, it is circling sunwise from its own point of view, but it appears to be flying moonwise to us who watch from below.

No matter how far we go, we are surrounded by members of our sacred family: the plant nations, the animal nations, the nations of two-leggeds, the spirit nations, the rock nations, the nations of the lakes and rivers and swamps and deserts and forests and mountains. As family members do, they help us, and we help them. Some help us with their fruits or flesh. Some help us by providing useful materials. Some provide us with their great healing powers. Some afford us protection. But all of them are made by the Great Mystery, all of them are therefore touched with the divine, all of them have their sacred message to teach us.

The traditional peoples understand the Stars as a nation of living beings, with their own natures and customs, the same as any other species. Far from being ignorant savages, the original peoples have always known, long before European scientists realized it, that the Stars are suns with planets of their own with life on them, and that the Sun is a Star with his own family of planets. His presence fills the day and marks the Red Road, while the Moon and Stars fill the night and mark the Blue Road. Traditional peoples worldwide honored these celestial nations with great stone circles like Stonehenge and Avebury in Great Britain, the pyramids and ziggurats of Africa, Asia and South America, and the great medicine wheels of North America.

Like all cultures, nations in this continent have their stories of how this or that constellation came to be. And long before science fiction writers did, they spoke about people coming here from other stars and planets. Many of them tell of an earthly man falling in love with a star woman, or vice versa. A medicine woman I knew spoke of star people, human beings with the reincarnated souls of individuals from other planets. The Hodenasaunee (Iroquois Confederacy) speak of Sky Woman, also known as Iotsitsisen (Mature Flower), who fell through an opening beneath a removable "tree" in the Star World, hurtling through the Heavens on a beam of light toward a watery world beneath, her fall slowed by waterfowl, and guided by Beaver to the safety of Turtle, the only solid surface in all this ocean. The Anishinabeg (Ojibweh or Chippewa) tell how the Creator involved the Star People in the creation of humanity. Their elders, according to John Boatman, tell of seeing circular sky-vehicles bringing people from other planets. The Hopi and Diné, among others, say they lived on several worlds before coming to this one. The Blackfeet have a story about a hunter who sees seven women coming to visit Earth in a "star basket;" he falls in love with one, and she agrees to take him in the star basket to ask permission of her father, the Sun, to marry her. The Hidatsa speak of coming to Earth in a "flaming arrow," or space ship. Similarly, the Dogon of West Africa say they came here from the Pleiades.

At the same time, traditional people are aware that the people in the Star Nations (the stars, planets, comets and so on) are physical presences, but also spiritual entities. This is no different from the beings in the world around us: an eagle or a bear is both a physical presence and a spiritual entity. So traditional peoples can accept that human beings have walked on the Moon, but they do not think the astronauts ever came near Grandmother Moon, the spiritual entity. Whatever beings may live there the astronauts were entirely unable to perceive, for the doors of their perception were closed, as William Blake put it, letting them see only through narrow chinks in their cavern. In the same way, it is doubtful whether the vast majority of mainstream Americans have ever been aware of the sacred Mother Earth (the spiritual entity) or the spirits that move about on her.

Traditional people have always been aware from observation that some stars remain stationary and other members of the Star Nations move in predictable ways (the Moon, planets, comets), and yet others move in unpredictable ways (meteors). On almost any clear night—especially at the time of the Perseid and Leonid meteor showers—one can see members of the Star Nations coming back down to Mother Earth to be reborn.

The Stars are spirit presences to and through whom we can pray, who can mediate for us with the Creator. They constitute a celestial map that can guide us, a pattern of meaning and familiarity. The pattern in the night Sky is reflected by the patterns in the Earth. So, by observing the Star Nations, we can be prepared for what is coming to us. They are high above us, and can see all our paths, just as an eagle sees farther than a groundling. Like a mirror in the Sky, the Stars help us to see far, and know what is on our path. Many nations speak of the Stars as the campfires their ancestors light on their way to the blessed lands; for most of the traditional nations they represent in some way the guiding, protective presence of our ancestors.

Tim Giago (Nanwica Kciji) has written about how the Lakota elder Jim Holy Eagle, who lived to be more than one hundred years old, spoke of the Grandfathers of past generations looking at the Heavens by night and pondering the vastness of the universe, and wondering if there is an end to it or if it goes on forever. Such immensity, Holy Eagle taught, gives the people their spirituality and their strength. It also gives the great gifts of humility, and awe and wonder in the face of the truly infinite: the Great Mystery beyond any knowing, the Creator.

The newcomers and the original peoples mark the passage of time in different ways. The European calendar is cobbled together from many sources. It borrows from the Roman (two months, for example, being named for the Roman Emperors Julius and Augustus Cæsar), from the Scandinavians (hence weekdays named for Thor and Freya), from the Druids (hence a weekday named for Odin), and so on. It is strictly a solar calendar, since it stays with the 365¼-day length of the solar year by adding a leap day every four years.

Some ethnic groups, such as Jews and Muslims, are familiar with another kind of calendar, based on the lunar year, which is based on the Moon's cycle. The Moon's cycle lasts 29½ days. Therefore, a twelve-month lunar year is 354 days. This is 11¼ days short of completing the 365¼-day solar year. A thirteen-month lunar year is 18¼ days longer than the solar year. The European calendar solved this problem by adding half-days to some months and a day and a half to all the others (except for February, which is still a lunar month in its length). As a result, they're not lunar months ("moonths") any longer.

Each of the original peoples have their own way of correlating the solar and lunar years. Most nations solve this by adding in most years a thirteenth moon, a thirteenth month, to either the preceding or succeeding year, comprising the intercalary days. In the traditional Hodenasaunee (Iroquois Confederacy) calendar, the year begins on the winter solstice, and progresses through twelve lunar months. If there are days left over between the end of the last lunar cycle and the winter solstice, or days between the solstice and the beginning of the next lunar cycle, these intercalary days form the most sacred thirteenth moon, during which the New Year ceremonies take place. Among many nations, including the Hodenasaunee and Tsalagi (Cherokee), these ceremonies were times of sacred chaos, of completely unrestrained behavior, and cleansing. At the New Year itself, the usual patterns of appropriate behavior were suspended. All debts were forgiven. All those punished were released from punishment. Inebriation, sexual activity and other bawdy behavior were the "rule" rather than the exception.

The purpose of the chaos was to cleanse the psychological detritus from the previous year, so the new year could begin with a clean slate. The newcomers to this continent still have a lingering cultural memory of this ancient worldwide tribal tradition in the exuberant behavior they exhibit on New Year's Eve and *Mardi Gras*—though it is, ironically, now limited by law and custom, forbidding the healthiest and most purgative kinds of chaotic behavior, such as sexuality, and limiting revelers to the most unhealthy kinds of license, such as drunkenness and rowdy behavior.

In the midst of all this madness the medicine people would remain "sane," going about and watching to ensure everyone's safety. They would also watch the night skies and call an end to the intercalary days when the Heavens declared it was time.

Among the original peoples, specific sacred days vary from nation to nation, but generally they include the summer and winter solstices, fall and spring equinoxes, either the full or new Moon or both, the beginning of planting season, the beginning of harvest season, the migrations of the geese, the first snow, the breakup of the ice and the like—very clear and practical days that anyone can observe. The Kanien'kéha:ka (Mohawk), for example, have ceremonies for the vernal return to life of the maple, the coming of the thunder, the planting of the seeds, the gathering of the strawberries and of course autumn's ingathering. In every nation other important festivals, such as namings, weddings or the investiture of a new chief, take place in harmony with the movements of the Sun, Moon and Stars.

What months are called varies from nation to nation, and within the same nation. There is no official, standardized *name* for each month but rather signifiers. The same individual may even use different signifiers at different times. If somebody says, "the Moon when the apple tree blossoms," it is presumed that the hearer knows when that is, which is only possible if the hearer knows the local seasons. The same person next time might say, "the Moon when robins lay eggs," using a different signifier for what is to most Americans the same Moon. Anthropologists mistakenly think of these signifiers as names— leading to much misunderstanding of the traditional ways. To the traditional mind, they are not the "same month," since there is no "reality" separate from the event itself. These are two *different* months that, to the most Americans' way of thinking, happen to come at the same time (something like the way, in Judaism, that Pesach (Passover), the Feast of Unleavened Bread, and the Feast of First Fruits all arrive concurrently).

The dominant culture names years with numerals. Thanks to an arithmetical error by Medieval monk Dionysius Exiguus (Dennis the Short), A.D. 1 is several years after the birth of Jesus Christ. All the celebrations of the beginning of the third millennium were, therefore, based on a mistake! Traditional peoples, rather, use descriptors that evoke the story behind "the year the buffalo went West" or "the year of the forest fire," and so on. Peter Nabokov describes, in *A Forest of Time*, the history sticks that recorded these descriptors. As with moons, outsiders will never fully understand the descriptors used by any particular nation—in other words, this heritage of cultural history is protected from outsiders.

Comets, novae, eclipses, and other unusual astronomical events were always traditionally seen as auguries of significant, unusual events on the Earth. These events were extraordinary, and thus clearly *wakan*: sacred, disconcerting, mysterious and portentous. Scientists now can predict these events well in advance, but that only robs them of their *wakan* nature, rendering them *washte*, common and ordinary, as "civilized" as the arrival of the next crosstown bus. This scientific worldview has tried to suggest that there is no correlation between stellar and earthly events, but the Native traditions are axiomatically based on the belief that there is one.

For us who walk the Red Road it is important to pay attention to the teachings of the stellar beings and, as much as possible, to live in accordance with them. If we plant our crops with the Moon, and reap with the Moon, for instance, our crops will grow better. If we live as well in accordance with the interpenetrating circles of the Heavens, we will be happier and wax stronger.

In the dominant culture, it is assumed that all units of time, such as seconds, minutes and hours are equal in length. The assumption that time is a steady flow is so strong that atomic clocks are reputed to be accurate enough to show that the Earth itself is inaccurate, inasmuch as days vary in length by infinitesimal fractions of a second. But is it not, as Einstein taught, all relative? The scientists assume that atomic clocks are wholly accurate; could not one say with equal truth that the atomic clocks are inaccurate when compared to the Earth?

In the same way, units of place are also considered to be always of the same length, whether they are in Manhattan, the Himalayas, or even beyond the galaxy. As a result of these assumptions, the dominant culture sees little relationship between time and place. Still, for members of all cultures, the experience of time is that two units of time are not the same in length. When one is anxiously awaiting the birth of a child, or staring at test questions without knowing the answers, or sleeping on the beach in the warm Sun, time passes at varying rates. Children experience a year as passing much more slowly than adults do, and for the very old days blur into just "the day" as they leave χρονος (*chronos*) altogether and move into pure καιρος (*kairos*).

The dominant culture insists on an "objective reality" beyond our senses, measured by the clock, and concludes that our variable experience of time is inaccurate. Since the arrow of time (as Stephen Jay Gould put it) flies so fleetingly, Benjamin Franklin's alter ego Poor Richard advised, "Time is money." People often try to slow time to maximize its utility, setting schedules and quotas to contain it—and to forestall the ultimate strike by time's arrow: death and destruction. Hence the demand to produce ever faster within the allotted time, creating a subliminal malaise that causes time's arrow to speed faster yet.

Often mainstream Americans are frustrated by the apparent lack of a "decent time sense" on the part of original people, seeing them as typically late and lazy, imprecise in their calibrations of time. Once a Tsalagi (Cherokee) friend invited me to a Sacred Stone People's Lodge ceremony that night at 8:00. When I got to his home, however, there was no sign of him. Unconcerned, I just got the fire going to heat the rocks. Most people would probably have been quite frustrated by his absence. Even Native Americans joke about "Indian Standard Time" and other peoples about their own equivalents—one-ish, two-ish, and so on. But time for him was a circle, not an arrow; the ceremony would come at the right time, not a moment sooner.

Einstein's General Theory of Relativity and Heisenberg's Principle of Indeterminacy both suggest a complex relationship between time and place resulting in the conclusion that time is not an inexorable flow. Preliminary studies of "black holes" in space and of a split photon beam suggest that even the supposedly absolute laws regarding matter and energy and the speed of light are flexible. Superstring theory suggests many more spatial and temporal dimensions than the ones the most people are familiar with. Despite this growing understanding of reality (which in my view coheres with the traditional peoples' understandings of time and place), the dominant culture continues to treat particular units of time and place as always identical.

Western physicists also say there are only three physical dimensions and one temporal dimension, though in traditional physics there are an infinite number of both. It is possible to move in spirit through many dimensions of space and time; in fact, that is how medicine women and men can change the flow of events and visit civilizations far removed in time and place. For traditional peoples, time is both constantly flowing and yet constantly still, like a river or a waterfall.

Place and time are measured in terms of each other, so that one could say (as Einstein did) that they are aspects of each other. Both time and place are measured in terms of experience. For example, the distance between rests on a long journey is a smaller unit of measurement, and the distance traveled in a day is a larger unit of measurement. From a traditional point of view, a mile through rough terrain contains more "rests," hence is a longer distance.

The units familiar to traditional peoples are derived from the body of the world and our own bodies. The Sun provides us with the day. The Moon provides us with the month. The seasons provide us with the circle of the year. Our bodies provide us with such units as the lifetime, the month (women's moon times), the day (sleep and waking cycles), the breath and the heartbeat.

The Sun serves for original people not only as a celestial timepiece, but also as a compass. One knows, for example, that the Sun follows the Red Road through the day, rising in the East, circling to the South at noon, and setting in the West. One knows that the Sun rises farther North in the summer or when one travels to the far South, and farther South in the winter or when one travels to the far North. Thus, with one glance at the Sun, traditional people know where they are located in both time and place.

Another important measure of time for traditional peoples is found in the rhythms of our bodies. Our breath reminds us of the wind, of Father Sky. Our hearts, like the voice of the Sacred Drum, remind us of Mother Earth. Our heartbeat and breathing rates speed up in rough terrain and slow down in an easy walk, in harmony with the changes in our experience of time and place.

When we die our hearts and breathing stop: we are now no longer in a single time and place, but one with our Creator and all creation.

It is often difficult for those who walk the Red Road to name a moment of time for members of the dominant culture, because of these cultural differences. It can even be difficult for Native Americans to talk with each other about time because the conversation is usually in English, not in the traditional language, and English is constructed in a way that incorporates the dominant culture's understanding of time and place. Benjamin Lee Whorf's amazing book *Language, Thought and Reality* shows how English is based on a "the subject verbs the object" linguistic system, while Hopi has subject and object participating in the verbing. Gary Witherspoon's *Language and Art in the Navajo Universe* similarly stresses the dominance of verbs in the Diné language, implying how the World and everything in it is in constant movement—of transformation, deformation and restoration.

A Native American using English may mean something other than what the words say. If a pastor of a mainstream American church says, "Come to the church by 8:00, for that's when the service starts," you can be sure it will start when the clock says 8:00, or as close to that as is possible. When my Tsalagi friend said, "Come over at 8:00 and we'll go in the lodge," he meant, "We will enter the lodge when it is the right time to have it, and the best I can do to translate that into time terminology is to say '8:00'."

Both Native Americans and members of the dominant culture would probably agree that, in terms of our experience, winter days pass quickly and winter nights pass slowly. But members of the dominant culture would say winter nights have more (equal-length) hours in them than summer nights, while traditional people would say that winter nights have the same number of hours as summer nights, but the hours pass more slowly in winter (if they were to speak in terms of "hours"—a dominant culture concept). This is entirely coherent with experience.

Time for traditional peoples is nonlinear in another way: when we climb a mountain in the midst of summer, we move through the seasons to winter. In another sense, we move gradually through the aeons to the time when conifers reigned supreme, to the time of mosses and lichens, to the time of bare rocks waiting for life to begin. In yet another sense, we move to the deep north, from the conifer forests to the tundra, where it is colder and yet where the Sun's light lasts longest into the evening. Similarly, time moves differently in the village and in the wilderness; in the summer and in the winter, at different phases of the Moon, at different times in the individual's life and so on. Traditional peoples know that everything has its own rhythm. We have craved rhythm since we were infants rocked in the cradle—and even before, listening to our mother's heartbeat above her womb and rocking within her as she walked about.

Traditional peoples see time and place as sacred. Decisions about when and where to do things are made carefully in order to be in alignment with the circles of time and place. A traditional person *only* does something if it is clearly the right time and place to do it. This is because all ceremonies are in effect microcosms of all time and place.

The Native American peoples honor sacred places that are not too close to where they live. One reason is that the sacred places must be protected from enemies. Even before the coming of the Europeans, one nation would not want its sacred places to be discovered by another, lest the nation lose its sources of power and wisdom. Since the European invasion, this became even more critical when the Black Robes, the military and the government attempted to wipe out the traditional ceremonies. Today they remain hidden mainly because of the continual concern for "wannabes" who want to arrogate these traditions, as well as self-appointed Native American "judges" and religious or political reactionaries who want to destroy them. In ancient times and still today, the wilderness helps to protect the sacred ceremonial places from intrusion. Ironically, it is in the place associated with chaos, the uncivilized region, where the sacred things are most safe.

Even among respected fellow traditionals I notice a mutual reserve with regard to sacred places. If one accidentally comes upon a Sacred Stone People's Lodge in the wilderness, one leaves it strictly alone and even averts one's eyes. Likewise one does not ask another where her or his lodge is located—not out of a lack of mutual trust, but out of respect for the integrity of another's spiritual resource. For, if we talk about these places the way we talk about where we shop or go to the movies, we can rob them of some of their sacredness.

The second reason the sacred places are out in the wild regions is to remind us that the ceremonies are *lela wakan* (very sacred, powerful, mysterious and dangerous). If the sacred places were located right where we live, we would treat sacred ceremonies like any other part of life. They would become *washte*: ordinary, comfortable and benign. Even if you know exactly where they are, ceremonial grounds in my experience are often hard to see. Unlike the mainstream

American houses of worship, they blend in with the wilderness: they are small, made of natural materials and, when the leaves of autumn or snows of winter fall on them, when mosses grow on them, these elements are allowed to stay. Moreover, they can often be reached only after a strenuous walk, in places where there are no paths—up steep hills, or over broken rocks, through brambles, and the like. Ideally, holy places are in the wilderness, all but completely inaccessible, to remind us who seek them out that spirituality is not an easy thing to attain, and that it takes a great deal of persistent effort.

One Grandfather taught me how important it is not to overuse the *wakan*. Our sacred places are difficult to reach to remind us not to overuse them and deplete their power, lest some day we *really* need it and it isn't available. The effort it takes to reach the ceremonial grounds also gives us time to put the ordinary *washte* world behind us—to empty out of us our mundane concerns so that we are ready to be filled with the *wakan*, the sacred.

When over time our feet beat down a path to a certain sacred place, when the lodge we erected there gets too comfortable and familiar, when it starts falling apart, then it is time for us to let it naturally die of old age and move on. Indeed, the word "lodge" suggests, as does סֻכָּה (*sukkah*) in the Jewish tradition, a structure of a temporary nature, built while on a pilgrimage. If we stay too long in one spot, it becomes too *washte*, too humanized. We are tempted not to continue our pilgimage. *Wakan* beings, such as the wild animals and the *nagipi* (spirit beings), will stay away, repelled by the stench of human sweat and human troubles that we have allowed to drain into the soil and tinge the air. When it begins to stink and fall apart from too much wear, it is time to let the lodge go and give this spot the opportunity to cleanse itself of these toxins and recover its *wakan* wildness. Better to move on to a place where we are again aware of the possibility that a bear might tear its way into the lodge or lightning might strike—where the *wakan* can still pull us out of our comfortable lives.

Another reason for locating the spirit grounds well away from inhabited areas is that the ceremonies tend to attract and collect *wakan*. Just as too much *washte* is not good for the *wakan,* too much *wakan* is not good for the *washte*. It is better to keep ceremonial spots, which can draw *wakan* forces such as fire or flood spirits or wild animals, at some distance from our living places. Ceremonial lodges, indeed, do attract the *wakan* more quickly than a tipi or a wigwam; the lodges I have built over the years have often been taken apart by snowstorms, lightning or wild animals—a sign that they are powerful accumulators of the *wakan* energies.

And one last reason we traditionally locate the Sacred Stone People's Lodge in a difficult-to-reach spot is so that—like the prince fighting to get to Sleeping Beauty through the forest of thorns—by the time we have walked long and hard to get there, we *fully* appreciate it. There are difficulties ahead in anyone's life, but the difficulties are *wakan*; they bring the sacred into our lives. Walking that difficult path to our sacred grounds is, in a way, symbolic of walking through life, seeking union with the Creator, *Skan*, or *Wakan-Tanka*, with all living creatures, and with all one's ancestors. By walking this path to the sacred grounds, we show our commitment to the ceremony, our honor and respect to the Creator, the spirits and the ancestors: the walking becomes a part of the ceremony itself.

Before the European invasion, the traditional peoples also moved their whole communities from time to time so the stench of human habitation would not become increasingly unbearable for the people themselves and increasingly repel the *wakan,* the spirits and wild animals. Chief Sealth, more than a century and a half ago, spoke of the stench of the invaders' cities. Never cleansed, never relieved, these cities remain fixed in one spot, growing larger like cancers, rotting fastest in their centers. Imagine if he could have seen the cities of today!—perhaps, in vision, he did.

Robert Burton, in *The Anatomy of Melancholy*, taught: "The heavens themselves run continually round, the Sun riseth and sets, the Moon increaseth, stars and planets keep their constant motions, the air is still tossed by the winds, the waters ebb and flow, to their conservation, no doubt, to teach us that we should ever be in motion." Traditional peoples of the world know this. It is in our nature to move; this is the nature of life.

With a few exceptions, the members of the dominant culture see travel as the solution to the problem of getting from point A to point B. The faster that travel can be accomplished, the better. In an effort to minimize this perceived problem, people in modern society drive their cars swiftly down superhighways, take fast planes from coast to coast—until they suffer constantly from soul lag, because their souls never have a chance to catch up. Bruce Chatwin, in his travel memoir, *The Songlines*, tells of some traditional people in the Kalahari who were pushed into a forced march by a European explorer. They finally refused to walk another step until their souls had had a chance to catch up.

For traditional peoples, travel is itself a sacred and beautiful thing, good in its own right. As Gautama Buddha said, "It is better to travel well than to arrive." If you are going to visit a friend, for instance, your traveling thither is part of the gift you bring. If you are going to a sacred place, the journey itself is part of the gift you make to the Creator. And it helps keep us close to our ancestors who walked the same spiritual paths. When the traditional peoples of Australia speak of walking the same paths their ancestors walked, they say: "Many people afterwards become country, in that place, ancestors."

In these Eastern woodlands where I have always lived, it used to be rare to have a full view of the landscape as one traveled—because the trees beneath which one walked blocked the view. When one did encounter a break in the trees and found a wider vista, one stopped and paused, compelled by the rarity of such views to observe it—not only for the pleasure, but to determine if there were any approaching dangers. But the European settlers cut down the trees to make farms and villages and highways, opening up these views. Now it seems that, far from being unexpected and powerful, these views have gone to the other extreme of being made commonplace, *washte*. They have been robbed of their *wakan* power. Even in lands with open landscapes, such as deserts and prairies, when one walked, slowly encountering the revelation of new vistas, one had time enough to adjust to the personal language of the land, to allow one's soul to keep pace and enter into dialogue with one's situation. Now even the desert is something to rush through quickly on a superhighway.

The sacred way to move is to walk. Rather than sitting inside cars, our bodies stationary even as we are moved at great speeds, we must learn to walk. "We should walk lightly on the Earth," one elder taught me. That means to carry few possessions (physical and nonphysical) on our backs, and also to make our decisions with care lest they cause harm to ourselves or others. Heavy-footed walking—"making a big presence" or "a loud presence" as that elder often put it—pounds the air out of the soil and nothing can grow. We must remember that we walk on the dust of our ancestors and that from beneath the ground the faces of our descendants look up at us. Heavy-footed walking, with the heel first, is unnatural.

We learn best from our elder brothers and sisters how to walk. Their movements are clean, silent, smooth and simple. No energy is wasted. Watch the snake and the spider, how they move. Observe the fluid leap of the catamount, the perfect grace of the trout. This is one reason why the traditional peoples dance the Eagle Dance, the Bear Dance, and so on, not just to learn the dancing, the movements, of our elder relations, but to *become* them in spirit. Thus, when we glide in our walking like the hawk, we pick up more of her observant nature; when we thunder silently like the bear, we evidence his adoration for the Earth; when we step as lightly as the vanishing deer, we too leave no trace in our passing or in our standing still. Our first step is as imperceptible as our last.

Traditional people can walk for many miles because they learn ways of walking that are restful. Their bodies are resting even as they walk. It is good to go barefoot to be in contact with Grandmother, or at least with your feet shod in natural, soft materials. Try to step with the ball of your foot and your toes touching first, then the heel. Keep your knees slightly forward when your weight is on them, not locked. This way of walking is much more silent—respectful of the quiet of nature around us. It is much easier on natural pathways and on steep slopes—and of course better when one is hunting.

Walking like this isn't easy at first, especially if you wear built-up heels, but, with practice, it becomes natural. When done smoothly and well, you will seem to glide across the land. Remember to breathe well and taste the air with your senses. As you walk, pay attention to the world around you. Be one with your environment, not an intruder into it. Watch the Earth for animal tracks and learn to read their stories. Watch the weather and the courses of birds in the Sky. Listen to sounds. Pay attention to prints in the Earth and skytrails of birds and spirits overhead. All the time you are walking, there are stories being told to you.

As Yoshida Kenkō wrote in *Tsurezure-Gusa* ("Essays in Idleness"): "A certain recluse, whose name I do not know, said that no bonds attached him to this life, and that the only thing he would regret leaving behind was the sky."

As William Blake sang:

> *How do you know but ev'ry Bird that cuts the airy way,*
> *Is an immense world of delight, clos'd by your senses five?*

And as Grandfather Black Elk heard sung to him in his great vision:

> *Behold, a sacred voice is calling you;*
> *All over the Sky a sacred voice is calling.*

II

Washte & Wakan

Lᴇᴛ ᴍᴇ ʙᴇɢɪɴ ʙʏ ᴛᴇʟʟɪɴɢ you a story.

A long time ago, the people found a good place where there were plenty of good things, so they decided to stay there and not move around. In this fertile location, they were fertile too. They began having lots of children, and as a result there were many mouths to feed. But they did not remember to keep balances. With all the abundance that was around them, they did not see any need to thank the plants and animals they took for food, or to leave tobacco gifts behind. There was such plenty in this land that they saw no reason to avoid hunting mother animals lest there be no generation next year to hunt, and they saw no reason to leave some plants behind to ensure another crop next year. Worst of all, they offered no thanks from their hearts for all this plenty—neither to the Creator nor to these created beings.

A few individuals among the people said that perhaps this practice needed to be rethought, and warned of environmental collapse, but others laughed at them and called them doomsayers. "Is there not plenty for all?" they asked. The change was so gradual that many did not see it coming until it was too late. Eventually the area was overharvested, leading to breaks in the food chain. Plants and animals became scarce, either because they were dying out, or because they learned to avoid this area with the stench of many humans. Erosion spread as grasses and trees disappeared, and water became brackish. Summers were unbearably hot, and rains and snows often came out of season.

The people had to go farther and farther for their food. So great was the need for food that even children had to help with finding it. Two boys among these people had adopted each other as brothers, though they were not brothers by birth. They went off to find food, hoping to be honored if their hunt should be successful.

These two boys loved each other very much, although they were quite different in nature. One was bold and brave. He was impetuous at times, but known already for his courage. He already had a way with women and "hunted" for them as well, but he had not yet found one with whom he wanted to spend his life—although this is understandable because he was yet young. People said of him that he would be a great warrior or even a chief.

The other was reserved by nature, even shy, given to going off alone to contemplate the world around him. He had not been with a woman yet, and had not had much success hunting. He would listen to his honorary brother tell of his exploits with a vicarious thrill and yet also some embarrassment that though his brother had so many exciting stories to tell these conquests evidently meant little to him. People thought this quiet brother might some day be a medicine man.

They complemented each other well, and it was on the sharing of their strengths that their friendship was built. One learned to appreciate from the other, and the other learned courage from the first.

After four days of walking away from the village they saw a white-furred buffalo cow. This creature, they knew, would have abundant flesh to feed their people and that beautiful fur would be highly prized. They agreed to split up and circle around from either direction toward the buffalo cow. The brave brother went sunwise, circling toward the right, and the thoughtful brother went moonwise, circling toward the left.

But, when both of them came through the bushes, what they saw before them was not the buffalo cow they expected, but a woman. Some now say she was wearing a beautiful gown made of white buffalo fur that fit closely about her lovely figure; but the way I heard the story is that she wore no earthly clothing, but had long shining white hair that draped her back and shoulders like a robe: the hair of a wise Grandmother and the face and figure of a lovely young woman. But, in any case, there was no doubt in the mind of either boy that this was a sacred shapeshifter: that somehow the creature they had been hunting had now appeared before them as a woman.

Both boys were very aware that she was both owanyanka washte *(very beautiful) and* lela wakan *(very sacred, powerful, mysterious, dangerous).*

The courageous brother was more aware of her washte *qualities, and the other was more aware of the* wakan *aspect of her nature.*

The one, overwhelmed with her beauty, conceived a powerful desire for her physical body. For him the hunt continued, but now it was another kind of hunt—yet one with which he was also very familiar. It was not his custom to ask for what he wanted. It was his way to say and do whatever was necessary to get what he wanted, as his people had done to the land around them, to take without asking, without thanking and without giving back. This boy took a step toward the woman, intending to act on his desires. She held up one hand in warning. He then took another step toward her. She held up her second hand in warning. He took yet another step toward her. This time she spoke, warning him, "Do not take another step forward, or you will get what you want—but in the end you will be left with nothing." Believing her to mean that he could take from her what he wanted, he took the fourth and final step forward.

Time stood still. The brave brother experienced a whole lifetime with this woman—living with her, having children with her, growing old with her and eventually dying. But what the other brother saw was quite different. At the very moment that his companion first reached to embrace the woman, a mist surrounded them, and he could not see what was happening. When the cloud—the cloud being all that was left of his brother's spirit—dissipated, he saw the woman standing alone. Looking closer, he saw that there was nothing left of his brother but putrefied bones already grown over with moss and fading back into the soil—a sign that many years had gone by.

Seeing this, the other boy, the pensive one, was now full of fear in the presence of a spirit so clearly lela wakan. *He did not dare look directly at her, out of respect and shame, and for fear that he might meet the same fate as his brother. He took a step backwards. She held up one hand, motioning him closer. He took another step backwards. She held up her other hand to motion him closer. He took a third step backwards, and this time she spoke, and said, "Come closer to me, for I have a message, which I want you to deliver to your people." Fortunately he did not take the final step backwards, which would surely have led to his running away. He came close to her, but with his eyes still turned aside, his desire and fear pouring out of him onto the Earth, leaving him empty. She then told him this: "Go back to your people and tell them that I will come to them when* the Moon is full, and I will give them a gift, which will be for their salvation. Tell them that they are to prepare a sacred lodge and meet me there."

The boy turned away obediently—and then turned back again, but she was already gone, disappearing the same way the mist vanishes in the morning. So he returned to his people. But, sadly, for the most part they did not believe his story. They, who now were so often liars and cheaters themselves, could not discern his honest nature. They decided that he must have made it up, to cover up what they assumed had really happened, that he had murdered his adoptive brother. Only the chief, Standing Hollow Horn, believed his story, knowing this boy was not prone to murder or to lying. He told the people to build a lodge to welcome the sacred woman. They did so, but they grumbled. Then he told them, on the Full Moon, to gather there. Again, they did so, grumbling, mostly hoping to see the chief humiliated so someone more to their liking could be put in his place.

They waited a long time in the night beneath the Moon. Some, in fact, left, complaining of the cold and desiring to be in their warm, comfortable beds. More and more began to depart, shaking their heads. But then someone said, "Look!" And those who remained in the lodge looked—and in the distance they saw a silver cloud. It was approaching them. As the cloud got closer, they could see a woman beneath it. As it got closer yet they could hear the woman was singing, and what she was singing was, "Behold! I am coming! With a visible breath I am coming!" As she came closer yet they saw that she was owanyanka washte and lela wakan. As she continued to approach them, they could see that the silver cloud was issuing from her mouth, and that she was holding something in her hands.

The men lowered their heads in respect and shame as she approached—ashamed at the way this sacred messenger had been first received by members of their nation, ashamed at their doubt and their own greedy ways. Many of the women too, especially the younger ones, turned their eyes downward, out of sorrow that the sons of their own bodies could treat a woman like them, the grandmothers, mothers, sisters, wives and daughters of these men, in such a way. As she walked among them, the men heard the grandmothers whisper quiet exclamations of awe and admiration at her great beauty and her sacred appearance, and they felt their shame even more deeply. Then she motioned with her hands, and all of the people looked up. They gazed on the woman, beautiful and sacred, clothed only in her own silver hair and the shimmering silver cloud, both of which shone brightly in the moonlight. Tears streamed down their faces. None of them could say a word.

When she came to the chief, she held out to him on her outstretched palms the object she was carrying, telling him it was called the Chanunpa Wakan (Sacred Pipe). She said, "This gift is for the salvation of your people. With it you will remember to pray with and for all living creatures, all your relations. If you keep it well, you will always have plenty and live in safety."

The people were starving; they had no food to share with the woman, only some water. So they dipped sweetgrass into a bowl of water and gave it to her. She sprinkled the water on them with the sweetgrass, and thus, to this day, the people use this as a means of purification. Then she prepared sacred food for them, and served it with her own hands, first to the elders, then to the little children and mothers and last to the warriors.

After they had eaten together, the woman taught the chief the sacred meaning and use of the Chanunpa Wakan. "With your feet on the Earth and the pipestem lifted into the Sky," she said, "you become a living bridge of prayer, uniting the Sacred Above with the Sacred Below." She also brought out a sacred white stone with seven circles indented into it, ranging in size from very large to very small. These circles represent the seven great ceremonies that she taught to the people.

Her last words to them were, "Toksha ake wa chin yanktin ktelo" (I will see you again). When they need her the most, she said, when their need is desperate, she will return.

Some say that, as she left, she rolled onto the ground and became a yellow buffalo: yellow for the East and the beginning of life. The buffalo rolled over and became red: red for the South and the height of life. Then she rolled again and became black: black for the West and the ending of life. Then she rolled one last time and was once again a white buffalo cow: white for the North and the time between death and rebirth. In so doing she gave one final teaching: the nature of the Four Sacred Directions, bound together in the Changleshka Wakan, the Sacred Hoop.

Others say that, at her direction, the women lit a great bonfire of dried cottonwood, and the people all stood in a circle around it. When the flames had burned down, she told the elders to throw sweetgrass onto the glowing coals. This they did, and a great cloud of smoke rose up. When it had dissipated, she was gone. This way of telling the story shows that the people were forgiven for their sicha ways, and reminded to keep the sacred cere-

monies with great care, and remember, as the smoke rises from the Pipe, and the steam rises from the Lodge, that she rises with it, that her spirit is ever with them when they do these things.

People often say that she is the daughter of Skan *(the ancient Lakota word for G-d and Sky/Heaven), a messenger sent from* Skan, *and that she will come again when the people need her most. Many white buffalo calves have been born in recent years—but the old medicine men say that the Beautiful Woman, whom they call* Wohpe, *first came as a meteor, a falling star, and will come again from the Star Nations, which are the campfires of those who lived on this Earth long ago. That is how we can expect her to come again, as a falling star. In the meanwhile, it is important to remember that the Sacred Pipe still exists. I have met people who have seen it. It is also important to remember that every Sacred Pipe that is carried by any of our legitimate Pipe Carriers is not a Pipe, but the Pipe. In this way we all have access to the Sacred Pipe she gave us.*

We will consider the teaching this story carries a little later. First, however, I need to explain some things that will help me do that.

An elder I once knew introduced me to a useful way of categorizing living beings. He liked to point out that there are two kinds of plants and animals: the friendly ones and the unfriendly ones. Some plants commonly grow close to where human beings live. They clearly like us. Moreover, they are usually valuable to us in some way: they are nice to look at, or are good to eat, or their materials are useful for making things. Maple trees are of this kind; they give us shade, firewood and sweet syrup. Dandelions are another good example. Despite often being considered worthless "weeds" by those who force nature to produce only grass in their lawns, they are pretty to look at, and their greens are delicious in the spring. Others include clover, sorrel, watercress, fiddlehead fern and cattail. These plants are considered *washte*.

But there are also many kinds of plants that do not like us, that grow rather far from us. Not only do they offer us no common usefulness, but they often show their dislike for us with camouflage or an unattractive appearance, a poisonous nature or thorny protections. Yet these plants often excel as powerful healing drugs, when taken in minuscule doses. Some nations also seek out those rare poisonous plants that enable one to break through to the sacred realm of visions and dreams. These plants are considered *wakan*.

There are exceptions, of course. Some plants grow in profusion near human beings and yet are dangerous, such as poison ivy. If we are nature-wise, we know it well and know to respect it, just as we know how to live with an unruly neighbor or relative. And we remember that a great friend to humans, jewel weed, almost always can be found near poison ivy. Jewel weed is good for healing the kind of skin rashes caused by poison ivy, as long as it is applied before the infection spreads. We are also more susceptible to poison ivy rashes when we haven't taken care of ourselves, body and spirit. So, when you think about it, poison ivy is really a friend too, since it reminds us to take care of ourselves and to be aware of our environment.

As with plants, so also with animals. The animals who live near us like us. Squirrels, chipmunks, robins and dogs all provide us with goodness of various kinds. Songbirds are pleasant to hear and, when they *stop* singing, warn us of dangers such as an approaching storm or enemy warriors. But the truly wild animals do not particularly like us or want to help us. It is very rare to come close to an eagle or a bear, because they are wary of us. Whenever one comes close to me in the wild it is always a dramatic event and in its way a sacred vision, because I know it wouldn't willingly come near me unless it were for a specific purpose. They are great teachers and very wise beings. While we should not seek out these powerful *wakan* beings except with great care and respect, their ways are of immense healing value. Like the rare poisonous plants, we seek them out only when we really need to, at great peril to ourselves, when we have no other choice.

The traditional way of categorizing beings is based on direct observation of appearance and behavior. It makes careful distinctions between diurnal and nocturnal animals and plants, and those who appear in one season and not another, for example. Traditional taxonomy also distinguishes between creatures who are Sky-oriented (seek sustenance or safety by going upward), such as birds, bats, butterflies, bobcats, squirrels, pines and vines, and those who are Earth-oriented (seek sustenance or safety by going underground), such as prairie dogs, moles, worms, fungi and many ground-hugging herbs. It makes distinctions among creatures based on their preferred diet—plant or animal—and environment—lakes, rivers, woods, grasslands, caves, mountains, deserts, and so on. Finally, it recognizes that pretty much everything comes in male and female form: some rocks are definitely female and others male, for instance.

Another traditional way of categorizing is according to the number of legs a living creature has. Beings with no legs include fish, spirits, amoebae and rocks—which are considered alive in this tradition, as in the views of Père Pierre Teilhard de Chardin. These beings generally live at or below the surface of Mother Earth, within her soil or water, and help us understand better her ways. The deeper beneath the surface they prefer to be, the more likely they are to be *wakan*.

Among our eldest brothers and sisters are such no-leggeds as rocks and ponds, and such one-leggeds as trees and rivers. One-legged beings also include snakes, worms, eels, snails, slugs and stemmed plants. The essential quality about plants, especially trees, is that they join together Earth and Sky, by being deeply rooted in one and reaching with their arms for the other. When we burn trees, we send smoke into the Great Above, smoke carrying the spirit of the trees. And bodies of water embrace the sky too, in reflection. The farther from human habitation these beings live, the more likely they are to be *wakan*—sacred, powerful, mysterious, awe-inspiring, dangerous, frightening.

Two-legged beings include ghosts, humans, bear and birds. Their home is in the Sky, or Heaven (in many languages other than English "sky" and "heaven" are the same word). Although for bear and humans their home is in Heaven, in this life they are limited physically to the lateral dimensions, and only travel there in vision and dream and after death. Bear and humans are two earthbound creatures who (like wolves) look especially steadfastly and yearn-ingly into Heaven, because deep inside both lies the collective memory that they came here from other worlds and the knowing that, when they spirit-travel, in visions and dreams and when they die, they visit or return there again. Thus, bear and humans have a special affinity with each other, and in the traditional way of thinking, the bear is humanity's closest relative.

Unlike bear and human, ghosts and birds can travel the sky path at will. Ghosts, unfettered by a physical body, have particular power to help or harm us—as do birds, on the physical plane. This is one reason why the bird nations include many great teachers in the traditional heritage, especially among those birds who fly far up into the Heavens above, into the distant *wakan* regions. Frank Fools Crow taught that, when we become "hollow bones" (spiritually light, like the birds), the sacred powers can do spiritual things in and through us without limit.

There are quite a few varieties of four-legged beings, as well as of six-legged, eight-legged and and many-legged beings. These beings generally live on or near the surface of Mother Earth (land or sea), and they help us learn about how best to live here, at the juncture of land or sea and sky. Again, the farther from human habitation they live, the more likely they are to be *wakan*—to be sacred, powerful, mysterious, awe-inspiring, dangerous, frightening.

The dominant culture is destroying the rare precious plants and animals of the wild, either intentionally or with pollution or the destruction of ecosystems for monetary gain. Wild animals are being slaughtered or robbed of their natural habitats. For most of us, our only encounter with wild sacred animals, such as eagle and bear, is in zoos. *Wakan* becomes *sicha* (out of balance) when it is restrained, forced to be *washte* in parks, in zoos, in animal shows in which wild creatures are forcibly "trained" to certain "cute" behavior. As with a dog who is chained or cooped up all day, eventually the creature's spirit either breaks or becomes destructive—the power of the *wakan* is put out of balance. This happens to cultures too; it is already happening to the dominant culture and has happened to many others.

Mainstream religions often say the sacred (the *wakan*) has evil as its opposite or complement. But that is not so for the traditional peoples of this continent. For them, the opposite of the *wakan* is the *washte*. The *wakan* is the sacredness that is found in times and places alien to human society, and the *washte* is the ordinariness found within human society—the goodness of routine, tradition and habitual activity. Both, it must be emphasized, are good, provided they are allowed to thrive in balance, each in its natural times and places. Among the traditional peoples of this continent there is no concept of evil, *per se*, but there is the somewhat similar concept of *sicha*. When the *washte* or the *wakan* is allowed to get out of balance, to thrive in times or places not theirs by nature, or to disappear from times and places natural to them, conditions become *sicha*.

Sicha is not quite the same thing, however, as the concept of evil found in Judaism, Christianity and Islam. The concept of evil presumes certain activities, forbidden by G-d, are by their very nature evil, regardless of circumstances. The concept of *sicha*, however, relates not to particular actions, but to the upsetting of natural balances. *Sicha* is activity, or the failure to act, that results in imbalance. It is forcing into movement what should remain in stasis, or restraining what should remain flowing. In Kantian terms, *sicha* is turning *Sein* (being) into *Werden* (becoming), and vice versa. This is why the Native Americans were upset when the Europeans started damming rivers, razing forests and mountains and cutting through four-legged migration routes by fencing in the land and building highways. That was clearly *sicha* to them, since it was holding back what should flow freely—and now nature is out of balance. Now, rivers like the

Mississippi are prone to flooding, the great forests are prone to major fires, some wild creatures are dying out and others are venturing into human communities or, like the whales, committing suicide on shores near human habitation.

The traditional aim is to ensure that our actions flow with nature, rather than against it. I have been told that, among the Southeastern nations, people show respect to flowing water by drawing water out with the current, rather than against it—just as one brushes hair or fur the way it grows, or cuts meat or shapes wood or stone with the grain. This, literally, is going with the flow of nature.

It is also *sicha* to indulge in the *wakan* indiscriminately, to the degree that it becomes *washte*. Traditional peoples are appalled at how unrestrainedly many people drink alcohol, smoke tobacco and engage in sexuality, with no thought to approaching these sacred things with care and respect. Tobacco is a sacred herb to be used in prayer; when one smokes it frequently, with a mind full of petty anger, greed and boredom, that becomes in effect one's "prayer." True prayer then becomes more difficult, just as overusing healing herbs diminishes their effect. *Sicha* is certainly evident when men force themselves sexually on women—and I don't mean only rape here, but also the tricks and wiles, the "lines" men use to "get sex." Sexuality, like storms and river rapids and winter, like anything *wakan*, is to be respected—and we must not try to force it to manifest itself when or with whom it doesn't want to. It is less often realized that sexuality must not be resrained when it wishes to flow; that, too, is *sicha*.

Sacred, rare and powerful visions and dreams are *wakan*. These most often come upon us unawares; certainly we do not seek them out unless we are in great need, and not without careful precautions. Like seeking out poisonous plants for their healing properties or seeking out dangerous wild animals for their great teaching wisdom, we have to go deep into a certain kind of spiritual wilderness to find the sacred visions and dreams. We can "hunt" the sacred dreams and visions through ceremony as we experience extreme conditions such as sleep or sensory deprivation, fasting, intense humidity, physical pain, sexual activity (such as in some maturity rites and during the intercalary days), hyperventilation, and drumming, dancing or chanting for many hours. Some nations use certain powerful wild plants, such as peyote, in order to find powerful dangerous dreams or visions—but this should *only* be done under the tutelage of an experienced medicine man or woman.

Old people experience the *wakan* frequently. In today's dominant culture, elderly individuals often experience constant pain, ringing in their ears or other strange sensory phenomena, and have trouble coping with sudden change. They tend to remember past events or see into the far future much better than what someone told them a few minutes ago. Among the traditional peoples, these are understood not as problems, as failures or losses, but as irruptions of the *wakan*. And, for that reason, they are welcome.

Every child of any culture knows how to break through into the *wakan*. The child's world is largely unexplored, "untamed," so children need hardly venture out of sight of home to be surrounded by the *wakan*. Besides, children explore their own bodies and learn all sorts of amazing things that happen when, for example, they press hard on their eyelids and see colorful patterns, hold their breath until they feel dissociation or faintness, or run very hard until their blood is pounding, or masturbate to explore the mysterious feelings, or spin until they are dizzy and fall and the world goes upside-down.

The Lakota story of how the Sacred Pipe came to us through Pte Ska Winyan, the White Buffalo Calf Woman, is similar in spirit to other stories told by many nations. These stories deliver the core teaching that there was a time when the People neglected their responsibilities of giving thanks to all life, and giving back to those beings who share their lives with the two-leggeds. The Hodenasaunee (Iroquois Confederacy), for example, tell this one:

> *When the people found a land of plenty, they settled into it but began to take for granted all the abundance around them. They neglected the songs and prayers of thanksgiving given to them by the Creator. They began to argue among themselves, splitting off into separate, constantly feuding bands. They told their children to stay home, lest their enemies should abduct them, even punishing their children severely whenever they tried to play with their friends.*
>
> *But seven children secretly met together at night—despite the punishments of their parents—and planned to hold a great thanksgiving ceremony in the way they had heard of from their grandparents. Only one of them, Gathering Wind, was loved by his parents, but he, too, joined the others because he knew how important it was to give thanks. The children chose the oldest boy, Broken Ice, and the oldest girl, Bright Day, as their faithkeepers. After weeks of careful, surreptitious preparations, they gathered in the night around a fire kindled by Broken Ice on a bare hilltop deep*

*in the forest, joining hands in a sacred dance, singing the ancient thanks-
giving song.*

    *Eventually the parents noticed their children were missing, and came
searching for them in the forest. Even as their parents approached, they kept
dancing, slowly rising toward the Sky World. Most of the parents angrily
shouted for their children to return. Later on, they would regret their cruel
treatment and vow to remain thankful to all life and always kind to their
children. But, at the time, only Gathering Wind's parents grieved his
passing. As he rose into the Heavens, he was moved to see them weeping, and
broke hands with the others and dropped again toward the world below. He
gathered speed as he fell, becoming a falling star. For this reason, to this day
the people renew their vows to be thankful whenever they see a falling star.
And, later on, from where the falling star of Gathering Wind touched the
Earth, the great Tree of Peace would grow, reminding the people to walk in
peace with all the nations of the Sacred Hoop.*

This Hodenasaunee story, like the Lakota story, features a universal failure to
be thankful, children who are wiser than their parents, and even a falling star
who brings back the ways of peace and gratitude.

    In the Lakota story, as I told you, two boys are the first to encounter the
sacred woman, the Falling Star. Both see that she is *washte* (in this context,
beautiful and desirable) as well as *wakan* (powerful, sacred, mysterious,
even frightening and dangerous). One boy is more aware of the *washte*, and
wants to have that beauty for himself. The other, however, is more aware of
the *wakan*.

    Most people, when telling or interpreting the story, assume that the first
boy behaved badly and that the second boy's behavior was good, and they suggest or imply that we should try to be more like the second boy. And, indeed,
Native Americans have largely adopted an approach toward life more like that
of the second boy. But let's look more closely at the story.

    Certainly the first boy was *sicha* (out of balance) to want to "take" sexuality
from the woman without giving back. By desiring to take what hadn't been
freely given, he was, in effect, determining to rape her. Rape is *sicha* not just
because it is theft of a most egregious kind, but because it tries to control the
wakan—for every individual is *wakan*, and beauty and sexuality themselves
are *wakan*. Rape forces it to be *washte*. This boy was wrong (*sicha*) for only
seeing the beauty of the woman's body and not her essentially sacred nature.

The sight of beauty—of an eagle in flight, of deer grazing in a field of wild-flowers or of a beautiful woman—is pleasant, *washte* to behold; but the beauty itself, by nature, is not *washte* but *wakan* and therefore worthy of reverence, not covetousness. The sight of a woman's beauty is pleasant, but entering sexually into the woman, like entering the wilderness, is entering into the *wakan*—and must be done only if invited, and only with humility and respect.

As Nikos Kazantzakis said: "The only way we can apprehend the appearance of the face of G-d is through looking at beautiful things." Like anything *wakan*, beauty is not a creation of human ingenuity, but of the Creator. Even what appears to be the beauty of artifice—the beauty of a carving or beadwork or a woven blanket, for instance—isn't inserted into the object by human intention, but is simply *there*, appearing mysteriously beneath our hands. We carve or weave objects; we do not carve or weave *beauty* itself. I myself do not carve or weave, but I do compose stories and poems and songs, and if beauty comes it is uncontrived. If I *try* to make a poem beautiful, I fail. In the same way, beauty in the individual is not a matter of human initiative but an accident, a genetic happenstance that one has without seeking it.

In the Diné (Navajo) language, the word *hózhó*, usually translated as "beauty," also means "harmony" and "peace." Bear that in mind as you read, in very poor translation, two Diné prayers—that are ultimately the same prayer:

> *With beauty behind me, I walk.*
> *With beauty above me, I walk.*
> *With beauty below me, I walk.*
> *From the east beauty has been restored.*
> *From the south beauty has been restored.*
> *From the west beauty has been restored.*
> *From the north beauty has been restored.*
> *From the zenith beauty has been restored.*
> *From the nadir beauty has been restored.*
> *From all around me beauty has been restored.*
>
> *Creator, may we walk in beauty.*
> *May beauty be above us so that we dream of beauty.*
> *May beauty precede us so that we are led by beauty.*
> *May beauty be to the left of us so that we may receive beauty.*
> *May beauty be to the right of us so that we may give out beauty.*

May beauty be behind us so that those who come after us may see beauty. Creator, may we walk in beauty.

One warm summer day, when I was about seventeen summers old, I was walking a trail in the eastern Adirondacks. Coming around a bend, I saw before me a waterfall. A woman was standing naked in the cold cataract, combing out her long, glistening black hair with her fingers. As the sunlight and water poured shining silver over the beauty of her face and figure, she sang a low song I could not quite make out over the thunder of the fall. Immediately I froze, unable and unwilling to move, transfixed by this unexpected wonder. In the traditional way we are taught that it is not improper to look respectfully at the unexpected revelation of the *wakan*, but I could not know if her ethics required that I should avert my eyes. I was afraid that I might catch her attention and disturb her if I moved to leave, but felt that nevertheless I should leave her to the privacy of her communion with nature. So, for a moment that was an eternity, I stood and looked in silent, respectful awe at this breathtaking vision. I wonder to this day whether she was aware of me, whether she allowed me the gift of staying to watch or if she wished me to go. Seeing no sign from her of permission granted, no acknowledgment even of my presence, I left as quietly as I could, still almost hearing her song over the thundering water as the trail turned away from the waterfall and back into the quiet woods.

I do not doubt that on one level of reality this was some ordinary woman, a tired hiker on a hot, humid day, enjoying the cool water washing the sweat off her body, even though in my memory of this scene there is no knapsack, no pile of clothing nearby, even though the song she sang was no popular melody but the simple pentatones of a chant. At the same time I am equally sure that this was, for me, a sacred vision, in the Platonic sense the ιδεα (*idea*) of *Woman* in all Her sacred glory, perhaps even of the White Buffalo Calf Woman, the Beautiful One herself, and the same choice given to the two brothers had been put before me as well. Perhaps, by telling you this story, I pass her message on.

As William Blake put it in one of his songs, "The nakedness of woman is the work of G-d." This vision was at the conjunction of contrasts where the *wakan* is so often to be found: the hot day and cold water, the shining white light on black rocks, the silence of the forest and the thunder of the falls, the nakedness clothed in lucid transparency, the motionless cataract composed of fast-falling water. Indeed, at the sight of this beauty I did feel a momentary tightening of sexual attraction—I was at that time when manhood is in its first flowering—but I also felt wonder and fear at the unexpected sight of a G-d-desslike vision, a boyish shyness and an overwhelming awareness of the vital need to be respectful. I am not certain that I made the right choice, but I believe that I did—and have prayed ever since that that was so.

To each of the two brothers the Beautiful One gave instructions, guiding their choices, and they chose whether or not to abide by her guidance. To me— if indeed this was *She*, and even if it was not—she gave no sign at all. Yet she did give me a teaching: that each of us must in such moments recognize that all women are *She*, and choose to act wisely and well, to the best of our ability, on the basis of the fundamental rule of *Respect*.

Indeed, sexuality, sexual desire, is not the issue here, any more than it is the "point" in the story of Adam and Eve. Neither story teaches that sexual desire is wrong. Rather, both stories are essentially about hubris and fear, about taking what has not been freely offered and cowering from the consequences of doing so. Sexuality is simply a part of being alive and is natural and normal, provided it is welcome to each person involved. Moreover, it is *lela wakan*— very sacred and powerful and mysterious.

Old medicine men, I have been told, call this woman not the White Buffalo Calf Woman, as everybody else does, but the Beautiful One, acknowledging her teaching that the respectful appreciation of beauty, including the beauty of woman, is truly a sacred thing. Appreciation without respect (like the one brother) and respect without appreciation (like the other brother) are both *sicha*. The Beautiful One taught us this truth by showing that even an entire life of ordinary goodness (*washte*) with no sense of the sacred (*wakan*) in it comes to naught in the end: just a pile of bones vanishing into time. She revealed this truth also by telling the shy brother, the one who saw her as *wakan*, to come forward and look at her beauty, so he could take her message to the people, and later by allowing the men to raise their heads and observe her unadorned loveliness when she walked among them.

In the Lakota story, the courageous brother, who normally embraced only the *washte*, here desired to appropriate something very sacred, *wakan*, and forcibly make it *washte*. Likewise, the thoughtful brother, who normally was comfortable with the *wakan*, was actually, if unwittingly, arrogating the *washte*, seeking refuge in the ordinary, when he let his fears of her nature as *wakan* take hold of him. Both, indeed, were exhibiting the two mistakes their own people were making at that time. The first brother was *sicha* in that he shared with the majority its mistake of taking without giving back, and the second brother was *sicha* in that he shared with the minority its failure to act decisively to stop the other's arrogation.

Both boys in this definitive moment went to the extremes of their wonted behavior. The one, overly bold with women to the point of turning them into objects for conquest, here treats a Messenger from the Creator in a most dehumanizing way. The other, overly shy with women to the point of denying the humanity they share with him, fails to see the essential goodness of this Beautiful Woman. There's a particular lesson in all this for men: we men should treat woman in all her individual varieties as if she were the Beautiful One herself, and we also should attempt to get past the outer appearance of a woman to see her essential goodness, her essential humanity. While the sight of a woman's beauty is, for us, *washte* indeed, and in many nations it is not considered rude to look openly with respectful appreciation at a beautiful woman, still we must look with absolute respect, whether a woman is completely covered or completely naked. It is common for traditional people who don't know each other well to look at the ground in front of them, rather than directly at each other, lest they show disrespect. They will, however, look up when they are welcomed so to do—as the Beautiful One invited the people to do when she walked among them.

It is not commonly remembered that our path through life is so constituted that we must give something in order to receive something. This concept of balances, of Sacred Giveaway, is at the very heart of Native American culture and spirituality. To achieve something, we must take risks. We risk rejection when we offer our love to another person. We risk great sorrow when we accept the love of another. We risk the darkness and heat within the Sacred Stone People's Lodge, or risk losing our laden table and comfortable bed in the Vision Seeking Ceremony, or risk losing some of our skin in the Sun Dance Ceremony. This is why Native Americans today, even if they abhor the warlike ways of the dominant culture, still honor their military veterans just as they did the warriors of old: because these brave souls gave much. Without sacrificing, without losing, we cannot receive. Many *washichu* people (people who are interested primarily in their own gain, notwithstanding the cost to others) want to experience the sacred power of the Native American spiritual ways, but don't want to give of themselves or their property.

Both boys were *washichu,* individuals unwilling to give of themselves, to risk vulnerability. The first boy wanted to take from the woman what was not his to take, without taking the risk of vulnerability that characterizes real love, which is always *wakan*. And the second boy wanted not to take what was freely offered but to stay in his safe, comfortable life, without taking the risk of approaching the truly sacred and mighty, the *wakan*.

The first boy got his wish and lived a *washte* lifetime with the woman, free from the *wakan*, but, to bring balance, was consumed down to putrefying ashes. The second boy got his wish, to return to familiar *washte* society and leave her frightening *wakan* presence, but, to bring balance, he first had to come closer to her and accept her message and then deliver it. This story, in fact, points to two alternate realities—neither one entirely ideal. Native Americans perhaps have chosen the better alternative, by attempting to live in the reality of the thoughtful brother, wherein this woman brought to us the means to maintain balances. The dominant culture suffers from the imbalance of taking without giving back, the reality of the brave brother who lived out a lifetime with the woman, capturing her *wakan* beauty and power and making it *washte*. The path of imbalance is ostensibly pleasant and easy, but will lead to environmental or nuclear catastrophe that could reduce the Earth and its inhabitants to ashes.

We must choose. As Moses says at the end of Deuteronomy: "Behold, this day I have set before you life and prosperity, death and adversity; ... therefore, choose life so that you and your descendants may live...." The Two-Minded Generation Prophecy, which I will tell you about later, also teaches that we must choose which brother to emulate, which vessel to take on the river of life.

The poet W. H. Auden sums up nicely the difference between the *washte* and the *wakan*: "The value of a profane [*washte*] thing lies in what it usefully does; the value of a sacred [*wakan*] thing lies in what it is." Of course, Auden is typically Western in assigning a value to sacred things; moreover, he forgets that all things are ultimately sacred, since all things come from the Creator. But, from our subjective human point of view, Auden is correct. The *wakan* is constantly at flow, like the river or the wind; it is constantly flowing through everything, but without ever resting in anything. The *washte*, however, is at rest. When the *wakan* does pause, it becomes *washte*. That is why it is *washte* at home, among our own people, where we can be at rest. The *washte* provides us security and comfort, allowing us to relax and be content.

Another useful formulation is based on the teachings of the Taoist master Lao-tse. The first line in his *Tao-te Ching* is: "The Tao that can be named/

described is not the eternal/real Tao." *Tao* (pronounced "dow") is something like *x* in mathematics. It refers to the inscrutable, indescribable substrate that is deeper than the division of existence and nonexistence, deeper than the division of single and multiple. *Wakan* events and things are unique in a way beyond depiction or description; they are neither strictly one nor plural. Thus, for instance, it is often taught that all Sacred Pipes are representations of the one original Sacred Pipe, which is spiritual and beyond differentiation in terms of appearance or number or existence/nonexistence.

The dialectic between *washte* and *wakan* may also be understood in terms of the bicameral mind, explored by Julian Jaynes in *The Origin of Consciousness in the Breakdown of the Bicameral Mind.* The left hemisphere of the brain is more commonly involved with logic and reason (*washte*) and the right hemisphere with insight, intuition, dream, vision and creativity (*wakan*). This dialectic is known by other terms to many traditional nations. The Diné (Navajo), for instance, speak of the Blessing Way, associated with the feminine principle and equivalent to *wakan*, and the Protection Shield Way, associated with the masculine principle and equivalent to *washte*.

Washte events and things can be easily counted, compared and described, and their existence easily proven. But this is not so with *wakan* events and things. One remembers that one had a spiritual experience, or a dream or a vision, one knows one watched the birth of one's child or the death of one's parents, one knows one expressed love sexually. Perhaps, haltingly, clumsily, one can find words that to some small degree point toward the experience as, in the Buddhist analogy, a finger can point to the Moon but is not the Moon herself. One remembers that one was there, that one saw, what one did. One can describe the experience but one cannot truly recapture it—make the moment come again. Memory cannot encompass this burden, and words fail utterly. I quote from "Ode to an Astronaut in Winter," a poem I wrote many years ago:

> *...but now I am here, held down by gravity, and she is out there;*
> *there are tapes of every sound, films of every moment, and*
> *hundreds and hundreds of pounds of rock, and all the world*
> *to say I was there, but*
> *was*
> *I?   Can I really say I remember.*

The greatest poets and painters and composers are those who sometimes evoke the *wakan,* but the *wakan* can never be described; it cannot be captured; it cannot be proven. The *wakan* is beyond all the petty arguments among theists, atheists and agnostics, which deal only with *washte* questions of demonstrability and provability.

The *washte* is a function of our physical reality, our robe. Thus, what is *washte* for a mole or a fish is not what is *washte* for a human or a wildflower. Being with your *oyatë,* your nation, is *washte,* since the *oyatë* shares the communality of the same robe. But the *wakan* is a function of our spiritual reality, of the spirit *within* the robe. Since spirit is one, what is *wakan* for one species is *wakan* for all species. And the surprising, non-repetitive, intuitive, unteachable, unlearnable wisdom (not knowledge) of the soul is *wakan* wisdom. And to be alone, to be outside the robe of your *oyatë,* is to be exposed to the *wakan* of the wilderness—the wilderness of trees or desert or mountain or sea, and also the wilderness of dream or vision or ceremony or death, the places where your *oyatë* is not to be found. Since the *washte* is associated with the outer robe, the body, when we come back to a new life, our essential spirit remains the same, but our likes and dislikes (what is *washte* to us) may change.

The *washte* is the goodness that is nurtured by human civilization. It is cultivated and preserved through routine and repetition. It is what we enjoy in our day-to-day lives—delicious food, the comforts of home and companionship, the delight of being with our families. The *washte* is immanent, marked by ordinary place and time, τοπος (*topos*) and χρονος (*chronos*), and is therefore transient in nature. Its pleasures do not last.

The *washte* is the result of deliberate decisions and effort and must be maintained to exist at all. It is supported by the effort of an entire community, and it can be owned by individuals or groups. I think of my neighbors here in the Catskills where I live, or the fellow members of our regional Native American association. The members of each group help each other out when someone has an inundation of the *wakan,* such as damage to one's home from snow or flood or fire. The *washte* tends to congregate, to form *oyatë,* nations— of humans, of community-forming birds, of bees and ants, of various plants, and so on. The *washte* is governed by human, prescriptive law that can be broken. Life without surprise, without the unexpected, is *washte.* Unbalanced by the *wakan,* it leads to boredom and dissatisfaction.

The *wakan* is what makes life sacred. The things that are *wakan* are frightening, powerful, dangerous and mysterious, but they bring sacred meaning to our lives. The *wakan* cannot be cultivated. Its presence cannot be reliably invoked, its behavior cannot be predicted. The *wakan* simply happens; it never directly results from deliberate decisions or effort. If it is corraled behind fences, made familiar, it ceases to be *wakan* and becomes *washte*. The *wakan* is self-sustaining; it does not need to be, and in fact cannot be, maintained in community, and is never owned by anyone or anything. The *wakan* has a nature unto itself, free from human intention or intervention. It is transcendent; above, beyond, outside of ordinary human experience.

If the *washte* is walking the familiar path worn from frequent use, then the *wakan* is walking an unfamiliar path; even more, it is leaving all paths behind—as the medicine man or woman does in seeking the *wakan* plants or animals, as one does in fasting or depriving oneself of sleep, as during the sacred ceremonies. The coming of the Thunder Beings, the smoking of the Sacred Pipe, the experience of powerful dreams and visions: these things are *wakan*. The *wakan* exists in sacred time, καιρος (*kairos*), the eternity-instant that marks life-changing events. While woven blankets, delicious meals and individual lives do not last, the spirit within them, the traditions behind them, go on forever. The *wakan* is to be found in the extremes: the heat of midsummer day, the frigid dark of midwinter night, the summit of the mountain, the exultation of the storm, the depths of the lake and river and cavern. The *wakan* tends to be solitary, or appear in twos or threes at most—the eagle soaring alone on the updrafts, the bear sleeping and dreaming alone all winter, the single powerful vision or dream that is remembered for years.

When free in its solitary nature, it tends to strengthen as it travels on its way becoming broader and deeper and more powerful. If captured and stilled, however, if made *washte*, the *wakan* weakens and loses power. The *wakan* is governed by natural, descriptive law, which cannot be broken except at greatest peril. Marked by sacred place and time, γαια (*gaia*) and καιρος (*kairos*), it comes without expectation or repetition. Unbalanced by the *washte* (as during wars or natural disasters, or under despotic rulers), it leads to fear and madness.

As Little Wound put it in *Lakota Belief and Ritual* (edited by James R. Walker), the prefix *wa-* refers to "anything which is something" or "anything with which something can be done." Remove this prefix from *wakan* and *washte* and you have *Kan* and *Shte*. These are complementary elemental forces, not unlike the Taoist forces *Yin* and *Yang*. *Kan* (according to Little Wound) refers to the quality common to ancientness, eternality, creativity, incomprehensibility, strangeness, wonderfulness, sacredness, supernaturalness. *Shte* refers to the pleasure derived from goodness, comfort, good health, beauty, companionship.

Every culture makes the *wakan washte* in some ways. Whenever this happens, the *wakan* loses its free-flowing nature, and hence loses its natural tendency to build in energy, tending instead to dissipate energy as does the *washte*. Moreover, the *washte*, when separated from the *wakan*, tends to become *sicha*. "Everything that proceeds from the hands of the Creator of all things is good," said Jean-Jacques Rousseau in *Émile*, "but everything degenerates in the hands of humanity." The water that is brought in for drinking or cooking from the *wakan* flow of the river must be replenished and eventually changed, or it grows brackish—just as the water in the freely flowing river stays clean but the water in a still pool can become brackish. The *wakan* fire in the *washte* wigwam, tipi, longhouse or hogan must be maintained, or it goes out; the air in a closed room quickly becomes impure and unbreathable. Skin wrapped tightly in clothing or bandages becomes putrid. And like wild animals caged in zoos, humans densely packed in cities suffer a loss of clarity, peace and moral bearings.

The traditional peoples tend to minimize the frequency with which they make the *wakan washte*, to keep the inevitable *sicha* to a minimum. Only what water is needed is taken from the river. It is taken with respect and used immediately, so none is wasted or allowed to become putrid. The dominant culture puts a much greater amount of the *washte* under its control than do the traditional peoples, which forces it to spend a great deal of effort on maintaining that control, on keeping pollution and putrefaction at bay, and keeping the captive *wakan* from either roaring out of control or dissipating entirely.

Rather than controlling the *wakan*, the traditional peoples welcome it from time to time so it can cleanse and purify. They know the *wakan* washes (no pun intended) the *washte*. Jesus and Han-shan understood this and entered the wilderness to rid themselves of the unwholesome effects of closed, stultified society. Members of nations like the Nehiyawok (Cree), who are fortunate enough to exist in lands largely not yet coveted by the dominant culture, are still able to go back "into the bush" from time to time to cleanse their spirits.

A good storm renews the Earth and cleanses the air. Forest and grass fires consume old dying growth and make room for new growth. Running water ("living water", מים חיים [*mayim hayyim*] in Hebrew, ὑδρος ξοον [*hydros zoön*] in Greek) heals; the Tsalagi (Cherokee) like the Jews, Hindus and Jains enter into a river for spiritual renewal. The Sacred Stone People's Lodge in the midst of the wilderness also purifies. The light of the full Moon has this power, which is why medicine men and women leave their sacred bundles and sacred stones (*wotai*) on a rock beneath the Moon to be purified.

Ceremonies help to concentrate the *wakan* in one place for more intense purification. A ceremony concentrates it naturally, as does the midwinter night, the midsummer day, the storm, the river, the mountain top. The ceremonial place is a *wakan* site in a hard-to-reach place in the wilderness that is *only* entered for ceremony, not for hunting, gathering or any other purpose. Ceremonies, however, use two hallmarks of the *washte* to find the *wakan*— community and repetition. But it is a community in which our clothing of societal conventions is stripped away and the ordinary relationships and patterns of the *washte* are firmly set aside. Likewise, repetition in ceremony does not wear the familiar *washte* mask, but serves to break us free from the *washte*. The repetition of drumming, dancing, chanting and dramatic repetition in storytelling: these are repetitions that we *only* use in the context of ceremony.

The *washte* offers paths into the *wakan* through the little rituals that people use, for example, when preparing to go to sleep or to engage in the hunt or a battle. In fact, we can define ceremony or ritual as a specific kind of *washte* path that leads us surely out to the edge of the pathless *wakan* wilderness and, later, leads us surely back in to the ordinary, the *washte*, once again. To head out into the *wakan* without walking one of these sure paths is fruitless and can be dangerous, except for the medicine man or woman, who often acts as an explorer. These paths ultimately represent the path of life, for life is a sure path that leads through youth to old age to the *wakan* of what happens beyond death.

There is much more *wakan* than *washte* in the universe, or at least there was until Western culture squeezed the *wakan* out to the edges. Now that the inhabited regions of the earth are almost entirely within the circle of human *washte*, it is hard to reach a place where one does not find the constructs of human habitation and commerce replacing and subduing the wilderness. It is difficult for humans, as creatures who congregate and prefer to be largely surrounded by the *washte,* to step outside their nature and actually be wild themselves as they enter into the *wakan*. People in modern society carry their *washte* with them, bringing along cellular phones, high-tech weapons, recreational vehicles and so on. However, traditional people—defined as such by how they live, not their ancestry—leave behind all the *accoutrements* of the *washte* and become *wakan* themselves: vulnerable to the dangers but open to the generosity of the *wakan*.

Like the two brothers, some humans tend more toward the *washte* and others toward the *wakan*. Many individuals prefer order and sameness and don't welcome the unexpected. These people are happiest in the company of others, and find delight and comfort in the ordinary events of life. Others prefer to spend more time alone, to cherish the unexpected and the miraculous. They often seek out the wildernesses of the Earth as well as of dream and vision. It is believed that left-handed people (and I've read that there is a higher percentage of them among Native Americans than any other people) tend to be more *wakan*, and right-handed people to be more *washte*. Needless to say, both ways are perfectly fine; they are simply different.

On the macrocosmic level, the *wakan* is dependable in its own way. Imagine a leaf floating down a river toward a half-submerged rock. Will it pass by the rock on the near side or the far side? No one can know. But no matter where the leaf goes, we know it will go; the water will flow. We can make an ironclad prediction about the *wakan*: Like the river, like the wind, the πνευμα (*pneuma*) Jesus talked about with Nikodemos, it flows where it will, it flows where it should (unless humanity interferes with it). If we accept that the *wakan* flows as it will and should, even if we cannot be sure exactly where or how, then we see that, while it can be frightening, it's not malevolent. For those who find the concept of *wakan* frightening, that's exactly what it should be! But the *wakan*, while not exactly a *washte* friend, is most assuredly not an enemy either. It just goes on its sacred way with little regard for our personal *washte* concerns.

The friendly plants and animals are *washte* and tend to form communities. The behavior of communities (human included) is usually predictable. Bees in community will fly from flower to flower. Low-flying birds tend to develop routines and lay down "paths" of *washte* in the midst of the *wakan*. For all living creatures, the places where they spend most of their time and the things they do most often are *washte*-for-them. For these friendly beings, their circle of *washte* places and activities considerably overlaps our human *washte* circle.

The unfriendly beings, which are dangerous yet are good for healing or teaching, are *wakan*. They tend to be solitary, or at most to form small groups whose behavior is still unpredictable. And the most unfriendly, the most *wakan* creatures, are those who are considered mythical by scientists: the unicorns of Europe and Asia, the Great White Giant and *Wakinyan Wakan* (Thunder Beings) and *Unchegila* (Dragon) of this continent, the two species of dragons known in Europe and China, the Little People (I was once vouchsafed a glimpse of one beside a country road near my home) and the yeti or sasquatch, as well as ghosts and spirits. Humans rarely go to the places where these unfriendly beings live and spend most of their time, so our paths almost never cross.

In the eighteenth century, European Americans came to the Chiefs of the Hodenasaunee (Iroquois Confederacy) to learn about their ancient Constitution, the *Kaienerekowa*, or Great Law of Peace, represented by the Tree of Peace. The Europeans later used many of its tenets when they wrote the United States Constitution, but one they failed to adopt. When the newcomers consulted with the Chiefs of the Hodenasaunee, they were warned never to "separate the spirit from the body" of their new nation. This warning ran counter to the Enlightenment notion of "the separation of church and state." The Chiefs applauded freedom of religion, but warned that a government separate from all spirituality would become unbalanced, greedy, corrupt and prone to violence (like the first of the two boys), and that those who practice the spiritual ways, being isolated from true leadership, would become marginalized, weak or fearful, holding onto the comfortable illusions of the past (like the second of the two boys). Although conservative Christian forces, in alliance with mercantile interests, extreme wealth and the military, have now infiltrated government, their veneer of piety is not to be trusted; they, too, have become "whited sepulchres" filled with corruption, devoid of genuine spirituality.

The psychologist R. D. Laing correctly says that the line between "sane" and "insane" is a matter of societal definition, and that it is arbitrarily drawn. Most people see a person who claims to talk with G-d or angels or wild animals as mentally ill. Such a person is often put into therapy and on drugs that dampen the spirit's ability to perceive these *wakan* entities. Traditional peoples, however, respect such individuals for their special gifts. People from modern society admire Saint Francis of Assisi, William Blake and others for their spiritual gifts (their contact with the numinous), yet find it nearly impossible to admit that the numinous *(wakan)* visits with people living today.

For Western cultures as a whole, the physical world is body without spirit, and hence is available for exploitation. Like the first of the two brothers who find the sacred woman, they see only the *washte* and want to dominate it. They have farmed or urbanized the world until much of it is expended and barren. They make considerable use of metals and coal and crude oil (which are *wakan*, since they come from deep within the body of the Earth) for *washte* purposes of convenience. They have dumped their unwanted byproducts—toxic chemicals and nuclear waste—in the wildernesses, destroying wildlife and ecosystems. The few ancient wildernesses that remain are becoming ever more powerful, since those that survive are by necessity strong, and their *wakan* energy is increasingly concentrated into ever-shrinking spaces.

For the few people who still hunt or fish, it takes a proportionally greater amount of humility, listening and patience to catch one of the wise, angry creatures who inhabit these areas. Fish have learned to see even perfectly safe food—*any* worm or insect in the water—not as a potential meal but as a potential threat. They have learned to fear the hook. And this fear, combined with greedy overfishing, leads to starvation and smaller adult fish. In the far North of Turtle Island there are still lakes and rivers where the fish grow large and seem eager to be caught—just as the trees and the deer and bear and eagles there also have a better chance to grow to the great size of old age. This is no longer true in the more exploited regions farther south.

These days, traditional people who see the *wakan* in the world around them are inclined to be afraid of it, and are tempted to run away, like the second brother, and return to the familiar and easy life style offered by the dominant culture. But we must not run away. We must deliver the message that Mother Earth gives us—the same message that the second brother gave to the people. The White Buffalo Calf Woman, the Beautiful One, is coming back soon. Her message is that we must seek balance and show respect for all our relations, before we destroy this Earth and Sky.

Let me tell you a story one Spirit Grandfather told me.

Once there was a woman who had two suitors who were identical twins. But, though they were indistinguishable in outward appearance, they were completely opposite in all other ways. One built and the other destroyed. One always told the truth and the other always lied. One brought things to life and the other took life.

The two brothers often wrestled with each other, for each one wanted to be supreme, and to prove to the woman that he was the right man for her to marry. Each one often asked her to marry him, but she could never give an answer.

Finally she decided that the fair thing to do was to give them both a trial. So first she lived with the one brother. He built a home for her. He grew plants for her to eat. Everything was wonderful. But he kept on building and growing until there was no room for anything else.

"Why do you keep on building like this," she asked, "when there is already too much?"

He answered, "I am the truthful brother. I only build and never destroy."

Then she lived with the other brother. He took apart the excess of beautiful things his brother had made. He killed animals for her to eat. Everything was again wonderful. But then he kept on destroying and killing until there was nothing left.

"Why do you keep on destroying like this," she asked, "until there is nothing left?"

He answered, "I am the truthful brother. I only build and never destroy."

But she knew he was the lying brother, so she realized that he was actually saying the exact opposite of the truth.

The brothers demanded her now to decide which one she would marry. She did not like the idea of living with either one who made too much or one who destroyed too much. She prayed to the Great Mystery to know what to do. As she prayed, the two brothers started fighting again. They wrestled and struggled, sending up great clouds of dust as they strove with each other. At last, only one young man was left standing. He approached her. She could not tell which one it was.

She asked him, "Are you the building brother or the destroying brother? Are you the truthful brother or the one who always lies?"

"I am the truthful brother," he replied, which told her nothing. Perhaps it was the truthful brother, in which case he was telling the truth, or perhaps it was the lying brother, in which case that was a lie. She could not be sure.

She watched him. He built a home for her, but only one. He planted herbs for her, and hunted animals for her. He cleared away what she did not want and made good things for her. She was happy to live with this man, and told him so.

The Great Mystery told her in a dream that this man contained both brothers. And so, to this day, every person contains both brothers. We carry within us both creation and destruction, beauty and sacred power. Sometimes one brother shows his nature through us, and sometimes the other; it is wisdom if we know when it is proper for one or the other to manifest himself.

So it was indeed the truthful brother who had come to live with her. But he, and all of us, must be conscious that the lying brother is within us,

and that sometimes to call ourselves truthful is a lie. Yet that is neither
good nor bad, but just how things are.

Have you ever struggled to capture a thought or memory, and the harder you
tried the farther it ran from your conscious mind—only to have it suddenly
occur to you when you had stopped seeking it? Or have you had a thought or
memory burst upon your consciousness unexpectedly, leaving you shaking
with its immensity? Some thoughts are clearly *wakan* by nature. Dreams often
surprise us the same way: we awaken and we remember dreaming an amazing
dream, but it slips away from our grasp like a wild creature before we can lay
our hands on it. Traditional peoples, who are experienced in hunting this kind
of quarry, have little trouble recalling memories or dreams. The medicine
woman or man is particularly adept at hunting not only *wakan* plants and animals, but *wakan* thoughts, dreams and visions—including, in fact, dreams not
yet dreamt, thoughts not yet thought, visions not yet seen.

While most words used in ordinary conversation are "friendly," there are
other words that are "unfriendly." The latter have great power in them. The
medicine man or woman often searches for powerful words and "harvests"
them to use in healing or sacred ceremony. The older and wiser a person
becomes, the greater the percentage of *wakan* speech; the traditional elder
speaks little but, when she or he does, we *listen*, because we know the words will
be well worth our undivided attention. When speech is extremely *wakan*, it may
well surprise and even shock us. Sadly, modern culture is dissipating the sacred
power in certain words through overuse. Poets are perhaps the only people
among the dominant culture who intuitively know and respect the *wakan*
power of some words—I think, for instance, of the profoundly magical use of
the "f" word in Lawrence Ferlinghetti's poem "The Situation in the West,
Followed by a Holy Proposal," and, indeed, much of the Beat poets' *œuvre*.

Among traditional peoples, communication is in essence a living being, a
spirit being, in its own right. It does what it wishes and exists on its own terms.
It's not that some person decides to communicate, but that Spirit decides to
speak through that person to the people listening. Spirit can choose to be
evoked anywhere, at any time, and not necessarily in linear terms. That is to
say, the "speaking" may come after the "hearing," or there may be hearing
without any apparent "speaker." Spirit can at any time choose to join individuals together in a magical experience that transcends time and space, without

their even being consciously aware of it. This, in fact, is much of what dreaming and visioning is all about.

When you tell a good joke, the person who hears it laughs. In that moment of laughter the person is, for just a moment, pulled out of ordinary *washte* experience into *wakan* experience. Why? Because the unexpectedness of the punch line is *wakan*. After the joke has been told a few times, it's no longer funny, because now it has become *washte*, ordinary. However, if the hearer doesn't "get" the joke, if it must be explained, then the hearer never leaves the *washte*.

Using humor in the face of tragedy and hard times has long been a hall-mark of the traditional peoples. Piapot, a chief of the Nehiyawok (Cree), once remarked, "The white man who is our agent is so stingy that he carries a linen rag in his pocket into which he blows his nose, for fear that he might blow away something of value."—an incisive comment not only on the newcomers' greed, but on their strange and unhealthy personal habits.

Or, there's this more recent story:

> *A white woman driving her car one day sees an Indian woman thumbing for a ride beside the highway. As the trip has been long and dull, she stops the car and lets the woman get in.*
>
> *After a bit of small talk, the Indian woman notices a brown bag on the front seat. "What's in the bag?" the Indian woman asks.*
>
> *"It's a bottle of wine. I got it for my husband," the white woman replies.*
>
> *For a moment the Indian lady is silent. Then she says, "Good trade."*

That joke draws subtle allusions to the different views of marriage held by patri-archal whites and matriarchal Indians, even the serious issue of alcoholism. This next one touches lightly on the loss of traditional natural wisdom, forcing dependence on non-Indian expertise, and the romantic newcomer image of Native omniscience:

> *Everybody kept asking the chief if it was going to be a hard winter. "Come on, you have to know," they would say; "after all, you're the chief!" But he really had no idea.*
>
> *Not wanting to admit his ignorance, he told them he would consult with the spirits.*
>
> *Then the chief went into town to the phone booth, called the National Weather Service, and asked, "Hey, what's this winter going to be like?"*

"It's going to be cold," said the meteorologist who answered the phone. So the chief came back home and reported to his people that, according to the spirits, it was going to be cold, and they began to gather wood in preparation. After a few days, they came and asked him, "Have we gathered enough wood yet? How cold is this winter going to be?"

So again the chief said he'd consult with the spirits. He went to town and called the National Weather Service, and asked the meteorologist exactly how cold it was going to be. "Very cold," the man said. The chief went back and told the people, "The spirits say, very cold." And they went out and gathered even more wood.

After a few more days of hard labor gathering wood, the people came again to the chief and asked, "So, do we have enough wood yet? Is this winter going to be really, really cold?"

Once again, the chief went to town to consult with the spirits by telephone. He called the meteorologist and asked the same question. "Oh, yes," he said to the chief, "it is going to be really, really cold."

"How do you know this?" the chief asked.

"Easy," the meteorologist replied. "Those Indians up on the rez, they're gathering wood like crazy!"

Within a lot of traditional humor is a very sacred principle called *heyoka* among the Lakota, *gagosa* among the Hodenasaunee (Iroquois Confederacy). *Heyoka* is the contrary principle. What is bizarre for us is ordinary for *heyoka*. There are *heyoka* animals and plants, and *heyoka* humans. Medicine men and women often act in *heyoka* ways; other people often do too because it is in their nature. These people often make us laugh with their antics—but, as Black Elk taught, this laughter helps us to be open to the *wakan*, in the same way that a good joke pulls us momentarily out of the ordinary (*washte*).

Heyoka people are traditionally described as follows. They say "yes" when they mean "no" and "no" when they mean "yes." They are awake at night and asleep by day. They ride horses backwards. They wear lots of clothes in the summer and go around naked in the winter. They pick up red-hot rocks like there's nothing wrong with them, but rocks at normal temperature they cannot bear to touch. Unlike the rest of us, who leave footprints behind us, they pick up their footprints as they walk. If a heyoka enters the Sacred Stone People's Lodge, it is obviously time to leave; when the heyoka leaves, it is clearly time to go in. And when *heyoka* joke around they are very serious, and when they are serious you should not take them seriously. In the story I told you about the always truthful brother and the always lying brother, the latter was *heyoka*.

People with *heyoka* tendencies have several important traditional roles. If you need a powerful sacred name (the kind you don't use in ordinary daily existence, but rather in ceremony, for healing, or for seeking out the *nagipi* (spirits), you go to a *heyoka*. But don't accept the name that is suggested to you in all seriousness, but the silly, strange name that is suggested to you in what appears to be humor. When a child is born, it is often brought to a *heyoka* for blessing—which may be given in some ridiculous way. When you are stuck in trying to solve a problem, a *heyoka* will help you, often by pointing out in effect how you're getting all too serious about your problem.

Heyoka have the vital function of keeping balance between *washte* and *wakan*. While around other humans and human habitation, they serve like lightning rods, drawing off *wakan*—which in large measure could be risky for the *washte* nature of communities, but on which the *heyoka* thrive. I have been told that likewise, in the wilderness, they protect the *wakan* from inundations of *washte*. I haven't seen or learned about this in the Native American context, but I believe that this is essentially what environmentalists are doing who employ unusual, even hilarious means to protect forests or wild species—sitting for days in a tree threatened by loggers, holding hands and singing songs in front of earthmoving equipment, appearing naked in public as members of one organization do and saying that that's preferable to wearing furs.

One extremely important role the *heyoka*—especially *heyoka* medicine men and women—play is to help keep balances during the New Year Festival. During the intercalary time between the end of the lunar year and the Winter Solstice, anarchy reigns, all debts are forgiven, all agreements voided and license becomes normal. Among the Hodenasaunee, for instance, people would run naked through the wintry streets between the longhouses, openly engage in unusual sexual activity and generally do the most outrageous things. At the New Year Festival, everyone in the nation became, for a while, *heyoka*. Except for the *heyoka* themselves—they became normal! The *heyoka* watched over all the other people, together with the medicine men and women, to make sure they were safe, and watched the skies so they could call an end to the Festival. (Needless to say, these ceremonies are no longer practiced, or continue but in milder forms—because of pressures exerted by religions and government.)

The *Wakinyan Wakan*, the Thunder Beings, are also *heyoka*. In talking about them, I need to be very clear on one point: I am using plurals in talking about them, but they are neither male nor female, singular nor plural, real nor imaginary. They live in the thunderclouds in the West, where the Grandfathers live. They are both contrary and dangerously powerful, and so are great sources of healing and cleansing. The Thunder Beings—like the Great White Giant of the North, the *nagipi* (spirit beings), the *Unchegila* (Dragon) and the Little People—are entities unknown to scientists. They are traditionally described as having no beaks, yet they speak the voice of thunder from their beaks. They have no eyes, yet lightning shoots from their eyes. They have no claws, yet they drop rain from their claws. They have no wings, but when their gigantic wings beat the winds come. They make a nest of dry bones in which they lay a gigantic egg from which their young continually come forth. They devour these young, which then become Thunder Beings too, in their infinite manifestations. They are guardians of the truth. Remember this: when the rain and wind lash your face, when you see the flash of lightning, when you hear the voice of thunder, when your home is shaking, they are there. When they are there, shut up and listen to them. But, even when you don't observe these man-ifestations of their presence, bear in mind that they are never far from us and can hear us, even our thoughts, especially when they are silent themselves. So be truthful, be good, be generous, be humble, be respectful.

Nobody carries Thunder Being medicine; never claim any connection with them, as they do not take kindly to that and are never to be trifled with. When you're sure they're there, they're not. When you are sure they aren't there, they come full force. They are beyond good and evil. They are cleansers, and they can cleanse away *everything*, good and evil. That is to say, they lead to new beginnings. They are beyond fear and courage. If you are afraid of them, you have no reason to be afraid of them, because that means you respect them. But if you are *not* afraid of them, you *should* be afraid of them, because that means you do *not* respect them! And, in conclusion, if you rely on anything I can say about them, you'll find that it's completely unreliable. I jokingly summarize the Thunder Being teaching in what I call Audlin's Law: "No law applies if you expect it to, including this one."

European-American historians say that Native Americans didn't know about electricity before the Europeans came. But that is not so. In fact, Native Americans still know some facts about electricity that the Europeans have yet to learn. It's not widely recognized, for example, that electric and magnetic fields cause nervousness and anxiety. When the Thunder Beings come, as they sometimes do during the Fourth Age of the Sacred Stone People's Lodge, they create such a field. We feel the mounting tension as a kind of "buzzing" fills the lodge. Once when I was a boy, lightning struck close to the lodge, no doubt attracted by the same field-presence. This presence serves as a kind of cleansing, a kind of "jolt" that wakes us up and heals us.

But, while they're unusual in traditional culture, electric and magnetic fields are all-pervasive among people in modern society. Far from cleansing us or opening us up, as it does in small measure, like any medicine, the constant bombardment of our bodies and souls by electromagnetic radiation—from fluorescent lights, cathode ray tubes, microwaves and cellular telephone energy—has the cumulative effect of so overloading our spirits that they wind up deadened. Overexposure to these kinds of radiation damages creativity, insight and initiative, as well as physical health.

I remember several years ago when a hurricane crossed the Connecticut shoreline where I was then living. For several days, there was a power outage. All the electrical machinery stopped, all the telephones, microwaves, computers, copiers, fax machines, fluorescent lights, all the things that emanate a powerful radiation that affects one's thinking and moods. When the electricity stopped, people slowed down, relaxed and became more friendly. Time seemed to steady itself into a slower, gentler rhythm. However, when the power came back on, people went back to their usual frenzied pace.

Modern society is drowning in too much of these effects, which are similar to those brought by the Thunder Beings. Even more forebodingly, it is rendering these *wakan* effects *washte*: it is turning the sacred powers into electronic, fossil-fueled and nuclear slaves. Even while most people don't know the Thunder Beings exist, they are being overwhelmed by electrical emanations similar to those of the Thunder Beings and getting nothing *but* these "jolts," without any rest. In using that *wakan* energy to destroy nature, they have really welcomed the power of the Thunder Beings, which will eventually destroy their culture.

In the traditional way, when storms or the Thunder Beings occasionally come during the Sacred Stone People's Lodge, the electric "jolt" we receive is a good one. It wakes us up, straightens us out, cleans us out and sets us right. How well I remember that time when as a boy I foolishly prayed for a sign, and a lightning bolt hit a tree next to the lodge! That surely set me right!

In Christianity, different denominations and theologians argue as to the meaning of the Sacrament of Holy Communion. Is it, for instance, literal transubstantiation of the bread and wine into the body and blood of Christ, or is it a remembrance of an historical event, or is it yet something else? My view as an ordained Christian clergyperson is that it is a *mysterium tremendum*, a sacred mystery that, fortunately, is not explicable. As with a joke, explaining it ruins it.

In Dorothy Bryant's fine novel, *The Kin of Ata are Waiting for You* (also published as *The Comforter*), there is a scene in which a student and his teacher are watching a sacred dance of the tribe. He asks the teacher its meaning and her reply suggests that he is foolish to want to replace meaning-as-implicit-in-dance with meaning-as-explicit-in-words. If he does that, she tells him, the words will get in between him and the dance. Instead, she advises, he should go *through* the dance—and find the meaning on the other side. I believe that the "other side," the far side of words and dance, is the uncharted wilderness, the realm of the *wakan*. To force the meaning from that other side to this side, the *washte* side, where logic and reason rule, is to rob sacred meaning of its dynamic power.

Yesterday I hiked up a mountain in the Catskills with a friend, to look at a petroglyph she had found years before, in a quarry used centuries ago by Native people. We looked at this beautiful work, a single line curved and angled into a complex pattern, carefully incised into the rock, and discussed what its meaning and purpose might be. I was conscious of the fact that we were looking at it through the distorting lens of our "modern" ways of thinking, and that the ancient person responsible for this work would surely have laughed at our foolish guesses! Rather, though we modern humans have forgotten how to "read" it, this glyph means exactly what it says in the First Language. Better put, it means exactly what it is: itself. Looking at it, I was reminded of prehistoric cave paintings I was once privileged to see near the home of one Grandmother in the Ozark Mountains. Even though those works were clearly representational, it seems to me somehow sacrilegious to assign to such renderings a certain meaning or purpose, as anthropologists do. They are mute to modern minds because these works are *wakan*, not *washte*. Their power lies in their very being, not in any imputed meaning or purpose.

There is a great temptation for anyone who walks the spiritual path, the *wakan* path, to seek to become a "shaman"—a Tungusic word that has been so over-used and misused in recent years as to be rendered devoid of any real meaning. This temptation is modeled on the dominant culture, in which the religious leader is in the foreground, occluding the view of the sacred, attracting attention instead to himself or herself. In traditional cultures, those that lack organized religion, the elders stand apart from the mainstream of society; they are, like the *wakan* itself, contrary, sacred, mysterious and solitary. To borrow Thomas Carlyle's analogy, they are like an underground river: they nourish the Earth without their presence being seen.

This is why—to the consternation of well-meaning members of modern society—these elders often live alone, apart, in crumbling shacks or rusting old trailers, way out on the rez or well outside of town where the poor folks live. They practice a kind of creative asceticism—not, as in the Western religions a "giving up" of pleasures in order to "chastise the flesh" but rather a determined abandoning of conventions, of *washte* paths, to find the *wakan* or, more accurately, to allow themselves to be found by it. To prepare themselves for this encounter, they use different means—including fasting, sleep deprivation, psychoactive drugs, chanting, dancing, sweating, drumming, solitude, physical pain, consorting with dead bodies, going on quests, sexuality, mountain climbing, long-distance running—in the service of a higher rule: that what the medicine person does is done for the good of all and with the greatest care, attention and humility.

The members of the nation see little of the medicine person, since he or she is most often about when other people are asleep or at home—during the night, during the winter, during the dark of the Moon—seeking the elusive herbs that bloom at these times, watching the night Sky for the return of the crescent Moon, the stars for signs of the Solstice and the Earth for signs of winter beginning to recede. At times of $\mu\varepsilon\tau\alpha\tau\alpha\xi\iota\varsigma$ (*metataxis*)—the chaotic, mutable, shifting region between one stable system and its complementary stable system (in this case, the time outside of time between two years)—the medicine person, like the *heyoka*, is strangely normal, while the people are enwrapped in sacred chaos. This normality is the "string on the kite" that keeps the nation's anarchy from spinning out of control, such that he or she can guide the people back into normal ways as the new cycle begins.

You can learn to be a priest, a minister, an 'imam, a rabbi. But you can't learn to be a medicine man or woman. People are born with this gift or are called to it through dreams and visions. While one cannot be taught how to *be* one, one *must* be taught how to *cope* with being one. Walking the medicine path has a radical effect on one's life. Indeed, it is not something one should envy.

To experience the *wakan*, you need to abandon the known and familiar and go into the wordless, trackless wilderness within your soul. Gautama Buddha once said, "To reach a destination you have never found, you must take a path you do not know." An old saying goes, "If you don't know where you're going, any path wll take you there." The poet Antonio Machado wrote these exquisite and truthful lines:

> *Caminante, son tus huellas*
> *el camino, y nada más,*
> *caminante, no hay camino,*
> *se hace camino al andar,*
> *Al andar se hace el camino…*
>
> *(Wayfarer, your tracks are*
> *the way, and nothing else;*
> *wayfarer, there is no way,*
> *it becomes the way when you walk it,*
> *When you walk it it becomes the way…)*

George Armstrong Custer's Crow scouts told him, on the eve of the Battle of Little Big Horn, "Today, my friend, we go home by a road we do not know." Ohiyesa's (Charles A. Eastman's) *Uncheeda,* or Grandmother, taught him to follow any new path or footprint he found "to the point of knowing." In all of these teachings the truth is clear: You will find what you seek only if you let go of the safe and familiar and risk venturing into the unknown—the sacred, powerful, mysterious, dangerous. If you are *not* taking risks, if you feel no fear in your spiritual walk, you have not left the *washte* realm.

I could just get up behind a podium and lecture people about these matters—and I have—but none of my hearers is going to leave the *washte* behind merely because of anything I say. Indeed, it would be ὑβρις (*hubris*) even to try to help someone to find the *wakan*. I can only tell you where the pathless wilderness of the *wakan* begins—in such sacred actions as drumming, chanting, fasting, sleep deprivation, sweating, sacred sexuality, even drugs. But I cannot guide you any further. You must find your way into the sacred by yourself, if you wish and if you dare.

III

Reality & Awareness

GRANDFATHER SINGS-ALONE ONCE WROTE an essay reminding us to beware of thinking, when we see something unusual happen in the natural world, that it's a message from the Creator sent especially to us. In *The New Phoenix*, he wrote: "Let the natural world be natural. Allow yourself to be present for spiritual experiences without analyzing everything.... There is a place for analysis, a time to use the mind, but not in the middle of a sacred event."

People in the the dominant culture commonly have one of two kinds of responses to the unusual natural events they observe. The first is that they are simply the mundane movements of natural processes governed by descriptive laws, without any other significance. From this perspective, the natural world offers sensory data that are devoid of larger relevance. Based on an assumption that humanity is extrinsic to nature, this attitude leads to the valuation of nature for its pragmatic benefits only.

The other typical response is to inflate natural events with personal meaning. Such an observer values natural events in personal and allegorical terms. Interpreting larger events in terms of himself or herself, this observer asks, "What is this event's meaning for me?" This attitude toward the world leads to the valuation of nature for its purportedly psychic or spiritual benefit. Such individuals may see an eagle circling overhead and believe it is a powerful vision sent specifically to them—even concluding that it means they have been given eagle medicine!

People in the dominant culture often think those are the only two choices. In both cases the observers stand outside of nature, failing to recognize their intimate relationship with the family of living beings. Observers set themselves up as *above* nature, as if nature were a show being put on for their benefit and they were the arbiter of its value. The same is true for dreams and visions. Those who take them seriously still tend to think of them as containing information, but encoded in a nearly incomprehensible "language" that they must look up in "dream dictionaries" or have their psychoanalysts translate.

In the tradition of the original peoples, however, it is *the event itself* that is important; *the vision or dream itself* is the message. How we interpret it, or respond to it, is entirely personal. Rather than analyzing the event, squeezing it for any possible valuable meaning the way one might squeeze a fruit for its juice, traditional people consider it wise simply to observe the vision or dream on its own terms. Muslim teaching is similar; it says that, if we do not have sufficient knowledge or experience to understand the layers of meaning hidden in an event or story, we must be careful not to analyze, lest we assign some superfluous, self-serving or hazardously wrong "meaning" to it.

I remember, while dancing in a pow-wow one summer afternoon, one Grandfather called our attention to two eagles circling over our heads. I heard people around me saying, with what sounded to me like self-congratulatory ὕβρις (*hubris*), that the eagles were honoring our dancing. Grandfather did not say it was a vision or that the eagles were giving us any message. In fact, he did not say a single word. Rather, with an unrestrained, childlike joy, he simply pointed an eagle feather at them and offered tobacco to them in thanksgiving. He simply acknowledged these honored relatives visiting us, just as we might acknowledge a human acquaintance who joins us in the sacred dance circle.

My first teaching Grandfather taught me that there are no coincidences, that everything is connected and meaningful, even though some things may not be meaningful for you or me as individuals. He taught me that "there are four meanings to everything." Since the number four refers to the Sacred Hoop, it suggests completeness. So it can be inferred that what he meant by that teaching is that there is in fact no end to our quest for meaning—it is ultimately a circle that brings us back to the beginning. We understand a vision by simply embracing it.

While a sacred vision or dream is *wakan*, interpretations of it are *washte*. The sacredness must be taken on its own terms and not reduced to the *washte* of a message-for-me, real or imagined. That is no better than reducing the sacredness of the natural world around us to lumber and hides. To extract a meaning from a *wakan* event and then discard the event itself is *sicha*, wrong. That is as *washichu*, greedy, as killing a four-legged for the sport or even for its meat, and failing to honor its spirit or to use all of its body respectfully. The event itself is what is truly important, not our thoughts.

European views of "objective reality" have altered over time. Before Galileo, Copernicus and Kepler, Europeans believed that the planets turned around the Earth, until more accurate perceptions of objective reality forced them to abandon that conception. Basing their views on "proofs" drawn from sensory data, European peoples insist their conceptions of reality are the closest to the truth. They tend to look down their noses at traditional cultures for having different understandings of reality. If a tribe insists (let us say) that the Earth is a disc riding on a turtle's shell, the European says, "But we have looked at the Earth from space, and it is clearly an oblate spheroid." The European concludes that the traditional person's conception differs from "objective reality" as a result of insufficient perceptual data and incorrect conceptual analysis. "You can't prove your statement," the European says, "and I can." The European says there is only one reality, and two different conceptions of reality can't both be right.

In the philosophy of the traditional peoples, on the other hand, there is no such difference between reality and our perceptions and conceptions of it. What is real-for-us is what is real. If I see a vision, it is not only real-for-me, but also accepted by everyone else as real, even though others did not experience it, and even though their realities may not incorporate it. If I see three eagles soaring over the dance circle and you see four, we accept both perceptions as correct; we don't argue over who is right. When I tell others about a vision, my telling the story about it makes the vision not just real-for-me but real-for-them. I perceived the vision, they now have perceived my recreating of the vision in a sacred storytelling. In traditional culture, the fact that there is no "objective reality" out there beyond our senses means that it is perfectly possible for everyone to have a divergent reality, and everyone to be right in that reality. If a traditional person were taken in a space ship out past the Moon and shown the Earth from space, she or he would have no problem accepting this reality, the reality for the dominant culture, but it would in no way shake the foundations of his or her own reality. "That is your Earth," the traditional person would say; "not my Earth." Since traditional peoples are comfortable with accepting the divergent realities of others as also real, there is no need to determine which reality is "really real."

Traditional peoples see everything in terms of an interplay between the fundamental complementary opposites, *washte* and *wakan*. In this interplay, they find health-wholeness-holiness, the single concept expressed by these three English words. The words are in fact etymologically related, and often referred to in English as "medicine," from a French word, *médécin*, with a similar breadth of meaning.

Death and life, complementary opposites, are conjoined in sleep, which opens us up to the powerful medicine of dreams. Unfriendly plants and animals are deadly-dangerous and yet life-restoring. The most powerful ceremonies are likewise a conjunction of opposites: risk-involving and yet spiritually cleansing and nourishing, dramatically bringing the *washte* and the *wakan* together.

Sacred objects are made in such a way as to bring opposites together. The Sacred Pipe, the Sacred Drum, the Sacred Stone People's Lodge and the Sacred Rattle are all traditionally made of animal and plant and stone and spirit materials; all have the ordinary world of light outside and the mysterious world of darkness inside; inside each something rich with potential is placed and transmuted (respectively: tobacco, tobacco, human souls and seeds).

But the interplay of *washte* and *wakan* goes deeper than that. When a traditional person and a modern person look at the same thing, it is *not* the "same thing" because they perceive it in such fundamentally different ways. As Bishop George Berkeley taught, *esse est percipi*: essence and perception are one and the same. When I saw the woman bathing in the mountain waterfall, it was a sacred vision simply because I saw a concatenation of so many opposites: hot day and cold water, white light on black rocks, silent woods and thundering water, nakedness clothed in water. When traditional people (or others who have broken free from their cultural conditioning) watch the Eagle Dance, they see the story unfold, the change of shape from man to eagle, the dropping of the *washte* robe and the revelation of the *wakan* spirit.

For traditional peoples storytelling is a sacred act that brings people together and nourishes community. Jews are reminded of their common identity when they tell Haggadah at the Seder, Christians when they tell the story of the Last Supper at the Eucharist, and Muslims when they remember the coming of the Angel Gabriel to the Prophet during the holy month of Ramadan. Likewise, traditional peoples worldwide tell their sacred and traditional stories again and again, and, by so doing, remind themselves of who they are. These stories are a part of the people's nature; in hearing or telling them again, the stories and the personages in them are brought alive in that moment. So, when someone tells a story of a vision, the hearers in effect have had the vision too.

In the dominant culture culture, people whose perceptions and/or conceptions of reality diverge considerably from the socially agreed-upon norm are declared mentally ill. Today one is considered mentally ill if one sees angels, even though from Biblical times until the Enlightenment those who said they saw angels were believed. Today one is considered sane if one says the Earth circles 'round the Sun, but in the Middle Ages such a view was so radical that one might not be just considered crazy, but even executed for expressing it. The norms society agrees on change with the times, but in all of European cultural history one has had to adhere to the accepted norms or be cast out.

Among traditional peoples, persons who diverge considerably from the norm are not considered mentally ill but special persons—the Lakota term for them is *heyoka*—whose realities help us by challenging and energizing ours. As I have described, *heyoka* live in realities that are contrary or opposite: their realities are usually *wakan* but sometimes can be strangely ordinary, *washte*, when everyone else is *wakan*. Neither the ordinary person nor the *heyoka* person has a better view of reality; what each sees is universally accepted as fully real by everyone in the nation.

In human relationships, it is the same way for traditional people. If you *perceive* a problem in your relationship with someone, then there is a problem. It is a modern question, not a traditional question, to wonder if there "really" is a problem or if "I'm just perceiving one." Let's say you're married to someone you think is lazy. A traditional person married to this individual would realize that the problem is real simply because she or he *perceives* it. If another person were married to this individual, the other person might not perceive this individual as lazy. But that only means the laziness wouldn't be *a real problem* for the other person. All there is is perception, so the very fact that you perceive a problem makes the problem real.

Here is another thing about reality my Grandfathers have taught me. The modern view of reality is based on straight lines and angles. When someone goes somewhere or gives directions, the method of orientation is based on "straight ahead," "turn left" and "turn right." But Nature doesn't work that way, and neither does the traditional person. Everything in Nature goes in curves and circles, and the same is true in our going about. A traditional person doesn't necessarily walk in a straight line from Point A to Point B, but follows a curve that flows with the land. It is my personal view that Einstein, in his discovery of the curvature of space, learned something that traditional peoples have known for millennia. "Imagination is more important than knowledge," said Einstein; "I never came upon my discoveries through the process of rational thinking."

This story illustrates how the difference over "objective reality" and "perception" divides members of the dominant culture and traditional people:

> *Two people one day are walking through a forest. One is a member of the dominant culture, and the other is a traditional Native American. They both see something in a distant tree. "It looks like an owl," they both say. As they get closer they look again. Now they agree, "It looks like a pine cone."*
>
> *As they continue along the path, the two companions discuss what they have seen. "At first I thought it was an owl," says the member of the dominant culture, "but, as I got closer, I realized it was a pine cone. I only thought it was an owl because I was too far away." This person assumes the object had a certain objective reality the whole time, and that its nature did not change. Since the object appeared to change, he decides that his first conclusion was wrong.*
>
> *The Native American says, "When I was farther away it appeared to me as an owl, but, as I got closer, it changed its appearance into that of a pine cone. It was an owl at first, but, while I was walking closer, it became a pine cone." The Native American does not assume there is a certain unchanging objective reality to the object. Since the object appeared to change, he believes it did change its nature.*
>
> *The two friends don't reach any consensus, but they do emerge from their conversations with very different feelings. The Native American is happy to have had a vision—a small vision, perhaps, but still one that affirms for him the presence of the Creator and the spirits all around him. The member of the dominant culture may feel foolish for having misperceived the pine cone as an owl and wonder if he should make an appointment with an optometrist.*

Which of these two people is right? Was it a pine cone all along, or was it an owl who turned into a pine cone? And which of the two companions can prove the other wrong? Even if there is a "reality out there" beyond our senses, all we have is our sense perceptions. Ultimately, both individuals are equally right, or wrong—not just because we create our own reality with what we believe, but also because spirits can borrow, for example, a pine cone stuck in a tree to render visible their owl semblance, or an owl to manifest their pine cone semblance. As Hui-neng, the Sixth Patriarch of Zen, once taught, when he overheard two monks arguing over whether it was the flag moving in the wind or the wind moving the flag, "It is your minds moving!" Or, as Wild Witch High Priestess Manx Starfire puts it, in words almost identical to those of a Native American elder I know: "In science, seeing is believing; in magic, believing is seeing." Science seeks proof within its preconceptions (its system of laws), while magic is open to whatever chooses to reveal itself. In either case, cultural conditioning builds the framework of our expectations. Whether the two walkers in the story see an owl or a pine cone is indeed a matter of their minds moving and says more about each of them than it does about the entity in question.

A medicine woman or man sees with pure perception, with the "enlarged and numerous senses" Blake the artist yearned for. And such a person carries, he said, "the desire of raising other men into a perception of the infinite[;] this the North American tribes practise." If a traditional elder had accompanied our two walking companions, she or he might well have looked into the tree, from both far and near, and seen both the owl *and* the pine cone simultaneously—or seen, more deeply yet, the imperceptible sacred spirit in or of the tree, which has the potential to robe itself in either outer form and most likely an infinity of other forms as well. The medicine person sees beyond such outer robes, the "glamour" the spirit deliberately throws over itself as camouflage. With the mind still and the senses wide open, the medicine person sees past the outer coverings and finds there, in the entity's heart and soul, how it perceives itself—its essential nature. As Pierre Abélard sang in one of his hymns, "*Est in re veritas, jam non in schemate*" ("Truth is in the thing itself, never in the reasoning"). The eyes of our robe (body) see other robes (bodies), but the eyes of our spirit see spirit. The spirit in the tree remains one in nature whatever the two walkers' perceptions of its outer appearance.

Members of the dominant culture are dispassionate observers, separating themselves as much as possible from the thing observed. They prefer to observe birds with binoculars, from a distance, from behind a blind. But, in failing to interact with the birds, perception is limited. Conversely, the way of the traditional peoples is to recognize one's relatedness to—ultimately, one's oneness with—the thing being observed, such that one truly knows and loves the thing itself and thus can fully perceive and understand its nature. "Before we can *see* we must *learn how to look*," Barre Toelken once observed. This way of observing takes considerable patience and quietude within; it means putting aside preconceptions and remaining fully open to the experience itself, becoming fully one with the experience, as is taught in Zen. William Blake wrote, "If the doors of perception were cleansed every thing would appear to man as it is, infinite."

When I saw one old medicine man do the Eagle Dance, I can honestly say I saw him become an eagle. No longer did I see an old man dancing on the Earth, but an eagle soaring above. While a member of the dominant society would ask whether the physical reality of the old man actually changes, the Native American knows that existence is perception. The Native American recognizes the dance as the Eagle Dance and the symbolic movements of outstretched arms and hooked fingers as the movements of Eagle. The sensory data the Native American receives all clearly say, "This is Eagle." The Native American has no trouble accepting the reality of shapeshifting and therefore sees Eagle.

Even a member of the dominant culture may overcome cultural conditioning enough to see the old man become Eagle. After all, shapeshifting occurs even in the dominant culture, though usually explained as the eyes "playing tricks." One Native Grandmother told me the story of attending the ballet *Swan Lake* at Carnegie Hall. In the final scenes, she and the hundreds of others in the audience saw the ballerina Maya Plisetskaya not simply dance the part, but actually physically *become* the dying swan.

It's not that the Eagle dancer in some objective sense ceases to be human and becomes an eagle, but that he recognizes Eagle within himself, and allows us to share in that recognition. Anyone can learn to do the dance, and even to do it well. But these outer actions are not some kind of "magic spell" with repeatable results. They are simply evocative; if Eagle is not already present in the inner spirit—if the dancer does not carry Eagle medicine—then no shifting of shape will occur, no matter how good the dancing. If this were not the case, then anyone doing the Eagle Dance anywhere, even on a stage in front of a paying audience, would become Eagle.

The dance—being essentially a sacred ceremony—strips away surface appearances (*washte*) to reveal the deeper, spiritual reality (*wakan*). The dance is, therefore, a deliberate self-deprivation of the *washte*: it is a ceremony in which one puts aside the pleasures of the *washte* so that the *wakan* may flow more freely. Without emptying oneself first (as Zen Master Nan-in once taught his guest by pouring tea into a teacup that was already full), it cannot happen.

But observers of the dance and, often, dancers themselves hold on to the *washte* out of fear, ignorance or selfish desire, and so nothing *wakan* happens, and they conclude there is no such thing as the *wakan*. For the same reason, if they enter the Sacred Stone People's Lodge and never let go of their comfortable *washte*, they will have no more positive outcome than the physically healthy and cleansing effects of a steam bath. Perhaps this is a way the *wakan* protects itself: the *wakan* chooses its own, and thus is not subject to command or coercion.

Since visions and dreams do not fit comfortably within the framework of modern society's reality, they are considered less-than-real. But in recognizing perceptions as the very nature of physical existence, the traditional culture welcomes dreams and visions as a means of maintaining a vital relationship with the spirits and the Creator. Dreams and visions are considered powerful and far more real than the perceptual robes (corporeal natures) they cloak themselves in—as even more real than ordinary experience, simply because they are *wakan*.

It is my understanding that shapeshifting is also a changing of perceptions, though the distinction between "appearing" to shift appearance and "actually" shifting appearance is one made in modern ontology, not traditional ontology. Shapeshifting is often a matter of adaptation and camouflage. Many birds, trees and plants, as well as some fur-bearing creatures such as ermines, change their appearance between winter and summer. Other creatures shift their appearance to adapt during the course of their lives: caterpillars become butterflies; tadpoles become frogs. For camouflage, the appearance of certain insects, reptiles and birds mimics their environment. Likewise, a spirit can shapeshift from owl appearance to pine cone appearance as you approach so you won't focus your attention on it.

The old medicine men and women know how to change their appearance by changing perceptions for better adaptation and more effective camouflage. This is why shapeshifting is not done "on stage" to convince an audience, or to prove to scientists that it can be done. It is done not to *draw* attention, but most often to *deflect* attention (the only exception being to draw the attention of certain beings, such as spirit peoples). It is not a matter of changing their objective reality, as the dominant culture assumes, since in traditional ontology there is no "reality out there beyond the senses," but a matter of changing the observer's perception of them. If a medicine man wishes you to see him as an eagle, you will see an eagle and, moreover, since perceptions are reality, he *is* an eagle in that moment.

The outer physical shape is a robe a spirit puts on. Every spirit, theoretically, carries the potential of appearing in (putting on) an infinity of shapes—though individual nature tends to favor certain shapes above others. The medicine one carries leads to that natural affinity for certain shapes. In the ancient traditional stories, the natures of all living creatures were fluid, metamorphic—flowing with infinite *wakan* possibility—until eventually each kind of creature got a name that "fixed" its nature into a certain form. Shapeshifters know how to put aside this name and go back to their original fluid nature (or, to paraphrase the Zen Buddhist *koön*, their original face before they were born). Coyote and Hare and Spider in these stories are not fixed in outer appearance; they are not specifically animals or humans, but spirits that can take on either kind of shape. In these stories it often happens that a young man or woman marries a Bear or a Star who appears variously in bear or star or human shape. Nâlungiaq, an Inuit elder, told the early twentieth century ethnologist Knud Rasmussen that, in the earliest times, "sometimes they were people and other times animals, and there was no difference."

Whatever shape a spirit has gives it the characteristics, and medicine, inherent within that shape. Every living being—eagle, bear, tree, star, even an ordinary housecat, even an amoeba—has its special characteristics. If a medicine person takes on the shape of wolf, let's say, then, even if the individual has no sense of smell in her or his "normal" (*washte*) robe, then she or he does have an acute sense of smell as wolf. Though the elder may have poor eyesight normally, as eagle the elder has powerful visionary ability. The medicine people also know that, when we are reborn, we come back to the robe that is right for us on our journey toward wisdom—for example to a living being that has medicine that we need to learn, or learn better.

Today, our elder brothers and sisters (the spirit beings, the rocks, the plants, the two-leggeds, the four-leggeds, the six-leggeds, the eight-leggeds), especially the "unfriendly" ones, still remember how to do this shapeshifting, though they are careful not to attract notice from *washichu* humans, and still today a few old medicine men and women remember how to do this. Moreover, still today, the Landkeepers walk abroad, doing their best to care for the natural world and its wild inhabitants, and even occasionally enter into the city when the need is there, for example, to succor a lost or frightened creature. These sacred spirit-beings may appear in any kind of robe, two- or four-legged, for example, and even sometimes in a combination, such as a wolf's head on a human body dressed in wolf fur. (Bear in mind, however, that these are *wild, wakan* beings that cannot be invoked or bound to human will. If you see one, be wary and respectful as you would with any dangerous wild creature: do not approach or accost it.) But, for most humans, this medicine is not only lost but believed to be impossible.

Shapeshifting is a part of storytelling. Stories told aloud do more than just entertain. Stories are powerful ceremonies that, told well, evoke powerful sacred presences. The repetitive nature of story and song evokes the beat of the heart, the breath of the lungs: it brings the universe around us alive. As the storyteller is telling it, the story is vivid in the minds of both teller and hearers; the hearers enter into the story themselves, becoming a part of it. Storytelling is a kind of shapeshifting: as the story is told, the listeners can just about see the story's ghost or monster in the darkness just beyond the firelight, the hero and the heroine in the stars overhead, the roaring beast in the flickering flames. Among traditional people, storytelling needs no highly technological "special effects;" it brings the wilderness closer rather than pushing it farther away. As a story is being told, the storyteller and the hearers, together with the mysterious shapes in the darkness of night around the council fire, *become* the figures in the sacred story itself.

Hunting, too, is shapeshifting: a successful hunter becomes in essence the creature he is hunting. And, in ceremony, we take off not only our clothes to enter the Sacred Stone People's Lodge, but our common everyday identities too, in order to become the essential First Man or First Woman who inhabits the Dreamtime (as the traditional people of Australia call it).

Words—such as these words I am sharing with you—are a robe for thoughts. A thought is evoked in the shape of words. When those words are translated into another language, the robe of words has in effect shapeshifted. When a story is told in different ways by different persons or different nations, that too is a shapeshifting of the sacred spirit of the story. The physical presence of a Sacred Pipe is but a robe of the one single Sacred Pipe, the spirit of the Pipe that is within each and all the physical robes that it wears. In all these cases, the spirit, the ἰδέα (*idea*) in Platonic terms, remains the same.

Shapeshifting pervades all our reality, for those of us who walk the traditional way. When the fetus dies in becoming a child, the child dies in becoming an adult, when the adult dies in becoming an elder, when the elder dies in becoming a spirit presence, this is shapeshifting; the spirit remains the same. When we sleep and dream, and when we walk in visions, we are very rarely robed in our everyday body; rather, we seem to walk more often as different people, even four-leggeds or spirits. The physical changes wrought by sexuality (arousal, gestation, parturition, lactation) are shapeshifting. Likewise, a relationship can shift its shape — change its robe — people moving from friends to lovers or back again, from friends to enemies and back again, and so on.

Ceremonies are especially powerful at night, when the darkness doesn't hide but more fully reveals the infinite multiplicity of potential shapes that every being carries. But, even in daylight, this multiplicity is there. I think of a woman who told me about what she saw one dizzyingly hot summer day (for the extremes of torrid heat and humidity and light can pull us out of the *washte* as surely as can the darkness of night or the cold of winter). The air was buzzing like bees with the *wakan,* just as often there is a sacred buzzing of Spirit inside the Sacred Stone People's Lodge. She saw in her back yard an old woman, a Grandmother, standing silently in the grass with her long hair sweeping down and her arms outstretched. When the woman looked later, she saw once again the old apple tree that had stood for years in that spot. As Gautama Buddha taught, we must detach from our preconceptions and expectations, which limit us and the things around us to one outer nature only, such that we can see what the Buddhists call *tathata,* reality as it really is — an infinity of potential shapes carried by every being. *Tat tvam asi,* as the Hindus teach: That thou art.

A newborn infant has a very limited sense of reality because it has not yet developed a mental structure (concepts) enabling it to order raw sensory data. In modern society, children are taught to be observant only of sensory data considered relevant and meaningful; other data are to be denied or ignored. Traditionals are taught to pay attention to *all* sensory data, since all of them are significant in various ways. Historians chip data out of a petrified past; traditional historians, as Peter Nabokov describes, know the past is still present.

Individuals, as they go through life, learn from their elders the traditional stories and ways of doing things, in the process of creating their own reality. By the time the elders become Grandmothers and Grandfathers, they have each created for themselves a reality that enables them to live well. We respect our elders because they carry wisdom that enables us too to shape our reality well. A Tsalagi (Cherokee) friend showed me many years ago how to twist my hair to make a fine fishing line. The making involves both moonwise and sun-wise twists. As he deftly made a strong slender thread, and I managed to hold the other end in my comparatively clumsy fingers, he quietly taught me, "This is the way life is. We weave together sunwise and moonwise, man and woman, summer and winter, and in that weaving there is life."

The elders remember times and people the young ones do not recall. In them we are all connected to the living presence of the Grandfathers and Grandmothers who have gone on before us. So, while we honor all people with the ethical respect that is due to everyone, we also honor elders with sacred respect because they carry the sacredness of the past and all its wisdom. Traditional wisdom has gone from generation to generation, twisted deftly one way by men and another way by women, and has proven itself to be a strong thread. The truths embodied in traditional stories bind us from generation to generation.

From our elders we seek to learn wisdom that is practical. One elder I met said, "I don't want to hear your philosophy unless it grows corn." Hin-mut-too-yah-lat-kekht (Thunder that Rises to a Higher Plane), more often known as Chief Joseph, said, "I believe much trouble and blood would be saved if we opened our hearts more. I will tell you in my way how the Indian sees things. The white people have more words to tell you how things look to them, but it does not require many words to speak the truth." Or, as Percy Lomaquahu said, "Humbleness means peace, honesty—all mean Hopi. True, honest, perfect words—that's what we call Hopi words. In all languages, not just in Hopi."

In the traditional world, the young person knows that her or his perceptual reality hasn't yet been *proven* by living many years successfully. The older one lives to be, the more clearly one's world view has been proven effective for living. When young people don't gain the respect and honor of their elders, or when they die young—unless their death is from disease or a necessary act of self-sacrifice—they show that their perspectives, their realities, haven't worked very well. That is not to say the realities of those who die young are wrong in some absolute sense, but that their realities hadn't yet come to full flower. Though they may have died bravely, they might have found another way to be courageous—and live on. That is why, among the original peoples, the young see a brave death as a good thing, but the old see battle and death as something to mourn.

In the dominant culture, meaning is something the observer imposes on reality. Children are trained from infancy to restrict their actual perceptions to fit a single, preestablished "consensus" reality. They take in some data as significant, ignoring all others, and arrange them into meaningful patterns. In this understanding, reality is a mindless and meaningless flow of events, each event the cause of subsequent events, and reality only worthy of attention to the degree that it is of value to the observer.

For Native Americans all reality is inherently meaningful. Meaning is a fundamental characteristic of all things, not something that originates in our minds but in nature itself. Children are guided into observing reality patiently, without drawing conclusions, and attend to it until the meaning within it becomes clear. Nature itself is didactic. Put in Native American terms, we are to pay attention, because reality is constantly speaking to us and teaching us.

Several things become apparent from this axiomatic understanding of the nature of reality:

> *For traditional peoples, if reality is always meaningful, then there is no entity and no event without meaning: if no meaning is apparent, that is because we have failed to perceive the meaning, not because there is none.* Example: If a Native American sees, for instance, an eagle circling overhead, he or she would be sure the event has great meaning and importance, though not necessarily for him or her, even if that significance is not immediately apparent.

> *If all things are teaching us, then there are no inanimate objects (in the sense of being unable to communicate with us because they have no spirit).* Example: Native Americans see rocks as living beings who have much to teach us.

> *An entity is primarily known to exist not because we perceive it through the senses, but because we realize that we are being taught.* Example: A Native American believes in the existence of spirit beings of many kinds, whose presence is known not by their being observed, for they may not even be observable, but because the individual is aware of being taught—even when the teaching comes without any empirical evidence of a teacher, as in dreams and visions.

The dominant culture sees the connection between events primarily in terms of cause and effect. It may be subtle, but a butterfly fanning its wings in

Argentina may be one of the causes of a typhoon in Bangladesh. According to the dominant culture, events with similarities that have no cause-and-effect relationship are coincidences. Most people are conditioned to believe that if one dreams of one's grandfather the same night he dies, it is merely a coincidence.

The traditional peoples' culture says that meaning connects events. According to this culture, events with similarities are meaningfully related whether or not they share a common antecedent cause. If one dreams of one's grandfather the same night he dies (as I, for example, did), that is not a coincidence but a significant event, a *wakan* event.

Persons who hold the modern literal understanding of reality become observing minds separated from reality, unable to bridge the gap into reality, which is forever out there beyond their perceptions. (One can explore this difficulty in the writings of René Descartes.) Conversely, the traditional person does not feel divorced from reality, but closely interrelated with it. Rather than imposing meaning, traditional peoples participate in a world of meaningfulness.

Put another way, meaningfulness is story: the world around us, and every entity within it, is constantly telling us a story. And we too are constantly participating in the unfolding of an infinite number of stories. Our lives are stories, and the life of all entities are stories, and these stories connect with each other in meaningful ways through space and time when these stories are shared.

This is why traditional peoples believe in the efficacy of what anthropologists call sympathetic magic, performing actions that have no apparent cause-and-effect relationship with a natural event and believing the magic will promote or inhibit the natural event. Since traditionals believe, as I have said, that all events are meaningfully connected, there is not a cause-and-effect relationship, but a participation in a network of meaning—among, for instance, menstruating women, the dark of the Moon, and the planting of crops in the spring. To amplify this network of meaning, menstruating Hodenasaunee (Iroquois Confederacy) women traditionally planted the seeds of the Three Sisters (corn, beans and squash), then walked naked through the fields on a moonless night at the Equinox, dragging their long robes on the ground behind them to promote good growth. These traditions spiritually evoked Iotsitsisen, the primordial woman from whose naked body the Three Sisters and tobacco first grew. It was traditional in other nations, for the same reason, for couples to have sexual relations in the newly seeded fields, as a necessary part of the sacred art of farming. And it was traditional among many peoples for the hunter to abstain from sexuality before entering the dark, moist, feminine tangle of the woods. In all these ways, a clear relationship is seen between the fruitfulness of human beings and the fruitfulness of the world they inhabit.

This is why a healer does things that medical science says will have no effect, such as touching the patient with sacred stones, or shaking a rattle, or sucking at the pain—not as an example of "sympathetic magic," as ethnologists characterize it, but because of this meaningful connection. (Mainstream European medicine is quite efficacious in some matters, but in many others, such as allergies, fevers and various kinds of cancer, it is ineffective and even sometimes does more damage than good. For concerns like these, I would rather turn to an effective medicine man or woman [including one trained in foreign traditional ways, such as acupuncture] than a Western doctor.)

As Bishop Berkeley knew, the very act of perceiving is the act of "creating our reality." In Martin Buber's terms, the world and everything in it is seen not as "it" (object) but as "thou," living Spirit-filled *wakan* entities. It is seen, more subtly, as the One Entity, the Great Mystery, the Tao, who puts on the robe of the "thousand and one things" (to quote Lao-tse). Mother Earth is a living being, and all entities are living beings, her children. The world is a powerful sacred being with its family of sacred beings, of which we are all an integral part. Being alive, the world is meaningful; every event has its meaning, every creature its message and teaching. Traditional peoples look at the world and everything in it as "wholes," as universals: each a universe in itself, a microcosm of the macrocosm, each whole a part of an infinity of other wholes, and itself comprising an infinity of other smaller wholes.

The traditional tribal way is one of magic. Magic seeks no rules: every medicine man or woman works in her or his own unique way, and no one expects the same results every time a certain action is taken. That is why no one can be *taught* to be a medicine woman or man—either you have it in you or you do not. I do believe everyone potentially could learn at least a little of the sacred medicine, the tribal magic, if only one first learned to love and respect the unknown and not be afraid of or deny the reality of the miraculous. And everyone is involved with the *wakan* from time to time, in dreaming dreams, perhaps in experiencing visions, and certainly in the sacred ceremonies of sexuality.

Magic is one and the same as the *wakan*—which is to say that, unlike science, it is not founded on a search for verifiable, repeatable results, but on ways to integrate the *washte* of human society meaningfully with the *wakan* of the individual and the wilderness. Traditional peoples are, of course, perfectly aware of the need for repeatable results, but these are to be found in the *washte*—in cooking, in making useful objects, and so on. Repeatable results—the hallmark of the *washte*—are the familiar, well-worn path as opposed to the mysterious trackless wilderness. Genuine medicine men and women offer no guarantees. Only those vaunted "shamans" who charge money pretend guaranteed results, but they try to turn magic (*wakan*) into science (*washte*), to take all the mystery out of life.

Here is what I can tell you:

> *Traditional magic works with nature, not against it.* Nothing that is unnatural is ever done. (Those few people in the traditional cultures who try to work against nature bring *sicha*, imbalance, into the world, which carries its own unfortunate consequences.)
>
> *Traditional magic is based not on re-creation, but recognition.* As I have said, it's not that the Eagle Dance literally turs the dancer into an eagle, but that it allows Eagle, present as medicine within the dancer's spirit, to come forth through the dancer.
>
> *Traditional magic is a process of asking, not manipulating.* The Rain Dance, for example, is not done to force the skies to rain, but to ask the spirits, respectfully and prayerfully in the First Language, if they would be willing to let the rain come forth.
>
> *Traditional magic is also a matter of balances: you don't get something for nothing, and you don't get something from nothing.* If the prayer for rain is granted, that means the rain is taken from somewhere or some-when else. That raises the possibility that others in the Circle of Life might suffer; a point that must be kept in mind. Also, you must give of yourself as a part of the prayer, to keep balances.

Once a lady of European ancestry told me about a conversation she had had with someone she met from Maine. As they talked, she felt within her the powerful conviction that he hailed from a certain tiny town in the northern part of the state that she had heard of but had never visited. She asked, *à propos* of nothing, "You wouldn't be from Eagle Lake, would you?" She expected him to say no, but his astonished reply was, "How did you know that?" The woman believed that, amazing as it was, it was only a coincidence, and she was sure she had no special gifts of insight.

Often among traditional peoples I have seen amazing examples of fore-knowledge. Sometimes they can be explained in terms of the the dominant culture's science and beliefs. For instance, older people are particularly sensitive to changes in air pressure and humidity and know well in advance when a storm is coming. They can commonly predict to the day when a woman's child will be born, evidently simply from their experience with these matters.

Yet I have also seen many examples of individuals knowing things that—according to scientists—they could not possibly know. This expanded awareness is often visionary, coming directly from the spirits. Indeed, it is the seeing of the multiplicity of robes that all beings carry and, moreover, seeing *through* the robe to the spirit within. It is how the cats and dogs who share their lives with me always immediately know whether a human coming to the door can be trusted, and why they hiss or bark (speaking in the First Language) at presences in the night that my dulled human senses are utterly unable to perceive.

When I first met a medicine man from the Great Plains and, years later, an elderly medicine woman in northern Vermont, each immediately told me quite significant things about myself (past, present and future), even though neither of them had even been told of my existence before these meetings. When I went once to Arkansas, a stranger walked up to me and handed me a Sacred Drum, saying, "Here's your drum." It turned out he had had a dream telling him that he would be meeting someone with my name, and that this person needed a drum—as indeed I did, for my drum had been ruined in an accident. Before meeting a certain Grandmother wise in the sacred ways, I dreamed about her. In my dream, she was sitting and talking with me about sacred matters in my maternal grandmother's parlor. I was not surprised to learn, when I met her, that she had put the kettle on in expectation of my arrival, having had similar dreams herself. Years before that, my first teaching Grandfather startled me often with his astonishing powers of perception and insight. I have long since ceased to be amazed at examples of expanded awareness. Perhaps the reason is that I have found I have this expanded awareness myself to a degree—because I don't tell myself it's impossible, it *is* possible.

In the late eighteenth century, the great poet and prophet William Blake was aware of and enamored with Native American culture. As I've mentioned, he believed that the European culture closes "the doors of perception," blocking out everything that is not empirically self-evident, demonstrably present in time and place. This culture insists we cannot know the future, or the past, unless it's been objectively recorded, and we cannot perceive anything that is not immediately apparent. Hamlet's rejoinder is appropriate:

> *There are more things in heaven and earth, Horatio,*
> *Than are dreamt of in your philosophy.*

Traditional people are expected to be observant, pay attention, and practice using expanded awareness. Gregory Cajete (in his book *Native Science: Natural Laws of Interdependence*) talks about "night walking," in which one intentionally sets out in the dark relying entirely on balance, listening and touch—and, though he doesn't mention it, a sixth sense and an inner confidence that comes from knowing one is surrounded by spirits who protect and guide. Modern people have flashlights; the traditional people learn to rely instead on more powerful tools. Even today we learn to be aware of our surroundings when walking through the wilderness, lest we have a mishap. If we are hunting, we learn to expand our awareness so we know where the deer or rabbit are. If we are walking in unsafe areas (which these days might well be a murky city street late at night), we learn not to broadcast fear but to expand the sphere of our awareness so we have sufficient forewarning of impending danger. If we are talking with or even just thinking about a friend, we learn to pay attention to her or his inner spirit, so we can be aware of any concerns or needs to which we might be able to respond.

We use our expanded awareness to walk along the pathways of connectedness in the world around us. The dominant culture calls such expanded awareness a talent, or even a parapsychological ability, and says few if any have it. Among the original peoples the belief is that everyone has at least some potential for such expanded awareness and it can be fostered through practice; it is not a talent but something that flows through one. It is, as the elders say, not something we possess, but something we carry.

Having slammed shut "the doors of perception," many in the dominant culture are unwilling to take the risk of opening themselves to things they do not understand. Frederick J. Chiaventone, in his book *A Road We Do Not Know*, suggests that the difference in perceptual ability between traditionals and others is in expectations: people born and bred in four-cornered rooms have a relatively limited field of vision, while those born and raised in the open see the great circles of the horizon and celestial phenomena.

The traditional understanding is that you can learn to cultivate this expanded awareness if you first accept it as a reality, and stop convincing yourself that you cannot do such things. Second, when you find you have used expanded awareness, you should not dismiss it (as the woman I know did) as an odd coincidence, but affirm it as a natural aspect of perception and interrelatedness. Third, you should learn to trust it: when you have a sense that a friend is in need, or when you sense impending danger, and so on, you should act upon this sense, and later on affirm that this was a good and natural thing to do. But while you must affirm this experience, you must remember not to take personal credit for it, or fall into the trap of ὕβρις (*hubris*). Remember, it is something that flows through you and me and all living beings.

Like all abilities, different people are able to use it to different degrees. Just as some people are sharp-eyed and others have poor vision, just as some people are fleet of foot and others are not, so too some people are acutely aware of the perceptions of expanded awareness and others are not. No one should feel ashamed for not having this skill in abundance; surely, if you do not, the Creator has balanced this in you, making up for this lack with other strengths. Besides, that's one of the benefits of living in community: everyone has some special skill to contribute to the good of all. Still, even if you do not have it in abundance, you can learn to cultivate it and rely on it, just as you can learn to overcome other deficiencies.

We can develop this perception by relying less on unnatural things. The invention of the electric light bulb led to a banishment of the *wakan* spirits of the night; candles and oil lamps and fires do not repel spirits but allow them to manifest if they choose. To strengthen our perceptive abilities we can go out for a walk in the early dawn or on the verge of night without the use of any artificial lighting. As the medicine men and women do, we can walk in the blackest hour of the night, in the depths of winter, at the dark of the Moon — at the times which are most *wakan*, most alien to us. In the words of Igjugarjuk, the great Inuit *angakoq*, or medicine man: "To learn to see, to learn to hear, you must do this — go into the wilderness. It is not I who can teach you the ways of the G-ds. Such things are learned only in solitude."

I sincerely believe that a vital way to cultivate this ability is by participating in the ceremonial traditions of the Red Road. Let us take, for example, the Sacred Stone People's Lodge Ceremony (often called *Inipi* or the sweat lodge). Once the door is closed, it is pitch dark inside and silent, with only a ruddy glow and a low hissing coming from the Grandfather Rocks. The common experience of those participating for the first time is that all their senses are cut off once the door is closed: there is no light for sight, and hearing is significantly diminished by the steam that gets in one's ears. However, if one seeks, one finds there are other, subtler senses—not the "five senses" we use in a *washte* environment, but others, more attuned to the *wakan*. As Shakespeare said,

> *Such harmony is in immortal souls;*
> *But whilst this muddy vesture of decay*
> *Doth grossly close it in, we cannot hear it.*

Slowly one becomes aware of the others in the lodge. While one cannot see them visually, still one can perceive them. (There are no words in English to explain what I mean. John Milton, who was blind, comes close, speaking of "darkness visible." Just be open to it, and you may sense them too.) With practice one can perceive not just the living humans in the lodge, but also the subtler presences of medicine animals, ancestors and *nagipi* (spirit beings). Tachcha Hushtë (Lame Deer) taught that it is what we see with our eyes closed that most matters.

Similarly, in the Vision Crying Ceremony (*Hanblecheyapi*), we learn through sitting alone within a sacred circle, fasting, remaining awake and aware, to clear away all the dross that occludes our perceptions, until we can see clearly the vision that is given. As one Grandfather taught me, the vision is there the whole time, but we have to cleanse our sight to be able to see it.

We can also cultivate this ability by paying careful attention to our dreams and visions. I've mentioned dreaming of my maternal grandfather the night he died. Though I was asleep near Boston and he was in northern New York, we were obviously together in spirit. Similarly, I have dreamed of friends as in need and, when I contacted them, found it was indeed so.

The Native American tradition does not conceive of time as a line extending from a fixed past into an indefinite future, but as an intermingling of circles. Place too is an intermingling of circles. Therefore, we believe we are always connected with everyone and everything, that each of us is at the center of the Sacred Hoop, and that we are, if we are open to it, able to see and to communicate with others notwithstanding the supposed limitations of time and place.

Wachin tsapa yo! Be attentive! I encourage you to be open to this ability, to cultivate it, to trust it, and to honor it in yourself and others. Through it you will learn much of great value for all of us and help to mend the Sacred Hoop of All the Nations.

Have you ever looked into someone's eyes and thought to yourself, "I am going to spend the rest of my life loving this person!"? Have you ever seen someone's eyes and had the feeling that this person was *sicha*, and to be avoided at all costs? How true it is, the old saying that "the eyes are the windows of the soul."

You can learn a lot about people by looking into their eyes. By observation, you can pick out signs of intensity, duplicity, sorrow, stress, wisdom, love and so on. In traditional Native American culture, people tend not to look long into someone else's eyes out of respect, and also because they are aware of the risk of the other person learning a lot about them. As is true in some other cultures, such as those of East Asia and South Asia, they do not look deeply into each other's eyes unless they are close friends, relatives or lovers—in a relationship where there is enough trust for both to bare their souls in this way. It is otherwise usually considered rude to stare, so one learns to pick up with a quick glance the clues another person's eyes reveal. Learning to do this is an example of expanded awareness.

In the dominant culture, on the other hand, it is considered polite to look constantly into the other's eyes while having a conversation. Traditional peoples find this confrontive and rude, and often also disconcerting. For them, eye contact, like physical touch, is customarily infrequent and fleeting in *washte* society. (In the context of the *wakan*, as in ceremony, touch and looking, even of a most intimate nature, is actually frequent and welcome, even among relative strangers.) In the dominant culture making eye contact is usually meant to deliver a message of strength and sincerity and to indicate that the listener is attentively paying attention. It often becomes a kind of optical wrestling match, seeing who will look away first.

In their dealings with each other, these two cultures have experienced much misunderstanding and anger. Members of the dominant culture thought Native Americans were weak, duplicitous or cowardly because of their averted gaze and hesitation to shake hands, and the traditional peoples thought these strangers with their stares were trying to invade not only their lands but their souls.

The eyes and ears of members of the dominant culture are so constantly bombarded by bright lights and loud noise that some of the fine observational abilities found in traditional people have been burned right out of them. The ability to perceive spirit-presences with a sense other than the five that Western scientists know, or the ability to use extended awareness in other ways, is severely blunted. Simply to see at night, for instance, is virtually impossible for most modern people; without artificial illumination, they quickly become unable to navigate in the darkness.

Traditional peoples are much more often sharpsighted, even when they get old. Still, there are traditionals whose vision is not sharp, but it is not seen as a problem; rather, as a sign that this individual has, in balance, another kind of seeing. Those who are not able to see clearly with their eyes see in other ways. Traditionals do not say the sharpsighted person sees reality more accurately than the myopic person does, but that each sees a different reality. Claude Monet, who had poor physical vision, beautifully painted the spirit of what he saw: he was freed from the outer sight that sees the *washte*, and thus could see the inner spirit, the *wakan*, more easily.

Looked at another way, it is not that some eyes are better and other eyes are worse, but that different people's eyes are suited to different purposes. Some eyes are better for hunting, some are better for doing close work (stringing beads, carving, etc.), and some are better for seeing in Spirit. Each of these tasks is needed and respected in its own right, and none is considered "greater" or "lesser." Various species have better or worse sensory abilities than humans, but always in balance. The weak eyesight of canines, for instance, is made up for by their superb scenting and hearing capabilities.

I remember, when I was very little, looking at the snowflakes falling, as big soft fuzzy shapes, and thinking that's just how they looked, at least until they fell on my outstretched hand, briefly becoming finely detailed hexagons of infinite variety before they melted in the warmth of my palm. I remember looking at the Moon as a swirl of light swimming through the Sky, like a shapeless pat of butter melting across the plate. A few years later in school, I felt ashamed when I could not read the letters on the test chart. Before I was given glasses, I had to sit in the front desk in the classroom and make pinhole lenses with my cupped hands to try to read the blackboard. However, my first Grandfather teacher told me I had excellent vision; just of a different kind. He taught me that, in Lakota, this is called seeing with *chantë ishta*, the eye of the heart. He taught me that my inability to see the physical appearance of people or things very well could help me to see their inner spirit far better. My eyes have grown even more myopic as I've grown older. But, as an adult, I have learned to wear eyeglasses when they're helpful (especially for dealing with technical matters), but not when I want to walk more closely with Spirit.

One thing I like about being in the Sacred Stone People's Lodge is that my poor outer eyesight doesn't matter: in the darkness, the sharp-eyed, the totally blind and people like me are all at the same level of physical sight. Since in the lodge I cannot see at all with my physical eyes, I strive to see more clearly with the sight that we use in visions and dreams. I strive with the eye of the heart to see the souls about me, to see the future before me, such that I may walk better on the Red Road. I hope you too will cultivate this inner seeing, so you too may walk as well as you can on the Red Road.

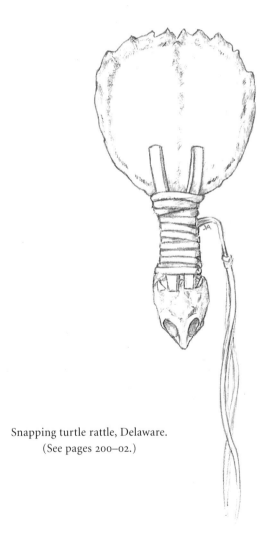

Snapping turtle rattle, Delaware.
(See pages 200–02.)

IV

Human Relationships

IN THE DOMINANT CULTURE, the primacy of the individual goes hand in hand with the concept that all things in the environment are also individual and separate and can therefore be owned. In Europe, ownership developed through the exploitation of nature: as forests were turned into farmland, large-scale agriculture created concentrations of wealth to be defended and traded. Competition for these prizes led to conquests that gradually brought the land and everything in it under the "ownership" of emperors, kings, princes of the Church, the nobility—with the majority of human beings functioning as commodities in the process of creating wealth and power for others, valuable only for what they produced. Ownership had come to seem natural and normal, and the newcomers brought it to Turtle Island with them. Since the people arriving had to count entirely on themselves and their families for survival, they usually sought to possess as much as they could.

Inevitably, great wealth comes in part at the expense of someone else. The most powerful members of society tend to accumulate a larger and larger share of the available wealth, creating want, suffering and conflict. With this comes an attitude of arrogation, the belief in the right to amass as many possessions as possible lest others acquire them and strengthen their own position. The labor and even the bodies and minds of less powerful people are exploited as virtual possessions; therefore, people come to think of their own selves, including their bodies, thoughts, words and actions, as personal possessions that they in turn must defend. In this situation, society can only be held together by applied force—the massive, sometimes brutal, imposition of prescriptive law. Against this power the individual must always press back, defending the self against exploitation.

My experience has always been that the original peoples—those worthy of inclusion in that company, at least—treat all individuals with respect, no matter what their gender, age, race, sexual orientation, physical appearance or condition. They do not judge or criticize others or compare them in terms of "better" and "worse," they do not talk behind someone's back, they do not gang up on individuals. Rather than taking, they seek ways to be giving, to be generous—not only to those they care about, but if anything even more so to those they don't particularly like.

Since the traditional culture is based on balances, individuals commonly share what they do not need with others within the community. This is not prescriptive law—law that can be broken and mandates punishments for its violation—but descriptive law. Certain birds migrate at certain times of the year, the seasons always follow in their proper order; descriptive law describes natural behavior. For humans, it is natural behavior, and logical besides, for each individual to take only what she or he needs, and to share any further bounty with others (of whatever species) because fostering the survival and well-being of others ultimately fosters one's own. At another time, one may need to rely on the good will of others to share their bounty in return. This philosophy also is the teaching of the White Buffalo Calf Woman: the sacred descriptive law of *mitaquye oyashin* ("all my relations"), remaining mindful of all one's relations.

This philosophy is well known by most people, since it was taught by Moses, Jesus and Muhammed, and even by Karl Marx in his famous dictum, "From each according to his ability and to each according to his need." Only a few Jews, Muslims and Christians fully practice the ideals set forth by their claimed founders, however, and the governments that claimed to follow Marx's model never truly did so. While before the coming of the invaders there certainly were selfish and greedy Native Americans, more often than not the Native American peoples did follow the way of *mitaquye oyashin*. The early colonist Roger Williams, in *A Key into the Languages of America* (1643), wrote that the essential difference between most Christians in the Massachusetts Bay Colony and the Native Americans he knew was that the latter actually kept their faith. He shrewdly observed, "It is a strange truth that a man shall generally find more free entertainment and refreshment among these barbarians, than amongst thousands that call themselves Christians."

The difference is also illustrated in the original peoples' relationship with the sacred. Traditionals don't say that they own sacred things, but that they *carry* them. A Sacred Pipe carrier, for instance, carries the great burden of that holy object with respect and care in behalf of and for the sake of the people. In the same way, the understanding of the original peoples is that we do not own ourselves but carry our selves as sacred trusts, in behalf of and for the sake of the people. "Those who would keep [own] their life will lose it," says Jesus, "but those who lose [give away] their life for my sake will keep it."

Our own selves are a sacred gift handed down from our ancestors. Each of us carries the *sichun*, the *potens* of our descendants. We grow out of the soil nourished by our ancestors; we bend down and become the seed of our children's children. This is why, for instance, at the *Tatanka Lowanpi* (Buffalo Sing), the ceremony that recognizes girls becoming women, the people are always reminded of how important it is to respect ourselves and each other in body, spirit and mind. We all must carry ourselves as a sacred trust given to us by the Grandfathers and Grandmothers *for the people*, past, present and future.

When one thinks of oneself as a possession, loss of control and changes such as sickness and pain, old age and death are perceived as threats to one's possession of oneself. If you think of yourself as a sacred trust (as in the traditional culture), it's likely that you will be at peace with yourself and the world. Even when you experience adversity, it will be understood not as an assault on you, but simply as a part of the story. If you think of yourself as a sacred trust, you will be less afraid of losing control of yourself in nightmares or visions (what some may call hallucinations). Knowing these things are *wakan*, traditional people more often welcome them despite their fear. As you grow older, you will carry the living memory of what the previous generations taught you, and that living memory is a sacred trust. As you draw near the time of your joining the Grandfathers and Grandmothers, you will be aware of the sacred importance in passing it on to those who come after you.

In the traditional peoples' culture, individuals seek not the affirmation of others, but to satisfy themselves that they are living their lives as honorably as possible. Traditionals realize it is impossible to satisfy every other person since each person has a different set of priorities, and that it is best rather to satisfy yourself that you are doing the best you can to live life rightly. An Aztec Grandfather recently told me his people teach: "Respect for others is peace." One elder said many years ago that the spiritual heritage of the original peoples can be summed up in one word: *Respect*. In this one word one finds the wisdom of many traditions: the Golden Rule ("Do unto others as you would have them do unto you."); K'ung fu-tse (Confucius) ("Do not do unto others as you would not have them do unto you."); the Torah ("Love your neighbor as yourself."); and the Wiccan Rede of the Pagan traditions ("An it harm none, do what thou wilst.")

The principle of balance in giving and receiving is similar. We give to others, but not to the degree that we deny ourselves the necessities we need to survive, except when a greater good is served, such as saving the lives of others. We give to others, but close off that giving when they seek to take advantage. We receive from others when they freely and willingly give, and we accept humbly and gratefully. If we do not need what they give us, we share it with someone who does.

These balances operate in the Sacred Giveaway and when an herbalist asks for permission before taking a good healing plant, leaving a tobacco gift behind in thanks. We see these balances operating also in love. In the original peoples' way, to love another is to give yourself freely and fully to that person, accepting the other's gift of herself or himself to you in return. Since ultimately the only gift that is truly ours to give is ourselves, this is a very sacred kind of giving.

Where the dominant culture is inclined to look on old people, "retarded" people and significantly disabled people as nearly worthless, the traditional culture considers its Grandfathers and Grandmothers, as well as its people whose lack of certain *washte* abilities means they are particularly strong in certain *wakan* abilities, to be valuable guides and teachers who are very close to the spirits. While many in the dominant culture still consider gays and lesbians to be aberrant, if not mentally ill or "sinful," the traditional culture respects their *winkte*—those who are considered neither male nor female, or both—as very sacred people. Some, like a certain Lakota *winkte* known as both Pipe Man and Pipe Woman, were famous for their courage.

The traditional peoples' coming-of-age rituals for both boys and girls remind them and everyone of the sacredness of the flower of sexuality now blossoming in their bodies—while unfortunatelymost modern people have no rituals to mark this momentous change, unless it be the acquisition of a driver's license and the right to see "adult" movies and purchase alcohol and cigarettes. At the *Tatanka Lowanpi*, the Buffalo Sing Ceremony, the members of the nation and the new women themselves are reminded that their bodies are sacred with the ability to bring new life into the world, just as the Creator has made all life. With the Sacred Pipe our leaders often remind us that our greatest teachers have been women—perhaps the same Woman: White Buffalo Calf Woman, Corn Woman, Sky Woman, Changing Woman, and others.

Some years ago, in the Sacred Stone People's Lodge, the Grandmothers gave a teaching that older women should bear their sinking breasts and stretch marks with dignity, and consider them as signs of wisdom and beautiful badges of honor for their carrying the sacred responsibility of being mothers and grandmothers! As we all grow older, the Grandmothers said, the signs of age in our bodies are manifestations of wisdom coming to fullest fruitage. I remember another time when one Grandmother, whose body not only showed manifest signs of age, but had undergone a mastectomy, said that she loved to come to the lodge—because it was one place where she still felt beautiful. We all told her, sincerely, that she was indeed beautiful to us. Indeed, traditional people see and respect the beauty in everyone whatever their age. Such is the *wakan* spirit of the Beautiful Woman who brought us the Sacred Pipe.

Changes that come with aging are another example of balance. As we give away our youthful vitality and beauty, we gain other things (if we are open to receiving them!). Elders may no longer be able to bend down to pick up a large rock, let alone carry it, but they are mighty in carrying the *wakan.* Very old people I have known seem to me to have all but outgrown any need for their bodies; their bodies are but frail wisps, but their minds are strong and beautiful with wisdom, compassion and memory. When death comes, we give away whatever is left of our bodies and receive in balance the wisdom of our ancestor Grandfathers and Grandmothers—such that, in the time of our death, we become truly all-wise. This is why we listen carefully to what people say in the last moments of this life.

Life is a circle, as all things are a circle, the Sacred Hoop of All the Nations. We see the circle in all things around us: the turning of the seasons, the phases of the Moon, the circle of the horizon. For this reason our ends are close to our beginnings: death and birth are found next to each other, completing the Sacred Hoop. Most traditional peoples the world over associate the East with our birth and the West with our death, and respectively with learning and teaching. The day in between sunrise and sunset represents our adult years, the time of doing, and this is associated with the South, since the Sun travels southward as it approaches its zenith. The night, associated with the North, represents the Spirit World, the time of being, in which we move between physical lives.

Have you noticed how often the death of a beloved relative comes around the same time as a new birth in the family? Grandparents and grandchildren usually have very close relationships, often far closer than those between parents and children. They seem to understand each other better, and to seek each other's company out more.

According to Frank Waters, the Pawnee speak of two kinds of familial relationships—"joking" and "serious"—and recognize the grandparent-grandchild relationship as a "joking" relationship, and the parent-child one as "serious." Adults (as opposed to elders) watch out for the welfare of children (and elders), as "serious" protectors (protection is associated with the South when the Sun is at the zenith). Elders, associated with the West and North, are sharers of wisdom, and they share it in a warm, affectionate, "joking" way. This kind of relationship, epitomized in the saying, "It takes a village to raise a child," is still found in North America among people who have to some degree preserved the extended family. An African-American friend told me, for instance, how once she skipped school as a child, and, when she was heading home about the time she should be getting back from school, every mother was out on her porch, shaking an admonishing finger at her. Even without the full benefits of an extended family, children thrive when they have a close relationship with their living ancestors. A study described in *The New York Times* suggests strongly that children worldwide raised near or with their grandmothers do better in life than those deprived of their grandmothers.

In many nations the most important leaders, before the Europeans demanded only male leaders to negotiate with, were the women. According to Paula Gunn Allen, the word "squaw," came originally from the Narragansett word *sunksquuaog*, which literally means a chief—and this nation often had women serve as chiefs. (Others, including Suzan Shown Harjo, object to the use of this word, saying it refers to a woman's private parts. I do not know which derivation is correct, but the fact remains that women served the Narragansett as chiefs.) Still today, those who really know the Native traditions know that the best learning comes from the Grandmothers. Natives often laugh about the anthropologists who think they have gotten a lot of profound teaching from the men, who never even bother to ask the women, when traditional peoples know their women carry even wiser teachings that the men do not know!

I was taught four reasons for the closeness of elders and children. ("There are," one Grandfather often said to me, "four reasons for everything.") The first is the similarity of those stages of life: lacking the basic tools of survival, children and elders are both more vulnerable to the vicissitudes of nature and depend on the adults for sustenance and protection. They both sleep a lot, and in traditional cultures sleep more deeply—enter more deeply into the *wakan* darkness-like-death—than do adults. The adults must awaken occasionally during the night to tend to the fire or the children or the old ones and must remain subliminally aware of the *wakan* in the waking world: the possible advent of wild animals, enemy humans or extreme weather. Elders and children both are relatively hairless and small compared to adults, with softer skin, missing teeth and rounder bellies. Gender-related features are less prominent and there is less interest in sexuality. For both, nakedness is mostly for fun and play, where for adults it's most often serious, for ceremony. The closer they are to birth and death the more help they need with activities of life, especially at the moments closest to birth and death. Both usually find nonverbal communication—talking in the First Language—easy and eloquent. Being closer to the Spirit World, they both are more vulnerable in famine, plague and disaster. They are far less encumbered with life than adults.

The second reason is found in storytelling and teaching. Children and elders see no essential difference between story (fantasy) and "reality" as adults usually do. Elders often find they cannot help but pass on stories in order to instruct the young, and the children love to hear these stories. One elder told me how, when the children would want to stay in the longhouse past their bedtimes, so they could hear more stories, the elders would tell them ghost stories—then send them out into the night, knowing they'd hurry home through the mysterious dark! Since the children will live farther into the future than their parents will, the elders bridge through them the seven generations, from their own grandparents, whom they remember, to their grandchildren's grandchildren, who will hear their stories. This helps the grandparents build a strong bond with these children, whom they will remain close to in spirit to guide, admonish and protect.

The third reason is that children and elders both have great freedom to behave as they wish, no matter how outrageously, as long as no hurt is given, because they are both so precious to the whole community. They have a blissful freedom from the responsibilities of adulthood. "Be like little children," Jesus taught. Children love to become various kinds of animals when they play, and elders, too, know and practice the magical ways of sacred shapeshifting. Children and elders both can talk even to trees and spirits with a free, confident expectation that they will *answer;* adults find this far more difficult. And the wild creatures respect little ones and elders (or did respect them, until they recognized that even these humans have become unpredictably violent and cannot be trusted any longer). I remember a woman in the

Sacred Stone People's Lodge who was praying for a vision. When the door was opened, she saw to her horror that her little child was seated on the ground just outside, playing with a gigantic black snake. She scooped up her son and chased the snake away—even though black snakes are no threat to humans— not at all realizing that *this* was the vision, and that her child, not she, had seen it properly.

But the most important reason is that both elders and children are very close to the Spirit World. Hehaka Sapa (Black Elk) told Joseph Epes Brown that children have just come from the Creator, and that he, as an old man, was soon to return to the Creator; thus, he and they were very close. This is why children and elders are more comfortable with, and more familiar with, the *wakan*, such as the presence of spirits. Children in the dominant culture are taught that the spirits they sense are not real, but in the traditional culture there really is no difference between what is real-for-us and what is real-out-there. When a child plays with an "imaginary playmate" or has a vivid dream, the child has no question about the reality thereof, unless adults try to discourage such knowing. I remember being so dissuaded when I was a child, and made it a point not to do so with my children. My daughter saw black birdlike creatures flying about, not unlike the Thunder Beings, which she called chih-chihs because of the sound of their voices. I did not doubt her then nor do I now, and to this day, though as an adult she no longer sees them, she *remembers* seeing them, and she remains convinced that they were real.

Like children, elders do not perceive reality as do adults. Both are more naturally attuned to the presence of spirits. They often see and hold conversations with people who died long before or may not have been born yet, or visit places in spirit. I still have the accurate floor plans my daughter drew of both of my grandparents' homes when she was just a few years old. She even described the *décor* of the rooms, even though physically she had only visited one of the homes as a babe-in-arms and had never been to the other at all.

We can disparage the elder as "suffering from the delusions and mental debilitations associated with old age," and we can disparage the child as "unfamiliar yet with the difference between fantasy and reality." Or we can recognize that such statements are merely cultural axioms, and affirm that the elder and the child are experiencing things we adults have lost the ability to perceive and comprehend—except with great difficulty. The hearts of children are pure, Hehaka Sapa said, which is why the Creator reveals to them many things that adults fail to see.

In childhood, as in the sacred mythic time (the Spirit World—what the traditional peoples of Australia call the Dreamtime), magic and miracle are common. In old age, just as in the twilight of evening, nature again unhooks itself from its moorings and becomes more fluid, and spirits are more apparent than the physical realm.

Adults, on the other hand, are farthest from the Spirit World. In the part of the circle of life that is adulthood, they are like the brightness of summer day, the time when the *washte* is dominant, the time for activity. Busy with repetitive chores and responsibilities, adults rarely get to relax. As a result, adults often have trouble sensing spirits and are sometimes even cynical about the validity of such experiences.

For this reason, adults achieve entry into the Spirit World by and large only through ceremonies such as the Sacred Stone People's Lodge. Children do not yet need ceremonies, because they are still so close to the Spirit World, but as they grow older they should become familiar with ceremonies. Similarly, elders do not need ceremonies any longer, because they are with every breath growing closer to their last breath, when their breath, their spirit—the same word in many languages, if not in English—leaves the body and enters the Spirit World, but they participate when they wish to help the adults and children to find the right path.

This helps us to understand the traditional peoples' circular understanding of the nature of time. Elders embody the past that they vividly remember, but adults look at them and see their own future. And children embody the future that they will live to see, but adults look at them and see their own past. Adults, who are associated with the South, the *washte* height of summer and daytime, are at the farthest distance from both their *wakan* past and *wakan* future; they need ceremonies to bring them closer in place and time.

Where elders most often teach their grandchildren the *wakan* matters—old stories, recollections of past generations, songs, prayers and ceremonies— adults teach their children the practical things. This is right and proper, since adults, farthest from the Spirit World, are most deeply involved in the practical aspects of life.

So mothers teach their daughters about planting and reaping, about food preparation, about weaving, about healing, and about caring for babies and the aged. Fathers teach their sons how to construct shelters, how to hunt and fish, how to fight and play organized games, how to survive under difficult conditions, how to find wild foods and healing plants, and how to seek visions.

All of these learnings, while ostensibly practical, are also in their way very *wakan*, sacred, as well.

In traditional culture a child learns not so much how to do as how to be: behind any actual skills that are imparted is the everpresent teaching that leads to character formation. When one is taught how to weave a rug, for example, one is taught the sacred stories of one's ancestors that are customarily depicted in the patterns, or how the very art of rug weaving itself was brought to us like all skills by ancestors or sacred medicine animals, such as, in this case, Grandmother Spider. Thus, whenever the individual weaves a rug, she or he is honoring her or his ancestors and all our other relatives in the Sacred Hoop. I have several very old Native American baskets in my home and also a couple bird's nests—and it impresses me how both kinds of weaving are simple, sturdy, beautiful, useful and similar in design.

The theme of respecting one's ancestors and every part of the Sacred Hoop is in all one's learning. Education is not separated from other activities, but is integral to them. Each of one's relatives has a particular gift to give the child as it grows. While this varies from nation to nation, the experience I'm most aware of is that even today still the Grandfathers teach boys the old stories, the uncles teach them how to hunt or to make practical things, and the fathers teach ethics (self-reliance, self-discipline, respect for others, and so on), and that the Grandmothers, aunts and mothers teach girls in a like manner. Each of these relationships is unique and satisfying, and the individual is only going to learn these things by fostering a healthy loving relationship with each of these people. As the individual grows older, she or he will in time be teaching as an uncle or aunt, a parent, a grandparent. A strong web of sharing binds all these free individuals together into a strong but supple society.

Education is lifelong. I remember hearing how one Chief declined an offer from members of the dominant society to build a school on his people's reservation. He said, "You go to school until you are eighteen or twenty, and come out thinking you know everything you need to know for the rest of your lives. For us," and his hand circled round, pointing at the world around them, "this is our classroom. We never leave it."

When I was a child I was told things like "Big boys don't cry." Western culture has traditionally taught that men may show anger, happiness and courage, but not fear or sorrow. It has also taught that women may show happiness, fear and sorrow, but not anger or courage. But even the expression of happiness must be muted for men—exuberance is frowned upon, and they must be careful not to exhibit too much love for their fellow men lest they be labeled "queer."

In recent years people have begun, rightly, to insist that it is all right for men to show fear or sorrow, and for women to show anger or courage, since by nature both men and women are capable of expressing the whole range of emotions. The original peoples' understanding, as it has been taught to me, is that no emotion, in the proper context, is wrong to express. One great warrior was known as Young Man Afraid of His Horses, and one medicine man was called Afraid of Bear; both carried their names with great dignity. And many Native women, such as Sacajawea and Jikonshaseh, are still renowned for their bravery and dignity.

A Grandfather once taught me that expressing your emotions is like eliminating bodily waste. Emotions, like the fertilizer our bodies produce, may not all be pleasant, but they do good, making things grow. Just as by-products of digestion complete the circle of living things, so too emotions enable our spirits, or others' spirits, to grow. But, on the other hand, just as we do not move our bowels right where people walk all the time, we do not want to express our emotions indiscriminately, but to express them in the right time and place.

People in modern society have problems with emotions that are conceived of as "negative," such as anger, fear and depression. The traditional understanding is that emotions like happiness and content are *washte*, and others, like sexual desire, anger, awe, battle-lust and fear are *wakan*. The latter are wild and uncontrollable, potentially destructive by nature. They draw us out of our regular day-to-day mentality into regions of sacred power. As with wild *wakan* animals, we don't want them around all the time! They are emotions that we can only have in or around us for brief times.

A good time to express these is in the context of ceremony, such as in the Sacred Stone People's Lodge, or with the Sacred Pipe, or by dancing. One of the finest ceremonies for expressing them is the Condolence of the Hoden-asaunee (Iroquois Confederacy). It was originally given by Skennenrahawi (the Peacemaker) to Aionwantha (Hiawatha) when he was weeping inconsolably for his murdered children. It is actually a prayer to console people who are overcome with grief or anger because of the death of someone they love. These feelings are natural and healthy, the Peacemaker taught, but they must be released so those burdened with them can again see, hear and speak clearly.

Sorrow is the other side of love. When a relationship is broken off, or the loved one dies or moves far away, we feel sorrow, which is an emptiness that reminds us we still love. We must not try to repress the sorrow or to fill it up with meaningless involvements. We should rather learn that the sorrow is a friend and a teacher that reminds us of the sacred importance of love.

Depression is strongly resisted by Western culture, which categorizes it as a "problem" and medicates it to make it go away. We are told there is something wrong with us if we are not happy all the time. But, if it were *not* resisted, a Native friend once said to me, it could perhaps be a door to another type of experience. And she is right: many of the world's great creative artists and spiritual teachers were manic-depressives. Emotions can be a portal to greater aesthetic and spiritual awareness.

The Tewa tell this story of their great leader Long Sash:

There was a time when the people were lost, and became frightened that they would never again find their way. Long Sash himself became full of doubts and fears, and was confused by the many voices he heard in his mind, urging him to do many different things.

Long Sash asked the voices to speak clearly. He prayed hard for guidance, and left his body. The people thought at first he was asleep, and then, when he didn't come back, that he had died. But, indeed, he had left his body for a while and eventually came back. He promised the people that now he knew the way, and that their difficult journey would soon be over.

And he taught them: "Sometimes you will come to this place of doubt. When you do, pray to the Creator and the spirits, as I did, for guidance." To provide his people with a permanent reminder of this teaching, he placed his headdress in the night Sky—it now shines as a group of stars to remind us what to do when we are doubtful and afraid.

Fear reminds us that we must follow the way of the Creator. The phrase from the King James Version of the Bible, "Thou shalt fear the Lord thy G-d" is actually an accurate translation, even if the Hebrew verb carries more a connotation of "honor," "respect" and "obey." Our fear keeps us honest and true, keeps us listening to make sure we are doing what the Creator wants.

Fear, properly, is balanced by love. Fear keeps love respectful, and from becoming too possessive, too *washte*. Love keeps fear from turning into blind, helpless panic. Love conjoined with fear—whether for a loved one or for the Creator—says, "You may be a mystery to me, filled with unknowns that I will never plumb, but I feel your love for me and I love you."

Fear reminds us to pay close attention, lest we be taken by surprise. It reminds us to take care of and respect Nature, and not think we should subdue it to our wishes. When a boy prayed in the Sacred Stone People's Lodge for a sign that he was walking the right spiritual path, the Grandfather with him laughed. The boy soon learned why. I've told you already—while they were in the lodge a powerful storm came, and lightning hit a tree right next to it. The boy was more afraid than he had ever been before. Coming out, he saw the marks on the side of the lodge, showing how close it had come to hitting them. The boy learned his lesson, not to pray for signs, but just let them come when they do.

When we fight our fear, when we try to repress it, it becomes difficult and dangerous. When we accept our fear and flow with it, it helps us. Although I have been a frequent public speaker for decades, I still feel fear. But I have learned over the years that fear is a friend: when I am speaking before others, I remind myself that I feel fear because I am aware I am talking about the sacred ways of a noble people who are struggling to survive, and that, while I am in my person unworthy, what I carry is *wakan*, and must be spoken of with the greatest of care and respect. I let the fear express itself as conviction in my voice, so people hear the respect I have for the sacred ways.

Rather than fighting our fear, we let it teach us. In George MacDonald's novel *At the Back of the North Wind*, the wind teaches a little boy not to defy her, but to move in harmony with her. When he opposes her, the wind's cold breath is on his face; it becomes warm when he stays with her. Lao-tse, the Taoist master, teaches us that it is the strong, hard branch that is broken by the wind, but the weaker, green branch bends with the wind and survives the storm. So Hehaka Sapa (Black Elk), as recorded in *The Sixth Grandfather*, becomes so filled, so suffused, so empathically one with the *wakan* force of the storm that his song about the storm becomes the song that the storm itself sings:

> *I myself made them fear.*
> *Myself I wore an eagle relic....*
> *Myself, hail-like powers I wore....*

I myself made them fear.
Behold me!

Love begins with trust. If two people love each other, they do not need to hide behind psychological defenses. They are entirely honest with each other. This means, rather than building their relationship on mutual taking (which is the essence of *washichu*, greediness), they base it on mutual giving. Furthermore, if two people genuinely love each other, they champion each other's freedom and do not seek to coerce each other. Long-term relationships are seen as an ideal, of course, but among traditional people they are built not on the basis of mutual obligations or demands, on a sense of possessive "ownership" of each other, but on the basis of mutual trust and respect—and there is nothing inherently wrong about a short-term relationship.

There is relatively little categorization and stratification among traditional peoples. People are respected as individuals, and their individual choices are just that; if they lead to difficulty, they find out for themselves, but the difficulty will not be a result of criticism from other members of their nation. Likewise, relationships are allowed to develop however they do. If the sexual ardor between two people eventually cools off, no problem; the relationship has just changed. If two friends share physical love with each other, for a little or a long while, that's fine too. If someone who has always been attracted sexually to members of one sex should once or occasionally enjoy physical love with a member of the other sex, no one questions it.

Among the traditionals, love is recognized as a kind of energy or power, neutral in itself, just as fire or electricity or flowing water are neutral powers, but that like them can be channeled in nourishing or destructive ways. So it's not how often, or how many, or with whom, we become involved with love or the physical expression of love, but rather whether we respectfully invoke this *wakan* power in positive, healing, life-affirming ways.

Individuals are respectful of other individuals among the traditional peoples. Above all, men are especially respectful of women—for they bear the particularly *wakan* responsibility of bleeding in synchronicity with the Moon, and also, like *Maka Ina*, Mother Earth, of bringing new life into the world and nourishing it from their own bodies. As one elder said, "Remember that, at every stage in your life, Woman has her hand over you: at birth, in your childhood, in your adulthood, when you're old, and when you die." He spoke of the hand holding us to her breast, the hand that guides us in learning, the hand that we are joined with in marriage, the hand that cares for us when we can no longer care for ourselves, and the hand that prepares our dead body for its return beneath the hand of our mother the Earth.

A man who disrespects women is shunned and dishonored. In the Egyptian and Babylonian creation stories, Man came from Woman, not the other way around. These stories speak of the First Woman, the Woman Who Fell From the Sky, whom they called Inanna, Ishtar, Astarte—all names that mean "Star" (and the English word is an etymological descendant of "Ishtar" and "Astarte"). Those are the same stories that Native Americans and other traditional peoples tell worldwide. It was a woman who, in the traditions of many nations, came from the Star Nations to teach us how to live. In many of these stories, including the Mohawk and Lakota stories about two brothers, disrespect is shown to this sacred woman. The stories remind us to behave differently. The Beautiful Woman promised, *"Toksha ake wa chin yanktin ktelo"* (I will see you again), and, indeed, according to the Moon Lodge teachings, we do see her again—for every woman we meet is She, and this beautiful world we walk upon is She. We should no more fence in and claim ownership over a woman than over this Mother Earth on which we walk: both are sacred. Therefore, a husband has as an inviolable duty to be courteous and respectful toward and supportive of his wife in all things. Among many nations, she is the master of the home, and he fears most of all coming home and finding his belongings piled in a heap outside the door. There could be no greater shame than that suffered by a man rejected by his wife. This fear of being shamed compels him to treat her with constant respect.

Love is like a well or a spring, which offers a *wakan* abundance of "living water." We remember that—in a beautiful paradox—emptying it keeps it flowing: if we neglect to draw water, the well of love silts up and goes dry. But the more love we draw out the more there is to draw. Also, love is not quantitative but qualitative. It is not that one loves one person to a greater or lesser degree than another, but *differently*: I love this person in one way and that person in another according to the unique contours of each particular relationship. The nature and expression of the love change as the relationship changes. My wise friend Saba Ali cherishes this dazzlingly radiant line from Jane Austen's *Mansfield Park*: "There are as many types of love as there are moments in life."

By following these basic principles, traditional peoples—or any peoples— are able to get to know each other as persons, and to learn from each other the unique "personal language" of what makes oneself and the other feel loved. Therefore, love involves a great deal of attentive listening, in order to learn how best to love the other person. As one Grandmother used to say to me, "G-d gave us two ears and one mouth so we'd listen twice as much."

The original peoples recognize that each person is a unique creation, both *washte* and *wakan* at times, constantly evolving, and full of mystery. The mystery of the human individual tends to make her or him ultimately unknowable. Traditionals are not afraid of the shadowy, the mysterious, the *wakan*, but welcome and cherish it and, above all, respect it.

There are two kinds of knowing. One is the knowing of information, and the other is the knowing of recognition. The first, which is *washte*, has more to do with facts, and the second, which is *wakan*, has more to do with Spirit. The first is knowing *about* the person, but the second is knowing the *person herself or himself.* While English makes do with one word for both kinds, other languages have separate words. French, for instance, has the verb *savoir* for the knowing of facts, and German has the verb *wissen.* French has the verb *connaître* for the knowing of recognition, and German has the verb *kennen.*

Traditional peoples tend to emphasize the *wakan* kind of knowing, the knowing of recognition, while Western culture tends to emphasize the knowing of facts. Saba Ali has written, "We have become so dependent on our minds that we do not use our inner understanding, our subconscious, any more....Our minds store information for necessity, not endearment." If you meet someone and, in the instant of meeting, recognize this person as someone you love, you cannot help but love that person even if you know next to nothing about that person. The beginning of truly knowing a person is to recognize that she or he *is* a person, and a *person* is *wakan*, unpredictable—not a machine, but a life endowed with free will, the ability to choose. One cannot "know" a person by acquiring facts.

In genuine love it is recognized that the nature of the other is ultimately unknowable. Neither seeks to dispel the mysteries about the other, but to cherish them. So love is a paradox: "I cannot ever fully know you, but I love you for being that 'you' I cannot know." This is why, when you hold your newborn child in your arms, you love it even though its life-to-be is at this moment entirely unknown. This is why brave warriors in Native American history have wept when their honorable enemies were killed. This is why lovers cherish more *being* with each other than *doing* with each other.

The embrace is a sign of love that symbolizes the Sacred Hoop: both persons are within the circle. When we embrace, first we open our arms, becoming vulnerable in a sense, exposing our hearts both literally and figuratively, to create space in ourselves to welcome the other into us. Then we close our arms around each other, one with each other within the Sacred Hoop. (Sexuality is an extension of the embrace, of course—an even closer joining.) Then, when the ceremony of embrace ends, we open again, and return to our separate identities, but enriched by the moment in which we were one together. Now and forever after, we are connected, and carry a little bit of the other in us.

Years ago, someone told me about a college professor who used to say hello to everyone in the morning on the way to his office. After some time he began to feel a slow diminishing of his spiritual strength. Fortunately he talked to a wise spiritual person who told him he was "leaking" his spiritual strength by going to all this effort of greeting everyone. He took this advice to heart, and stopped trying to be friendly to everyone and greeted only those he cared about, whose sincere greetings in return balanced his giving and replenished his spirit. After a while he felt his spiritual strength returning. It has become common in the dominant culture to try to show how open, peaceable and sensitive people are by greeting everyone warmly, even people they don't know well or dislike, often with an embrace. Embraces have become so common, so *washte*, that eventually they mean nothing. When you embrace indiscriminately, the act loses its sacred, *wakan* value.

Just as the Sacred Hoop comprises both the *washte* and the *wakan*, so greeting another person carries both of these aspects in varying degrees. The encounter of enemies tends to be more *wakan*: events can quickly become unpredictable and dangerous. One does not want to meet one's enemy often just as one does not want to consume too much of a *wakan* plant, but those rare encounters are powerful experiences that lead to learning and growth. The encounter of friends or relatives tends to be *washte*: it is predictable, comfortable, without risk. The encounter of lovers tends to have both aspects in full measure: to be in the arms of one's beloved is comforting, but it also changes one utterly.

This is why the original peoples tend to take their time getting to know someone, and not to be particularly effusive in their greetings, except with those whom they love. When a traditional person embraces someone, you can be sure that the embrace is fully meant, because the embrace is a sacred ceremony.

Let me tell you a love story:

A long time ago there was a man who had been much noted for not only his bravery and his hunting skills, but for his courteous, respectful ways. Many were the grandmothers who nodded to each other, agreeing together without a word being said that he would make a wonderful husband and father, capable not only of providing plenty of food to his family but of giving them the more precious gifts of good teaching and kind example.

But time went on, the seasons went round and round, and he did not find a mate. In fact, none of the women among the people seemed even to catch his eye. But not from lack of trying! There could not have been even one of the young, single women—indeed, even a few bolder ones among those who were married!—who did not do her best to catch his eye, to give him the sight of a pretty ankle as she danced, to make sure good smells came from her home. Yet, alas, for all their efforts it might just as well have been naught; the young man seemed entirely uninterested in finding himself a good woman.

Instead, his attention seemed to be entirely focused on hunting. He disappeared for days at a time and never came back empty-handed. He carefully prepared the game he returned with and shared it with the grandfathers and grandmothers, with the poor and orphaned. This endeared him yet more in the thoughts of everyone in the nation. Grandmothers took to ruse, asking him to sit with them and it would just happen that one of their pretty granddaughters would happen along as well. But all to no avail; he would unfailingly smile and be polite, but never did his interests stray from cordial pleasantries.

One day he was hunting in a land unfamiliar to him, where his people—and, for that matter, other people—never went. The land was rumored to be haunted. But he, as a practical, sensible young fellow, would have none of that. In fact, he saw to his delight that game was plentiful in this valley, and that it was an attractive place: a lush valley surrounded by tree-covered hills. Through it a river wound, its waters flashing with fish.

By the bank of the river he saw a tipi. It was decorated with strange designs that seemed to slide away from his eyes like the images in a dream when you awake. However it was not the tipi that commanded his attention, but the woman who was by the fire just outside the entrance, weaving at a small loom. She was not merely the most beautiful woman he had ever seen; she was the most beautiful woman imaginable. In his eyes her long hair was as black as night but it shone with the light of the Moon and the stars. In his eyes her skin glowed like the Sun. In his eyes her eyes were as deep as lakes, her breasts as round as the hills, her waist like a sapling in the spring, and her fingers danced at their work like a flock of birds.

He came down to her and took down from his shoulders the deer he had killed, and placed it before her. She took it and soon meat was roasting above the fire. As the inviting scent of the coming meal filled the air, she continued to weave, and he to watch her. She simply kept at the shuttling back and forth, creating a pattern with the ball of multicolored yarn in her lap, once in a while looking up briefly at him and giving him a small smile. Eventually she served up the deer meat with some vegetables and wojapi. The two of them ate plentifully and well.

All this time, not a word was spoken between them.

When their meal was done, the day was coming to an end and night was beginning to gather. She picked up her weaving and showed it to him. He looked at it and went with her into the tipi. There they spent the night together and sweet was their enjoyment of their mutual gift to each other.

Morning came too soon. The man lay in the bed, warm and content, his eyes shut still. But something seemed wrong. It seemed to him that the light inside the tipi was too bright, the air too still and dusty. He opened his eyes and saw that the tipi around him was fraying and rent, and sunlight was pouring in through the tears. He did not want to turn to look around himself and see what was with him inside the tipi, but he knew he would not be able to restrain his eyes forever. He turned his head and saw beside him in bed a body, dried and shrunken as if it had been dead many years.

In its bony hands he found the weaving still, held up slightly as if he were meant to take it. And he did, leaving quietly and, strange as it may sound, not with a little regret. He returned to his people, and they could see that he was a little sadder and a little wiser than he had been before. The only change he was aware of was that now he saw something of the mystery of the woman he had met in all women. For he saw that love comes like a flash in the night, and old age steals upon us when we least expect it. Eventually he did find a woman he could love, and he settled down with her and had a family. But no one knew why sometimes he took out a bit of old, unfinished weaving and looked at it and wept.

Traditional peoples rarely talk about sexuality—by and large, they are very modest in their speech and deportment. They see the sexual excess in mass culture and want no part of that, and they remember when their ancestors were persecuted as sexual "sinners," based on the rigid tenets expressed in an alien religion's holy book—which even the newcomers often themselves disobeyed and obey even less today.

The root of this problem lies in the history of treating the human body—persons—as *washichu*, subject to ownership. As wealth was created, it came to involve the ownership of other people through slavery and other forms of subjugation and exploitation. Western culture long subjugated women to the point that they and their children were without rights or possessions, the virtual property of their husbands or fathers—and their sexuality in particular was considered the property of these men. When people of a culture understand themselves as "things"—something that can be owned, the individual loses a sense of connectedness to the world, to family, even to her or his own body and the consciousness of self. In this situation, sexuality is robbed of its sacred *wakan* power.

Possessiveness in relationships springs from this sense of ownership: individuals feel that they own exclusive rights not only to their loved ones' attention and sexuality, but to their loved ones themselves. Ultimately, the beauty of love, of unencumbered and unencumbering desire, freely given and freely received, dies in the chains of possessiveness and the cage of jealousy.

For the original people, sexuality is *wakan*. They welcome it when it comes and let it flow freely on when it chooses, whether it comes often or rarely, no matter with whom. They know that, if we try to hold on to love as a possession, it loses its sacred power. They know that if they *need* sexuality and can't go long without it, they are becoming "hooked" on it; far better to be able to go without sexuality, without regret or demand, and yet to welcome it respectfully, humbly, gratefully when it does come. This should not be understood to mean that for traditionals sexual activity is indiscriminate and relatively meaningless. Quite the contrary. Being *wakan*, it is treated with the greatest respect—for sexuality *is* a ceremony; perhaps the greatest ceremony. It pulls us out of our *washte* lives to unite us with another life. Moreover, it connects us with future and past generations since it is what began our own lives and can lead to the creation of new life. All life is about interchange, relationships, which is to say, sexuality—in a sense much wider than merely coitus.

Traditional men must treat all women, young and old, pretty and plain, married and unmarried, heterosexual and homosexual, as if they were the White Buffalo Calf Woman, the Beautiful Woman herself. An honorable man does not expect or demand "sexual favors" from women, but lets the woman take the lead in any kind of relationship (unless the woman wants him to take the lead). It is men's role to let their love for woman flow freely and naturally, as pure *wakan* energy, letting it be shaped by the wishes of the woman. The woman directs his love into the love of friendship, of romance and so on, or reshapes it into another form later on. Just as women, as mothers, can put spirit into bodies, they also put the love of men into physical form. As an extension of this, the woman is mistress of the home and all its contents (excepting ony the man's clothing and weapons), for the home is the body of love.

Let me explain this through an analogy to hunting. Just as it is man's province to hunt (ceremonially seeking a sacred animal spirit willing to let its robe be turned into sacred flesh) and woman's province to cook (ceremonially turning sacred flesh into sacred food), so also a man hunts for the wild creature called love in the Spirit World. He hunts, or more properly watches out, just as he watches out for a deer, for a love that is willing to give itself to him in a Sacred Giveaway. He then pierces its body, woman or deer, and magically shapeshifts it from sacred spirit being into sacred flesh, which is given to him in a pure gift of undifferentiated raw love. He then presents this gift to the woman, who then with the heat of passion magically shapeshifts it from the sacred flesh of love into sacred food, creating a sacred meal of love. How truly William Blake knew that love is shapeshifting, dying to our old single selves so we may be reborn as a new, dual being:

> *Wouldest thou love one who never died*
> *For thee or ever die for one who had not died for thee[?]*

Like men, traditional women seek to be worthy of this honor. They offer the sacred gift of sexuality only to those who are worthy of it, as they were taught at their coming-of-age ceremony. People who have shared this *wakan* gift with someone are not jealous or envious when later that person shares the gift with someone else. Rather, true love honors all love. And any persons who have ever shared this sacred gift have a bond, and treat each other forever after with the utmost respect and kindness—as they do after joining together in any of the sacred ceremonies.

Years ago, a famous science fiction writer now deceased—known to be something of a lecher—asked me, in all seriousness, if I would tell him the "Indian love secrets." I responded by telling him, in equal seriousness, to read the novel *Stranger in a Strange Land*. In this brilliant work, his colleague, Robert A. Heinlein, tells how Earthly women are overwhelmed by a man from Mars who does something men from this planet so rarely do—he *groks* them: he gives them his undivided, fully respectful attention. Unfortunately, my advice was not heeded.

If there *is* any "Indian love secret," it is to give the same fully respectful and devoted attention as Heinlein's Martian did. Walking the traditional way, people learn to look at a person's soul first, rather than judge by external appearance. For traditional peoples, the ideal of love is to seek with all that is within you to give the other person happiness, expecting and demanding nothing in return, yet being open to whatever is freely given to you. Traditional people don't often say the word "love," but rather express it in their actions, through generosity, respect and trust. When they do say the word, they mean it to signify a total gift of self to other.

In sexuality we can, for moments at least, forget "who we are," and enter into a sacred realm where all is one, where individuals join into a single greater being. The sweat of sexuality reminds me of the sweat in the Sacred Stone People's Lodge; in both cases, ritual gives way to an explosive irruption of the *wakan* in a moment we do not deliberately choose but that chooses us, a moment in which there is no self or other but an experience that is ultimately indescribable. As Blake put it:

> We are put on earth a little space,
> That we may learn to bear the beams of love.

We are all *one*. We must treat ourselves and all others with respect because we are parts of the same whole—to mistreat another person is to mistreat ourselves. We understand our individual selves and those of others to be body and soul, *together*. The body has its spirituality, which is sexuality, and the soul has its sexuality, which is spirituality. Spiritual experiences have often been compared to sexual climax, as for instance Saint Theresa d'Avila, Saint John of the Cross, John Donne, William Blake, Walt Whitman, Lame Deer, Lawrence Ferlinghetti and many others have done. The two have even been found to be ultimately one by Hindus, Charvakian Jains, Muslim and Hindi Bauls of Eastern India, Taoists and Tantric Buddhists, as well as certain mystical branches of Judaism, Christianity and Islam (Sufi). In sexuality, individuals complete each other, creating a greater whole.

Here is a delightful story told by the Blood and Piegan Nations:

In the beginning, men and women lived separately. Though both made homes and both hunted for game, the men were able to get bigger game with their superior weapons. On the other hand, their homes were pretty unpleasant. The women lived well and comfortably, though they only foraged for plants for their sustenance. The Creator realized that this was a mistake, to have set them down in different places, and decided that putting some pleasure into it would bring men and women together.

By and by, at the nudging of the Creator, a man wandered over and saw the women's camp. He went back and described their fine, comfortable homes. He said that these creatures looked very different, but that the differences were interesting and exciting. The men all said, "Let's go over and get together with these creatures!"

Meanwhile, a woman saw the footprints of the man who had spied on them, and followed them back. She saw the men's camp in the distance. She came back and told the other women, "There are humans living over there. They are bigger and stronger, and their houses are shabby and filthy, but they live better than we, because they shoot sharp sticks that can bring down birds or buffalo. They are never hungry!"

Not long after she made her report, the women saw the men coming over the hill toward them. They saw the men were ugly and muddy, with matted hair, and realized that these humans smelled terrible. Disgusted, they threw rocks at the men and shouted at them to go away.

After the men left, the women talked. Their chief said, "They are just poor creatures. They don't know any better. Instead of throwing rocks at them and yelling, instead of making them ashamed, we should have welcomed them, and taught them how to live well." The women talked about it, and decided they should make themselves look muddy and matted like the men, in order not to shame them.

Meanwhile, in the men's camp, the men were talking. The men realized these other human creatures lived in a different way, and were probably scared to see the men. The chief said, "We should wash ourselves, and dress up in a manner like theirs, in that way to show them we have good intentions."

So the men all washed themselves carefully and put on nice skins and combed out their ragged knotty hair, and approached the women's camp. But what they saw when they looked over the hill was the women, all dirty and ugly, slaughtering a buffalo. "Those women are disgusting!" the men agreed. "We want nothing to do with them!"

The women watched the men retreat with sorrow, because they really wanted to get together with these other humans. Their chief said, "We have made a mistake." So they washed, braided their hair, and dressed in their good skins again. They put on beautiful beads and painted their faces with sacred colors.

The chief of the men, back in their camp, grumbled, "How I wish the women were beautiful, instead of being ugly and smelly!" All the men agreed with him.

A lookout came running to say the women were coming. The men were afraid they were coming to kill the men. "Quick!" they all shouted. "Get your bows and arrows!"

"No, wait!" the chief shouted. "Instead, go to the river and get clean. Comb out your hair and put feathers in them. Smudge yourselves carefully. Put on your best fur clothing. Put on your bear claw necklaces!" The men hurried to comply.

The women arrived, and they were singing beautifully as they came. The men were all astonished at their loveliness. But the men were too shy to approach them. "I will go talk with their chief," said the chief of the men.

Meanwhile, the women whispered among themselves that the men weren't as bad as they had thought. "Their strength is not ugliness, but another kind of beauty!"

The man chief approached the woman chief. "Let us talk," he suggested. But neither could think of anything to say. Yet, as they faced each other, both found that their hearts were pounding with delight in each other.

"Let us try something new," the woman chief said.

"Yes, that would be good," the man chief replied.

They started exploring each other's bodies, to get familiar with their differences. Each found the differences of the other most pleasing. They soon found some very interesting things to do with each other. They completely forgot that their two peoples were all around them.

Later on, they agreed they should get up and explain to the others what they had discovered men and women could do together. But, when the two chiefs looked up, they found nobody around. All the men and women had paired off and gone away couple by couple. Each couple was discovering the same things the two chiefs had enjoyed.

When, later on, the couples came back, they were smiling with their whole bodies. The men moved in with the women, who had nicer homes. From now on the men hunted for the women, and the women still gathered berries, eggs and nuts. The women also made beautiful beadwork and clothing. Together they made love, and happiness and children.

The Creator smiled.

The *washichu* attitude focuses on body parts. One is encouraged to determine where one's erogenous zones are, for instance—as if they were always in the same places, and stimulation of them will invariably result in sexual arousal, like flipping up an electric switch. Yet experience tells us that we might one time caress our lover's genitalia and get no response, and another time get a powerful response with just a glance or a brief touch of hands. If traditional people had to say where their "erogenous zones" are, they would say everywhere—from head to foot!—at least potentially, or that their location is variable. Finding the *wakan* of sexuality is a search as difficult in its way as finding an eagle or a rare healing plant or a medicine teacher: only *washte* things can be found where you expect them. It is better to let the eagle, the medicine teacher or the sexual experience find you. Sexuality calls for the expanded awareness I've already talked with you about—attentively perceiving oneself or one's lover in order to determine where the unpredictable *wakan* is to be found and how it is to be heeded at any moment.

A woman's or a man's outer appearance is a mere genetic accident for which the person should neither take nor be given any credit. Beauty is not a mundane (*washte*) possession, but a sacred (*wakan*) thing, utterly unique and to be respected on its own terms. From the point of view of men, women are "friendly," like the friendly animals and plants, and men are likewise "friendly" from the point of view of women. But *Man*, and *Woman*, and the beauty they carry is *wakan*.

Ultimately, beauty brings with it a certain responsibility, just as sharp-sightedness or great strength does: the responsibility to carry it honorably and for the good of the people. While an individual's beauty can be aesthetically pleasing, it is entirely irrelevant to the genuine worthiness of the individual. It is, after all, instinctual for us to look at others, especially those belonging to the gender we are attracted to. Among the traditional people it would be considered disrespectful to look away from this sacred beauty that has chosen to reveal itself. Every individual is beautiful in her or his own way, and since it's not a matter of comparison, beauty is affirmed at all stages of life, not just youth. Beauty that simply *is*—appreciated humbly and gratefully with a child-like delight and wonder—is true beauty.

It could be said that the newcomers' "gift" of self-consciousness, in the form of mirrors and cameras, was as terrible and frightening in its way as the "gift" of strongly alcoholic drinks (*mni wakan*, or wild/dangerous water) and the "gift" of weapons that kill from a distance. Before they had mirrors and photographs, traditional individuals were less aware of their outer appearance. They saw it only in *wakan* ways—on the surface of a still pool or a sheet of ice, but more in the love of others, or perhaps in dreams or visions. Therefore, while they kept themselves clean and well-groomed, they were not particularly self-conscious about their outer appearance. They therefore thought of themselves more easily as spirits perceiving the world through their robes, rather than thinking of the robe first. They did not seek to accentuate the (sexual) appeal of their outer robe, and did not carry or present themselves in a way meant to manipulate others.

I'm thinking, for example, of a Mic-Mac woman I knew years ago. She would laughingly scoff if she knew I were telling you that, truly, she is one of the most beautiful women I have ever known. However, she is also one of the most clumsy. The first time we encountered each other, she came running to meet me, having heard about me, and stumbled, falling into my lap where I sat by the council fire, spilling hot tea all over the Sacred Drum I had made when I was a boy and had carried ever since, ruining it. Indeed, her beauty was so evident largely because she was utterly unaware of it, or of her intrinsic kind-hearted, generous nature. It was just that—part of her nature, just as it is part of the nature of distant mountains or scent of autumn leaves or the songs of birds to be beautiful. She, like they, could not be otherwise, and her goodness and beauty flowed from her as naturally as the flow of the river or the wind.

Men who have the *washichu* mentality approach women in a kind of war-motif: they set siege against women, their bodies and their sexuality. Most of these men have absolutely no idea what women like. Foreplay is considered just a chore, not very interesting to them, but necessary to get to what, to these men, is the goal—overthrow of the battlements. For men of this sort, it's all about their sexual climax. The woman's satisfaction is rarely an important consideration. Worse, men all too often grow tired of a woman once they have seduced her, and move on to others. They become addicted to sex. *Washichu* women sometimes become sexual predators too, but often they experience sexuality as something extrinsic to themselves that is used against them. They use sexuality to get other benefits, or guard against being laid siege to and taken. Because of this and early indoctrination about the sinfulness of sex, it is difficult for them to enjoy it fully or come to a full understanding of their own sexuality.

Traditionals don't touch indiscriminately or even shake hands very much. Before the coming of the newcomers, they touched even less. Touch shared for mutual pleasure is comforting and agreeable, hence *washte*; but this kind of touch occurs only in the presence of trust—when one is with a close family member or friend, or a stranger when Spirit says it's all right. When it's this rare, the power of touch is carefully reserved against need, just as herbal teas are more efficacious when sparingly used. This boosts the *wakan* nature of touch when ceremonies of healing or sexuality are being invoked. Also, when it's this rare, if one is touched (or bitten or scratched) by a wild creature in dream, vision or waking life, it is much more likely to confer strong medicine.

In every culture, children naturally and normally explore their own bodies, and each other's too. Even before puberty, even in the womb, they stimulate, they masturbate, they learn what feels good, they learn the powerful *wakan* that can be evoked through these things. Though traditional peoples are proper and respectful in these matters, and teach their children to be respectful as well, they also understand the need for children to learn. Children in traditional society are given considerable latitude at all times, as I've already told you; thus they are free to learn from practice about the significance of touch. Among traditionals, at least when unencumbered by a foreign morality, touch is to be given and received with deliberate care, neither forced unwillingly on others nor withheld out of fear—as we learn from the two brothers who met the White Buffalo Calf Woman. Children, like adults, are entirely free to touch and be touched as they wish. The only rule is that one always maintains one's honor and give others respect. Rather than being taught that sexuality is shameful, they are assured that it's a sacred gift from the Creator.

Because of confusions in the dominant culture concerning touch, there is at the same time too much touch and too little touch. People touch hands a lot, to the point that their hands are largely desensitized. Yet the rest of their bodies are often starving for that simple, nourishing kind of touch. Typically, the four-leggeds who live with them get more strokes and caresses than they do.

In the traditional culture, individuals carry the childlike sense of "sacred play" into adulthood: far from either being ashamed and repressed or avaricious and indiscriminate, the extremes of the two brothers, they learn the Middle Way, as Gautama Buddha called it. They learn to be respectful of the *wakan* that they can release in themselves and each other. They learn that the "sacred play" of touch is part of the First Language, spoken by all creatures as they court each other, the language of dance, of caresses, of scent, of looking, of a full silence, the language spoken by spirit to spirit through the medium of their outer robes, their bodies. And they learn that simple physical closeness is good in and of itself—whether there is potential sexual attraction or not. In continental Europe, men still kiss when they greet each other without worrying whether they will be accused of being homosexual. The Maori and Inuit still greet each other, whatever the relationship, in the same way many four-leggeds do, by touching and stroking each other's nose; and in a number of African tribes, men often hold hands as they walk together, as an expression of friendship.

An episode of *Nova* several years ago showed an experiment in which a mother monkey was divided by a thin gauze screen from half of her children, and allowed to interact normally with the rest. In this experiment, as in others like it, the children who had an abundance of touch lived longer and healthier lives. Indeed, our elder brothers and sisters, those who live in the wilderness of *wakan*, know the vital importance of touch. I have seen bear lick and caress each other, otters playing together, and, once, two wolves approach and kiss each other with their noses.

Traditional peoples well knew the difference between sensuality and sexuality. Sensuality is the intentional delighting of the senses, especially through touch; it is for the sake of pleasure, and has no particular need for anything else. We need to recover today the goodness of sensuality, of what a Tsalagi (Cherokee) woman who taught me when I was young called sacred play. Before the Black Robes decreed otherwise, no part of the body was seen as better or worse than any other, so individual or mutual sharing of pleasurable touch did not avoid, or focus exclusively on, the so-called erogenous zones. Thus, with your friends, pay attention to the entire robe equally, yours and the other persons'—don't use just your hands, which likely have been desensitized; don't be afraid to caress with your entire body and soul, and don't be afraid to touch beyond socially accepted areas—you may have seen four-leggeds giving each other pleasure by grooming or licking each other all over, including their genitalia. This is not sexuality, but sensuality. Sensuality may or may not evoke orgasm or even arousal—that is up to the *wakan*, not us—but, if arousal or orgasm come, they are not unwelcome, and certainly nothing to be embarrassed about, since in any case they too are pleasurable.

In mainstream society, the physical signs of arousal are considered at best unmannerly and at worst indecent, embarrassing, and even implicitly confrontational or demanding. This seems strange to the traditional way of thinking, since one does not have conscious control over this, since indeed it is *wakan*. Individuals new to the Sacred Stone People's Lodge (most often men) have privately expressed to me concern that they might become aroused and feel publicly humiliated. Since arousal is *wakan*, and the *wakan* is what we are seeking through ceremony, they should be glad to receive this sign of its presence.

Among the traditional peoples (at least before the influence of European religions), arousal was considered an honest compliment. Simple arousal is by its nature truth literally incarnate. Needless to say, arousal carries no obligation; it does not require any response on the part of the other individual other than an appreciation of being appreciated. It is, in the sense of the Sacred Giveaway, a pure kind of giving, since what can we give another that is truly ours to give other than ourselves?

The Tsalagi woman's phrase "sacred play" aptly suggests this matter is both serious and joyful, that there is a connection between spirituality and play. Rather than approaching intimacy exclusively as something to be hurried through to reach a foreordained goal (climax), traditional peoples see every stage of the journeying itself as delightful. They can stop at any point along the way; they do not feel things are unfinished if there has not been climax. The attitude is to appreciate the fullness of every moment of togetherness and not lose the moment by thinking ahead, planning for a coming moment. As the Zen Buddhists teach, the idea is: "Be here now"—a phrase that suggests the importance of not letting expectations separate us from the experience itself.

The sense of "ownership"—that this woman or this man belongs to "me"— is alien to traditional people. True relationship is between "I" and "thou," as

Martin Buber wisely taught: not "I" and "it." The other person is seen as one's beloved, "thou," never as a sexual *object*, an "it." Buber says that G-d is also to be loved as "thou," which suggests to me that one ideally sees G-d in one's beloved, and that intimacy with one's beloved is also intimacy with the Divine. Likewise, in Islam, while sexuality is only to be expressed within marriage, it is *sadaqa*, a matter of holiness. "One of His signs is that he created mates for you from among yourselves, that you might find rest in them, and He put love and compassion between your hearts" (Qur'an, 30:21). The Qur'an (at 2:187) also says to men: "They [women] are your garments and you are their garments"— a passage that reminds us to be respectful to each other, a shelter for each other. Despite the later *hadith*, or traditional laws, of Islam, the Qur'an speaks of man and woman as completely equal and equally free and constrained by the Will of G-d.

Because among traditionals one does not "own" sexuality, one's own or another's, there is no unswerving insistence on monogamy or heterosexuality—or at least among most nations there wasn't until the coming of the Black Robes. And relationships are not categorized and socially strictured. Nor are people categorized as homosexual, heterosexual, bisexual, asexual or whatever—people just appreciate sexuality in whatever way seems appropriate and welcome to them. I remember a friend of mine telling me how once she and a female friend, who both considered themselves strictly heterosexual, decided one night to enjoy each other sexually. It was an astonishing experience, she told me, and it has never happened again, though if it ever does that would be perfectly fine. But the time shared, I was told, was a bonding; they both felt it made them closer to each other as friends.

In the longhouse, children often saw and heard people involved in sexual activity, and were familiar and comfortable with the concept. During the midwinter rites, sexuality could be quite open, and in many nations the *heyoka* engaged publicly in all sorts of sacred sexual play. There was no particular value attached to virginity or chastity. In fact, one who didn't engage in this vital part of life was seen as somehow antisocial, not taking part in the great Circle of Life, somewhat like the brother who was afraid of the *wakan* of the Beautiful Woman. Moreover, it was often traditional for young adults, male and female, to learn from older, respected teachers about this *wakan* aspect of life. I was fortunate in my early years to learn much of what I am now telling you from the young Tsalagi woman I mentioned, who, at nearly twice the age I was at the time, knew more about my male sexuality than I did, and was wonderful in helping me to understand hers and mine, through patient teaching, observation and practice. I learned that, cultural conditioning aside, men and women differ amazingly little in their sexuality when they come together with gentleness, generosity and respectful attention.

In the traditional way, it is not that people *make* love, not that they *decide* to have sex with a certain person at a certain time, but rather that sexuality, being *wakan*, is something they allow to happen to them when *it* chooses. Learning how to improve sexual "techniques" does not evoke sacredness, though it may help the inexperienced person, just as learning to fill the Sacred Pipe or sing the old sweat lodge songs correctly is fine. But these are just the "body" of ceremony, as technique is the "body" of sexuality. They're empty bodies, unless Spirit fills them—and that only happens by releasing our grasp on the *washte* and letting the *wakan* blow us wherever it chooses.

Years ago there was a woman who was coming regularly to the Sacred Stone People's Lodge at which I was the water pourer. She had overheard someone refer to the fact that I was the pastor of a Christian church. I remember noticing her turn visibly pale. After a few minutes, she asked me nervously if she could make an appointment to talk with me at my church. A couple of days later she came at the agreed-upon time. After a great deal of nervous chatter on her part, she finally confessed to me, with a great deal of shame, that, during the past several ceremonies, she had been masturbating (though she could scarcely say the word). She said it calmed her and made her feel good, and that it was for her a sort of prayer. She told me that she had tried often in her "ordinary" life, but was unable to arouse herself, to some degree because she believed it was a dirty, shameful thing to do. But, for some reason, in the lodge she felt "filled with love," relaxed and at peace. There in that sacred place she found she was able to climax very easily and powerfully and often. And, she added, it set her free from the anxious thoughts and worries and, for a while, sent her into "another world." Those were her exact words, but I knew she meant the *wakan*.

However, she went on, "I know it's a sin and that I shouldn't do it, but I can't stop myself." She talked about the training that had been given to her in her youth in a particularly misogynistically repressive branch of Christianity. She told me that she had tried to prevent herself from "doing it" in the lodge, but that repressing the feeling only made it come back more strongly, and she would find herself masturbating again, without conscious volition. She concluded by asking me to help her mend her ways. Indeed, in a strange way, she seemed to be hoping that I, with the power of the Christian church behind me, would command her, thus giving her the ability to stop.

Instead, I began by asking her what was wrong with doing something that harmed no one, and that gave her a sense of calm and goodness and prayerfulness. I told her that, while what she was doing was perhaps unusual in the lodge, there was nothing wrong with it, except according to the moral codes of certain religions imported into this land from elsewhere in the world. I reminded her that this ceremony was not part of those religions, but of the spiritual tradition indigenous to this Turtle Island. I said further that this is just one more wonderful way to break through the *washte* into the *wakan*, a repetitive act like drumming or chanting or hyperventilating or dancing. I explained to her that arousal and climax are in fact a kind of magical shapeshifting, since they precipitate significant changes in our robes, our physical selves. And they simply happen, without a deliberate decision, which means they are a sign of the presence of the *wakan*. It would be disrespectful ever to reject the *wakan*, out of shame or for any other reason, just as it would have been disrespectful if the shy brother had run away from the White Buffalo Calf Woman.

Besides, I told her, it was unlikely anybody in the darkness within the lodge knew, or, if they did, would particularly care—they would be happy for her if she felt close to Spirit and consider the means of invoking Spirit her business. Just as the lodge is a sacred place, and no one may enter without being welcomed, so too our bodies are lodges; one's own sexuality is one's own business until and if one chooses to welcome another person into it.

Sexuality is a part of life like any other part, I reminded her, so her arousal is just "there," a fact, and no more, not particularly different from sneezing, burping, farting, scratching an itch, or dozing in the comfortable embrace of the moist warm darkness—things we all have done in the lodge. She laughed when I told her about one old Grandfather whose loud, lengthy farts took the form of raucous melodies. Better that we fart or doze or attend to the unrelieved sexual arousal than sit through the ceremony so distracted and discomforted that we cannot fully participate. I told her that, for all I knew, others may well have masturbated in the darkness of the lodge. So what if they do? After all, touch is not uncommon in the lodge. Individuals often hold hands in mutual support or embrace each other in shared joy or sorrow. We often rub our own aching backs or feet simply because it feels good to do so, or rub each other's, as a shared act of kindness. In the traditional view, our genitals are just as much a part of us as our backs or feet, and rubbing them likewise feels good or can be a shared act of kindness.

As we discussed these matters, she realized that her *angst* about this matter, her inward resistance to the *wakan* wild freedom brought a negative element into the ceremony that *could* bother others in the lodge, even if her masturbating did not. In this regard, I told her that, if the spirits want us to do something, we are wise to obey. I told her how the Shona elders of Zimbabwe teach that the way to true happiness is to listen to what your spirits tell you, even if you are surprised by what they say.

Hearing these things, the woman began to cry. She wept for all the pain that the *washichu* mentality had put into her, a poisonous way of thinking that she now realized she did not need. Whenever she came to the ceremony after that, she did as the Shona elders recommended, no longer with shame, but with an uninhibited, infectious delight. Far from bothering or upsetting anybody, everyone was happy to see her childlike joy. By being so bold in walking the pathless path into the *wakan*, she encouraged us to be bolder in our own spiritual walk. We, too, became less afraid to do what our spirits told us to do, no matter how surprising.

I was and am proud of her, and honored at her trust in telling me about her pain and shame, and overjoyed at her courage in releasing herself from it. In this, as in all things, the traditional way is to give her—and all individuals who likewise respect themselves and others—the gift of respect. That word, one Grandfather said to me, is the most succinct description of the Red Road, the traditional way: *Respect*.

Wampum belt given in 1658 to Peter Stuyvesant, Governor of the New Netherlands, by the sachems of the Waronawonka (Munsee) Nation at Atharacton, now Kingston, New York as a record of their peace agreement with the Dutch immigrants. Within two years, Dutchmen murdered Preuwamakan, the great Waronawonka leader, destroying forever the fragile peace and beginning the slow decimation of the Nation. (See pages 328–29.)

V

Traditional Ways

BALANCES ARE ESSENTIAL to the free, efficient and harmonious flow of traditional society. Let me now explore with you some of its most essential characteristics, including its understandings of law and justice, ethics, reciprocity in giving, naming, and the maintenance of honor and respect. While I'll talk about them singly, they are closely related in the seamless weave of community as a whole.

The mainstream view that nature is a chaotic substrate which has *not yet* been brought within the human realm and made subject to human will is often linked to a particular interpretation of the beginning of Genesis: Human beings, the last to be created, are believed therefore to be the "crown of creation," appointed to "subdue the Earth and have dominion over it" (Genesis 1:26). What is ignored is G-d's call to serve (עבד [*'abad*]) the Earth and care for (שמר [*shamar*]) it (Genesis 2:15). This vaunted gift of dominion has been used to support the principle of property ownership and the exploitation of far corners of the Earth.

There is, however, a growing understanding among members of the dominant culture that nature is to be treated with care, since it is not an unlimited, inexhaustible resource. This is a positive development, although nature lovers can be as destructive as nature exploiters. So many are beginning to "get back to nature"—that national parks like Yosemite can be almost as crowded as a small city. And so many people want a "house with a view" that more and more natural places are being cut up to construct them. Less common, but also increasing, is the concept that nature should exist not because it's financially or aesthetically valuable to humans, but simply because it *is*—because all things in the earth are integral to a single living organism called Γαια (*Gaia*) by the classical Greeks, *Vasudhaiva Kutumbkam* (the Earth Family) or Indra's Net by the Hindus, and

Lethinistenha Ohontsia by the Kanien'kéha:ka (Mohawk). People with this view know that Nature prefers to be left alone, so they enter it with care and respect.

The traditional peoples do agree with the Bible and evolutionary scientists that the two-leggeds came most recently into being. In their view, however, human beings are not the greatest of creatures but, as the youngest of the Creator's children, the most ignorant and therefore the most prone to mistakes. Like an infant, the human being is weak and vulnerable compared to its elder siblings. It is relatively feeble in physical strength and in perceptive ability. Lacking protection against inclement weather, it needs the robes of these elders (furs or plant materials) to keep it warm; having little innate strength, it needs assistance from these elders (wood, bone, ivory, shell, metal, stone) to serve as weapons and tools. Our elder siblings still remember the First Language that humanity has forgotten, if we ever properly learned it. They still remember and live according to the way in which the Creator wishes us all to live, as human beings almost universally do not—so it is wise and essential for us to listen to and learn from our elder brothers and sisters of the other nations of life.

The traditional peoples look on the regions where humans do not live, but other beings do, in a different way than the mainstream culture. Their attitude is that "We have our abiding places and they have theirs, and we enter into theirs with respect, with no presumption that the status of guest is automatically granted." This philosophy parallels the Two-Row Wampum, the *Gaswentah,* which expresses an understanding held by the Hodenasaunee (Iroquois Confederacy), and supposedly accepted by the immigrants from Europe. The understanding was that the Hodenasaunee would stay in their own canoe and the newcomers would stay in their own boat on the river of life, and that those two vessels would never interfere with each other.

This do-not-interfere philosophy is found in the way the traditional peoples relate with the older nations of living beings. Just as one individual human would not enter the dwelling place of another human without first giving respect and receiving welcome, so a human should not enter the abiding places of other beings without giving respect and receiving welcome from those other beings. There is no difference here even in how the respect is offered: a human requesting welcome will show respect for any being in essentially the same way, by (for example) asking permission aloud before leaving human lands, by offering a tobacco gift, and by being prayerful, circumspect, quiet and humble. Whether welcome is being requested of another human or a bear or an eagle or the great grandfather trees; the being from whom the welcome is sought will reply according to the way of its own nation.

I remember years ago a woman who was learning to pour water from one of my teachers found that she had inadvertently built her Sacred Stone People's Lodge over a red ant colony. When her people began to be bitten by the ants as they sat upon the earth inside the lodge, they ran out of the lodge, yelling with pain and rubbing their sore behinds. Afterwards this woman told Grandfather and me that she was going to go inside the lodge by herself, and smudge and pray hard to the ants. "I will talk to the spirit of the ants," she said, "and I will ask them to move to another location." She went in and sweated and prayed hard, bravely withstanding the furious chomping on her naked derrière, but the ants refused to budge. My teacher and I smiled at each other; the message of the ants was clear to him and me if not to the lady: "Hey, two-legged fool, we've had our home here for many generations!" By biting her and her disciples, they were saying, "You have no right to put your lodge on top of our home, and make us uncomfortable with hot rocks and steam, and then do us the indignity of sitting on us!" In failing to respect—or even recognize—their refusal to give her welcome, she fell into a way of thinking common in the dominant culture, assuming that "of course" the ants should and would defer to her wishes.

There are some places where humans simply are never welcome, and some beings who will virtually never give welcome to humans; these places are most strongly *wakan*. The original peoples respect and honor the lack of welcome by leaving such places or beings strictly alone. We human beings too are *wakan* in part, and sometimes we find other humans will not welcome us. We should respect the *wakan* in all beings, human and otherwise. In the case of the medicine person or the holding of sacred ceremonies, however, welcome from very *wakan* beings or places may be given when asked; it may also be given unasked to a human being in dire need.

Our sisters and brothers in the Circle of Life, the Sacred Hoop of All the Nations, vary only in kind, not in worth. There are no weeds, there are no vermin, there are no worthless species or individuals. Every creature is a child of our Earth Mother, made by the Creator, and is to be given respect under all circumstances. To live in any other way is not the way of the original peoples.

In the traditional culture, giving back to our relations is vital, so we can remember prayerfully that we are all related. Giving back is not done simply by saying "thank you," which can become an empty phrase, a merely *washte* formula. It is, rather, genuine and spontaneous, from the heart, a humble expression of deep gratitude, a *wakan* manifestation rather than a socially required *washte* token of politeness. Among the original peoples, one is expected to keep balances, so generosity must not be a mere token gift or a show of ostentation, but, as K'ung Fu-tse (Confucius), Jesus and Moses Maimonides taught, a *real* giving out of humility and respect.

In Native (North) American culture, this balance of sharing is referred to as giving a tobacco gift. It doesn't necessarily have to be tobacco; tobacco is a good and common way to do this, hence the name, but it is not the only form. Other typical forms of a tobacco gift include sage, sweetgrass, cedar, a stone or feather or some kind of handcrafted article that you have made. But it can be anything, even a nod of respect, or a silent kindness.

Tobacco is often given because the smoke of this plant carries prayers. Therefore the gift says not only "I honor you for your generosity to me," but "I will lift you up in prayer." When we take a sapling (for the structure of a Sacred Stone People's Lodge, for example) or plants for healing, we leave a tobacco gift behind, on the North side, the side where the moss grows, the direction associated with the time between death and life. We are taking a life, so, with the tobacco gift, we are prayerfully helping the living being through this between-time to life again. We always say a prayer to its spirit, asking for its permission and forgiveness. We always leave enough individuals of the living being's nation behind to ensure there will be new life next year. If it is an animal, we never take a female except perhaps one past childbearing age. If there isn't enough to ensure new life next year, we take nothing. And, whether we take or not, we leave the tobacco gift, praying our thanks to the Creator. The Maya people say: "The roots of all living things are tied together. When a mighty tree is felled, a star falls from the sky. Before you cut down a mahogany, you should ask permission of the keeper of the forest and you should ask permission of the keeper of the star."

When we go to visit one of our Grandfathers or Grandmothers, we always bring a tobacco gift, as a way of respecting the *wakan* wisdom they carry, and as a way of helping them through the between-time which in not too long they will be entering. If the elder smokes cigarettes, we might provide a pack or two of his or her favored brand. Otherwise, we take loose tobacco. Best is pure tobacco (with no additives, fillers, sugars or chemicals). I am always pleased when people remember this tradition and give me a tobacco gift when they ask me to teach them something or when they come to a sacred ceremony.

A lot of people these days rightly have an aversion to the smoking of tobacco, since so many individuals are addicted to it and because overuse can lead to cancer and other diseases. But I note that the *pure* tobacco has been clinically proven to be far less addictive; it is the dextrose sugars and the chemical additives that are most harmful. At any rate, among the original peoples it is considered disrespectful to make decisions *for* one's elders, one's Grandfathers and Grandmothers. If they want to smoke tobacco, we who are younger have no right to "correct" them, or to disdain the ancient custom of giving a tobacco gift out of a misguided sense of "protecting" them from disease or addiction. I have seen many Grandmothers and Grandfathers smoke like fiends and still live to a healthy old age. Maybe that is because not only do they enjoy smoking, but they treat it as sacred. In fact, I've sometimes noticed the old ones turning a cigarette in their fingers to each of the Four Directions before they light it—making it a small ceremony. Blue Eagle (Luc Bourgault) tells how once someone asked an Anishinabe elder how to stop smoking; the elder replied, "Every time you light a cigarette, say a prayer. Either you will smoke less, or you will pray more!"

I remember reading years ago about Peter Freuchen's experience of accompanying some Eskimo hunters. When they had made their kill, they offered the anthropologist a section of the meat. Freuchen started effusively thanking them. But an elder upbraided him, saying that he must not thank them for his meat, for the portion he had been given was his right. Among these people, the elder said, no one is dependent on another, thus nobody gives or receives gifts, for these make one dependent—gifts make slaves just as whips make dogs. The point is: Freuchen had already "expressed his thanks," as it were, by participating in the hunt. He was not maintaining but upsetting the balances by adding to this his superfluous words of thanks.

Saying thanks with a tobacco gift is a way of keeping balances. You don't get something for nothing. When we sweat in the Sacred Stone People's Lodge, or give a bit of our flesh in the *Wiwanyag Wachipi* (Sun Dance), or get tied up in the *Yuwipi* (binding ceremony), and so on, we are giving a tobacco gift to the Grandfathers and Grandmothers, to the *nagipi* (spirits), to the medicine animals. And they give us the harvest of visions and protection, just as I give tobacco and the plants give me the harvest of their fruit. According to Blue Eagle, a Huichol elder once danced the rain dance to end a California drought and, when it rained, he told the amazed people, "The gratitude of human beings is the nourishment of the G-ds."

Some members of the dominant culture share the original peoples' commitment to give and take in balance. This is based on a respect for independence as well as interdependence. One doesn't give gifts that are unrequited, unbalanced (which could take the receiver's independence away), and one doesn't take without giving back (which destroys the web of interdependence).

A simple rule: *With rare exceptions, traditionals say "please" to their fellow creatures and say "thank you" to the Creator.* Saying "please" means giving the tobacco gift and asking other living beings for permission to enter their realm or to take their outer robe. To say "thank you" to a fellow creature is to create an imbalance of giving, and to say "please" to G-d runs the risk of suggesting that we know better than the Creator what we need. Watch the cats or dogs who live with you, and you will see that they say "please." Cats rub our legs and meow. Dogs pant, smile and woof their hope. Once you've fed them, they go off and radiate content—their way of thanking the Creator.

It's instructive that there is no way to say "You're welcome" in any Native American language I'm at all familiar with. The sharing and the thanks (tobacco gift) are a balanced exchange. Giving thanks in balanced exchange is the way we properly *should* behave; why, then, is further acknowledgement for normal, proper behavior necessary?

Gifts without balance lead to obligations, to the receiver being put in a lower status. Missionaries and explorers gave gifts to the natives as the first step toward annihilation. Today, the government hands out gifts (welfare checks and Indian Affairs handouts) to the poor and to Native Americans, perpetuating their lower, dependent status. "The proverb warns that 'You should not bite the hand that feeds you,'" Thomas Szasz says, "but maybe you should if it prevents you from feeding yourself."

The monetary gifts of the U.S. Bureau of Indian Affairs and the Canadian Department of Indian Affairs are handed out to recognized tribes. Many of these tribes are now being granted the privilege of legally operating casinos, from which they can make lots of money (though typically the non-Native "investors" make far more). It has also led to jealousy and mistrust among nations, as some nations with BIA or DIA status fight to keep other nations from getting it. Nowadays it seems many recognized nations are focused more on getting their hands on casino profits than on holding to their traditional ways. Even as I put the finishing touches on this book, some BIA-imposed tribal councils of the Hodenasaunee (Iroquois Confederacy) in New York are giving up on all land claims that are being prosecuted in federal court under historic treaties, in return for state permission to build casinos. In both ways they lose — they allow members of the dominant culture to replace their traditional governments with ones more amenable to the negotiations of greed, and they betray this sacred land and betray their ancestors who fought to protect it.

Listen to what one of the greatest Indian heroes, Tashunka Witko (Crazy Horse), said: "One does not sell the land upon which people walk." Which should remind you of what Chief Sealth said: "How can you buy or sell the Earth and Sky? These ideas are strange to us!" And hear what Leon Shenandoah, the great Tadodaho of the Hodenasaunee said: "We cannot trade the welfare of our future generations for profit now. We must abide by the Natural Law or be victims of its ultimate reality."

In traditional culture, giving is a sharing of what is universal — practical tools, useful or spiritual things (sage bundles, tobacco and so on), or sacred things (dreams, love, embraces, sexuality). It respects the independence of both giver and receiver.

When we do good to others, we should let the goodness go and move on. It's like the river. Should it hold on to every drop of water that flows through it? We should let goodness move through us in the same natural way, coming from sources outside us (the Grandfathers and Grandmothers, the Earth and Sky, the medicine beings) and flowing through us to our sister and brother living beings. That is what binds us together in the Sacred Hoop of All the Nations. A traditional person does not call attention to her or his acts of generosity or courage. One does not own goodness; it belongs to everyone and everything. Those who seek honor are less worthy of it, while those who seek instead to honor others, and prefer not to be honored themselves, are more worthy of it. I have always believed that the greatest honor goes to those who sincerely insist that they are least worthy of it.

Grandfather Tachcha Hushtë (Lame Deer) taught that the Creator "only sketches out the path of life roughly for all the creatures on earth, shows them where to go, where to arrive at, but leaves them to find their own way to get there. He wants them to act independently according to their nature, to the urges of each of them."

Quite a few years ago, when I was asked by a Grandfather to be a chief of a largely Cherokee intertribal organization, I immediately blurted out something like

"You've asked the wrong man! I'm nowhere near knowledgeable enough, or old enough. And I'm not even a Cherokee!" The Grandfather quietly replied to me in this way: "If I had thought you were going to say anything else, I wouldn't have asked you."

This conversation taught me a great deal about being a Chief, and about the nature of respect and traditional wisdom. As a *person*, a Chief doesn't deserve respect any more than anyone else—but respect for the *traditions that Chief teaches* is vital to the traditional peoples' way of life. Any chief, even the great chiefs of the past—Pontiac, Tecumseh, Sitting Bull and Joseph, as well as great chiefs of other lands, like Josiah the Hebrew king, Nezahualcoyotl the poet-king of the Alcohua, and Sundiata of the Mali—are just ordinary human beings, the same as anyone else. Chiefs put their breechclouts on one leg at a time. They can be grouchy. They get stomach aches and arthritis. They can be thoughtless and stupid. They make mistakes and often don't know what to do. As individuals, they deserve no more or less respect than anyone else.

But, as *Chiefs*, they deserve a special kind of respect. It is the responsibility of members of a nation to afford that special respect, when they are speaking to their people *as Chief*. And it is the responsibility of all Chiefs, of course, to know when they are speaking as ordinary persons and when they are speaking as Chiefs, and never to abuse the latter. When one is expressing his or her own personal thoughts or feelings on a subject, one just speaks as an individual. But when one is sharing the traditions as they have been taught to her or him, when the individual is simply the means through which the traditions express *themselves*, then one is speaking as Chief. A Chief must always be humble, and must never allow that title to go to her or his head. One must constantly be on guard, lest ὕβρις (*hubris*) take over, and make one think that *everything* one says is the epitome of ancient wisdom. I have seen some well-respected Chiefs fall victim to ὕβρις.

A Chief is not like a President or a King. These Western rulers, like the male G-d (whom Voltaire caustically referred to as an idol made in the image and likeness of man), assert and justify the system of ownership and dispense the right to take from the less powerful. A Chief is not a power broker or a judge. A Chief does not tell people what to do—except sometimes in dire emergencies, such as natural disasters or war. A Chief does not play favorites and pressure people into siding with him or he'll run them off the rez (as does one person I'm thinking of who has besmirched the great honor and burden given him). Rather, a Chief seeks consensus and harmony, and when necessary strives for reconciliation between disharmonious parties. It is a Chief's duty to live respectfully and honorably; to be a good spouse and a good parent; to avoid greed, envy, malice, avarice and the lust for power. A Chief works hard for the people and prays constantly for them. A Chief teaches, gently and quietly, with words, but mostly by example. A Chief does a great deal of listening and not so much talking; but, when a Chief speaks, the words are thoughtful and wise. To paraphrase Thomas Carlyle, the work of a Chief is like an underground river: it nourishes the landscape without its presence being seen.

The best Chiefs are those who are quiet in personality, who do not draw attention to themselves, who encourage and support others. The best Chiefs are those who have, as it is traditionally said, skin seven layers thick. The best Chiefs are those who hesitate before using that designation to describe themselves, who prefer to say, "All I can do is to do my best, what little I can do, for the sake of my people, in honor to our ancestors and the Creator, and for the sake of the future"—and then live humbly but courageously by those words.

Jean-Jacques Rousseau pointed to the commonly held Western belief that society is formed so that each individual gains by serving the rest. But, he insisted, that doesn't work. "We always gain more by hurting our neighbors than by doing good to them. Nothing is needed but the knowledge of how to do it with impunity; and, to this end, the mighty put all their strength, and the powerless all their cunning."

In Western civilization, justice is based on laws predicated on the assumption that human beings are basically greedy, even evil. It presumes a singleness of meaning to words, a specific measuring of land and accounting of belongings in its contracts and treaties. At core is the civilization's preoccupation with property ownership; virtually every law is a property issue at heart. Even the debate about abortion centers on whether the fetus "belongs" to, is a ward of, the mother or the state. The temptation to break the law is intensified by the greed that mercantile interests encourage, and the fact that respected authorities and leaders themselves all too often flout their own rules. These laws tend to be prescriptive in nature, naming activities that are forbidden, and by their very nature admit to the possibility of their being broken.

The great law codes of the world, from Hammurabi's Law, the Torah, the Qur'an and the Hodenasaunee (Iroquois Confederacy) Great Law of Peace to English common law and the United States Constitution, contain the explicit or implied promise that everyone will be accorded equal justice. But today money and power can "buy" leniency, while the poor and powerless get treated particularly harshly.

Justice and equality were woven, like the strands of a blanket, deep into the fabric of traditional society by such great teachers as Aionwantha (Hiawatha), the Peacemaker and Jikonshaseh of the Hodenasaunee (Iroquois Confederacy). The *Kaienerekowa*, the Great Law of Peace, the world's oldest living constitution and probably its most poetic and very possibly its greatest, was ratified on August 31, 1142, at a sacred place, now the site of a football field in Victor, New York. It binds everyone together in several ethical dimensions: the warp is one's belonging to a particular nation (the Seneca, Cayuga, Onondaga, Oneida, Mohawk or Tuscarora), and the weft is membership in a certain clan (the Wolf, Bear, Beaver, Turtle, Hawk, Heron, Deer, Eel or Snipe), which has brother and sister members in every nation. The woof of the blanket is spirituality: one might be a member of a certain medicine society, such as the False Face Society; individuals are also ethically woven together in society through such ceremonies as the Sacred Stone People's Lodge, which includes a commitment to treat those who have gone through the lodge with you with honor and respect, and the Moon Lodge, which ceremonially reminds men that every woman is ultimately *Woman*, the Beautiful One herself who brought us the Sacred Pipe that makes us one.

"Hear me!" said Tecumseh; "A single twig breaks, but a bundle of twigs is strong." Look to the Heavens and you will see a similar multidimensional binding: the circles of the Sun, the Moon, Planets, Comets and Stars. Look to the Earth and you will see the Great Law in the complex interplay and mutual dependence of all living creatures.

Authority and power are carefully balanced by the wise woman Jikonshaseh's teaching about the relationship between men and women: men are the chiefs and sachems, but they trace their lineage through their foremothers, and they know it is the women who both bestow these honors and can take them away for ethical transgressions. And one is taught always to act bearing in mind the consequences for the seven generations preceding and following. With such a weaving of relationships, how could one even conceive of harming anyone else in the Hodenasaunee?

Yet it happens, even among the Hodenasaunee. Justice among the original peoples is based on maintaining healthy relationships, and when the people neglect that responsibility, relationships break down into verbal and even physical infighting. An eighteenth-century Mohawk named Thayendanegea but better known as Joseph Brant allied himself with the British. This alliance and Brant's greed led to years of bloodshed and tyranny and the loss of vast amounts of Iroquois territory. Still suffering the effects of his leadership, his people today find themselves crowded onto tiny, heavily polluted reservations. Brant was *washichu*; he forgot that in traditional society every individual looks out for the welfare of all one's relations, which includes not only humans but all living things. He forgot that we are all a part of the same family, and that, as Sealth observed, if we hurt another member of the family we hurt ourselves. Many of his descendants, today's Iroquois leaders, forget the same things.

Among the traditional peoples, ethics are situational, with one's decisions made from the limited information available at any given time or place. When one walks through the wilderness one does one's best to decide the best way to go around a lake or mountain. Yet one may eventually find that it wasn't the best path after all, since it led to unforeseen difficulties later on. So it is with life: we sometimes make mistakes we deeply regret later, but, at the time, those decisions seemed to be the best. This ethical approach might be compared to the Buddhist Doctrine of Means.

There is no expectation of an inhuman, impossible perfection; rather, one is expected only to make decisions based on one's best judgment. As Carl Gustav Jung taught, one journeys not toward perfection, but wholeness. Mistakes, unsuccessful attempts, inaccurate assessments are seen as opportunities to grow, not as shameful failures and reasons for blame. As the *Mahabharata* states, "I made my first mistake the day I was born. By that path, I have ever since sought wisdom." I remember one Grandfather saying that just since he had gotten up that morning he had made enough mistakes to fill a deep valley! But, he added, "That's the only way we can learn."

Original peoples' justice is structured on the prevention of crime by maintaining balance in relationships through honesty and generosity and, when problems develop, healing them by reestablishing harmonious balances. One seeks harmony with others when the relationship has fallen into disrepair. One goes to the person to renew a good relationship—not through apologizing or arguing over who's right and who's wrong, but by seeking balance again. As the early Christian teacher, Saint Paul, advised: "Strive to outdo one another in generosity." Or, as Jesus taught his followers, if one realizes there's an unresolved issue with a friend when one goes to make an offering to G-d, one should leave the gift at the altar, reconcile oneself with the friend, and then go back to make the offering.

Native justice is not concerned with establishing objective facts—since traditional ontology does not assume there is an objective reality out there beyond our senses—but with harmoniously integrating the variations in our subjective perceptions. It is less concerned with "who actually did what" and "what really happened" than with maintaining and restoring balances. This is usually done by giving precious gifts to the offended party.

Of course, sometimes, with the irredeemably unrepentant, restoring balances was impossible. In such cases, shunning (loss of identity), physical scarring, banishment, or, rarely, executing might be invoked. Doug George-Kanentiio describes how the Hodenasaunee (Iroquois Confederacy) swiftly and soundly punished wife beaters, usually with divorce—which saw husbands evicted from their homes (which traditionally belonged to their wives) keeping only their clothing and hunting gear, losing any right to remarry. The punishment sometimes included beating (so the scars would signify this man was not to be trusted as a potential husband) and banishment.

Ideally, however, tensions and misunderstandings between individuals or groups would be detected and resolved before they led to the extreme of violence. While this sometimes might take the intervention of older and wiser people, largely the individual was responsible for being aware of any such problems and quickly making effort—perhaps through prayer or purification ceremonies, and perhaps by seeking resolution directly with the other party—to restore harmony once again. In the original peoples' way, if you realize another person feels angry toward you or sad, then, even if you don't think you did anything wrong, you express your sorrow for the disharmony and seek to restore harmony by giving that person a gift in order to restore the balances. It might be just a tobacco gift, or something as generous as (in traditional times) a horse, but the gift is to say, "I want to continue to have a good, healthy, trusting relationship with you." Ideally, the other person will also be motivated at the same time to give a gift to you for the same reason. In fact, I have often noticed traditional people who had fallen into a difficult relationship striving to give generously to each other, just as Saint Paul advised.

Among some nations, if you even dream of doing harm to your neighbor, you go to your neighbor the next morning and give her or him such a gift. As psychologists have long pointed out, our dreams can often point to repressed feelings; thus, if we seek to restore balances *before* we act on our negative attitudes, we will very probably prevent much unhappiness.

The Sacred Giveaway tradition is central to this philosophy, as I will explain later in more detail. When everyone in the nation from time to time gives gifts to each other, it tunes up relationships and maintains the balances. It also keeps people from becoming possessive of their belongings. Furthermore, in many nations, including those joined in the Hodenasaunee (Iroquois Confederacy), in the intercalary days at the New Year, during the time of sacred chaos, nobody owns anything and all ordinary relationships are suspended, leaving no *washte* societal rules at all. At this time, many things and even personal relationships are exchanged freely.

I will never forget how one respected Grandmother used to raise herself up to her full four feet five, stick her finger in my kneecap, and exhort me: "Distant Eagle, stand in your truth!" When she spoke this way to me or to others, her point was to be honorable and respectful in all our relationships, and to let our individual truth—not "the truth," a phrase that suggests an objective reality beyond the reach of our senses and our minds, but *our* truth, our convictions— be a bulwark against the dishonorable attacks of others, as well as our own tendencies to cut corners and bend our inner rules "just this once." So traditional people seek to stand in their truth, whether it coheres or not with another's truth, but they seek just as assiduously to maintain healthy balances with others. Thus, they live by the word that I already told you a wise Grandfather gave when asked about the essence of the traditional peoples' spiritual way: *Respect.* They respect their own perceptions and the perceptions of others, and respect the vital need to maintain harmonious relationships.

Honor and respect are among the most sacred things every individual carries. Among traditional peoples honor is not a personal possession but something *wakan*; each individual is responsible for carrying it, just as one carries sacred stories or ceremonies or objects, in behalf of all the people. Honor, being *wakan*; is something we treat with care because it is sacred and awe-full (these words suggest the literal meaning of *wakan*).

Honor is related to our knowing the stories and traditions of our people: to know these things is to honor our ancestors, whose deeds we remember because they help us define who *we* are. Knowing these things also honors our sisters and brothers of the current generation, because sharing this heritage with them means they are one with us. And knowing these things also honors our children's children to the seventh generation, because we carry these sacred stories and traditions so we can pass them on to our descendants: as they remember *us*, they will know who *they* are. Honor, then, is not defined as behaving within certain parameters established by law or convention, but as living in a way that gives respect to all beings. Honor is keeping balances with all beings; it is listening and being respectful.

In modern society it is officially deemed to be always dishonorable to engage in any kind of sexual talk or activity, even flirting, with anyone other than one's spouse—though, in fact, this convention is disrespected almost constantly. But in the traditional culture there is often a certain amount of free sexual banter, even sexual activity, provided only that it is humble and respectful, that it is a sharing and not a taking. (Different nations vary on what that "certain amount" is, of course.) The journals of the Black Robes suggest how shocked they were to see Native people behave in what they considered immoral, dishonorable ways. They did not realize that these Natives were being entirely honorable according to the ways of *their own* people. Still today the *heyoka* (sacred contrary) behavior of an elder often surprises people unfamiliar with the ways of the Red Road; such people do not realize that this behavior actually fosters strong relationships based on respect and love.

Anyone who behaves in a dishonorable way forgets the meaning in the sacred stories and traditions of their ancestors. Everyone makes mistakes from time to time, and I myself have made plenty more than my share, and I have found traditional peoples to be wonderfully forgiving. But sometimes there is an individual who willfully and repeatedly flouts the traditional ways, to the point that the people consider that person to have lost the honor he or she was carrying. No longer can that person be trusted to carry the honor of the nation and its sacred traditions and stories on to the coming generations. Such a person does not exist any longer, as far as the nation is concerned, and is no longer a part of the story. And a person without stories and without honor is no person. That person, moreover, does not even exist for himself or herself, for the same reason. Yet, although it is uncommon, even these non-persons can recover their existence and their honor through humility and respect, through brave deeds or other great sacrifices.

Lest we lose it, it is important that we maintain our sacred honor; even more important is the reason that the generations yet to come are depending on us to carry the sacred ways on to them.

In Native American tradition there are certain traditional ways in which one is given a name. These include:

> *A powerful dream* clearly given by the Grandfathers and Grandmothers.
> *A powerful vision* clearly given by the Grandfathers and Grandmothers.
> *A significant and life-changing event,* such as an act of bravery or a miraculous event.
> *The bestowing of a name* by an elder or a Chief.

The names given to children were usually *pro tempore*, to be supplanted by their "adult" names, received in one of these ways. It is virtually universal that adult names are confirmed after a great deal of prayer, meditation and thought, with smudging and the Sacred Pipe, often in the context of ceremonies such as the Sacred Stone People's Lodge, Vision Crying, or Buffalo Sing. An Onodowahgah (Seneca) elder told me that one only carried one's name for fifty years; after that time, it was given back to the ancestors and the nation, so future generations could use it.

There is a tendency among people who are not of Native ancestry but are attracted to the Native tradition to choose for themselves a "name" because it sounds appropriately mystical or aesthetic. I have heard elders laugh over names like "Singing Crystals" or "Wise Unicorn." One person I know has jokingly suggested names like "Squashed Bug on Windshield," "Runs With Scissors," and "Doesn't Play Well With Others." Another has offered "Walking Eagle" (too full of shit to fly).

I believe we must, in the matter of traditional names, let our names come to us in the old traditional ways. In this tradition, names are sacred and are given to one, not chosen by ourselves. Naming is a very sacred thing along the Red Road, and is not ever to be taken lightly. The names of traditional peoples manifest a connection with the universe around us, and express praise for the work of the Creator. So we do not appropriate a name, but let it come to us.

Of course most anybody would like a beautiful or noble-sounding name. But many of the great Chiefs had very ordinary or even ludicrous names. If you carry such a name, carry it with dignity. I think of a Chief named Worm, who, when people laughed at his name, reminded them that the worm stirs up the earth, aerating it and mixing good nutrients into the soil—indeed, that, without this noble creature, many plants would not be able to grow, and even that life as we know it might not be possible on this Earth. To his thinking, the worm is a great and important animal indeed. The names of some great leaders have also seemed foolish to the newcomers. The name Young Man Afraid of His Horses, for instance, shows the carrier of it knew that Horse, *Tashunka*, is truly *wakan*, something to be respectfully afraid of; in fact, translated more accurately, his name means Young Man Whose Very Horses are Feared. The great Chief Rain in the Face bore a name that has seemed ludicrous to many, but it teaches us of the courage of facing the rain, the storm, as an equal and letting it strengthen us. And his name teaches us of another kind of courage, and another kind of rain in the face: the courage to weep for all that has been done to break up the Sacred Hoop of All the Nations—and to weep with hope and joy for the vision of the Sacred Hoop one day restored.

Behind all such traditional names there is always a story. The way names are translated often leaves out a lot of implication. Chief Joseph is best known by that appellation given to him by the newcomers because his *real* name is too hard to translate: *Hin-mut-too-yah-lat-kekht*, or Thunder that Rises to a Higher Plane, is, in miniature, a story. It is, ultimately, a name in the First Language, the language of the Earth and her children. As N. Scott Momaday put it at the beginning of his book *The Names: A Memoir*, "The names are those of animals and of birds, of objects that have one definition in the eye, another in the hand, of forms and features on the rim of the world, or of sounds that carry on the bright wind and in the void. They are old and original in the mind, like the beat of rain on the river, and intrinsic in the native tongue, failing even as those who bear them turn once in the memory, go on, and are gone forever."

The story behind a name may be that one received it through a vision or a dream. A name may come from a significant experience. A name may be awarded to you in recognition of your own learning or hard work. My recommendation to you is to be patient in the matter of receiving a name. As one Grandmother often said (echoing the ancient Roman philosopher Seneca), "Haste is best made slowly."

In the way of the traditional peoples, names are everpresent, just as visions are everpresent, if only we have the eyes to see them. When I see an eagle way up in the Sky overhead, for instance, I see my own name in the Heavens; when the eagle is flying here and there all over the Sky, it is the name of a Grandfather who taught me. When I hear a mourning dove, I feel the presence of one of my teaching Grandmothers. When I see a star shining brightly overhead, my sister-by-honor is close to me in spirit. When I see a bear or an otter, I think of my dear honorary brothers, who are named after those brothers-in-fur. And so on.

Just this morning I was up very early and walking outside. It was cold, but the Sun was coming up and the springtime world around me was bright, peaceful and joyful. I was looking at a patch of primroses who had blossomed since last night and were lifting their newborn faces up to the dawn light. In the breeze I saw how their delicate, dewy skin trembled with a shy ecstasy. The words spoke themselves silently in my mind: "Why do you worry about clothing? Consider these lilies of the field, how they grow; they neither toil nor spin, yet I say that even Solomon in all his glory was not clothed like one of these." In an overwhelming rush, I realized that here all around me was the spirit of a friend of mine, whose name in Arabic means Morning Breeze That Opens the Flower. And here she was, unexpectedly all around me, in a powerful vision—not of her outer physical appearance, but her inner spiritual nature. It was a wonderful feeling; it was as if she and I were walking together in the quiet morning, enjoying each other's company.

So it is, when I see or hear certain things, I feel the presence of people I know or knew, with the "expanded awareness" I've told you about previously. No doubt there are other names, other presences around me too, at all times, or at least when I am not cooped up in buildings or cars but in a natural setting. This adds to my feeling of always being surrounded by the Grandfathers and Grandmothers, my ancestors, those whom I love, my friends and relatives, all my descendants and indeed every living thing. In sum, this enables me to feel the presence all around me of the Sacred Hoop of All the Nations.

We need to remain open and aware, with mind empty (in Buddhist terms), ready to be filled, so these presences may reveal themselves, at the time and place their own choosing. Our rational minds are simply not capable of such intuitive openness; this same friend who visited me in spirit has said, perceptively, "Our minds store information for necessity, not endearment."

This morning I was aware through my outer senses of flowers and morning sun and East breeze, when the inner spirit of my friend chose to unveil herself to me within the cloak of this landscape. Like *trompe-l'œil* puzzle-drawings (such as the one in which a face is hidden in the landscape), once my friend's presence-in-spirit was revealed to me in the world around me, it was impossible for me *not* to see her. Though now, later in the same day, as I write these words, the flowers have gone back to being just flowers, not the presence of this cherished friend—though they will always now and in future years remind me warmly of her whenever I look at them. When a name presents itself strongly and unexpectedly to me, as it did this morning, that usually means, in the Native tradition, that we are or should be communicating on some deeper level.

Yet, unbeknownst to me, all around me in the natural landscape are names—and spirits—beyond number. However, where I may not be able to recognize in the landscape around me the names of individuals or spirits whom I do not know in the ordinary, day-to-day sense ("know" in the sense of the French *connaître* or the German *kennen*), medicine women and men are able to perceive in and through their natural surroundings the *wakan* presences around them of all manner of individuals and spirits, whether known by name to them or not. They are far more able than I to clear their minds such that (again, in the Buddhist sense) their minds are perfect mirrors of the world around them. They even see the spirits take on their physical forms and converse with them.

By this sacred means the medicine women and men are able at any time and place to learn from the spirit-presences around them, communicating with them in a form of spiritual telepathy. It is through this freedom in time and space that, as I have told you, certain elders already knew all about me when (I thought) I was meeting them for the first time, even though nobody had ever mentioned even my existence to them before our meeting. So it is that in ancient times the elders were aware of the wise ones who lived on other continents and even communicated with them—which may explain why the elders of Turtle Island prophesied an invasion of white-skinned peoples from beyond the ocean to the East long before it came about. So it is that the elders of today have already communicated with the wise ones on other planets (our relations, the old stories say) and warned them to beware of ships from Earth bearing white-skinned strangers with big smiles and gaudy gifts.

I like the Tsalagi (Cherokee) tradition that keeps us humble about names: teasing friends by referring to them with overly ornate, high-falutin' versions of their names. I once called a Tsalagi Grandfather, Sings-Alone, "He Whose Voice is So Bad They Make Him Sing Out Behind the Outhouse." And, without skipping a beat, he referred to me as "He Who Flies High Over His Enemies Who Cower In Craven Terror That He's Going To Drop Poop On Them From Out Of The Sky." This humor helps us not to take our names or ourselves too seriously, and not—in a sense similar to that offered by Zen Buddhism—to become too attached to those names.

Medicine names, however, are not joked about, or even said aloud very frequently. Like the Hebrew name of G-d in Judaism, they are too sacred to be pronounced except in the context of ceremony. Ironically, these names often seem to be jokes. Most commonly given to us by a *heyoka*, one of the sacred contrary people, they are usually shocking, often scatological or sexually suggestive in nature. I have heard of individuals laughing when a *heyoka* gives them a medicine name, thinking that the *heyoka* is joking, since no medicine name could possibly be so bizarre. Yet these names are filled with sacred *wakan* power; for this reason, they are rarely said aloud, and never in ordinary discourse. It's not that they are secret (forbidden from being shared), though they are usually shared only with those who can be trusted to respect them. Among some nations, it is believed that, if an enemy knows your medicine name, he or she has power over you. I was taught, rather, that these names are not to be shared because they are understood as *wakan*—sacred medicine—and, as with anything *wakan*, they should be invoked sparingly so their power is not dissipated by frequent use or misuse, becoming *washte*. The common name can be joked about, can be shared with anyone, including even enemies, since it does not point to the sacred power within the individual. Both kinds of name are said with our breath. But common names are said with what might be called ordinary breath, while medicine names are spoken only with "visible breath"—in the course of ceremony, when our breath rises visibly to Heaven when we smoke and pray with the Sacred Pipe, or when our breath mists in the hot, humid air within the Sacred Stone People's Lodge, or when our breaths mingle in the sacred ceremony of sexuality. The Creator and the various kinds of spirit beings know us best and most truly by these medicine names. The power of our medicine names is the power of shapeshifting: when and where we are known by these names, we are no longer the "we" of common identity, but sacred participants in a powerful holy act that transcends ordinary time and place and enters the realm of dream, vision and myth.

When the newcomers invaded this continent, they gave most of the nations here new, often insulting names, at minimum evidencing a lack of respect for "lesser" peoples, and even meaning to dehumanize and demoralize them. Thus most of the names by which "Indian tribes" are known are not how they originally called, or still call, themselves. Likewise, the dominant society—often at their mission schools—gave children new European-Christian names and forbade them to use their original names, in order to force assimilation into white culture. To this day, Native Americans commonly have traditional names that do not appear on the documents and licenses and bank accounts of the dominant culture. Thus the *re*-naming hasn't always had the desired effect of dissipating the original people's identity and power. In fact it has often helped to protect them: their real names, the names that embody their sacred power, as individuals and as peoples, remain largely unknown to outsiders. It remains the responsibility of these traditional peoples to keep their names and their heritage alive within their hearts—not to let these true names become forgotten, unknown to themselves.

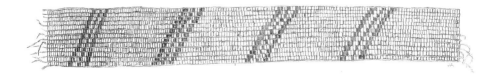

Hodenasaunee (Iroquois) wampum belt to mark their first sight of Europeans.
(See page 198.)

VI

Spiritual Realities

THE MESQUAKIE (FOX) NATION tells this story:

Long ago, one of our people became a Christian. In fact, he became a very good Christian. He attended church, he didn't overindulge in drink, and he was generous and polite to everyone. When he died, he went to the Indian Heaven, but they wouldn't take him in because he was a Christian. Then he went to the Christian Heaven, but they wouldn't take him in because he was an Indian. Then he went to Hell, but they wouldn't take him in because he was too good. So he came back to Earth again, and went to all the dances, including the Buffalo Dance. And he has taught all his children and grandchildren to do the same as he did.

An Onodowahgah (Seneca) elder, descended from Cornplanter, told me about a boyhood friend of his named Sparky, who didn't believe any longer in the "Indian religion"—meaning the old traditional ceremonies—and didn't believe in Christianity either. But Sparky did believe that you should worship G-d in your heart. I suggested to Grandfather that that seems to me to be the essence of the Indian spiritual way, and he emphatically agreed.

When the chiefs of the Hodenasaunee (Iroquois Confederacy) responded to the "Founding Fathers"' request for advice, they said the new-comers' idea of freedom of religion was just fine but the idea of separation of church and state would only lead to difficulty. For the original peoples, no such separation is possible. The individual or nation is always at the center of all things and the Creator; this attitude helps these peoples to see all things as living, sacred and filled with the presence of G-d, and all Creation as numinous.

Scholars like Åke Hultkrantz in his *Native Religions of North America* write of traditional spirituality as if it were a number of disparate religions. These are not organized religions but a single form of spirituality: it is essentially the same across this continent, although ceremonial and linguistic variations occur. From my encounters with elders of various traditional peoples worldwide, I have come to believe that they all share what is essentially the same spirituality. Because it lacks a charismatic founder, sacred books, a priestly hierarchy, permanent houses of worship, strict liturgies and codified rules for living, it is often referred to by Western scholars as "primitive." In describing it, you could perhaps use the term "Paganism," a word from the Latin, *paganus*, "country dweller." Indeed, today the remaining traditional people of the world are mostly found away from urbanized Western areas, in rural, outlying regions of Africa, Europe, Asia, the Pacific and the Arctic. But even at the root of certain "established" religions such as Taoism, Judaism, Islam, Shinto and Zoroastrianism, tribal traditions can still be detected.

This spirituality has also been referred to in scholastic works as "animistic," based on the belief that each inanimate object has a spirit, sometimes beneficent and sometimes malevolent. Rather, the traditionals believe that Spirit is universal, flowing in, through and from all things, and the spirit of each thing appears to be discrete just as an island seems to be a separate entity. Still, all spirits are ultimately one—*Spirit*—just as all islands are joined together by the land beneath the waves. Spirit, therefore, cannot be considered singular or plural; it just is.

This is a free-flowing spirituality, ultimately as simple as Zen and equally as profound. Instead of having as its "lens" of faith a book (like the Torah or the Qur'an) or a personality (like Krishna or Jesus), its "lens" is the world and everything in it; these, like all such lenses, enable us to perceive and understand more clearly the nature and will of G-d. Because all reality is alive with G-d, Native Americans seek and affirm the value of visions and dreams. They do far less talking in their prayers and much more listening—believing in a Creator and spirits that *really are* "closer to me than I am to myself" (to quote Saint Augustine).

G-d is often called *Wakan-Tanka* (the Great Mystery), in Lakota, accented on the second syllable, not the first and third. This name implies that the Creator is greater than the human mind can conceive. But in older Lakota the word for G-d is *Skan*, or *Taku Skanskan*. These terms suggest dynamic energy, and might be rendered in English with Thomas Aquinas's term, the First Cause or Prime Mover, but I prefer "the Creator," and use it throughout this book.

The Creator dwells at the center of the universe, which is everywhere and nowhere, at the center of the Sacred Hoop, the horizon, and in each of us.

The Creator is immanently known as *Atë* (Father), which has two syllables. He is represented for us by the Sky overhead, which nourishes and protects all living things. Beyond the immanent presence of *Atë* is the transcendent presence of *Tunkashila* (Grandfather), with the accent on the second syllable; he is unmanifested, unqualified and unlimited. *Skan* is also immanent in *Ina* (Mother), represented by the Earth beneath us, producing all living things and holding them to her bosom. Beyond *Ina* is the transcendent presence of *Unchi* (Grandmother), the level of potentiality, the ground or substratum for all life.

Wakan-Tanka is evidenced in the primal sacred beings: Sun, Rock, Spirit and Earth, and also in the next rank of sacred beings: Moon, Wind, Thunder Beings and *Wohpe* (the Meteor, the Messenger, the Beautiful Woman; that is, the White Buffalo Calf Woman). Note that each of the second set has a four within it: the four phases of the Moon, the Four Winds, the four parts of the Thunder Beings, and the four colors of the Beautiful Woman. Yet all these are one, are *Skan*.

Grandfather Luther Standing Bear taught: "From *Wakan-Tanka*, the Great Spirit, there came a great unifying life force that flowed in and through all things—the flowers of the plains, blowing winds, rocks, trees, birds, animals—and was the same force that had been breathed into the first man. Thus all things were kindred, and were brought together by the same Great Mystery." As the Abenaki elders say, "The Creator is in everything, and in the air we breathe."

Sacred energy is constantly flowing through everything, without resting in anything—for, if it stayed, it would become *washte*; like running water kept in a bowl, it would become stagnant. "All this visible universe proceeds from my invisible being," says Lord Krishna in the Bhagavad-Gìtà; "all beings find their rest in me, but I do not rest in them." The poet Gary Snyder (in an interview published in 1975 in the *California Quarterly*) described the Lakota concept of life as temporary energy swirls or turbulence patterns, which, he correctly noted, is far closer to the most recent understandings of subatomic physics than "modern" theories of all things as fixed. He was right; in fact, as Fritjof Capra and other writers have detailed, Buddhist, Taoist and Pagan teachings also anticipated by centuries, even millennia, the recently developed theories in subatomic physics. So much for "primitive"!

The spirit that flows in and through all things takes shape in the individual by way of four stages, which were taught to the elders by Bear. Using the Lakota terms, first there is *sichun*, the potential of being. Then there is *tun*, which transforms this potential into a noncorporeal, puissant essence. Next there is *ni*, loosely meaning breath, the continuous evidence of this essence. Finally, there is *nagi*, which protects and advises and carries the first three through the Circle of Life, through death to new life—that is, reincarnation. *Sichun* can be compared to the spark that brings fire into being, *tun* to the tinder that nourishes it into being, *ni* to the flame that bursts forth, and *nagi* to the smoke that rises to Heaven from the fire. You can see these same four aspects in storytelling or in singing the old songs with the Sacred Drum—the seed of the story or song carried in the storyteller's or lead singer's heart; the telling of the story or the singing of the song; the hearing of the story or song, leading to a fuller understanding of the nature of things in both teller and hearer. And you can see it in other things as well: for example the four stages of life (childhood, adulthood, old age and death) and the Four Directions, beginning with the East; and the Four Ages of the Sacred Stone People's Lodge.

We as human beings are called to be attentive, to know that in every act, every thing, every place, and every moment, G-d is present. The vital spirit-presence of the Creator in all things, in all places and times, is known in Lakota as *niya taniya*, in the Hodenasaunee (Iroquois Confederacy) languages as *orenda* or (specifically among the Onodowahgah [Seneca]) as *nigéh*, among the Algonquians as *kitchi manitou*. And there's the beautifully supple Yupiaq word *ella*, which (as Gregory Cajete points out, citing a study by Oscar Kawagley) can mean, depending on context, personal well-being, the weather, awareness, the World, the Creative Force or G-d, the Sky or the Universe. One must be constantly and intensely attentive, by means of extended awareness, to how G-d is manifest in all things, in various and abundant ways. Every creature is wise according to its own nature; if we are humbly attentive, each can teach us more about G-d. All beings are constantly at prayer each in its own special way: so, for instance, as Grandfather Hehaka Sapa (Black Elk) observed, no matter how softly the wind moves the trees whisper their own prayer to G-d. In the same way, the rocks remain in sublime meditation for centuries at a time, only occasionally getting up and moving about in earthquakes or storms. So, too, the lizard gazes out at the eye of G-d from the desert sand, and the eagle prays on high among the crags. All this is close to a wonderful Muslim teaching, which my friend Saba Ali described to me in phrasing evocative of the natural flow of things sunwise around the Sacred Hoop: "That when the wind blows and the trees move, they move in a motion that bows down in worship; that as the Sun rises and sets and the shadows of all things grow and recede, they too are bowing in worship."

Also, all events show the nature of *Skan*. A traditional person sees dawn, for example, as a holy event because it comes from *Wakan-Tanka*. As the morning Sun dispels the darkness of ignorance, the eye of the heart (*chantë ishta*) can open to see understanding. Thus, the traditional person begins each day praying that, just as the Sun ushers understanding into the world, so too may her or his soul find understanding. In the same way, the original peoples encounter the presence of G-d in and through all things and events. Similarly, in all things traditional peoples do, sacredness is central. Like the body itself, the Sacred Stone People's Lodge and the people's everyday dwellings are microcosms of the whole universe: they have a fire or hot rocks at the center, like the body's fiery heart, representing *Wakan-Tanka*'s centrality. Entrances are usually to the East, the source of first light. The place of wisdom (the elders' place) is to the West, the place of last light. Entering them and departing from them thus are also sacred acts, equivalent to conception and birth and death, and the beginning and end of sexual union.

The way G-d is understood in Native terms is not like the Christian understanding (except to the degree the latter has influenced the former). The Christian understanding is that G-d created all things *ex nihilo* ("out of nothingness" in Latin, even though the original Hebrew of the creation story in Genesis doesn't support this). The Native understanding is that the Great Mystery is a presence that pervades all things and speaks through all things. Rather than a "workman" or "creative artist" image (as in Christianity), the Native image is grandparental/parental, one in which we come to know the Great Mystery in and through all created things. Just as you and I resemble in certain ways our parents and grandparents, so too all created things resemble the Creator. And individuals resemble the Creator in particular ways, such as Eagle in omniscience (by flying highest, seeing the farthest), or Bear in wisdom and devotion to family. The Bible—itself in large measure the product of a tribal people—wisely teaches us both to love G-d and love our neighbor (*washte*) and fear/respect G-d and fear/respect other living things (*wakan*).

Living beings include not only plants and animals, but also rocks, *nagipi* (spirits, angels, and ghosts of those who have died), as well as creatures considered by the dominant culture to be of dubious authenticity at best, such as Dragons, the sasquatch and the Thunder Beings. Since all living beings were made by the Creator, all living beings have in them a certain part, a microcosm, of the Creator's wisdom. Those who are wise are quiet, so they can listen and learn from these living creatures who are all around us.

It is very common for traditional names to refer to living creatures, and those living creatures have a special importance for us as individuals. Since my name is Distant Eagle, I have a special connection to eagles, and try to listen to them and learn from them. Grandfather Worm, whom I've already mentioned to you, listened likewise to the wisdom of the worm, which is a wisdom no less sacred and valuable in its own way than that of the eagle or the bear. In the original peoples' culture all creatures are considered noble, since all were made by, and carry wisdom of, the Great Mystery.

People often find, over the course of their lives, that medicine animals work with them and/or through them. This is a very sacred thing, and one should never claim a medicine that is not truly one's own to carry, or brag about a medicine one has. (The *nagipi*, spirits, have a way of reminding us when we get carried away in our hubris.) A medicine animal often comes in visions or dreams, or through encounters in the wild. A friend once dreamed of being violently clawed by a bear, which could mean she had been offered the gift of bear medicine. Just the other night, another friend told me of her dream of crows, which may have meant she was being offered crow medicine. I have heard of a man who was bitten by a rattlesnake and nearly died, and who now has powerful snake medicine. If you think you are being offered the medicine of such a sacred animal, seek the creature out in the wild, if you can, and listen to it and learn from it. At least, go to a wild (*wakan*) place if you can, and speak to its spirit. Leave it tobacco gifts in thanks. Respect it. Do not use things made from it unless specifically directed to do so.

The Sacred Directions also have medicine animals associated with them. This varies from nation to nation, and often from person to person within nations, and even from day to day with the same person, but the general spirit is the same—these are wild beings, *wakan* beings, and by their very nature unpredictable! The Earth too is a living being, and has her medicine, including many healing herbs, which these medicine animals often help us find.

Evan Zuesse, in his excellent book *Ritual Cosmos*, suggests we think of spirituality as a series of concentric circles. When you start out, you are on the periphery, like a child who can't see what's going on at the center. As time goes by, you learn more and become familiar with the ceremony. Moving one circle at a time toward the center, you find yourself more fully able to participate. So, for instance, the first experience one has with the Sacred Stone People's Lodge may be to remain outside and pray with and for the people who enter the lodge. After a few times, the ceremonial leader (called the water pourer) may allow the person to assist those in charge of keeping the Sacred Fire or those who keep door, passing in water, heated rocks or sacred things as they are needed inside. Perhaps later the person will be allowed to be a firekeeper or doorkeeper. Later yet the person, after learning carefully and patiently listening to the elders, may be welcomed into an introductory ceremony.

Each juncture of life—birth, puberty, adolescence, adulthood, mid-life, old age, death—is marked by ceremony, by *rites de passage*, as sociologist Claude Lévi-Strauss called them. For traditional peoples each rite of passage is a chapter in the story, an initiation into a deeper level of understanding and of being. Each of them is marked by the "death" of the previous stage and the "birth" of the next stage—say, the "death" of the child and the "birth" of the adult. Worldwide, such ceremonies are marked by death-and-rebirth rituals often including such elements as the lamenting of the mothers for their dead children, a stripping-naked (a literal dropping of the robe to represent death, the dropping of the body-robe) and reclothing (to represent the new robe, the new persona), and the giving of a new name. We see this not only among traditional peoples in the Americas, Africa, Australia, and the Pacific Islands, but in many ancient and modern religions of the world. Though his comments have been widely misunderstood, it was to exactly this kind of ceremony that Jesus was referring when he said one must be born ἄνωθεν (*anūthen*)—meaning "born from above," in an initiation through water and spirit.

Thus, one's whole life becomes a meta-ritual. By the time death is close and one reaches the center of all these concentric circles, one has experienced death many times; one therefore understands life wholly. One realizes that serious illnesses are also a kind of death, and recovery of health a rebirth. One realizes that going on a hunt, going into battle, and engaging in sexual activity are varieties of death and rebirth—in fact, the French sometimes call sexuality *le petit mort*, the little death. One realizes that the nightly ritual of sleeping and entering into the untracked wilderness of dream also prepares us for life's final experience: as with formal ceremonies, one must let go of self and let the *wakan* blow where it listeth to enter into the trackless *wakan* of dream and vision.

One realizes that the simple act of walking is a transition between *wakan*, forsaking one's balance as in death, and *washte*, recovering that balance again, as in life. One realizes that simply exhaling is a kind of death and inhaling again fills one with life again just as it did at one's birth—and that, some day, one will "give up the spirit" and exhale one's last breath.

So experience and wisdom, marked by ceremonial initiation, slowly but surely bring one from the outer circles to the inner circles, ever closer to the innermost circle, where one actually is a leader in the ceremony, leading it for one's closest friends and relatives, and is helping those new to the Red Road to begin the walk toward the center. And then comes the time when one reaches the center—the opening to the Spirit World—and, as one embarks on this new journey, one no longer participates in, but *is* the ceremony; one sees all these circles, from the newly born to the oldest and wisest, carrying on the traditions even as one prepares to drop one's robe and take one's place among the ancestors.

Among traditional peoples worldwide, work, play and spirituality are not seen as sharply separated. Everything people do in their traditional ways is at the same time work (something necessary to daily survival), play (something enjoyable) and spiritual (something that enriches all aspects of life with sacred meaning).

One may think of weaving as work, but in the traditional culture it is enjoyable, because one often does it with friends and has fun doing it. It is also sacred, because one is creating patterns handed down by one's ancestors, and one prays to and through those ancestors and the descendants who will wrap themselves in this blanket.

One may think of games as play, but in the traditional culture they are also very serious. Playing lacrosse or snowsnake, to name two traditional Northeastern Native American games, helps one with one's hunting skills, affords one healthy exercise and helps one build *camaraderie*. It is also sacred to play: Black Elk, in his wonderful book, *The Sacred Pipe*, describes a sacred ball game as an example of that. On the rez you will often see kids involved in a good, rough-and-tumble game of football or basketball or baseball. In fact, baseball especially seems harmonious with the traditional spirit. It is the only team sport that is not ruled by the clock ($\chi\rho\sigma\nu\sigma\varsigma$ [chronos]) and that could at least theoretically go on to infinity ($\kappa\alpha\iota\rho\sigma\varsigma$ [kairos]). It features the wonderful concerto quality of the individual (the batter) balanced against the many (the defending team). Moreover, it is symbolic of our spiritual journey through life: as A. Bartlett Giamatti pointed out in his exquisite essays on the game, we begin at home, and, if we are fortunate, we make contact with the Spirit World beyond this mundane world (hitting a home run by sending a ball outside the field of play) and circle through the Four Sacred Directions, and then come home again knowing (connaître, kennen) it for the first time.

One may think of ceremonies as sacred, but they are also work and play. A lot of work goes into properly preparing a ceremony. To hold the Sacred Stone People's Lodge, for instance, we must gather rocks, chop wood, carry water and build the lodge. Often as I do this, I think of what Jesus Christ said in the non-canonical Gospel of Thomas: "Split wood, I am there. Pick up rocks, and you will find me there," or of the Zen exhortation to "Chop wood, carry water." The ceremony itself is work—as the fact that we sweat suggests: it takes a lot of work to sit through those four ages in the darkness and intense humidity, all the time praying hard. I think of the Hebrew word עבודה (avodah), which means both "work" and "worship," and of the Shaker teaching, "Hands to work and hearts to G-d."

And yet ceremony is also play; there is frequently great joy and laughter within the lodge. Often people will spontaneously tease, embrace, play with, massage each other in a simple sacred sharing of delight at the very goodness of life. I remember one time when a woman made mud by mixing her sweat and some of the sacred water with the Earth beneath her, and used it to paint first herself and then everyone else in the lodge from head to toe, paying particular attention to those areas that are never touched in the course of ordinary washte social interaction—evoking the wakan through a spontaneous act of lighthearted, innocent sensuality such as we experienced as little children. And I also think of the animals putting mud on Turtle to make the first land, in the Kanien'kéha:ka (Mohawk) creation story. Telling you about this makes me think of the noncanonical Gospel of Thomas: the disciples ask Jesus when the ἔσχατον (eschaton), the end of the age, will come—and he answers them, "When you take off your clothes without being ashamed, and take your clothes and put them under your feet as little children do, and tread on them; then you shall behold the Son of the Living One and you shall not fear."

Even entering a traditional home (wigwam, tipi, hogan) is sacred: we tend to progress through it in a sunwise manner. And I have seen old women on the rez give a simmering stew four sunwise stirs with the ladle and fold each article of laundry four times. I don't know if they are doing this consciously or not, but these fours are a way of honoring the Four Directions.

The work that traditional people do to provide for themselves and their families is both playful and spiritual. Traditional peoples didn't customarily have "jobs" in the *washichu* sense—until the Europeans came. Every individual was ready to do what was needed: even a child, even a highly respected medicine man or woman could be a warrior when necessary—I'm thinking of Tecumseh, Sitting Bull, Chief Joseph and others who were at the same time chiefs, warriors, medicine men, craftsmen and even poets in their utterances.

Most of us, though, live in a predominantly *washichu* environment, where we are taught to work when we're at work and only play after we are done with working. I have learned, as much as possible, to bring a sense of play into my work (to find ways to enjoy it, and to remain patient and peaceful), a sense of work into my play (by choosing activities that are beneficial to me or others), and to keep both as sacred. I try to do things in fours at work. I try to say little prayers for the lives I touch as I do my work. I try to move sunwise in my work. I refuse to let the hotheaded or demanding-critical types get to me. Even at work, I can imagine smelling good sage burning—the "Spirit Pipe" teaching that I will tell you about later on—and let the smoke wash over me and everyone I am dealing with so all is holy.

We need to break down the barriers that have been erected between work, play and spirituality, and recognize that all these are one.

One may think of storytelling as play, but it is sacred work too. For all traditional peoples, stories—even funny stories—are sacred. One elder I know is particularly adept at telling extremely hilarious stories, which get you laughing so hard that you find yourself gasping for breath and weeping tears, but then, sometimes days later, it suddenly strikes you that these funny stories were in fact powerful teachers of *wakan* truths. Indeed, the very act of telling and listening to a story is sacred work.

Why is storytelling sacred? The primary reason is that stories are living beings. Like any living being, they change over time, taking on different qualities, carrying different things. They are not static—unless they are put into a book or movie. Stories also create a common heritage seen in ceremony. When Jews come together for the Passover meal, they tell Haggadah, the story of the Exodus. When Christians celebrate the Eucharist, they tell the story of the Last Supper. During Ramadan, Muslims tell the story of the Angel Gabriel coming to the Prophet Muhammed, on whom let there be peace. When Native Americans pass the Sacred Pipe, they tell the story of the Coming of the Pipe; when someone grieves, they tell the Condolence, the story of Aionwantha (Hiawatha) and the Peacemaker. Although those who walk any of these spiritual paths have heard the stories many times before, it is always good to be nourished in spirit by hearing them again, and to be reminded by them of one's sacred community.

As one hears a story as a child, one gradually becomes "friends" with it, until at last, after hearing it many times, one tells the story oneself; one *becomes* the story. This process of gradually becoming one with the story is itself a story; to paraphrase Gautama Buddha, one cannot tell the story without becoming the story itself.

Scholars or editors cannot get the experience of storytelling into "anthologies of tribal literature." (As you read the few stories I've included in this book, perhaps you can sense how much better it would be if someone told them to you in person.) What this points to is the fact that stories are in their own way living beings. As living beings, they are something we cannot own, but (like the Sacred Pipe or the traditional ways) are sacred things we carry.

Storytelling can be seen as a sacred ceremony because it makes the past come alive. Through stories we transcend the contours of linear time and enrich the present moment with meaning. Through stories we experience the deeds, the very lives, of our ancestors, and gain perspective on our own lives. Every time we tell or hear a particular story we recharge it, making it come alive again in the here and now.

I think the anthropologists are wrong when they say folk tales have as a *primary* purpose explaining certain natural phenomena (such as why crows are black). These explanations are often no more than a kind of "flourish" tacked on to the end of a good story. I say rather that the natural phenomena are simply presences of the story in our daily life. Thus, whenever a Lakota sees a crow she or he thinks of the story of how crows used to warn the buffalo when the warriors were coming, until one brave, disguised as a buffalo, captured one and threw it in a fire to teach it a lesson, thus singeing its feathers.

When carried in such a manner, the story is a mnemonic, evocative way of *remembering* that there is more to the world than meets the physical eye. If we carry these stories in our hearts, then we see stories everywhere we go. Not only are we reminded of the stories handed down to us, but we see new stories unfolding all around us: seeing the tracks of animals in the Earth, for instance, might tell us a story of how a bobcat pounced on a mouse as its prey.

I believe there are two kinds of stories: *washte* and *wakan*. The *washte* stories are those that are engaging, those that make us laugh, or even cry. The *wakan* stories are those that speak powerfully to us, that call us out of our individual lives into the sacred realm. There are also *heyoka* stories that seem to be *washte*, pure entertainment, but behind their irreverence is profound teaching.

There is one rather unusual factor associated with storytelling among Native Americans. In most cultures, oral transmission of stories keeps the stories even more "fixed" than written transmission. For instance, before the Torah was written down about three thousand years ago, it was carefully memorized and passed on word for word for centuries. Inscribed on people's memories, it was very hard to change. On the other hand, Native American oral tradition allows, and indeed encourages, the story to change—to mature and grow, guided by the spirit of each successive person who tells it. I know I do not tell certain traditional stories in the same way as do those from whom I learned them. I have listened to my children as they let the story flow through their own natures—I have gathered new insights into the "same story" I thought I knew. (Ancient songs and prayers, however, remain unchanged.)

In the dominant culture, where stories are more and more often treated as mere entertainment, the tradition of learning to recite poetry from memory, as children were once expected to do, has been abandoned. This was a last vestige of the noble tradition of Mediaeval troubadours, Celtic bards, Germanic Minnesängers, West African griots and Scandinavian skalds, who recited lengthy epics and sagas. These great works, from the ancient Sumerian *Epic of Gilgamesh* to Homer's *Odyssey* to the stories of the great Mali king Sundiata to *Beowulf* and Wu Ch'eng-en's *Monkey*, were remembered and passed on from generation to generation not merely to entertain, but to teach and to inspire. These three tasks used to be one in Western culture. In modern times they are found together only in a few works, such as J. R. R. Tolkien's *Lord of the Rings*, E. R. Eddison's Zimiamvia books, Doris Lessing's *Canopus in Argos* pentalogy and Ursula K. Le Guin's Earthsea stories. Among tribal nations worldwide, too, the heritage of storytelling is dying out. I have heard that the Ainu, a tribe in Hokkaido, consider their culture to be dying or dead, because their traditional singers are no more.

The unwillingness to learn and pass on stories, unless they are entertaining or a potential source of income, has infected the Native American culture too. Young Native Americans are rarely eager to spend years studying with some old medicine man or woman, learning these boring old stories, chants, and ceremonies. At the same time, *washichu* (greedy) people are more than willing to arrogate them, without really understanding them, simply in order to make money. A few writers, such as Alfonso Ortiz and Richard Erdoes, have made magnificent efforts to save them in book form, but even they (as I do in this book) run the risk of turning a living, breathing heritage into something as lifeless as a stuffed and mounted moosehead. Some other writers, such as Sherman Alexie, Paula Gunn Allen, Joseph Bruchac, Louise Erdrich, Owl Goingback, Suzan Shown Harjo, N. Scott Momaday and Leslie Marmon Silko, have found ways to keep these stories alive through their beautifully written fiction.

Earlier, I gave you an example of the nature of traditional education. Let me expand on it now, again following the lines of Evan Zuesse. The example he uses is that of the ceremonies a nation holds at the time of an individual's death. Zuesse points out that a little child has no real experience with death or the ceremonies surrounding it. The child is, as it were, standing in the outermost of a series of concentric circles surrounding the dying person. The child is only distantly related to the dying person (for instance, a great-grandparent), and has not previously heard the traditional songs that are being sung. As time goes by, the child will gradually move further in among those concentric circles. Through his or her life, relatives will die who are gradually closer and closer: grandparents, uncles and aunts, parents and siblings and friends. As life goes by, the individual will become increasingly acquainted with the death ceremonies. By the time the individual is an elder, she or he has become a leader, standing in the innermost circle around the dying person, and teaching the sacred songs simply by singing, simply by example.

Throw a pebble into a still pond. Watch the ripples spread out and away from it. That's what it's like as the elder is dying—the ripples spread out through the generations, coming most strongly to those who knew the elder best and most gently to the children, who knew that one least.

Not only in the matter of dying, but in gaining all forms of wisdom, more is involved than simply a lifelong process of memorizing old songs or stories or ceremonies. It is far more importantly a lifelong process of growing in understanding. As young adults, we think we understand these songs and stories, the people we know, ceremonies, animals and the nature of sickness and death, courage and love, but that's it—we only *think* we understand. As Julian Jaynes explains it in *The Origin of Consciousness in the Breakdown of the Bicameral Mind*, understanding typically is a process of creating a familiar metaphor for the thing itself; as a result, we fail truly to understand the thing itself, we understand only a theoretical model for it. In other words, we attempt to grasp experience by converting the incomprehensible, unknowable *wakan* into the familiar contours of the *washte*. It's only much later in life that these concepts progress more deeply into our psychological viscera and reach full maturity, in which case the inner knowing is one with the outer being. As in Zen, the mind then becomes a perfect mirror reflecting reality. One can never know (understand) the *wakan*, but, when one gains the wisdom of age, one does know (become acquainted with) it.

When the individual comes to the end of her or his own physical life, she or he moves to the inmost circle, the center, the opening to the Spirit World. Surrounded by all the other circles, surrounded by everyone else in the tribe, all of whom are singing for the individual, the individual is supported by hearing the sacred ceremonies that he or she slowly learned and then taught by example. Since the individual has stood in every one of those concentric circles, the dying person identifies with every member of the tribe and passes on to join a circle in the spiritual dimension, surrounding the tribe with the presence of the Grandfathers and Grandmothers who have gone before. John Donne realized in one of his *Meditations*:

> *No man is an Iland, intire of itselfe*
> *every man is a peece of the Continent*
> *a part of the maine*
> *...any mans death diminishes me*
> *because I am involved in Mankinde;*
> *And therefore never send to know*
> *for whom the bell tolls;*
> *It tolls for thee.*

This progression from outer circles to inner circles is itself a circle, for the traditional teaching is that in many cases the individual comes back after death to begin that progression again. One day when my son was an infant, I was bathing him. He was laughing in the water, and I was laughing with him, getting almost as wet as he, as he splashed merrily about. Unexpectedly, a memory came back to me of myself as a child, being bathed by my father. And, as the memory filled me, I was sure that, on that day many years before, my father as he bathed me was remembering my grandfather washing him, and my grandfather had likewise remembered his father washing him, and that one day my son will remember this as he washes my grandson—and so on back and forth through the generations, the father washing the son, laughing joyfully with his child, and saying to himself, as in the Christian scriptures, "This is my beloved son, in whom I am well pleased." The story comes round again, always new, always alive, a circle of life through seven generations.

Once I was down in the southwestern corner of Georgia, with a family who lives near the banks of the Chattahoochee River. As the day cooled down one evening and shadows began flying across the cotton fields and pine woods, they brought their guitars out onto the farmhouse porch and started to sing the old songs. Knowing I play guitar, they put one in my hands so I could join in, and they were very gracious despite my disconcertingly Northern accent.

But what I found as I sang with them was that, while I knew these old songs, I didn't know them in the way *they* knew them. If you recall the difference between *savoir* and *connaître* in French and *wissen* and *kennen* in German, you know what I'm getting at. I only knew them in my head, having learned them from records, sheet music or radio. They knew them in their hearts, because they'd heard them and sung them all their lives. These songs were a part of them: they had first been sung right there among those fields by their ancestors now buried beneath them.

Every now and then I have people contact me who want me to teach them about the spiritual traditions of the Native Americans. Those spiritual traditions vary widely, and I only know in my heart and could conceivably pass on one way, and that is the way that was shared with me by my teacher Grandfathers and Grandmothers. And in fact, I cannot even "teach" that way, because it is only possible to teach *washte* matters, like how to weave or how to fletch an arrow; *wakan* matters are, by nature, unteachable. Thus, "teaching" the sacred traditions would be merely reducing them to *washte* "information," like capturing water from the river and putting it in a bucket; the water ceases to flow in a *wakan* manner; it becomes *washte*. The truth is that teaching the sacred traditions in this manner will not work. It would just leave you following along, like me on that Georgia porch, with head information as your only guide. These traditions must be learned in people's hearts. There are people who have learned some of the sacred ways from me, but I didn't set out to teach them. I simply told the stories and led the ceremonies, and they attended over a period of years, asking me questions when they needed to, and I answered insofar as it was appropriate.

According to a Maya teaching: "We need to use all our bodies to remember everything. The physical, mental, emotional and spiritual bodies are needed. Without desire, wonder and curiosity there is no intention to remember. Without study there is no understanding." This is to say, these *wakan* traditions cannot be learned in the head alone. The entire person, body and soul, is involved with the *wakan* act of thinking and understanding. And this understanding involves more than one person—it takes in the collective mind and memory of one's people and the Earth herself. Even the most powerful computers cannot carry such sacred information.

Once some friends asked me if I could provide them with an audiotape of the traditional songs I sing during the Sacred Stone People's Lodge. I told them I could not do that because I had promised my first Grandfather that I would never do so. The reason he asked that promise of me was because, like the songs I sang with my friends down in Georgia, the traditional sacred songs of the Native ancestors should only be learned and sung with the heart. There are recordings available of some of these songs, and of the songs of other nations as well, but the decision to make these recordings was made by others, and they are answerable to their teachers and ancestors and the spirits for their decision. I pass no judgment on it.

In this book I share what I do to guide people as they walk the Red Road, but I have shared nothing of the matters that are most sacred. I've told you *about* the walk, not the *walk itself.* If I tried, it would be like trying to teach you about swimming with a book or a video, when the only way to learn is to go into the water with someone who knows how to swim. If for instance you want to learn how to pour water (lead the Sacred Stone People's Lodge Ceremony), my advice to you is: *patience.* Take your time. Attend the ceremony as often as you can and be attentive (what my first Grandfather called *chantë ishta,* observing with the heart). If you are meant to learn the sacred songs and ceremonial ways, you will find yourself learning them without having to make any particular conscious effort. If the sacred ways don't stay in your head no matter how many ceremonies you attend, then perhaps you aren't meant to learn them: perhaps you aren't meant to walk the walk of a ceremonialist. Not everybody is going to walk the same exact path.

People these days look at knowledge as a commodity, as a property they can acquire. *Wisdom,* however, is a sacred trust. It belongs not to you but to the ancestors. You learn by observation, and you teach by example. In such teaching as this, hardly any words ever need be said. I learned to consider carefully before asking my first teaching Grandfather questions. He taught me that it was better if I were quiet and paid close attention, and that I would learn everything I needed to know in good time, provided only that I be patient.

One of the basic teachings in the traditional way is that respect be given at all times. Respect is one way in which one maintains the balances that are so central to the traditional way of living. One must never take without giving back. So, even in just encountering another living being, one must remember to give respect. Just to see an eagle is to be given something, since it is a sacred animal, so in return one gives the eagle one's respect. It saddened me some years ago to hear that a man who was trained in the ceremonial ways of the original peoples was known to shoot eagles out of the Sky so he could sell or trade with their wings and feathers. That is not respect. It would have been traditional, rather, when he saw an eagle, not to shoot it down, but to offer a tobacco gift to it.

In traditional Native American culture, the various disciplines were immensely practical. Artistic works were useful, and even playing games honed practical skills. The reason for this is that life was quite difficult, and the whole nation had to remain vigilant and prepared for such disasters as starvation, injury, wild animals, enemy nations, and extreme weather conditions. Respect, in this context, meant paying careful attention to those elders who carried essential skills and imitating their excellence. In other words, respect was essential to survival. Respect was learning to shoot with the bow by observing the best archers. Respect was paying close attention to the traditional stories until one had learned and understood them. Respect was shown in remaining silent until the elders had spoken first, for they had the greatest depth of experience, and remembered the teachings of the Grandfathers and Grandmothers.

In the traditional way, one honors the deed rather than the doer. Honoring the person instead of the skills smacks of potential favoritism, in that we might honor more those persons we prefer and admire instead of those we dislike, even though they may be equally proficient at the craft. Furthermore, in the traditional view, honoring the deed means we honor all striving, even if the results are not comparable. For a long time I carried a small medicine bag with beadwork that was the first such effort by a friend. It was not very well done, but I honored the considerable effort the friend made to do it as well as possible. I honored more this friend's great effort than an expert doing beautiful beadwork but without investing care and spirit in the craft.

What we need to remember is that there are two kinds of respect. These are old concepts that I call sacred respect and ethical respect.

It is one kind of respect that, for instance, we don't interrupt a sacred ceremony with questions or carry the Sacred Pipe in an egotistical or careless manner. We give sacred respect to sacred things, such as sacred ceremonies, sacred objects (such as drums, rattles, eagle feathers and the Sacred Pipe above all), the medicine animals, the sacred spirits, and the spiritual presence of the ancestors who have passed over.

And it is another kind of respect given to persons, to all living beings, that we treat them just as we would want to be treated ourselves. This, as already noted, is a matter of balances: "Love your neighbor as yourself." Ethical respect, the respect we pay to another human being, a plant or an animal, does not carry the same strong sacred connotations. It is simply a matter of courtesy to another living thing, a member of the family of "all my relations." Even enemies, even those who have done you wrong, are still, according to our traditional ways, to be accorded this ethical respect.

While an individual bear or deer, or any other creature, is to be treated with ethical respect, any member of any nation of beings embodies for us the ἰδέα (*idea*; the Greek word in Platonic philosophy that is usually translated as "form") of Bear or Deer—the sacred medicine animal itself, who is a great, wise teacher. We treat *a* bear with ethical respect; we treat *Bear* with sacred respect.

Persons (human or otherwise) who teach us about the sacred things or who conduct the sacred ceremonies are not sacred in and of themselves, but they are mediators of the sacred, so we treat them with both kinds of respect. Specifically, we treat the persons themselves with ethical respect, but we treat what they carry with sacred respect. A medicine teacher is, of course, just an individual, yet each one embodies Grandfather or Grandmother for us—the sacred presence of these aspects of the Creator. We treat *a* Grandmother or Grandfather with ethical respect; we treat *Grandmother* or *Grandfather* with sacred respect.

These people are most commonly our elders, who, being close to passing over, mediate for us the wisdom and protection of the spirits and medicine animals. That is why, when our elders are kind enough to teach us, we remain respectfully quiet, and our questions are carefully considered efforts to clarify our understanding, and are not attempts to "spar with the Master." Of course, you may find yourself disagreeing with some aspect of the traditional teachings that are shared with you; surely this will occur, for instance, as you consider everything I have been telling you. Paying respect does not mean you must blindly accept traditional teachings as absolute truth. How can you know something is true until you have tested it by trying it out in your own life? Rather, this means that *what is traditional* must be treated with respect and care, as it "belongs," if to anyone, to the ancestors and to the Creator. It is not a "commodity" that the "teacher" is passing on to the "students," for them to discuss and accept or reject as they choose, but wisdom that they must carry with humble respect. It is a sacred entity. Rather than vocally signifying agreement or disagreement when an elder speaks, among the original peoples a person does better by being *quiet* and listening carefully. Just as at the Sacred Giveaway or at communal meals the elder is always served first, so too it is traditionally proper for younger people to wait for their elders to speak first. If one does not understand something the elder said, then one may ask a question when the elder has finished speaking. Questions are asked respectfully, never argumentatively. One who is listening to an elder does well to absorb what is being taught, to ask questions only if necessary, and then later to discuss the teaching with one's peers. So there is room for dialogue and "critical thinking," but it is never done by passing judgment on the validity of the teaching. One doesn't argue, say, during the reading of the Gospel with the priest, or during the reading of the Torah or Qur'an with the rabbi or 'imam. One may discuss the meaning of the scriptural passage at another time, but the Qur'an, the Torah and the Gospel are *in themselves* sacred and not to be interrupted. These scriptures are, in essence, like the Grandfathers and Grandmothers of those other religious traditions. Our questions are respectful, humbly saying, "I do not understand," not "I do not agree."

There are variations in the way people walk the Red Road. When it comes to the Sacred Stone People's Lodge, for instance, there are all sorts of friendly arguments about how certain aspects of it are properly seen to. But these differences are superficial, like the differences among the various branches of any one of the world religions. At the core, the essence is the same. And we manage these differences quite easily by simply respecting: when it is time for ceremony, everybody puts aside these differences and accepts the way of the water pourer, the person who is leading the ceremony.

Sacred respect is itself sacred. We show respect to the Sacred Pipe, for instance, by turning it sunwise before we smoke from it. This is a matter of respect, since, by turning it, we are including all living beings in our prayer. This turning of the Sacred Pipe is itself a sacred act, since we are invoking the Circle of Life when we turn the Sacred Pipe sunwise. In respecting the sacredness of the Sacred Pipe, we are recognizing the fact that through the Sacred Pipe we are ourselves purified and made sacred and welcomed into the Sacred Hoop, and our prayers are heard.

Many of us have made mistakes early in our walking the Red Road. We may have turned the Sacred Pipe the wrong way, or accidentally stepped across the spirit trail when entering the Sacred Stone People's Lodge. But one Grandfather I knew said, "There are no mistakes if you do it with a good heart." What's worse: innocently turning the Sacred Pipe the wrong way or doing the ceremony punctiliously but with a better-than-thou or angry or selfish attitude? If we turn it the wrong way, we are only saying "I do not yet understand how to do it," not "I don't want to do it the sacred way." Doing all that we do with a good heart maintains balances with all our relations and gives respect to all things.

These teachings are not mine. I did not invent them, as philosophers of the European traditions invent new philosophies. Neither did my traditional teachers make all this up, nor did their teachers. These traditions are ancient. They are one with the Earth around us and all her children. They are the core of the traditional culture. If we lose them, we have no culture. The teachings are a whole thing; they are a *sacred* whole. They are not individual items among which you may choose in a "supermarket" of ideas. Rather, they are all connected in a non-linear fashion. You may have a question about something, but, if you keep listening, you may well find your question answered eventually by the elder without your having to ask.

Part of what I have been taught is that the teachings include not only the content, the information, but the form in which they are presented. In the traditional peoples' way of thinking, these two—their form and content—are inseparable. I have seen respected Grandfathers refuse to talk to some people, even though they were one hundred percent Native American in ancestry, because (as I heard one Grandfather put it once) "their spirits are too loud" to hear the teachings very well. And I have seen respected elders share a great deal with people who knew little to nothing about the Red Road, and who had little or no Native American ancestry, simply because they *listened*, quietly and respectfully—because they were ready to learn.

In fact, I believe the *way* these sacred ways are shared is more important than the content of the teachings themselves, which vary from tribe to tribe. Most, for example, carry the Sacred Pipe, but a few do not. The Tsalagi (Cherokee), unlike other nations, consider the Sun female and the Moon male, and they dance moonwise instead of sunwise. Some nations see the owl as a harbinger of death and others as a bearer of wisdom. But behind such relatively minor differences are essential truths based on direct observation of the reality of the universe all around us. And, despite such differences, *all* Native American tribes insist on being respectful when the teachings, in whatever way, are being shared with you.

No teacher, least of all I, deserves sacred respect, but rather the teachings themselves. Traditional peoples tend to honor the *wakan* thing or act carried (wisdom, ceremonies, memories of long ago, stories, etc.) while modern people tend to honor the carrier of things or acts to which they attach value. I, like anyone who carries the *wakan*, am as much in awe of this *wakan* that rides on my shoulders as others are! It is truly humbling! But the fact that I carry some *wakan* doesn't make me a better person, but gives me the responsibility of humility, and a constant awareness that I absolutely must not let my ego get fat (*washichu*—"stealing the fat") on the sweet taste of praise, lest I stumble beneath this heavy load—as, unfortunately, even some great medicine men and women have done.

Bear in mind that, when you give a tobacco gift after a Grandmother or Grandfather has shared something *wakan* with you, you are honoring not just that individual, but *all* of that elder's Native ancestors for passing on to us, generation to generation, these sacred traditions—yet, even more, the *wakan* itself. And bear in mind that, by accepting the teaching and giving the tobacco gift, you are pledging yourself to carrying that wisdom with humble respect, and to passing it on yourself, when it is appropriate to do so, just as it was passed on to you. Remember as well that the elder accepts that tobacco gift humbly, on behalf of the sacred traditions carried and shared.

I find it easy to be among traditional peoples. The wilderness and the silence cleanse my soul, stilling all the "head noise" the same way Buddhist *zazen* does, the same way the Earth cleanses all the *sicha* we pour into her when we are in the Sacred Stone People's Lodge. There is a tradition of silence in the European-American culture, represented by monastic tradition and the Society of Friends (miscalled the Quakers, who, I might note, were influenced in this regard by their Native American neighbors), but for the most part, members of the dominant culture seem to be frustrated by silence.

My first teaching Grandfather did not speak much. When I was young, I was quite baffled by the silence with which he often seemed to answer my questions, or by the hours and sometimes even days before, sometimes, he would finally give his considered reply. Now, many years after he dropped his robe and went on to join the Grandfathers and Grandmothers who have gone before us, I have come to appreciate his silence. Now I understand, and wish I had understood then, that it is for the young to be silent in the face of wisdom. Instead, I was often frustrated by the way of silence, even after I learned not to indulge the foolishness of my mind by putting it into words.

Yet now that his voice, in the physical sense, is forever stilled, I hear it more and better. When I was young, he taught me to *listen* and to respect the answers that came to my questions, including those that did not come in the short pre-digested form that I wanted and had been trained to expect by my schools. Now that he is physically gone from me, I find I hear his voice speaking to me in spirit, teaching me in his gentle simple way. I (and sometimes others) have felt his presence from time to time, particularly in the Sacred Stone People's Lodge. And I feel that his patience with me, when I was young and immeasurably impatient, has been rewarded.

These elders know that silence is essential on the path toward wisdom. If you are tramping noisily through the woods, you cannot hear the wisdom around you; in fact, you scare it away. Silence means more than simply being quiet; it also means stilling the voice within your head that tells you that you already know. In the Buddhist sense, it means emptying the mind of all foolish thought, so it can perfectly reflect reality—which is the essence of wisdom. The elders maintain silence because they have long since learned how essential it is to wisdom. (But do not be fooled into thinking that everyone who is silent is wise.)

The best teachers are, ironically, the ones who are best at learning. Hence the saying "Knowledge speaks, but wisdom listens." Knowledge is *washte*; it is information that can be manipulated, used to a purpose, even distorted. But wisdom is *wakan*; it comes unbidden, intuitively, out of the corner of the eye, like the stealthy approach of a wild animal.

As Ohiyesa (Charles Eastman) taught: "Silence is the absolute poise or balance of body, mind, and spirit. Silence is the cornerstone of character." Likewise, Chief Luther Standing Bear taught that among his people the "granting a space of silence before talking was done in the practice of true politeness and regardful of the rule that 'Thought comes before speech.'" And in the midst of sorrow, sickness, death or misfortune of any kind, and in the presence of the notable and great, silence was the mark of respect.

Many years ago, I took part in a multitribal council of Native Americans. We were following the traditional way of the Sacred Talking Stick in our discussions, passing it around the circle in which we were sitting, with only the one holding it allowed to speak. Those of us who were taking part in the discussion were having a great deal of difficulty hearing and understanding each other. In retrospect I realize we were each concentrating so hard on striving to explain *our own* points of view that we failed to *listen* well to each other. We failed, moreover, to listen to the Sacred Talking Stick itself.

After some time the Sacred Talking Stick came around to one honored Grandfather who was with us in the council circle. He held it in his hand. He looked at it. He looked at all of us. He looked out at the world around us. We waited expectantly for him to speak. Very likely each of us secretly hoped he would take our side and not that of others.

Time went by. He did not open his mouth. People began to shuffle in their places. Still he remained silent. We remained attentive to whatever he might say to us. But he said nothing. Instead we heard only the birds and the insects and the breathing of the Earth in the breeze that caressed our faces. Then, after several minutes, he passed the Sacred Talking Stick on to the next person.

The next person, who had not long before been "straining at the bit" for his turn to hold the Sacred Talking Stick and speak, now said nothing. The rest of us felt just as he did: ashamed of our loud words, our failure to listen. The Sacred Talking Stick went slowly around the circle, with each person reverently holding it, silent and respectful.

Slowly we began to speak again, as the Sacred Talking Stick continued to go around, but we now spoke quietly and hesitantly, weighing our words carefully, and diligently heeding what we and others were saying, what the Sacred Talking Stick was saying. Now we found ourselves moving toward consensus. We found ourselves making *good* decisions *together*.

I don't remember a single word of what was spoken that day. I don't even remember the subject we were discussing. But I *do* remember the silence of this Grandfather. It remains among the most profound "statements" I have ever heard. He could have lectured us, or railed at us, and with good reason. What he did was far more effective. He did what a true Chief, what a true elder, does so well: by the example of his quietude and attentiveness, he taught us to be quiet and attentive ourselves.

"There are times when we have had enough even of our Friends," Henry David Thoreau advises, "...and must withdraw religiously into solitude and silence, the better to prepare ourselves for a loftier intimacy. Silence is the ambrosial night in the intercourse of Friends, in which their sincerity is recruited and takes deeper root.... The language of Friendship is not words, but meanings. It is an intelligence above language."

Silence is the original language that was spoken by everything in creation. Humans have virtually all forgotten this language and replaced it with verbal languages, using unrelated sounds as "signs" to represent the things themselves. It is not possible to lie in the original language. This language, which is still spoken by four-leggeds, trees, and so on, is the language of love—not *saying* "I love you," but *showing* it, the spirit of it. When it's said in the original language to a cat or a dog, the four-legged being responds not to the words you say, but to the sincerity of love expressed through touch, through tone of voice, or simply through radiating the very love itself.

The First Language is *wakan*, natural and spontaneous and wild, and always truth, while ordinary human languages are *washte*, created by social convention, subject to manipulation and control, and distortions of the truth. In the First Language, words are not sounds associated by convention with certain meanings, with no inherent relationship between sound and meaning; they *are* the meaning. The purr of a wildcat, the scream of an eagle, the growl of a bear, the wind rustling through the grass, the roar of the river: all these things mean exactly what they are. Using the First Language, one could go anywhere in the world and communicate perfectly. A few medicine women and men of traditional nations worldwide have been able to communicate notwithstanding any physical separation in time and space, even talking with the elders of other dimensions and planets.

The First Language is the Λογος (*Logos*), the powerful Word so eloquently spoken by the Creator that the Christian scriptures say its very utterance called all things into being. As Igjugarjuk, the Inuit *angakoq*, or medicine man, told Knud Rasmussen, the Creator speaks to humanity "not through common words, but by storm and snow and rain and the fury of the sea; all the forces of nature that men fear." As traditional peoples worldwide have often said, for them the scriptures revealed by G-d are written not in books but on the very Earth herself.

Silence shows respect to others. When we are silent, we honor the words others say to us. When we are silent, we honor the sacred beings around us, including animals and plants and rocks and spirits, the human beings with us and all the ancestors.

Silence shows willingness to learn. When we are silent, we can hear what the sacred beings are teaching us. We attend to the teaching of others, including even the quietest of the nations of living things.

Silence shows humility. Humility means not self-effacement or self-abasement, but realizing we have more to learn than we have to say.

Silence shows attentiveness. In silence we attend to the ways of our Grandmother Earth, and Grandfather Sky and all their children, and can be prepared to take appropriate action when bounty or danger comes our way.

I suggest you go now and find a place where you can be silent. Perhaps you can do this with someone you love, just letting the silence be a way of expressing love for each other. Perhaps you can seek silence alone, finding that you are *not* alone, since silence expresses love for the sacred beings all around you in the Sacred Hoop. I'm going to be silent now, and go find a good place where I too can sit and be quiet.

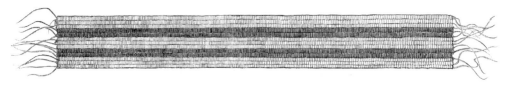

Two-Row Wampum. (See pages 333–35.)

VII

The Warrior's Way

In his book *De Bello Gallico* (*On the Gallic War*), Julius Caesar laughs at the British "primitives," who painted themselves blue with a pigment called woad—even as he and his soldiers were slapping at the annoying mosquitoes in the wet British climate, ignorant of the fact that woad is not only psychedelic, but has the power to drive mosquitoes away. Centuries later, when the descendants of those same British went forth to conquer the world, they felt just as superior to the "naked savages" they encountered. In fact, this condescending attitude remains common today—that nakedness and near-nakedness, as well as body-painting and the like are characteristic of "primitive" peoples. A few years ago, a cartoon (I think it was in the *New Yorker*) showed two young, pretty, stylishly dressed African women in a traditional kind of home. One, looking out the window with shock on her face, is shouting to the other, "Quick! Get your clothes off! Here comes an ethnologist!" One could easily extend the humor, having one of them later on look out the window and shout, "Quick! Get your clothes back on! Here comes a missionary!"

In the dominant culture clothing serves the practical function of protecting the body from excessive heat or cold, and the function of identifying a person by class, gender and relative wealth. But more fundamentally, the culture sees what is put on the human body—clothing, body-painting and jewelry—as an adornment of the flesh, since it sees the beautiful simplicity of the naked body as both fascinating and shameful. Seeing the body as both beautiful (*washte*) and sacred/mysterious/dangerous (*wakan*), but being unable to keep these two aspects in balance, it demands the body must be both hidden and sexually accentuated.

In modern society, clothing hides nakedness; among traditional people it is a natural extension of nakedness. The naked body represents the robe of the spirit, and the clothing put over it represents the spirit's ability to robe itself in various shapes, like the spirit that manifested itself as an owl and then as a pine cone. Traditionally, clothing is not made of synthetic fabrics, but natural materials most often coming from one-leggeds (plants) or four-leggeds. These materials are given by the elder beings out of compassion and pity, to clothe us humans, the youngest and most vulnerable of creatures. To put on clothing made from skins or woven fur or plant fibers is a sacred act that reminds the wearer of the sacred magic of shapeshifting. The design of traditional clothing is simple and practical, but often carries designs or decorations that, like body-painting, customarily have a sacred symbolism. The images and symbols, which typically come from dreams or visions, would be meaningful to one's people and to the sacred medicine animals and plants, and even to one's enemies.

Anthropologists have insisted that face- and body-painting by tribal peoples is a primitive mimicry of clothing arising out of an instinctive need to adorn and cover the body. But for such people it is a matter of further *uncovering* the body; clothing and painting actually are like windows, revealing the spirit within the body. Tribal peoples throughout the world, including on Turtle Island, do not see the body as a separate aspect of the individual self but an integral part of the whole person, as a sacred presence that one carries for the good of all. Adorning or painting the body is a way of evoking the right spirit in war, dance, hunting or ceremony. The painting of oneself helps attune the nature of one's spirit within to the nature of the world without. The adorning of oneself in materials found within one's Sacred Hoop —within one's horizon—brings the individual into harmony with the natural world all around.

Body-painting before going off to hunt or to war encourages the individual psychologically to move with the spirit of the hunted animal or enemy, and secondarily to remember that, as the animal or enemy is killed, the hunter or warrior also dies in a way (and takes upon himself the spirit of the honored animal or enemy). By such painting one *becomes* the enemy or quarry—in a way quite similar to the changes precipitated by the Eagle Dance. Body-painting is used to symbolize and evoke the spirit of the Sacred Other, so the hunter can better sense the spirit of the bear (for example) or the warrior of the enemy tribe, and anticipate the Sacred Other's actions in a spiritual encounter that symbolizes the struggle of life itself.

Often traditional warriors paint themselves or each other with the colors of death such that they are already in mourning, prepared for their own death and/or the death of the Sacred Other. At the same time, to be painted with the colors of death is to say Death itself is one's quarry as a hunter or one's enemy as a warrior.

When we go to pow-wows or watch movies supposedly depicting life in traditional Native American nations, the clothing we see, for all the insistence that it is accurate, is not. I hate to say it, but such garb is more of a costume. In traditional Native society, people were as unlikely to go around dressed in the overly ornate way they do at pow-wows—or as they did in the movie *Dances With Wolves*—as members of today's modern society are to go around wearing tuxedos or ballroom gowns. Imagine trying to slip through the woods on a hunt while wearing a long double-trailer headdress or roach, breastplate, and a big feathered bustle! And the women's clothing in many nations was far more practical than what is now worn at pow-wows; in fact, the ethics and laws of the dominant society now forbid the women of some nations from dressing traditionally in the summer by wearing nothing on their upper bodies.

Unlike in the dominant culture, modesty was not an issue. Before the "Black Robes" (missionaries) came, there was no concept that the sight of a woman nursing her child was shameful, or that one could only swim while wearing clothes over certain portions of one's body. Indeed, in many important ceremonies, the nakedness of one's body is a significant part (in those communities that have not internalized the European concept of shame). In the Vision Crying ceremony, for instance, nakedness represents humility, putting aside everything in order to be open to the vision, and in the Sacred Stone People's Lodge it represents the circle of birth and death and our openness to the Sacred Hoop around us.

Body-painting and clothing, or the lack thereof, serve to bring oneself into harmony with the world around one. All these things are an expression of the sacredness that flows in and out between oneself and the world about one. Through these things one learns to carry the sacredness of oneself in a way that is both expressive and beautiful.

Modern society has divided work from play—so people purchase their meat already prepared and wrapped in plastic, and hunt (if they do) mainly for pleasure. For traditional peoples, hunting is a practical necessity, an enjoyable undertaking and a sacred activity. It is an evident necessity because in traditional societies it is an important source of food.

Before setting out on the hunt, traditional hunters remove their telltale human scent of *washte* in the lodge (spiritually removing their bodies), where they also pray to the spirits of the animals, asking them for permission to hunt them and thanking through them the Creator for this gift of life for the sake of other living beings. They pay attention to dreams and visions, which often come from the spirits of the animals themselves, revealing where they may be found. The hunters smudge themselves carefully and offer tobacco to the Seven Directions. Among many nations it is customary for a hunter to paint himself with the colors and designs associated with the animal he intends to hunt, if not as I said with those associated with death and mourning. In hunting and in battle, it is also traditional to speak in the languages of various animals—the languages of the eagle, the owl, the coyote, the elk, and so on—which are really the First Language, to invoke the spirit of these elder nations, to be guided by their wisdom in the task that has been undertaken, and to become one with them.

After one has killed an animal, tobacco is given to the spirit of the animal, in balance for providing its robe as a Sacred Giveaway. The body is then smudged, then prepared, bearing a simple rule in mind: Nothing is to be wasted! Wasting any portion of a body is not only irresponsible, but disrespectful to the creature itself and sacrilegious to the Creator, who made it. Therefore proper preparation of all parts of the animal is *wakan*, a sacred activity, as well. One learns to prepare the skin by scraping away every bit of meat on the inner side, tanning it with brain and curing it over a fire. One learns how to make sinews into string by greasing them with fat while stretching them, how to prepare the ribs for roasts, the brains and intestines for soups and the entrails for fertilizer. The fat is carefully separated from between layers of meat and saved for winter, and meat strips too are smoked or dried for winter. When all these things are done, again a prayer is said to the Creator through the courageous spirit who has generously given its robe up for our sake.

How is it that the animal is courageous? Because it has *chosen* to die, to give itself to us. The animal gives its life and gives its death to its human brothers and sisters as its own Sacred Giveaway. The traditional stories often affirm this point, that it is not that we two-legged hunters outwit the dumb wild beasts, but rather that members of these elder nations choose to give themselves to us humans so that we may live.

Years ago a Spirit Grandfather helped me to understand this important wisdom. He said there is one place to which no animal will ever go until the proper time, and that is the place of its death. For every four-legged creature, and the rare truly wise two-legged as well, knows that place, but never enters it lest it die. A wise hunter knows this. You can shoot arrows at a deer all day, but you are wasting time and effort. You will never kill it except in that one place, the place of its death. Only the animal knows where it is, and so you must observe carefully where it goes and does not go when it is fleeing from you. From this you can determine the location of the place of its death. For it is not so much fleeing from you as it is fleeing from that place, the only place where it is mortally vulnerable to your arrows. That is why sometimes you will come upon, for instance, a family of deer and they will not run away from you but walk right past you. So, as you hunt, you must know the land around you very well, and be aware of the possible locations of the animal's death. And you must listen carefully to the deer, and it will actually teach you; it will tell you what place it is trying to avoid.

It often used to be the same with us two-legged creatures: the brave warriors of past generations often knew the place and time of their death, and woke up saying, "This is a good day to die!" Wise old Grandfathers and Grandmothers still actually know and choose the moment of their dying, as I have myself seen. It used to be each adult knew the death chant, but never sang it until death was actually coming, to welcome death. A secret of the Ghost Shirt warriors is that they knew the time and place of their death, and kept that knowledge from the white warriors. But the days of such wisdom being commonplace, alas, are all but completely gone.

On the other hand, there is also one place where the animal is completely safe from you, no matter what you do, and that is the place of its birth. In that place you will never see it. You will lose its track and possibly become lost yourself. It would be sacrilegious of you even to try to kill the deer in that place. So as you hunt you must let it be free enough to show you what place it is avoiding, but not so free that it can hide in the place it is seeking. So you are trying to keep it from escaping you into its past, but instead to send it into its future. By knowing these things your hunting will almost surely be successful.

This makes me think of the teaching of Jesus, in the Gospel of Thomas: "Where your beginning is, there shall your end be. Blessed is the one who stands in the beginning, for that one shall know the end and yet shall not taste of death."

I was taught that to kill old creatures is to kill your ancestors and to kill immature animals or a pregnant mother is to destroy your own children. All parts of time are everpresent; our ancestors and descendants are everpresent and to kill either is to sever the Circle of Life. There is an obvious practical aspect to this: the old ones are not as good to eat as those in their prime, and to kill pregnant mothers or young animals could lead to a smaller future generation and hunger for humans. This ecology is part of what the White Buffalo Calf Woman taught, that we should be careful to maintain balances with the world around us and not take without giving back. American farmers tend to use up the land and eventually must move on, as the people had failed to do in the time the two brothers encountered the White Buffalo Calf Woman. But hunters-and-gatherers never need to do this, because they take only enough to survive and leave plenty of wilderness (*wakan*) to sustain itself; they are more ecologically efficient. Farmers promote the *washte*, that is, repeatable results, ridding the Earth of unwanted plants, putting their crops in neat rows with well-worn pathways in between, forcing water out of its natural channels. Farmers push the *wakan* away, uprooting the weeds and scaring off the wild animals who might feed in their fields. Hunters seek out the *wakan*, the darkness of the forest where the wild creatures are to be found—the more *wakan* their surroundings, the more fruitful their hunting will be.

(Though some traditional nations are farmers, they don't farm like modern farmers, who impose an order on nature, but rather in harmony with nature. The Hopi, for example, grow corn at carefully spaced intervals, as did the Waronawonka [Munsee] and Esopus farmers near where I live: close enough that cross-pollination is possible, but not so close that the Earth is overtaxed.)

It is right to hunt creatures only like yourself. In most Native American nations women do not customarily hunt (unless they are *winkte*), not because of chauvinist regulations, but because the women of all nations, including the four-legged nations, are sacred, *wakan*. Human women should not hunt because their like, the females of other species, are also precious. When Grandfathers hunt, they hunt old animals, whose reflexes are slower, like their own. They are easier for Grandfathers to kill successfully, but, more importantly, these old animals are Grandfathers too. But, if you are in your prime, then you must only take life like your own: mature yet young, with reflexes like yours. In this way there is a balance and it is a fair contest.

In this sense, you may only kill your own self. You must always face your own death. Hunting with high-tech weaponry is anathema to this way. Traditionals hunt in a balance of vulnerability, in which their own vulnerability is a giving back. This is true love: not taking life, other's lives, but only your own, as represented by the animal—as Jesus asks Albion in William Blake's masterpiece, *Jerusalem*:

> *Wouldest thou love one who never died*
> *For thee or ever die for one who had not died for thee[?]*

This animal is not just giving meat to the people: it is teaching you about your own life and your own death. If you do not in this way learn about your life and your death, you are not a true hunter but a wanton slaughterer. True hunting is knowing and accepting your own death.

The wise hunter *becomes* the creature he seeks, in a form of shapeshifting. He joins in the traditional dances, which are magical ceremonies that help him become the creature he seeks. And the wild creatures shapeshift too—all the hunter takes is the robe of physical outer form, not their spirits. Their spirits return to their homes, where they shapeshift, taking on a new robe, a new body.

The robe left behind in a Sacred Giveaway is not merely a dead body, as people in the dominant culture believe; it is also shapeshifted, twice. First, the men invoke the shapeshifting magic of hunting, the sacred ceremony that (to paraphrase Calvin Luther Martin's helpful terminology) transforms sacred beings into sacred flesh. (This is why women [except *winkte*] never touch men's hunting weapons, for to do so would risk dissipating or diluting men's magic. The life-taking skills of hunting, fishing, sporting and battling, are *par excellence* the great male bonding rites.) The men then bring the sacred flesh to the women, who invoke the shapeshifting magic of smoking or seasoning and cooking, the sacred ceremony that transforms sacred flesh into sacred food. (Men [except *winkte*], likewise, must not touch women's cooking pots, for to do so would risk dissipating or diluting women's magic. The life-giving skills of planting and gathering herbs, cooking, midwiving and so on are *par excellence* the great female bonding rites.)

When they share this sacred food, when they consume the creature, they are also consumed *by* this creature: it is a Holy Communion: just as the shepherd becomes the lamb, so the hunter becomes the hunted, they are now again shapeshifted, transformed, into that sacred creature.

The hunter knows that the forest is the domain of the Beautiful One, the domain of Woman, and he enters it respectfully. The traditional peoples once respected the forest as the fragrant, fecund pubes of Earth herself, who feeds us with her bounty as does every woman, from her very flesh. Alberto Villoldo recorded (in his book, *Shaman, Healer, Sage)* what an Amazonian medicine woman told him: "Do you know why they are cutting down the rain forest? Because it is wet and dark and tangled and feminine." The newcomers of this continent saw the forests not only as fuel and as potential farming land, but as dangerous: in the dark moist shadows the wild people could still congregate to dance sacred invocations to the spirits around a bonfire. Connecticut still has Devil's Hopyard State Forest, a name that obviously reflects this fear.

Many in modern nations pen animals up in vast multitudes, trapped in a single robe of outer form, with their inner spirits and individual personalities utterly ignored, killing these pathetic creatures in spirit long before their bodies are unceremonially butchered. While many traditional nations also keep animals for food, they typically treat them with care, respecting each of them as an honored individual, and take their lives—just as traditional hunters do—after humbly seeking permission and giving a tobacco gift in return.

Modern hunting is typically done with high-tech weapons, which eliminate any need for skill, for a spiritual "dialogue" between hunter and hunted. And when one eats animals killed in these ways one is also ingesting all the humiliation, pain and terror that these poor creatures have been subjected to, in the long run further destroying one's own spirit, as well as one's body. If you don't hunt or raise farm animals yourself, then at least purchase organic, free-range meats, preferably kosher. Wild creatures are incapable of the shapeshifting magic when they are killed by an automobile or from a distance by weapons, or when their spirits slowly die penned up in a zoo or on a farm. There is no sacred hunter facilitating the magic; there is only an antiseptic but brutal inevitability. In a typical modern family, the husband brings home the "sacred paycheck," not an elder brother's robe, for his wife to transform into the "sacred TV dinner."

If you are a good hunter, the animals will show you honor by coming to you. A good hunter knows these wild creatures are his teachers, and he always shows respect to his teachers. A good hunter lives in harmony with self, world, tribe and the Creator. If you have done something wrong, *sicha,* transgressed the natural laws by which we are to live, the animals will remain far from you, and your hunting will be unsuccessful until you have reestablished these balances.

Hehaka Sapa (Black Elk) told Joseph Epes Brown, as recorded in *The Spiritual Legacy of the American Indian,* that hunting is not symbolically but literally a quest for the deepest truth of life. His teaching helps us understand what is truly meant by the widely misunderstood description of the Spirit World as the "happy hunting grounds." One's hunting for the wild animal flesh that nourishes our flesh is secondary in importance to one's hunt for the wild beasts and plants of spirit that nourish one's spirit. The wild creatures, our elder brothers and sisters, are among our teachers. So, too, are other kinds of spirits; I've already told you, for example, that love is a wild creature in the Spirit World that the man hunts for. Likewise, anger is a carnivore that we must come near only with care and cannot safely keep captive, because it is dangerous (*wakan*). Sorrow and depression are wild fungi that grow where the sacred animal love has died; like all *wakan* plants, they are a poison if we take in too much of them, but in small doses they can be healing. Fear is another wild animal, one that is often a companion to love, and helps it to remain free, to prevent it from being captured and rendered *washte*.

There's an old song in the dominant culture that speaks of being like a bird in a gilded cage. Modern culture puts people in cages, and teaches them to love the cages for the way they are gilded. People become caged by work, education, personal relationships, and religious and cultural conditioning. The cages are gilded with money, power, entertainment and addictive dependencies. Most people, as they go through their lives, grow more and more afraid of change. They would rather stay with the familiar, even when they loathe or fear it, simply because they have been taught to love the cage of familiarity, the *washte*, rather than venture into the unknown, wonderful though it may be, simply because they are afraid of the unknown, the *wakan*.

Traditional cultures worldwide believe that it is within the nature of human beings (and the nature of all living beings) to be both *washte* and *wakan*. They believe it is in our nature to be unpredictable. One should neither expect nor demand any person to act in a certain manner; to do so is to deprive the person of her or his free will, to put her or him in a cage of expectation. Yet simultaneously with this *wakan* freedom comes the responsibility to show respect to all life, including oneself. Being "wild" is never an excuse for foolhardiness or cruelty.

In the same way that the newcomers' culture sought to conquer the wilderness when it came to these shores, it also sought to conquer the people who lived in the wilderness. The natives of this continent were labeled "wild" and were "caged" onto reservations, in mission schools, and so on. Still today, their spirits are caged, and put on display like brightly feathered birds in "safe" environments such as pow-wows, books, movies and fairs and school presentations, where they can be observed like animals in the zoo.

I remember hearing the story of a medicine man seeing an old jade necklace for sale in a glass case at an "Indian Trading Post" and realizing its spirit was dying from lack of touch; he asked the young Native woman minding the shop to put it on, and, behold, it shone much more brightly as it lay across her breasts. Likewise, examples of the Sacred Pipe once carried by powerful medicine men now sit behind glass in museums, where their spirits are slowly dying from suffocation and the privation of contact with other living beings, with carriers to care for them and talk and listen to them, with the Circle of Life itself. The very bones of some elders remain in the hands of anthropologists. Meanwhile, the descendants of the original peoples are fast forgetting a very important thing: that, even though the newcomers meant the term "wild Indians" as a disparagement, they were right! We who follow the Red Road, whatever our ancestry, *are* wild, and we must never forget it. It pains me to see the sacred dances presented only as entertainment; the sacred wild herbs cultivated in gardens or, worse yet, processed into pills; the sacred ceremonies sold for money; or treaty-based tribal land claims bartered away in exchange for casinos. In doing or allowing these things we are allowing ourselves to be tamed. This is not the way of the original ancestors! We must not be afraid to be wild, to take risks, to allow ourselves to run free like the wind, the deer and the river. And we must seek freedom for all our relations as well, and encourage them to cherish it in their hearts.

What do you yearn for deep within your heart? Have you had a sacred vision or dream that tells you what you should do in your life? Has a Grandfather or Grandmother told you what you should do? Don't be afraid! Don't be tame! What, I ask you, what are you waiting for?

We are all warriors, and must never forget that. It is common for people to have the mistaken notion that a warrior is someone who carries weapons into battle. Adult males carrying weapons are not the only kind of warrior. Grandmothers and Grandfathers, children, women, every one of us is a warrior. I remember one Grandmother who, even as she lay dying, even though she could not leave her bed, showed me what a true warrior is like—challenging the mining company that had poisoned the air and ruined her health and the health of others.

Another common mistaken notion is that warriors replace fear with courage. That too is wrong. Every real warrior knows the value not only of courage, but of fear as well. Fear without courage breeds indecision and panic, which lead to failure. But courage without fear breeds foolhardiness, which also leads to failure. The young often find courage easy to come by—because they have yet to learn the respect for the *wakan*, the unknown and dangerous, that fear embodies. Sometimes young people, but more often older people, lack courage, becoming so afraid of the unknown that they prefer to stay in their golden cages of familiarity. Either courage or fear by itself will lead to failure, but, when they are allowed to work together, they lead to success.

However, there is at least one reason the Creator saw to it that the young often lack the kind of experience that teaches the wisdom of fear—to ensure that they won't refuse the gifts Spirit provides to them. One Grandfather told me, "If we knew what we were really getting into when we accept gifts from Spirit, we would be very afraid of accepting them—and might not at all. That's why Spirit usually offers those gifts to the young." He added with a chuckle, "They haven't learned yet to be afraid." I find it ironic that he said this when I was young; though I thought I understood, I didn't. Now, many years later, I am beginning truly to understand his teaching: the young have the strength to carry the great burdens put on them, yet lack the wisdom to hesitate accepting them. Unlike the pensive brother in the Lakota story, they are unlikely to run from the *wakan*. We human beings, as the youngest of the Creator's children, need to carry special burdens—such as the Sacred Pipe, and its equivalents in other cultures, the Torah, the Qur'an, the Dharma, and so on—but we don't fully understand as our siblings in fur and feather do what these grave responsibilities signify for Creation as a whole.

Courage is *washte*. The individual feels good within to be brave, and feels good when others honor her or him for bravery. Like the other *washte* things in life—good food, the love of family, and so on—one cannot have too much courage, as long as it doesn't lead to foolhardiness.

Fear is *wakan*. As with other *wakan* things, in great quantity it is overwhelming. Hence one can feel too much fear—so much that one is rendered helpless. The biggest fear we have is fear of change, fear of the future, fear of death. This leads to the fear of trying anything new, of trying anything that isn't "safe." Fear is dangerous: like the *wakan* herbs, it is poisonous. If we allow fear to feed on us, it will destroy us. But, in small amounts, fear is a good strong medicine in the same way as those *wakan* herbs. Fear, in fact, is a friend: it tells us what we need to work on, what we haven't yet faced with courage. Franklin Delano Roosevelt was wrong to say, "There is nothing to fear but fear itself;" he should have said, "The greatest thing to fear is ignoring what our fears teach us."

Fear is a teacher: it tells us what we need to grow in and what we still need to work on. Real courage doesn't repress fear but understands and welcomes it, listens to it and learns from it. On the other hand, courage keeps fear in its place so the fear does not overwhelm us.

A true warrior knows that the most important thing is to keep courage and fear, *washte* and *wakan*, together in balance. That is what the story of the two boys who first encountered the Bringer of the Pipe teaches us—one boy was courageous without fear and the other was fearful without courage. Each would have made a better choice in the face of the sacred if he had had a little of the other's gift.

One honored Grandfather I know told me that one of his teachers—whom I have also had the honor of meeting—once pointed to the Sacred Pipe and the eagle feathers on it, and said, "If you had any idea how much sacred power is in this, you would be afraid to come near!" What he meant is that we *should* be afraid of sacred things; we should not treat sacred things with the same kind of heedless disregard with which we handle a toothbrush. He did not mean that we should not touch the Pipe or the eagle feathers, but that we should do so with great care, with plenty of respectful fear, fully conscious of the power in them. In the same way, we should pull a plug from the wall socket or drive a car on a fast highway with a respectful consciousness of the *wakan* danger posed by the electric power surging through the naked prongs, or the speed at which we are traveling. If we have only courage, we will use sacred objects but remain oblivious to their great sacred power (what the elders call *wowashake wakan*), in which case smoking the Sacred Pipe will be hardly more for us than smoking a cigarette. On the other hand, if we have a balance of respectful fear, courageous fear, even smoking a cigarette can be a very sacred action. If, however, we have only fear unbalanced by courage, we will be too afraid to touch these sacred things at all, in which case we will never receive the sacred benefits that come from ceremony.

Sometimes I've had people come to the Sacred Stone People's Lodge who have had no fear in participating at all and join in the ceremony without a moment's hesitation. Such people rarely if ever have any kind of spiritual experience in the lodge because, lacking fear, they are unaware of the sacred power, the sacred medicine, found within. And sometimes I've had people who have had so much fear that they have been unable to attend at all: fear of passing out in the heat, fear of darkness, nakedness, claustrophobia and so on. People who have courage and fear conjoined feel fear but enter the lodge anyway. They neither ignore or repress their fear nor let their fear debilitate them. I myself have been carrying the ceremony for many years, and I still feel fear as I enter the lodge, but nevertheless I go in. It is my understanding and belief that even now, decades after the first time I entered the lodge, I should still enter the lodge the same way: not as a familiar, comfortable experience, but as a frightening, *wakan* ceremony where, literally, anything at all can happen. I thank my fears as the important teachers that they are.

A warrior knows that the usefulness of a bow lies in its ability to bend. If it bends too much, it has no strength to it. If it does not bend at all, it cannot release an arrow. As Lao-tse taught in the Tao-te Ching, the green branch bends in the storm and doesn't break, but the hard, firm branch snaps and falls. As persons, as warriors, we must combine the strength of courage and the bendingness of fear. Fear helps us remember how others feel who are not as far along the path as we, and courage enables us to help them. I always say the greatest courage is not found among those who bravely stand in the vanguard of battle, but among those who remain behind to protect the women as well as the children and the elderly—those who are most vulnerable and yet most precious because they are so close to the Spirit World.

There are so many true warriors who have been among us—only a few of whom have had their names recorded by history. I think of so many elders striving to pass on their heritage, such as those listed in the Note on Elders & Language (p. xiv). I think of heroes who have striven to keep their heritage alive, despite the pressures both within and outside their nations— heroes I have known who have striven boldly, often in the face of harsh criticism and rejection even from members of their own communities, to keep vitally alive the languages, songs, government and, above all, the spiritualities of their peoples.

Let me tell you about one of the most courageous people I have ever known. James Levi Tobias Bowier, Jr., came over to this continent from his West African homeland, when the Creator asked him to do so, and had with him only the clothes on his back and about twenty Liberian dollars. He was determined to get an American seminary education, get ordained and return to his people. By chance, or truly by the Creator's will, he met me, and we became very close, adopting each other as brothers. He even came once to the

Sacred Stone People's Lodge; I remember wondering how he, a Christian African, would respond to it, and was pleasantly surprised when he came out again afterwards, smiling broadly and saying, "This is just like what we do back in Africa!" We often shared with each other what we had learned about the traditions of the Native peoples of both continents. In the years he spent here, he never put aside his commitment to return to his own people and do what he could for them—even though many other Liberians who had also come here had chosen to stay, preferring a safe, pleasant American life over the privations and constant civil war back home.

James's elderly mother came over to visit him, and he immediately realized that she was seriously ill. Diagnosed with terminal cancer, she was placed in an American hospital. On the night in which this wise ancient one was to drop her robe, James insisted on telling my then-small children their accustomed bedtime story. I listened from the hallway as he told them traditional Grebo stories about the great trickster, Spider—stories amazingly similar to the Spider stories told by the traditional peoples of this continent!—and my children laughed with delight at Spider's escapades. I, however, was silently weeping, knowing exactly what James was doing. This was his own way of saying good-bye to his mother, I realized, for these were clearly stories that he remembered her telling him when he was little. He had now passed them on— he bade adieu to his mother by keeping her stories alive. My children still remember these stories, as adults, and they still remember James—which demonstrates the incredible power of storytelling.

I saw James off at the airport a few months later, knowing in my heart that I would never see him again, despite his promise that he would invite me to come to Liberia and, he hoped, sponsor my induction into the elders' society of his Grebo people. I heard from James occasionally by letter, as he struggled to set up a school to teach children of whatever tribal ancestry, whether the descendants of freed American slaves or indigenous ancestors, whether Christian or Muslim or of the traditional spirituality, whether urbanized folk or "hill folk." He was in his own way valiantly striving to restore the Sacred Hoop of All the Nations. But then came the devastating news, from members of his family, that one of the gangs of cutthroats that were fighting for control of the country had swept through Fendall, a suburb of the capital city of Monrovia, killing everyone they found. I eventually learned from the International Red Cross in Geneva that James, unarmed, lay dead on the floor of his little house in Fendall.

James never carried a weapon, as did the cowards who killed him, yet he taught nevertheless with his life what a true warrior is like. I remember his joyful demeanor, his astonishing talent on the tenor saxophone, and his astonishing *savoir faire* with women of all ages—all of them, from little girls (including my daughter) to aged Grandmothers, immediately "fell in love" with him. I tell you the story because I believe that, though his life was cut short, his spirit and his vision go on—through you and everyone who hears his story.

Life means constant change. We are on a constant journey of becoming who we really are; we are not that person yet, but we are walking in that direction. Fear, though *wakan*, wants us to stay with the *washte* of life as it is now: the safe comfortable life that is predictable and without risks. Courage, though *washte*, wants us to venture out of the *washte* of our comfortable life, take great risks and move into the *wakan* of the unknown future. To live is to change, to refuse to change is to die. To be afraid to change, then, is to be afraid to live. If we are not open to change, to growth, we die in spirit. The warrior, knowing this, keeps courage and fear together.

Do not be ashamed if you feel fear as you walk the Red Road of life. Just do not let your fear keep you from moving forward! And it is good if you are courageous, as long as you remember to join it together with a healthy dose of fear. If you keep courage and fear together, you are a true warrior.

From their first arrivals in Turtle Island until now, people from the dominant culture have often expressed abhorrence at the "barbarism" of the traditional ways. Many of them have, since their first encounters with Native Americans and still today, pointed to certain of the ceremonies that include physical pain, to the ancient wars among the nations and the sometimes harsh torturing of captives, and even to what appears to be a passive stoicism in the face of adversity, as examples of this barbarism. Others have also expressed incredulity at how Native American individuals, when they are fortunate, share their abundance with everyone. When a hunter kills an animal, it is shared with everyone who wishes to partake, and not just reserved to oneself or even one's family. In these latter times, when a Native American wins the lottery, it is still not unusual for him or her to distribute the winnings among the people.

It is very difficult for people outside the traditional cultures to understand these ways. Today, many descendants of the traditional peoples have themselves forgotten the reasons for them, losing a vital link to their heritage. These ways are rooted in the concepts of *wakan* and *washte,* but too often are understood in terms of good and evil.

The traditional peoples' view is that adversity, like serendipity, simply happens. There is no point in either complaining about or seeking out adversity for the sake of adversity, because no life is free of it. But not all adversity is right to accept, just as not all serendipity is right to accept. We do not accept either if it is not right to accept it: we do not accept serendipity at the expense of others' well-being, nor do we take adversity on ourselves for the sake of personal gain (pity or honor), for to do either is *washichu.* We do not brag about either or use either to get what we want, for that too is *washichu.*

As Buddhism teaches, so the traditional peoples teach: pleasure and pain are simply things that pass through us as we follow the course of our lives, without holding on to either. Individual lives are like different paths: some are easy to walk and some hard, but no path, no life, is entirely easy or entirely difficult. And all paths, no matter how easy or hard it is to walk them, no matter how long or short they are, reach their destination. Life, in other words, is a complex web of *wakan* and *washte.* Some lives have more of one and other lives have more of the other, but none is purely one or the other. As Taoism teaches, *yin* (*wakan*) and *yang* (*washte*) are never found pure; there is always at least a little of the one with the other. The traditional view is that, if you can do something to fend off adversity, then you do it; you don't wait for someone else to do it for you; provided only that you do not harm innocent beings by fending adversity off onto them. However, if you can't do anything about adversity, then you accept it without wasting energy foolishly quarreling with fate. This attitude is why traditional people have been described by others as stoic, even fatalistic, in the face of adversity.

How do we know whether or not to accept serendipity or adversity when it comes our way? The key is in the law of balances. Good and bad fortune alike are to be accepted if they are balanced by benefits that can be shared with the people. They are not to be accepted if they bring no such benefits. Good fortune is *washte* (pleasant), and adversity is *wakan* (difficult, dangerous, frightening). Adversity can bring *wakan* gifts and good fortune can bring *washte* gifts. We accept either kind of fortune if it brings such gifts, and we share both kinds of gifts with the people. If we keep either kind of gifts to ourselves alone, we are being *washichu.*

Knowing what adversity we should accept and what adversity we should eschew is like watching the world around us for sacred signs. As I have told you, not everything we see is a sacred sign: sometimes a deer crossing the road is only doing it to get to better grazing land, not to deliver a sacred sign to us. In the same way, not every adverse event is to be accepted; we accept it only if it gives us a sacred gift to share with the people. In both cases—as we should all the time—we listen to what Spirit is telling us.

A person of the traditional ways, like most people, avoids adversity if there is no good reason for welcoming it. We see no reason to accept or seek out needless adversity because that brings no benefit to the people. One does not foolishly step into the path of a stampeding herd of buffalo or a fast-moving train, for instance, if one does not need to. But there are circumstances in which one actually puts oneself into adversity, for the sake of gathering benefit for others. Before the coming of the Europeans, it was common among many of the traditional nations to hunt buffalo by sending one man, covered with the skin of a buffalo, out among them, to direct their course toward the other hunters. In fact, among all Americans, it is honorable to put one's life at risk to save the lives of others, for instance, in a fire or a flood.

One must always be watchful, aware of what's going on. Adequate preparation and anticipation is an essential part of being a true warrior: that way, actual confrontation can often be avoided. It is vital that we listen to Spirit in order to know what kind of adversity it is we are experiencing at any time. If the adversity serves a sacred purpose, if it brings a sacred gift, then we accept it, and share the sacred gift with the people. This is no different from sharing with the people any *washte* good fortune that comes to us.

We who walk in the traditional ways also welcome adversity when it makes us stronger. The strength of any individual is vital to the strength of the people, so it too is a gift to the people. If a storm blows, we flow with its strength, as Black Elk and George MacDonald taught. In fact, we should be grateful to the storm, for it gives us the gift of strength. Traditional peoples know they need to be strong, physically and spiritually, in order to face future adversity. When we are born our families shelter us from adversity. But as we grow our elders slowly let us experience more and more adversity, to make us strong. A life without adversity would be a life without any strength, and the least untoward event would snuff it out. This is why traditionally, as a child grew, its people would gradually expose it to the inevitable adversities of life (the *wakan*) and at the same rate remove safeguards (the *washte*) more and more. Through careful training, the child would learn to eschew those adversities that bring no gifts and accept those that do, taking care not to be harmed by them—and also would learn not to be overly afraid of the *wakan*.

Sometimes, too, adversity comes upon us as a result of mistakes we have made, and then we welcome the adversity because it teaches us how to live in a better way. This too is something the people help a child to understand as it grows: if one makes a mistake, one must bravely face the adverse consequences that follow it, so one does not make it again. How often I have heard parents say, "I wish I could protect my children from difficulty." How often I have seen parents try to shield their children from the consequences of their foolishness. But these consequences are not a malevolent force, "evil"; nor are they a punishment meted out by a vengeful deity, but simply the inevitable results of our choices—what is called *karma* by the Hindus.

Sometimes, however, adversity comes upon us because of the actions of others, either their inadvertent mistakes or intentional malevolence. In the case of the former we bear the results without anger because no harm was intended, and remember that the person who made the mistake will learn from seeing the sad results. In the case of the latter too, we respond with patience. Many of us have had persons unjustly seek to impugn our honor with attacks on our reputations. These experiences are not evil but a *wakan* kind of good, for they strengthen us. Such experiences help build up the "muscles" of our spirit. So we are foolish if we get angry or upset when such adversities come upon us. Instead, we should be glad for them. Jesus teaches, similarly, that we should love our enemies, and do good to those who would hurt us. Once I heard a Vajrayana (Tibetan Buddhist) lama say, "I am glad when people persecute me! I give thanks to them for their generosity, because they have given me this wonderful opportunity to learn better, through practice, the sacred arts of love and forgiveness." He doubtlessly was thinking of the teachings of the Gadamba Geshay Langritangba, about nine centuries ago: "When others out of jealousy treat me badly with abuse, slander and so on, I will learn to take all loss and offer the victory to them. When one whom I have benefited with great hope unreasonably hurts me very badly, I will learn to view that person as an excellent spiritual guide." Though Jesus and the two Vajrayana teachers come out of very different cultures, their understanding on this point is very similar to that of the traditional peoples of this continent.

In fact, there are very sensible, practical reasons to be glad for our enemies. Every species is improved by its predators, since—as the theory of natural selection points out—the fastest and the fittest are the individuals who will survive to breed.

Once I was in the mountains of Colorado to join others in ceremony. We were in a place where a *Wiwanyag Wachipi* (Sun Dance) had just been held by some Lakota from the reservation, and we were appalled at the mess they had left behind. At first I was tempted to criticize and complain about them, but Spirit reminded me they weren't there to hear me. So I just quietly started picking up their garbage and filling in the holes that had injured Grandmother Earth. After a while the others with me began slowly to join in. It became a very happy occasion, for we were expressing to our Grandmother Earth how much we love her.

And that brings us to an even more important reason for welcoming adversity, which is that it is sacred, *wakan*. Certainly no one enjoys adversity (except the *heyoka*, for whom adversity is *washte*), because adversity is dangerous and frightening, but one can also recognize the sacredness in it and realize that it brings sacred gifts to one. Traditional peoples believe that there are balances to everything. If we take pain on ourselves, then the Creator will bless us. Nothing is free. We must give for everything we receive, and we will receive for everything we give. Even in as small a thing as taking part of a plant useful for healing we give tobacco, because taking part of the plant causes pain to the plant, and giving tobacco is our way of recognizing its pain and, symbolically, feeling the pain ourselves. When we pray to an animal before killing it we acknowledge its pain as our own. When we share with others in the Sacred Giveaway, parting with emotional pain from things we treasure, we receive sacred gifts in return. As the visionary poet William Blake said, "Every kindness done to another is a little death in the Divine Image."

Let us take physical pain as an example. All people, in every culture, rid themselves of pain (the symptomology associated with an illness or injury) with medicines. But the traditional peoples believe that pain has a message for us, and that we are foolish not to listen to it. Native Americans have always had traditional medicines for the relieving of pain. One good example is the bark of the white willow, which contains a compound similar to aspirin. But, though traditionals may take medicine for it, they do not fear pain, for pain is a friend. When they have pain, they listen to what the pain is telling them. They believe that *washichu* persons, being afraid of pain, do not want to hear the message the pain is bringing, and do not receive the gifts that come with pain. *Washichu* run from pain in the same way that they avoid true spirituality. A truly traditional person—a true *human being*, as human beings are meant to live!—does not wantonly inflict pain on others, and does not fear pain or for that matter seek pain in a macho way, but rather accepts it when it comes, humbly and honorably. In fact, listening to pain tends to diminish it, while ignoring or avoiding pain tends to intensify it. So, when we experience physical pain, we listen to it, for it is a friend, as it has messages for us. On the most obvious level, pain tells us there is something wrong with our body, and the specific location and nature of the pain tells us what kind of healing to seek. But, more importantly, pain can help us to break through to a more sacred level of awareness.

Pain is not bad but *wakan*; it is a giving which can lead to our receiving great gifts. Many of the traditional ceremonies involve physical pain, and, as I have noted, members of the dominant culture have often expressed abhorrence at the "barbarism" of this aspect of the sacred ways. For a long time the most sacred ceremonies were made illegal, and those who tried to practice them were persecuted, simply because they were deemed too barbaric. But traditional people believe that the *wakan* way, the sacred way, is never easy; indeed, that, if it seems easy, we've gone astray. For other religions this is true too: it's easy to sit in a comfortable pew in church and sing hymns, but it's hard for people with a *washichu* (greedy) mind to give away all that they have and follow in the same path that Christ walked. Whatever your faith may be, if it is easy for you to practice your faith, you are not truly practicing it. The easiness in life is the *washte*. Of those who stay with the *washte*, like the first brother in the story of the White Buffalo Calf Woman, Jesus said, "Truly, they have already received their reward."

There have been many lately who have sought to make the ceremonies less difficult and threatening and painful, in order to make them more appealing to members of the dominant culture. But the degree to which we make them easier (*washte*) is the degree to which we make them less sacred (*wakan*). Just as with the sacred poisonous plants that, carefully administered, still can heal, we enter carefully into the *wakan*, the difficult and dangerous, in order to find what is truly holy. Think of the medicine men and women, who walk pretty much constantly in the *wakan*: you don't find them (the genuine ones, at least) in fancy homes with expensive cars parked out front. The truly sacred medicine people I have known have always lived humbly, often in tumbledown shacks with no plumbing or insulation. For many of them, pain, hunger, poverty and cold were constant companions. But I never heard them complain about these things. And I never heard them refuse any sincere request for the sacred medicine. I have seen them, despite the considerable physical pain I know some of them had, still lead ceremonies, walking about and doing things as if they had the body of a healthy teenager. I have seen them get up in the middle of the night to bring the Sacred Pipe where it was needed. I have seen them rise from their deathbeds to give healing to someone.

Indeed, I believe, the poverty and pain with which they live helps them. It keeps them focused on the *wakan*, the sacred. If they were surrounded with lots of nice things, with the trappings of a *washte* life, they might get distracted; they might even get greedy (*washichu*). One cannot deny that certain genuine medicine people—some of whom I knew—let themselves become trapped by the *washichu* spirit and allowed the sacred gifts they carried to be used to try to satisfy the insatiable hunger of greediness.

Moreover, the poverty and pain of life, as lived by the genuine medicine people, constitutes a sacred gift they are giving in order to receive in turn the gift of the medicine they carry. This is the sacred law of balances: nothing is received without a giving in return. These people, with their lives of great adversity, often seem to have "one foot in the grave." People in the dominant culture are afraid of the loss of control that pain and (above all) death represent, but the medicine people welcome the *wakan*, the wild, uncontrollable, and dangerous. Unlike most of us, who in the years between childhood and old age are far from death, they walk at all times very close to their deaths—and need to, because that helps them to stay close to the Spirit World.

It is important to remember that giving emotional or physical pain to others (except when it is *wakan*, as in healing work or war) is *sicha*, out of balance. We should never excuse the giving of pain to others as okay because it's *wakan*. Any pain inappropriately wreaked on others has its balances too and comes back to us. Yes, a healer may give pain to the patient in giving powerful *wakan* medicines or perhaps cutting off a seriously damaged limb, but of course this is in order to bring about release from greater pain. Yes, warriors inflict pain and kill, but war is supremely *wakan* when it is entered into for a greater good (for example, to prevent future mass starvation by protecting one's hunting grounds). Yes, the early ancestors used to torture war prisoners, but—though this is hard for modern people to understand—the captors gave their prisoners the opportunity to show great honor in the midst of the shame of captivity by withstanding the torture, which is very *wakan*. And yes, women too were often taken as captives, but many of them—including European-ancestry pioneer women—often preferred to stay with their captors, refusing opportunities to leave, because among Native Americans they were treated with a great respect they had never experienced among Europeans.

War is extremely *wakan*. This is clear by its very nature: *wakan* means dangerous, frightening and chaotic—and these are qualities that describe war. If we enter into war for the wrong reasons, or if we escalate it more than is absolutely necessary, the *wakan* will destroy us, just as misprescribing *wakan* (poisonous) medicines, or taking too much of them, will destroy the patient. (Political leaders of the world today, take note!) So we enter into war with great care, and with great respect for the enemy, since the pain we will inflict on them will bring them *wakan*, sacred gifts. War brings forth great pain—violence, revenge, torture, betrayal. But we know that in taking war to our enemies we come close to our own deaths, and we never do so except with a heavy heart.

One does what one must. The thing is, one only takes up weapons when one has no choice, when there is no other recourse. The traditional peoples are pacifists, but they are not fools. Traditional warriors often painted themselves black, realizing the need to mourn when there is no other choice but to fight, since in many instances it was a shameful failure to be diplomatic earlier that led to war. Their approach to war often led to a great nobility and dignity on the part of vanquisher and vanquished, captor and captive, killer and killed. But they knew they must maintain a great sorrow in their hearts when entering into war, for there is nothing to be proud of in making war.

One Grandmother explained to me why the Peacemaker persuaded Tadodaho, the Onoda'gega (Onondaga) chief who blocked the Peacemaker's efforts to bring peace to the warring Five Nations—Tadodaho, the most warlike of chiefs—to become just as zealous in peace. She told me that, when she was dancing the August Pueblo Corn Dance, the dance "grew me roots from the soles of my feet all the way down into the Earth; the dance gave me to finally understand all through and through why I am alive. And this alive had with it the fact that all the natural world and the natural place in every single person needs to be listened to and protected over everything else. Every single natural entity and every person." She went on: "I figure now, hearing the Peacemaker's story, that that is why Tadodaho was a major part of the journey to peace—him being a cannibal and so filled with war and death, eating his own people, snakes for hair. The Peacemaker makes him the Keeper of the Council Fires. Even him. Especially him. The story is deeper than the ocean and the great forests." Which, I add, is why we remember the implements of war buried deep beneath the stately white pine. Peace as well as war is *wakan*.

VIII

Carrying Wakan Objects

THE CONCEPT OF PERSONAL OWNERSHIP had very little provenance among the traditional peoples before the invasion of the Europeans. This was especially true of *wakan* things and actions. To this day, one does not own *wakan* objects or actions, but rather "carries" them. The responsibility of carrying something *wakan*, in fact, is quite the opposite of ownership: *It* owns *you*. The carrier acts only at the sacred entity's beck and call, and *nobody*, including the carrier, would ever dare to touch the *wakan* object or invoke the *wakan* activity, unless specifically told to do so by Spirit itself. These *wakan* objects have their own will and their own purpose, which is not necessarily the will and purpose of those who carry them, so carriers must be always respectful of *their* will—even to the point of being ready and willing to let them move on when they wish. These taboos, as anthropologists call them, are prominent among traditional nations of all times and places. Think of Aaron's sons, Nadab and Abihu, who (according to Deuteronomy 10) tried without permission to invoke the Creator with the Ark of the Covenant, and were killed by sacred fire.

Unfortunately, it is growing all too common to treat these *wakan* objects and actions as property. One increasingly sees the sacred ceremonies offered to unprepared strangers for money. One sees the Sacred Pipe, for instance, bought and sold at pow-wows and hung in museums. And one sees dream-catchers hung in such extremely unlikely locations as from rear-view mirrors in cars—one wonders why drivers would hang them there unless they intend to fall asleep at the wheel! Fortunately, these dreamcatchers are usually badly made; otherwise, they could cause great havoc.

There is another way in which these objects and actions are being treated as property. While certain nations, preeminently the Lakota, are justly concerned about the arrogation of the sacred ways by *washichu* (of whatever ancestry) who want to use the traditions for their own personal gain, some leaders in these nations have responded by proclaiming that no one has any right to these traditions but themselves. Instead of selfishly clutching the Sacred Pipe closer, the People should be extending it out to the entire world, sharing it with the Pope and the Dalai Lama and the leaders of every other faith, with the political leaders of the world's nations, with the CEOs in their boardrooms and the generals in their bunkers—those who have the power to destroy this world. And they should share it with the bum on the street, the sick in the hospital, the poor in the *barrios*, the forgotten and the ignored, and with everyone else. They should do what Black Elk and Lame Deer and their other wise elders did—and humbly, lovingly teach *all* the Creator's children how to walk the Red Road with honor and respect for every being in the Sacred Hoop.

So let us now do just that, and talk about some of these *wakan* objects as they are understood in the traditional way.

I would like to talk about stones and feathers at the same time for several reasons. First, they are both very sacred natural things. Second, they are both used a great deal for healing. And third, they complement each other: feathers come from the sky people above, and stones come from the earth people below.

As you walk on the Red Road before you, I hope you remain always attentive, in the way I have already discussed. If you are watchful, you will find good and useful things in your path, such as signs of nearby game animals or healing herbs. And you also might find a feather or a stone. I believe that such encounters are no accident, but part of the providential care the spirits and our Mother Earth give us.

There are those who say that feathers are more valuable because they are far less often encountered than stones. All too often stones are treated without respect, and feathers made the objects of greed and mercantilism. There are those too who say that some feathers, for instance the feathers of the spotted eagle, or certain stones, such as crystals, are intrinsically more valuable or powerful than others. American laws try to protect raptors by saying that anyone found possessing their feathers without the proper documentation can be prosecuted, but this has only fueled the black market, leading to the senseless murder of hawks and eagles by poachers, and has unfairly denied Native Americans not registered with Bureau of Indian Affairs-recognized nations the right to carry them for ceremonial purposes.

I have always been taught that *all* feathers and stones are both *washte* and *wakan*, though in varying proportions and qualities. In other words, they are all, each in its special way, beautiful and useful. Some feathers and stones are good for decoration and others make good tools; they are also all, each in a special way, powerful spirit presences. The feathers of the spotted eagle (also called the golden eagle) bring the medicine of Grandfather, because that bird flies higher into the Sky and hence sees farther than any other. But the feathers of a hummingbird or crow, for instance, also bring us important medicines. A crystal may have special healing properties, but so too may an unassuming pebble of basalt. Some of the most ancient Sacred Pipe bowls I have seen were carved centuries ago from basalt. (I chuckle at "New Age" people, paying lots of money for their crystals, and ignoring the sacred stones they trample underfoot!)

As we walk our path, we may have the experience not simply of finding such a feather or stone, but of one being *given* to us. Several people have told me they have had the experience of a bird flying near them and dropping a feather as a gift to them. And I have had the experience of coming out of the Sacred Stone People's Lodge and finding a healing stone or feather on the sacred mound that had not been there when I went in. In traditional stories, a bird sometimes brings the protagonist a sacred stone in its beak or claws. Even if, so it seems to us, we "simply happened to find" the stone or feather, still, how can we be sure that some medicine being or ancestor spirit didn't place it there for us and subtly direct our attention to it?

In whatever way a stone or a feather (or anything at all) comes to you, you should properly express your appreciation. Tobacco should be left where you picked up the feather or stone, or offered in the direction of the bird who dropped it. If you are sure this gift is for you personally to carry, then it is proper for you to do so. It is better, especially if you have the least doubt on this matter, that you consult with an elder. I suggest that the best alternative is to give it to the elder, even if the elder gives it right back to you. Remember, among the traditional peoples, there is no personal ownership; what was given to you was not the object, but the sacred responsibility of carrying that object in behalf of your people, and also in honor to the being(s) who put it in your path for you to find.

Stones and feathers have their homes, and where these homes are tells us something about their special medicines. The feathers of the birds who stay close to Mother Earth tend to be more *washte* than *wakan* (but not always; I have carried a wren wing that was a very powerful healer). These birds' feathers are more often colorful, hence particularly useful for decoration. The feathers of the birds whose spiritual home is high up in Father Sky aren't as pretty, but they carry a great sacred power. I told you that one Grandfather, pointing to a Sacred Pipe adorned with eagle feathers, said, "If you had the slightest idea how much power is there, you wouldn't even dare to come near!"

In the same way, some stones live near the surface of Mother Earth and some live deep down within her flesh. The surface stones are more often useful for arrowheads or mortars, or for building things. The ones from deep underground are more often the sacred crystals, or flints who carry fire within, or good igneous stones of the kind that is better for use in the Sacred Stone People's Lodge. That is why it is good to look beneath the roots of an uprooted tree or in the bed of a dried-up stream for such particularly *wakan* stones. That is why especially in spring we find sacred stones who have been brought up to the surface by natural processes (just as new plants come up, so do the stones, as any gardener knows!). That is why caves and kivas are very sacred places, because we are within Grandmother's womb, surrounded by these sacred stones. And that is why it distresses traditional peoples all around the world to see how other peoples tear into the flesh of Mother Earth to dig out her treasures and erect buildings and highways on her breasts and stomach.

My first teaching Grandfather taught me to look deeply into the sacred Grandfather Stones when they are first brought into the Sacred Stone People's Lodge. The stones may have seemed plain before they were put in the sacred fire, often still with some soil or moss or lichen—flesh of the Earth—still clinging to them. But now, in the lodge, we see their red glow that represents the blood that unites all living nations in the Sacred Hoop and the seven generations that came before us and will come after us. He also taught me a very important and sacred thing, that the heat of the fire makes them transparent; if we look closely into those glowing rocks we can see in the shimmering reds and oranges the dreams they have been dreaming while they slept deep within Mother Earth. It is true that in the shifting lights within the incandescent rocks we often see pictures; these are the rocks' dreams, which are for us visions, from which we can learn important things.

The conjunction of these two, the feathers from far up in the Sky and the stones from deep down in the Earth, is very powerful. They represent, respectively, the generations that have already dropped their robes and the generations yet unborn. In the Medicine Wheel, we mark the Sacred Hoop with stones, and mark the Four Directions with poles decorated with appropriately colored feathers. Bringing together medicine beings from the highest reaches of Father Sky and the bowels of Mother Earth is part of what makes the Sacred Pipe so strong a medicine: the spotted eagle's feathers and the red pipestone are both a part of it, bound together by wood from the skin of Mother Earth, where Earth and Sky touch, from trees that bind together, with their roots and branches and tall trunk between, the Earth and the Sky. We put the wooden stem to our lips, for that is where *we* live, at the juncture of Heaven and Earth, but at the other end of the Sacred Pipe we hold those feathers and that stone, and then we speak with "visible breath" (*niya taniya*, a term that refers to the everpresence of Spirit), exhaling the smoke that carries our prayers up to the highest Heaven. As the White Buffalo Calf Woman taught, when we stand on the Earth and reach up to Heaven with the stem of the Pipe, we become trees, our feet-roots going into the Earth, our arm-branches reaching into the Sky; as she taught, we become a living bridge of prayer, a rainbow, the Sacred Hoop itself, uniting the Sacred Above with the Sacred Below.

If you do carry sacred stones or feathers for healing and/or ceremony, they are to be given special care. Sacred feathers are best wrapped carefully in red cloth and kept in a medicine bundle that has in it the four sacred herbs (sweetgrass, cedar, tobacco and sage). It is good to smudge them from time to time. When sacred feathers or stones are taken out, it is proper for everyone in the vicinity to show respect by ceasing from idle chatter and being attentive and prayerful.

Making things with feathers or stones is a sacred task. It saddens me to see people working them into human-made objects with no care for the spirit in them. In doing this sacred task, one should smudge first and be sure to ask for permission from the object before working it. I was taught that stones are living beings, and feathers are part of living beings, so we must ask the spirits that live in them for permission and guidance in the work we are planning. In the same way, when we do things with them (such as dancing or healing) we should proceed with care and respect.

It is a good thing to hold a sacred feather or stone while praying; it will help you to focus your prayer, and the spirit in it will pray with you. Many people carry a *wotai*, a sacred stone that carries or mediates Spirit; such a stone is useful in prayer and healing.

I have been told by two Grandmothers that stones and feathers have a sacred language. I have learned a little about the language of stones, but all too little, and I despair at trying to explain it to you. These Grandmothers taught how the shape of a stone or feather, its color, any patterns in it, all tell us something of its message for us. But at the very least, if we quiet our minds and fully attend to them, patiently, we may hear what they are telling us. One of the Grandmothers would send out people who came to her for healing, telling them to bring a stone to her. By reading the message in the stone that attracted their notice, she know what needed to be done for healing to occur. Stones and feathers also can be placed on or around an individual in order to bring healing.

Smoke (*shota* in Lakota) is sacred, or *wakan*; it connects Heaven (*Atë Makpiyah* [Father Sky]) and Earth (*Maka Ina* [Mother Earth]). It represents the spirit being released by sacred fire, and is clearly *wakan* in that, while other things are susceptible to gravity, smoke rises. Because of this, smoke plays a significant role in ceremonies. There are four kinds of smoke that are most commonly used. You will see them used in many sacred ceremonies.

Tobacco smoke is smoke from a black thing (properly cured tobacco, when fresh, is black). Hence tobacco is to be associated with the West, and our Grandfathers. This is one reason why, when you go to visit a Grandfather, it is customary to give a "tobacco gift" as a way of expressing thanks. The best tobacco is grown and prepared without additives and fillers and the sugars that get you hooked. Early European visitors, including Cristóbal Colón (Christopher Columbus), reported the original people's smoking tobacco was so pure and powerful that its smoke, inhaled, left them "benumbed and almost drunk." Today, among traditionals, tobacco is most commonly associated with the Sacred Pipe, with which it is offered in a prayerful way to the Seven Directions. Tobacco is what we use for carrying our prayers up to the Creator.

Sage smoke is smoke from a white thing (sage is very commonly white, or pale green). Hence sage is to be associated with the North, and our Grandmothers. It is very proper, when visiting a Grandmother, to give her a gift of sage. I refer to wild sage; the cooking spice is another species. The smoke of sage is what we use for cleansing. Just as winter storms cleanse the Earth — the winter, with its white snows, is also associated with the North — so sage smoke purifies. Bear in mind that it is very powerful. If you attend any ceremony, you will be smudged: someone with a feather fan will wave at you smoke from a sage stick or sage brning in a shell. You may use your hands and arms to pull the smoke to you, as if you were laving yourself with water from a pond, and you may raise your arms and lift your feet, to be sure you are completely cleansed with the sage smoke. I also recommend sage tea to purify yourself inside (steep sage in boiling water, then strain; you may want to add a little honey or maple syrup, as it can be bitter). If you have a bad cold or the flu, be sure to smudge and drink this tea, so you have sage inside and out.

Sweetgrass smoke is smoke from a yellow thing (sweetgrass, when it has dried, is usually yellow). Hence sweetgrass is to be associated with the East and our Mothers. Sweetgrass smoke is what we use to gather the attention of the *nagipi*, the spirits. Just as dawn and the new fire kindled in the East represent the coming of the spirit into the body, so sweetgrass calls the spirits. You will see sweetgrass used by the water pourer (ceremonial leader) at the Sacred Stone People's Lodge Ceremony. She or he will light it on the glowing rocks in the pit, then beat it against the Earth along what is known as the spirit trail, from the rocks out to *Unchi* (literally, "Grandmother," but called the Sacred Mound in English), to ask the spirits to come and help us in the ceremony.

Finally, there is cedar smoke, which is smoke from a red thing (cedar bark is red). Hence cedar is to be associated with the South and our Fathers. Cedar smoke is what we use for protection. Just as a father protects his family, just as *Atë Makpiyah* protects the Earth, so cedar protects us. If you are afraid, burn some cedar on charcoal and smudge yourself. You will see cedar put on the glowing rocks as they come into the lodge for the Sacred Stone People's Lodge ceremony, to protect us from being burned, and to make the lodge a safe place where we may commune with our ancestors and descendants, whom the stones represent.

Any kind of smoke from the burning of any living thing is sacred because of its power of rising to Heaven. When we burn wood in a fire—an ordinary homefire, a campfire, or a sacred fire such as the *peta owankeshne* at the Sacred Stone People's Lodge—the smoke is carrying into the Great Above the living spirit of the trees who shared with us their branches, which once reached yearningly to the same Heaven. The ashes that remain behind go down into the Earth, our Grandmother. The fire must live carefully or it goes out or burns out of control. Thus, in many ways, from a simple fire we learn about our own life and our own death, and how our spirits too will go up to the Heaven, to Grandfather, and our bodies will sink into the Earth, to Grandmother.

There are seven especially sacred things. The first four are associated with the Four Directions—beginning in the West, they are the Sacred Pipe, the Sacred

Drum, the Sacred Flute, and the Sacred Talking Stick. The other three are associated with the other three directions—the Sacred Rattle, associated with the Zenith; the Sacred Faces (masks or false faces), associated with the Nadir; and the medicine shield and medicine bundle, carried respectively by the warrior and the medicine man or woman, associated with the Seventh Direction (the direction we go in our dreams and in our visions, and when we die). All of these speak with the voice of Spirit, and are capable of sacred medicine, including shapeshifting, healing, and travel in space and time.

The Sacred Pipe (*Chanunpa Wakan* in Lakota) is a gift to us from the Creator. Different nations tell different stories about how it came to us, but within all these stories is the same essential *Ur*-story: the Creator gave us the gift of the Sacred Pipe—usually by way of the sacred Beautiful Woman—so we can keep our center with it, remember where we came from, remember our relationships with all other living things and pray with it, seeking guidance. Therefore, whenever we hold the Sacred Pipe, we remember, at least subconsciously, the story of how it came to us.

The Sacred Pipe consists of a stem (usually wood, sometimes reed or bone) onto which a bowl (usually calumite [pipestone], sometimes basalt or another natural material) is inserted. Commonly, eagle feathers are hung from the joining of the bowl and stem. It is often decorated with animal effigies, beadwork, fetishes and the like.

One way to look at the symbolism of the Sacred Pipe is to recognize that all the sacred elements are in it—plant and animal and stone and spirit. The Sky is represented by the feathers, the Earth by the pipestone. Animals are represented by the effigies or grooves (in a "Four Winds" Pipe, for instance, there are four grooves for the animals of the Four Directions), and plants are represented by the stem. Pipestone is red, and so represents blood—the blood that unites all living things. So we recognize that, when we smoke with the Pipe, we pray with and for all things: the whole universe.

Another way to understand its symbolism is by seeing it as a living thing. It is always treated with great respect. The Pipe is our guide, our protector, our teacher, our mediator with the Creator. The bowl is seen as its beating heart, the stem as its body, the feathers as its wings. It is carried in its special pipe bag, which is its home, protected with sage, and is treated with care, and fed with tobacco.

When we pray with "visible breath" (*niya taniya*), our prayers rise to Heaven on the smoke; they are therefore heard. Thus, whatever we say while holding the Pipe is and must be true. This is why European Americans have often mistakenly called it the "peace pipe." They saw Native Americans "sign" the incomprehensible peace treaties thrust into their faces not with signatures, but with the Sacred Pipe. Sadly, the invders had no truth; not one treaty has been honored.

The Sacred Pipe is filled carefully with tobacco, sometimes with *kinnik-kinnik*, which is a mixture of blackberry leaves, red willow bark and other materials that make a sweet smoke. I always offer tobacco to the Seven Directions (West, North, East, South, Zenith, Nadir, and the Sacred or Seventh Direction) before putting it into the Pipe. Then it is lit with care. At the Sacred Stone People's Lodge, we light it with a coal from the *Peta Owankeshne* (Sacred Fire). Before it is smoked, the Pipe stem is turned four times sunwise (clockwise) around the bowl. The first puff is offered up to the Creator, as a thanksgiving. Subsequent puffs may be given to the directions, or motioned against oneself for a purification. If one is smoking with others, the Pipe is passed sunwise around the circle, stem first. It may be passed moonwise (counterclockwise) when the gathering is for mourning and/or at night, the New Moon, when *heyoka* (sacred contrary people) are leading the ceremony or when only women are participating in it. As each person receives it from the individual to her or his right, it is turned one more time before smoking. When it comes back around the circle to the first person, that individual smokes it down to ash.

One does not usually inhale the smoke of the Sacred Pipe. Usually it is simply taken in one's mouth and then gently expelled. One may pray aloud (or silently) as one releases the smoke. If one chooses not to partake of the Pipe as it goes around the circle, one should take the Pipe, raise it skyward for a moment, stem pointing upward and outward, then pass it along. Sometimes people inhale it if they are sick or need "medicine" for some reason. As the Pipe is smoked, a tamper (usually a small cylinder of wood—but any clean, small stick will do nicely) is used to push the tobacco down so it burns well. The extension of pipestone past the bowl is sometimes pressed into Grandmother Earth, so the stem can be angled upward, and the Creator can continue to smoke while the ceremony continues (among most nations, the presence of this extension is what differentiates the Sacred Pipe from a pleasure pipe). Often, however, the Pipe is simply passed until the tobacco is completely burned, or the Pipe carrier finishes it after everyone else has partaken. Once the tobacco has been thoroughly burned, the ash is gently (pipestone is soft!)

tapped or blown out, and the Pipe is cleaned and put away with great care, usually wrapped with sage in red cloth.

When you smoke the Sacred Pipe, think as you take in the smoke that you are breathing in the thoughts of others, welcoming them in among your own thoughts. Then, as you hold your breath, you reflect on these thoughts, so they become part of you. Then you breathe out your own thoughts and reflections, as a tobacco gift in return for sacred balance, a Sacred Giveaway. In this way, we unite through the interplay of thought and spirit with all living beings in all times and places—*Hau! Mitaquye oyashin!* (Ho! All my relations—Amen!) The Sacred Pipe, like the Sacred Stone People's Lodge, is a vehicle that takes us through all time and space.

In the most sacred sense, there is only one Sacred Pipe—just as there is only one Torah, one Last Supper, one Qur'an, and one Guru Granth Sahib. There are many Torah scrolls, for instance, but they are all representations of the one Torah. What appear to be many pipes carried by many people are all aspects of the original one, given by the White Buffalo Calf Woman and still carefully preserved on the Pine Ridge Reservation. In fact, even that one, *lela wakan* (very sacred) though it is, is just a physical object, and, like all the other aspects of it, it is a "reality check" that reminds us of the most sacred gift that the Woman brought us, the *Spirit Pipe*. The Spirit Pipe is not carried by some individual on Pine Ridge, but rather is something we all are responsible for respectfully carrying inwardly.

Carving a Sacred Pipe, like weaving a blanket or carving a tool from wood, is a *washte* activity consisting of the frequent repetition of basic actions that the body easily memorizes. The physical object that results, therefore, is in a sense, *washte*, but more importantly it is a robe for the *lela wakan* Spirit Pipe, just as our bodies are robes for our spirits. It eventually wears out and must be replaced, but its outer form of pipe represents *Pipe*, the Spirit Pipe, which is eternal.

Displaying a Sacred Pipe by itself in a museum or private collection, out of the cultural context of spirituality, is like taking a bucket of water from a mighty river and displaying it as a representation of the rushing torrent from which it came. A Sacred Pipe, like any ceremony or spiritual practice, is in fact nothing at all, unless the spirit is present in it. There is a parallel here to Platonic philosophy: a physical pipe is an embodiment of the ιδεα (*idea*), the "eternal form" of Sacred Pipe.

I recall one Grandmother telling me how, when she was young, she was fostered to a European-American couple. They would not let her speak her own language; they gave her a new Christian name and new European-style clothing. And they took from her all the sacred things that she carried, which had been given to her to carry by her grandfather, Moses Shango, a great medicine man in the nineteenth century. She had promised him that she would pray in the traditional way every day, and was very upset by this turn of events. But Grandfather came to her in a dream and said, "Do not weep, my child; you do not need the physical pipe. All you need to do is shut your eyes and visualize carefully taking the Pipe out, putting the pieces together, filling it carefully with tobacco offered to the Seven Directions, turning it in the proper way, and offering your prayers with visible breath." She followed his instructions—and, of course, her foster parents were none the wiser that she was still following the medicine path. I have talked with Native American prisoners who have likewise continued faithfully to walk their spiritual path by smoking the Spirit Pipe in their spirits, even in the Big House.

The physical Sacred Pipe some of us carry is just a physical representation of the Spirit Pipe, to help us to smoke the Spirit Pipe in our souls. Similarly, all *wakan* physical objects (Sacred Pipe, Sacred Drum, Sacred Rattle, and so on) are a "reality check" to help us evoke the spiritual objects. Anybody can go through the physical motions of smoking the Sacred Pipe, but unless we mean it with our souls, the motions themselves are hollow and fruitless. If we smoke the Spirit Pipe in our souls, then we are *truly* praying a good prayer.

The Drum and the Flute are sacred because they give expression to our inmost nature and to the nature of the world around us. The Drum evokes the beating of our heart and the rhythm of the days, moons and seasons, while the Flute evokes the flowing of our breath and voice and the songs of the wind and river. Music and dance both comprise the heartbeat and the breath—the beat and the phrase. When we dance, we fly up like eagles into Grandfather Sky, the land of visions, and our feet touch down again onto Grandmother Earth, touching not just on the drum's downbeat, but with her heartbeat. Our movements and our melodies are based on the breath of Grandmother Earth: a phrase, an inhalation, a phrase, an inhalation.

European instruments are based on a scale of notes ultimately derived from the harmonics of a vibrating string. However, this natural scale has been replaced since Bach's day with an unnatural scale based on tonal compromises so instruments can be played together in any key, in the fine polyphonic musical tradition that originated in that continent. From the perspective of that musical heritage, the scales of traditional peoples' instruments worldwide sound off key—because they are derived from the intrinsic nature of instruments, and no compromise is made. Every instrument, from Drum to Flute, is allowed to sing with its own personal scale. This varies from individual instrument to instrument even of the same type, as the maker allows it to find its own music—its own voicing, to use the technical term. The overall result is that ensemble playing in the European sense is not really possible, which is appropriate, since the instruments are carriers of the *wakan*, and the *wakan* is by nature solitary. These natural instruments *do* harmonize with the natural sounds of the environment—the wind through the trees, the rushing of the stream, the cries of the birds. All voices of our elder sisters and brothers, like those of traditional instruments, being natural, are likewise *wakan*.

Different nations make different kinds of drums. Drums, of course, are found worldwide, and many cultures use them in sacred ways. I know African and African-descended people who carry, for instance, the traditional *dhumbek*, which is an open-ended clay pot with a head made of skin. Japanese Zen Buddhists, like the Nipponzan Myohoji, with whom I've had conversations, use a small hand-drum in their peace practice.

In the Native North American tradition, there are individual drums, often called tom-toms or hand-drums in the modern culture, and council drums. These differ mainly in size; the latter are so large that they are suspended from a frame. A group of people (most often just men, but some are mixed gender or all-woman, depending on the spirit of the particular drum) sits around a council drum, striking it rhythmically with beaters while singing traditional songs. This, for me, is a powerful spiritual experience; I often find myself going into a trancelike state, deeply aware of the heart of the drum beating while it sings through us.

Indeed, these council drums are very strong spirits. For some thirty years, the intertribal Native American community of which I'm a part has carried a magnificent drum, first blessed by Crow Dog, and still speaking with a powerful and eloquent voice. Its voice is slower and quieter than no doubt was once the case, but you can easily hear the wisdom in it when we strike it. Recently, our Cloudbreakers' Society acquired a new drum, saving the old drum for special ceremonies. This new drum doesn't have the same aged authority, but it does have the vitality of youth. Our beaters bounce with a new vigor, and the songs come out faster and more vibrantly: here, palpably, is a different personality. And I was pleased to meet the drum-maker, from the

Thunder Bay region of Ontario, and find that he clearly makes drums not only with an artisan's care, but also with a great deal of prayer and smudging. Some day this new drum will also age, and will give forth the same quieter wisdom of the older drum. Physical drums age, just as do all other robes for spirits, including our own bodies—but the spirit in the Drum, like the spirit in other physical robes, goes on.

Individual drums are carried and struck by one person alone. I still have a drum that I made myself. I made it for the *Hanblecheyapi* (The Vision Crying Ceremony). It has nearly fallen apart, but I still love it, even if it is no longer really usable. I've told you the story of how, several years ago, an honored Tsalagi (Cherokee) brother made a new drum for me to carry, also in the Plains style of rawhide stretched over a circular wooden frame and held in place with sinew. He told me the Grandmothers and Grandfathers had instructed him to make me a drum, though I had not said anything to him about needing one—indeed, we had not yet even met. The one I made is decorated with symbols of the Red and Blue Roads, of the Twelve Sacred Mountains (in black), and has the circle of the Sun near the periphery. The one the Tsalagi brother made for me to carry has an Eagle design on it, brought out of the natural pigments in the hide.

Think about the Sacred Drum. It is a circle. That circle should call to mind the *Changleshka Wakan*, the Sacred Hoop of All the Nations, the Circle of Life, the circle of the horizon, the circles of the year and (lunar) month and so on. Everything we do is in a circle: we sit in our tipi or wigwam in a circle, we sit in the Sacred Stone People's Lodge in a circle, we dance around the pole for the Sun Dance in a circle. The circle of the drum reminds us of all these things.

The physical objects we carry are reminders of the One Drum, *Chan Chega*, the Sacred Drum, that never ceases to beat in the Spirit World. The physical drum is made of wood and rawhide (plants and animals) and often decorated with feathers and other things, as is a two-headed drum I also carry. As with the Sacred Pipe, the materials of the drum bring all things into it, and so all things speak through it when it speaks.

The drums we carry are alive with the spirit of the one Sacred Drum. If you carry a drum, I advise you to take good care of it and to feed it. Give it tobacco (place tobacco to the sacred directions around the drumhead, and/or put some inside) from time to time; it likes that. Keep it in good condition. And thank it—a traditional way to give it your thanks is to touch the beater to the drumhead and move it around in a small sunwise circle, perhaps preceding or following this with a small, silent tap.

The Sacred Drum speaks in the First Language. Therefore, not only does it speak with the voice of all living things, but it also speaks with the voice of the Creator. When first we were conceived inside our mother's womb, the first sound we heard was our mother's heartbeat. The drum speaks with the heartbeat of our Great Mother. It is not you making the sound of the drum; rather, the drum is speaking by itself. The drum and its voice are sacred.

In the First Language, the word is the same as the thing itself, and every word is a world of wisdom. For this reason the Sacred Drum, like all *wakan* things, can evoke the shapechanging magic, and can take us to other times, other places, even other dimensions and planets. This magic occurs most often when the person or persons playing the drum brings out certain special rhythms, but it can occur at any time, whether we wish it or not, if the Sacred Drum wishes it. Because the Sacred Drum is associated with the North, it can bring to us the voices of our ancestors, who are still alive, their hearts beating in the universe around us.

For these reasons, people should not engage in idle chatter when *Chan Chega* is speaking. People should listen respectfully, or chant with it, or dance with it, and be prepared to go wherever it takes them, for it can bring healing. Once at a Native gathering down in Georgia, I saw a Kiowa man who was pretty seriously drunk. He stumbled and shambled over to the fire where I was sitting with some other people. The *sicha* of his polluted spirit made us uncomfortable. We became even more uncomfortable when he sat down and picked up the drum I carry and started beating on it. At first there was no appreciable rhythm to his haphazard banging, and I considered getting up and taking it away from him lest he disrespect it and himself. In a sign-language conversation I had with the people with me, we agreed that this was necessary. But then the drum spoke. The sacred rhythm manifested itself, so far as we could tell, of its own accord. The drum ministered to him. It healed him. He sobered up. He started talking about his pain, and the pain of his people, in an incredibly moving way. We embraced him. I was in tears. So were we all.

If you carry the Sacred Drum, get to know it; listen to it. Try beating it without conscious thought, and letting it give you a drum song. Beat the center. Move to the edge. Beat the middle of the stick against the edge. Listen to the different timbres. Try swirling the beater on the drumhead. Try turning the drum to different angles. Listen to the different voices with which it speaks.

If you know a good traditional teacher, perhaps she or he will share with you a drum song. (Remember these drum songs are sacred, and are not the "property" of the elder, but a sacred trust, which they carry for the people. If the elder says no, accept that. Whether the elder says yes or no, be sure to give a tobacco gift.)

A dear Abenaki-descended friend of mine was instructed by an honored Grandfather we both knew and loved in the making of the Sacred Flute. My friend took months of careful work in the making, for it meant learning more than simply crafting a wooden object, but the spirituality of the Sacred Flute. This instrument was made in the traditional Anishinabe (Ojibweh) style, fashioned from wood, with a small, adjustable piece of wood to split the airstream. The process of hollowing it and tuning it took him months, and he had to have a lot of faith as he carved it out that his incisions would bring it truly to life.

I myself carry a flute made by a Tsalagi (Cherokee) elder in Tennessee, given to me by another dear friend, this one of Tsalagi ancestry. It is made of cedar, with floral designs carved into it. It is kept in a special deerskin flute bag decorated with fox fur. Though I did not make it myself, I carry it with great joy and honor.

Traditional Native American flutes are end-blown, with holes stopped by the fingers. They are unlike the classical European instrument, which, as a transverse flute, is sounded by blowing at an angle across the hole into the resonating chamber. The closest European equivalent to the Native American flute is the recorder. I find the flute tradition of this continent more similar to those of other traditional people, such as the bamboo flutes of the Pacific, one of which I happen to carry, or the shakuhachi of Japan.

Native American flutes are commonly made from wood, sometimes of two pieces that are grooved and glued together, and sometimes of one piece hollowed out with, for example, a stone drill or a glowing hot stone. Flutes can also be made from hardened clay, reed, or other such materials. One important traditional flute is the eagle bone flute made by the Plains Nations to be employed during the *Wiwanyag Wachipi* (Sun Dance).

If you carry a flute, I recommend you do so with care and respect. As with the Sacred Drum, the other most important instrument, the Sacred Flute should be honored with sacred respect. Traditional peoples believe the flute, like the drum, is sleeping when it is not being played. Therefore we should awaken it carefully when it is time for it to sing, and we should put it away with equal care so it will sleep comfortably. For this reason we take it, or the drum, gently and slowly out of its coverings, as if we were rousing someone from sleep. We always ask its permission before we play it and listen with our spirit to ensure we have it. We also always thank it afterwards, perhaps by giving tobacco to express our appreciation. And we also always treat the flute with great care so it will remain healthy. In other words, we should think of it and treat it (like all things, especially those we consider sacred) not as an article or possession, but as a living being, as an elder; moreover, as a teacher.

One can learn to play traditional songs that have been passed down the seven generations in one or many nations. One may learn these songs either from elders or (if there is no other choice) from some of the commercially recorded tapes that are available—but be aware that many recorded songs are not genuine traditional songs. (Though that is not to say they are not worth learning; if you find yourself drawn to one, if it "speaks" to you, by all means, learn it and play it!) If you learn a traditional song, give tobacco in thanks for the gift and for the trust put in you, and play it with respect and honor, especially to the ancestors who brought it to you, and to Grandmother Earth and all her children who hear you play.

I have heard traditional songs of the dominant culture played in a Native American fashion on traditional flutes, and this can be effective and is not necessarily wrong. This is most commonly done with hymn tunes. "Amazing Grace" was adopted by the Tsalagi (Cherokee) as their national anthem, and was sung during the Trail of Tears, when a large portion of that nation was forced out of their traditional land in the Carolinas and into Oklahoma. Remember when you play it that the words were composed by John Newton, a slave ship captain who had a miraculous change of heart. It is an exceptionally good hymn to play on the traditional flute.

Another wonderful thing you can do is to learn songs from our sisters and brothers of other living nations. Songs can be taught to you by the birds, the frogs, the crickets, the katydids, even by the wind soughing through the trees or rocks. I have heard recordings of whale and porpoise songs, and have often thought they would be beautiful to play on the flute, though I have never tried. But certainly our feathered sisters and brothers have the vastest tradition of songs, and they are glad to teach them to us as long as we are patient and quiet enough to learn.

It is also a very good thing to try playing the flute you carry by simply letting the spirit of the flute give you its own inner songs. As I said, we believe the flute is sleeping when it is not being played, and in its dreams it is playing sacred songs our physical ears cannot hear—just as the Grandfather Rocks dream dreams for thousands of years until they come glowing into the lodge and we can see their dreams within. We also believe that the *nagipi*, the spirit beings, can teach us songs. If you wish to hear and learn the flute's own songs, or the songs of the *nagipi*, let your mind relax, let your breathing be gentle and easy, and let your fingers play freely. If you allow yourself to enter a meditative spirit in which you don't try to control the flute but let it speak for itself, the flute may give you its own music.

When you play the flute, think of *the flute* as doing the singing, not as you making it (forcing it to) sing. Think of the flute as your Grandfather or Grandmother, and of yourself as the flute's grandchild, as its servant, its student, assisting it to sing. Assist humbly, gratefully listening to its wisdom. Just as we living today tell stories which we learned from our Grandfathers and Grandmothers who have since dropped their robes, thereby giving them voice through our own voices, so too we give the Sacred Flute voice by breathing into it. The flute is the breath of the people.

The Sacred Flute, like the Sacred Pipe and Sacred Drum and all other sacred objects, combines fullness and emptiness. It is the emptiness within it that enables it to sing for us, and it is the precise balance of emptiness to fullness that makes it sing best. For this reason you will see the most expert flutemakers, those who work closest with the spirits, taking utmost care to put the finger holes in the right places, and painstakingly sanding minute amounts of wood away to bring out the tone of the flute as fully and perfectly as possible.

The Sacred Flute has a special relationship with the Sacred Pipe, in that we breathe through both of them. It is a complementary similarity: we exhale through the Sacred Flute, and inhale through the Sacred Pipe. Because of this similarity, it is good if we carry both and listen to and learn from each of them.

Playing the Sacred Flute can help us meditate. Like chanting, drumming, fasting, dancing, sweating and so on, it enables us to break through, out of the *washte*, the realm of mundane human society, and into the *wakan*, the spiritual realm. The songs it sings for us help us to walk the Red Road better, accompanied by the Grandfathers and Grandmothers, feathered elders, *nagipi*, or whoever else gave us these sacred songs.

The Sacred Flute, like the Sacred Drum, is also a healer. We cannot play it well if we are distraught, so it forces us to modulate our breath and to calm down. More than that, its vibrations sink deep into us when we play, and bring back our own natural rhythms when we are out of sorts. Realizing this, a healer can use the Sacred Flute to bring healing to others. While I do not know much about this myself, I have seen it done, and have a few times tried this healing technique.

The Sacred Flute, as I mentioned, is used in ceremony, such as in the Sun Dance. It is also often a part of the Sacred Stone People's Lodge Ceremony, and those who go up on the hill for the Vision Crying Ceremony may take a flute along. The Sacred Flute, like the Sacred Drum, can evoke powerful medicine, including enabling us to change our robe (physical appearance), and take us to other times and other places, even other worlds.

Today, when a man falls in love with a woman he often woos her by getting a radio station to play a recorded song in her honor over the air. But in the old days he would sneak up near her home in the darkness of night and play the Sacred Flute for her, letting the sacred magic of a love song weave itself into the weft of her dreaming. Did she perhaps partly awaken during the night and lie in her blankets listening to the song? Did she go about the next day looking at all the handsome men and wonder which one it was who had played for her in the darkness? Or perhaps did she not consciously know what sacred magic was performed during the night? Only the Sacred Flute would know for certain, and it would only tell its children when the time was right.

One of the most important and sacred things a person can carry is the Sacred Pipe. It is normally carried by the ceremonialist. Sometimes this person is called the Medicine Chief, or "water pourer" (the one who leads the Sacred Stone People's Lodge ceremony) of a band. If the ceremonialist carries the Sacred Pipe (and other sacred things too, no doubt), then what does the Chief carry? The Chief carries the Sacred Talking Stick.

The Sacred Talking Stick is as sacred in its way as the Pipe. Neither should ever take precedence over the other. Both represent the Sacred Hoop of All the Nations. Just as the Pipe is turned around as one smokes it, and goes around the circle if there is more than one person smoking it, so too the Sacred Talking Stick goes around the circle whenever there is a discussion of important matters.

Someone who carries the Sacred Talking Stick should be a person who assiduously seeks consensus and is determined to ensure that every person has her or his say during that quest. The person should be just as much above reproach as a Pipe Carrier. The person should carry the Sacred Talking Stick with the same care and respect that is accorded the Sacred Pipe.

I have seen Sacred Talking Sticks of many descriptions. There is far more variety to their physical nature than there is to the Sacred Pipe. Often they have wooden handles wrapped with skin or fur, on the other end of which are artful arrangements of feathers, fur, stones on threads and the like. A Hodenasaunee (Iroquois Confederacy) Talking Stick I've seen is a rectangular block of white pine (to represent the sacred White Roots of Peace, which calls to mind the Hodenasaunee Constitution, the *Kaienerekowa*, the Great Law of Peace). It was about one inch square by one foot and decorated with sacred drawings. An Abenaki Talking Stick I carry is a piece of sacred ash, with the tips bent to form circles, to represent the Sacred Hoop in its many manifestations. I've heard that some Mic-Macs carry a Talking Feather, which reminds them to speak gently lest they blow it away, and that the Suquamish use a Sacred Talking Stick six feet long—with the understanding that one may talk only as long as one can hold it up in the air—a good way to minimize long-winded speech-making! I've heard it said that certain nations, including I think the Anishinabeg, make Sacred Talking Sticks from the same wood that they use for flutes, with the idea that the words people say while holding them should be soft and melodious and conducive to healing.

When not in use, Sacred Talking Sticks should be kept wrapped in a sacred bundle, surrounded with sage and cedar. Whenever the band meets in council, the Chief should take the Sacred Talking Stick out. Everyone present should be smudged, and the Sacred Talking Stick as well. After the Chief offers a prayer, the Sacred Talking Stick is passed sunwise around the circle of the band. As it comes to each person's hand, that person "has the floor," and everyone gives her or him their undivided prayerful attention. If that person has nothing to say aloud, he or she should still hold it for a moment, and let silence be the statement. If that person asks you a question, or if you feel a strong urge to reply to something said, wait patiently until the Sacred Talking Stick comes around to you before replying. By the time it comes to you, someone else may have said what you wanted to say (and perhaps better than you), or you may find, upon inner reflection, that what you wanted at first to say was ill-advised. The Sacred Talking Stick continues to go around in this manner (with the Chief praying, at least silently, every time it passes through her or his hands) until the consensus is that everything that needs to be said has been said—just as the Sacred Pipe is smoked until the tobacco has been burned completely to ash. Then the Sacred Talking Stick should be put away with the same respectful care given to the Sacred Pipe.

Obviously, to counsel with each other in this manner calls for great patience and great listening skills. The Sacred Talking Stick itself helps us to learn these important skills. Whether you're holding the Sacred Talking Stick or not, you should at all times during this ceremony be actively listening. When it is in your hands, you're listening within to Spirit speaking, not just the great and impressive sound of your own words; when it is in others' hands, you're listening not just to their words, but always to Spirit as well. Words, remember, are but a robe that Spirit wears.

The relationship between Sacred Pipe and Sacred Talking Stick is an important one. One might think of the Sacred Pipe as *wakan* and the Sacred Talking Stick as *washte.* If the band's Pipe Carrier has received a powerful message from the Grandfathers and Grandmothers through the Pipe, she or he should bring it to the Sacred Talking Stick Carrier (the Chief) and ask for a council. At the council, the Pipe Carrier should sit to the Chief's left, and, once the Sacred Talking Stick has been handed to him or her by the Chief, speak first about what has been said through the Pipe. Never, however, should what has been given through the Pipe be misused to squelch full and free discussion in council.

If there is no such message given ahead of time through the Pipe, then the Pipe Carrier should still sit to the Chief's left and, after the Talking Stick has been passed to everyone's content, the Pipe should then be passed in the sacred way around the circle. This act both ratifies the agreement that has been reached in council, and allows the band to be sure the Grandfathers and Grandmothers concur with the decision reached.

For the traditional peoples of this continent, the Sacred Rattle is considered something very powerful and holy. The main purpose of rattles is to call the spirit beings. All other purposes are basically extensions of that primary one. The Sacred Rattle is made of any natural chamber, affixed to a handle of some sort, with seeds or small stones placed inside it. Not uncommonly the rattle is decorated with such things as stones, feathers, pigments or carving. Rattles are made from materials such as dried gourd, turtle shell, hardened rawhide, hardened bladder, seashell, horn or bone. You will note that almost all of these natural chambers are from animals; therefore the presence of the animal nation is invoked when the rattle is used.

Seeds or stones (or sometimes small shells) are put into the chamber. Seeds invoke the plant nations; shells the sea nations and stones the earth nations. Best, of course, is to put seeds in animal-based chambers, or shells in plant-based chambers, or stones in either, so that as many nations as possible bring their medicine into the rattle. The nations of the Eastern Woodlands favor dried kernels of corn, to honor the Sacred Corn Woman. I have heard that the Southwestern Desert nations also use corn to honor Changing Woman, who is her equivalent. The handle, too, may come from the plant nations (wood) or the animal nations (bone or a preserved leg). So you see that the Sacred Rattle, like the Sacred Pipe and the Sacred Stone People's Lodge, is made from four sacred things—animal materials, plant materials, stone materials, and spirit materials.

Besides representing the plant nations, seeds suggest *potential*, the future, new beginnings. The seeds are sitting in darkness within the chamber, just as sitting in the darkness beneath the soil they harbor their potential during the winter, before resurrecting in the spring. But this darkness inside the rattle is a special darkness, reminding us of the darkness of the spiritual path, the darkness of the path on which we walk by seeing with our heart (*chantë ishta*). Rattles also invoke the *wakan* healing presence of the rattlesnake, whose venom is deadly yet a powerful healer, who is reborn every time it sloughs its old skin. The bringing together of materials from the animal and plant nations, combined with a chamber of darkness in which are found seeds of potential, evokes the kind of medicine associated with the Sacred Stone People's Lodge—in fact, the Sacred Rattle is, in effect, that ceremony in microcosm. For that reason, when the Sacred Rattle is invoked within the lodge, the medicine is especially powerful.

Just as with the Sacred Drum, there are several rhythms that can be offered with the Sacred Rattle. But where the sound of the former reminds us of the beating of the heart, the sound of the latter invokes the power of the storm. The rattle can be shaken vertically, using the wrist, to sound like driving rain or hail, or it can be spun in a circular motion with the wrist to create a constant hissing sound like a steady rain or snow. You can also shake it vertically with your wrist while, at the same time, your arm moves it in a rotating orbit parallel to the ground. If you are sitting in a circle (in the Sacred Stone People's Lodge, for instance), each person in the circle will hear the powerful sound of the rattle repeatedly coming and going right in front of her or his face, just as happens when wind whips the storm around.

The Sacred Rattle can be used thus over a sick person, to bring spiritual cleansing or to nurture healing, by calling spirit beings to cure and protect. Certainly the Sacred Rattle is something a healer will want to have among her or his tools, along with herbs, sacred stones and feathers, and so on, as all these things work together very well for healing. The same circular motion might also be offered over a person needing healing, who is lying down on Mother Earth. In either case the sound will seem to come from everywhere and nowhere, just as during a powerful thunderstorm.

All these factors together help us see how the Sacred Rattle calls the spirit beings. The seeds in the darkness, the invocation of animal and plant nations, the invocation of the sacred woman, and the sound of the rain and wind all suggest the spirit beings whose presence is *wakan.* A gentle rain promotes growth in Mother Earth's children, and the circular wrist motion invokes such nurture. A fierce storm cleanses Mother Earth's children, and the vertical wrist motion, like the straight lines of driving rain or lightning, invokes those aspects of nature. The Sacred Rattle can be used to invoke the Thunder Beings, as sometimes is done during the Sacred Stone People's Lodge, circling the rattle around in the fierce darkness, shaking it hard like lightning while a Thunder Being song is sung.

Masks are found throughout the world. In the European culture alone, they are most commonly used to hide identity. Robbers and spies often wear them; on Halloween and at costume parties, people wear masks to tantalize others with their anonymity. Elsewhere in the world, however, the purpose is entirely different.

Sacred Faces—to use a different term to denote the different purpose— are used in tribal traditions, both in Turtle Island and elsewhere in the world, not to hide ordinary identity, but to evoke sacred identity. Faces used in the Nōh dramas of Japan, classical Greek theatre, and in classical Mithraism, like the ceremonial faces of Africa and New Guinea are or were all made and used for this sacred purpose. Among the Pagans of pre-Christian Europe, Sacred Faces served this sacred purpose at Samhain, to evoke or honor the dead, the gods and goddesses, the fey, or other creatures of Nature; a last vestige of this remains in Halloween costumes.

Traditional peoples believe that there is a two-way relationship between our spirits and our experiences. We create our own reality, and our reality creates us. The nature of our spirit, therefore, is a major determinant of the nature of the world around us. If we are happy within, we will be happy even if our environment is austere or adverse. If we are unhappy within, no amount of pleasant things in our environment will make us happy. In everything you do as you walk the Red Road, if you walk in harmony with your world, at peace with yourself, you will have happiness within, and therefore happiness will be likelier without.

Sacred Faces are like windows in the same way that medicine shields are: they help us to see the sacredness within ourselves and within the world around us. A person will do things wearing a mask that he or she would never do as an "ordinary person." This is because the mask represents and welcomes a sacred being who comes to the person, or helps to evoke one who is implicitly present within the person, and who enables the person to do very sacred and powerful things. These things are not of our *washte* ordinary world, but of the *wakan* realm: dangerous and holy things that lead to healing.

The Onodowahgah (Seneca) word *gagosa* means "face," referring to the sacred face of the Left-Hand Twin who was vanquished by the Right-Hand Twin and made to promise to help humanity. Those cured by the rituals of the False Face Society are customarily invited to become members of it. The society's rituals are traditionally performed at the New Year and Green Corn Festivals.

The faces are carefully carved directly from living basswood trees, without harming the trees. They are painted black, red, or black and red. They have large eyes, often of pressed-in metal, with pupil-holes. The mouth and nose are exaggerated and distorted, often with a few large snaggly teeth and/or lolling tongue. A long hank of hair always hangs down the face. The particular form of the face comes from a dream the person has had. I spent some time recently with a Mohawk-Blackfoot Grandmother who was close to the time of dropping her robe, and I realized that her face now looked like a Sacred Face, twisted, with one tooth left, and her hair long and stringy. In the eyes of some she may have appeared to have lost all her appeal, but to the eyes of spirit she was ever so beautiful with all the wisdom she carried.

Besides the *gagosa*, carved from the basswood trees, there are also the *gadisa*, made from straw, which are used only at the New Year. A Onodowahgah (Seneca) elder descended from Cornplanter told me how, traditionally, four men wearing the *gadisa* would bring the message of the New Year to the longhouse. They came, he said, from the Land of the Burning Stumps. While running from the East door to the West door of the longhouse, they would tell the Chief what was to happen in the near future. Then the Chief would raise the pole on the door, allowing them to depart. They would dance and then disappear.

These Sacred Faces are considered alive. When not in use, they are hung facing the wall or wrapped in red cloth and put away in a safe place. They are occasionally "fed" by smearing a thick gruel of parched cornmeal with maple sugar on their lips. They are also often wiped with sunflower seed oil to help "keep their skin soft." Old ones, thus, will have a bright shine from many such applications. Each one has a name and personality; it is always addressed as "Grandfather." They are often talked or sung to.

Sacred Faces have the same ceremonial power as nakedness: they are a symbolic way of temporarily putting aside our *washte* selves, putting aside our physical bodies in a symbolism of death and a welcoming of the *wakan* beyond mortal existence. Sacred Faces serve as windows, making our robes, our bodies, spiritually transparent so our spirits can likewise flow freely. Freed from the constraints of *washte* societal norms, the spirits within are fully released. When ceremonially naked or wearing Sacred Faces, or both, one finds the spirit enables us to speak and do things that we would not "normally" say or do.

Sacred Faces are another way to listen to the Grandfathers and Grand-mothers, and to learn from them. They help us to cleanse our inner spirits, and to bring healing to ourselves and others. Even if you yourself do not carry a Sacred Face, you can still learn from them that it is important to recognize the sacred powers, the *wakan*, within yourself and not be afraid to let it come out when appropriate for healing and cleansing—to follow what spirit wants you to do, especially in ceremonial contexts, even if it seems strange or socially inappropriate.

It is not Native American custom to use shields in war, as they were among the Xhosa, Zulu, Europeans and Japanese during their respective feudal ages. The Sacred Shields of Turtle Island traditionally are a part of one's spiritual life. A medicine shield is, in a sense, one's Medicine Wheel. That is why they are cir-cular: they remind us of all the circles in our lives: the horizon, the cycles of the Moon, the year, the day and the cycle of our lives.

They represent the juncture between the spiritual and physical worlds. You might think of a medicine shield as a window enabling us to look through to the spiritual world, and enabling the *nagipi* (spirit beings) to look through the other way, into the physical world. Do medicine shields mediate between two worlds? I am speaking of two worlds, but, in the traditional view, there is no separation. The traditional view sees spirit as the groundroot of reality, though spirits often take up residence for a time in physical forms.

Medicine shields can be made in many different ways, but a common way is to make a circle from a stripped willow branch, and stretch a skin or hide on it. The skin or hide is then decorated with pictures, beads, feathers, stones or whatever the person is directed through dreams or visions to put on it. I carry one of this type, with birchbark instead of skin, that was made by one of my brothers-by-honor. Another way is to decorate a turtle's shell—in honor of Turtle Island, and the Sacred Stone People's Lodge, which takes the form of a turtle. I carry one of this kind as well, made by an honored brother who studied with a Hodenasaunee (Iroquois Confederacy) medicine man. The skin-over-wood and turtle shell varieties both evoke the turtle-shaped skin-over-wood structure of the Sacred Stone People's Lodge.

These shields are often used in ceremonies. They are, for instance, put on a staff outside the lodge during the Sacred Stone People's Lodge Ceremony or at the entrance to the circle in the Vision Crying Ceremony to tell the spirits who is there and to give the spirits a gate into this world. They may be displayed at socials and traditional dances. A person may go off alone with her or his medicine shield and pray with it, using it as a focus for good strong spirit prayers.

Each medicine bundle is entirely personal and sacred. There is only one medicine bundle whose contents I am familiar with, and about its contents I cannot tell you. Nobody teaches you how to make one, since it is a matter between you and the medicine you carry (spirits, sacred animals, Grandfathers, Grandmothers, etc.). But I can give you some general guidelines.

No artificial ingredients go in it. Steer clear of "New Age" materials, or anything of other traditions than that of the Red Road, unless specifically directed to do so by Spirit. You want to put in it things that keep you connected with your ancestors, your teachers, your medicine animals and your loved ones. You will want things that you use for healing. Medicine bundles should *never* contain materials made from your medicine animal. That would dilute the sacred power the bags carry. Everything should be purified and blessed. One good way is to put things on *Unchi*, the Sacred Mound outside the Sacred Stone People's Lodge, during the ceremony. Another way is to leave things out on a rock under the Full Moon or during a good thunderstorm on a regular basis. And you should have lots of tobacco (a spiritual "conductor"), cedar (a spiritual "insulator"), and sage (a spiritual "filter") in the bundle.

Think of the medicine bundle as alive. Work with it, listen to it. And, like a living creature, it will ingest and egest: things will come to you from time to time that are to be added, and you will likewise be moved to take things out of it and give them to people who need them (for example, for healing), or to offer them as Sacred Giveaway when you receive a teaching vision.

The Lakota word for medicine bundle is *washichun*, which is very similar to *washichu*, which means a greedy person. I will talk more about this later, but, for now, suffice it to say that this fact should remind us to be very humble in carrying a medicine bundle.

Oneida deer hoof rattle.
(See pages 200–02).

IX

Sacred Ceremonies

THERE IS NOTHING MORE HOLY in this tradition than the gift of the Beautiful Woman, the Sacred Pipe. In certain sacred ways it brings in the presence of all living things, and its smoke, in rising up to the Creator, binds together Heaven and Earth. It is always smoked in a circle, and turned in a circle before and after smoking, such that all living things are a part of one's prayer. It is essential to all the great ceremonies and is itself the greatest ceremony.

To teach about the Pipe is to teach about prayer. One cannot teach about the one without teaching about the other. Our prayers are made not just for ourselves, but with and for all living creatures. Prayer is not so much petitionary, as it is in the Western religions, but creative visualization, as Maxwell Maltz taught, and a thanking for a gift to be given in response to our own giving. As the smoke of the Sacred Pipe rises, our prayers of believing, knowing, visualizing and thanking—the four stages by which spirit takes on being—rise up to the Grandfathers and Grandmothers.

Remember when you pray that it is not *a* Sacred Pipe you lift up, but *the* Sacred Pipe. Remember that all the hands of everyone who has ever raised the Pipe are raising it with you—all your ancestors and descendants, all your teachers, and their teachers, right back to the Beautiful One herself. Remember that you are surrounded by all the Sacred Hoop. Approach this Pipe with respect, and remember that you are praying in the presence of the Creator.

The way of the *Chanunpa Wakan* (Sacred Pipe) varies slightly from nation to nation and carrier to carrier within the same nation, in words and to some degree in the sacred actions done. Here is what I do. I take the Chanunpah out of the wrappings carefully and assemble it respectfully, turn it four times, and then put it down on red cloth on the Earth. Then I light sage and smudge the Chanunpah and myself.

Next, I take a small pinch of tobacco for each of the Seven Directions, offering them in turn to that direction and saying a short prayer to the spirits of that direction, then place the tobacco in the pipe. For zenith, I circle the pinch sunwise against the Sky. For nadir, I circle the pinch sunwise against the Earth and give part of the pinch to the Earth. For the Sacred Direction, I hold the pinch to my heart. When the Chanunpah is filled, I put on top of the tobacco a bit of sage leaf, called a sage plug, to keep everything pure. Then I lift it and turn it four times again, after which I hold it stem outward toward the West, and sing the medicine song that was given to me. (I was taught to do this very quietly, since it's just between me and the spirits.)

At this point, if it is not to be shared immediately, it can be leaned against an altar (usually the Buffalo Altar, such as outside the Sacred Stone People's Lodge), with the extension of the bowl going into the Earth. When the time comes to smoke it, it is shared going sunwise around the circle, with each person turning it once sunwise before smoking. People don't have to partake; if they don't actually take any smoke, they can just lift it stem outward toward the Heavens. Smoke is normally just taken into the mouth, but sometimes people take it into their lungs for courage, healing or deep prayer. Individuals may smudge with it (draw the smoke in with their hands) if they wish. I'm probably making it sound way too complicated. Grandfather taught me to keep it simple, and he tended to frown on those who make this and other ceremonies highly liturgical, like ceremonies practiced in the dominant culture.

Among the traditional peoples, prayers are rarely memorized and repeated verbatim, but, rather, are offered spontaneously from the heart. The teaching is the same as that which Jesus gave to his students, that prayers should be simple and eloquent, said more in private than in public, and directed to the Great Mystery—not at impressing those around us. I'm thinking, for example, of a simple Tsalagi (Cherokee) prayer: *Ogedoda Galun'lati ogadosgi, osda nuwati Elohino, yolda hoyona, wado.* (O Great One who dwells in the Sky illuminating all that is, giving Good Medicine of life and the Great Creation, our Mother Earth, knowing that all things are as they should be, we give thanks for the beauty of all things.) Or this little Lakota prayer: *Unshimala ye oyate wachin cha. Mitaquye oyashin.* (Take pity on all the people. All my relations [Amen].)

But prayers should be from the heart, not from books. Silently holding up the Sacred Pipe when it is passed to you, pointing the stem to the Sky and then touching it to the Earth; this is a good prayer! Medicine names should be used in praying (if one has one), because the sacred beings know us by those names. Employers, salespeople and bill collectors call me by my American culture "legal" name; friends know me by my traditional name; my most intimate friends and the spirits and medicine beings and the Creator know me by another name entirely.

As a conversation with sacred beings, prayer is an opportunity to talk about what's going on—just as one would with a living human elder—as well as to give thanks and to make petitions. Prayer is humbly asking respected elders, the spirits in the Heavens, to help us learn how to cope with our need. It is important to recognize that the spirits may know, better than we, that there is a similar need, for example, for rain elsewhere and whether that need supersedes our own.

Praying must be done in a way that maintains balances. If we are asking for something, we must give something too. In the morning, I give some tobacco to our mother, the Earth. Then, and then only, I say my prayers. When we sweat in the Sacred Stone People's Lodge, or give our skin at the Sun Dance, or give up our sleep and meals and our comfortable lives at the Vision Crying, we can make strong prayers, because we have made sacrifice.

As I understand it, the word "traditional" can be used in two ways. The first way is to refer to the mimicking of an ancient cultural practice—mere anachronism and entertainment, like the dances put on for tourists that have little historical root. It also includes mimicking the traditional ceremonies by memorizing and reciting a prayer found in a book. (If one echoes the words "with a good heart," as one elder taught, making them new in that moment, that is another matter.) Another variation is found in the archly pious, overly structured ceremonies that some people put on, trying to be ultra-purist and claiming that only one way of doing things is traditional. This ignores the constant free flow of Spirit in oral cultures, wherein traditions are never fixed by texts and constricted by hierarchy. The super-traditionalists leave no room for laughter or spontaneity or, least of all, for Spirit.

The second way to use the word "traditional," which I prefer, is to refer to a flow. I can invent or create a ceremony that's entirely original with me, but it is still traditional—because it flows naturally out of the training and cultural experience I have had and it partakes of the same artistic and magical wellsprings. There's a universality to the sacred ways. An elder of the Pagan traditions once said to me, "We perform our rituals *exactly* as our ancestors did: we make them up!"

What people often don't understand is that what happens in a "traditional" ritual is an actual reliving (not just a reenacting) of a mythic event—the parallel being to the understanding of Roman Catholic, Orthodox, and Episcopal Christians that the bread and wine at the Eucharist *literally* become the body and blood of Jesus Christ, rather than being a memorialization of the historic Last Supper. What occurs within the ritual reality can in fact change the tradition slightly—keeping the tradition living, without falling into extremes of either artifice or stultification. We aren't mimicking the lives of the Prototypical Ancestors—as Mircea Eliade well explains in his books—but *becoming* them. A ceremony is not necessarily going to flow every time exactly as it "historically" did. Just as a story told by a living person is alive, filled with Spirit, it's the *livingness* of true ceremony, true magic, that is essential.

For this reason it is perfectly acceptable to create a new ceremony for a specific purpose, as long as it is done in a respectful and traditional way. A woman I once knew who had never resolved her anger toward her deceased mother developed a private ceremony to alleviate that burden. These new ceremonies are most effective if they are not eclectic, if they use the "language" (the common symbols) of one heritage. One would be unlikely to center a new Native American ceremony around the Buddhist chant in homage to Kuan-Yin or the Shahadah of Islam, but it would be good to raise the Sacred Pipe during the ceremony, or offer a prayer to the Grandfathers and Grandmothers of the Seven Directions. On the other hand, I am delighted when the followers of other traditions come into the Sacred Stone People's Lodge and share some of their prayers or chants—I believe it helps in the healing of the Sacred Hoop.

There is a certain amount of controversy in Native American circles about whether ceremonial welcome should be shared with anyone who has little or no Native American ancestry. Ancestry should not be an issue. Those whom I have welcomed into the ceremonies are people whose calling to walk the Red Road is honorable and strong. I never exclude *anyone* who has a strong spiritual commitment to any sacred path—for, ultimately, all these paths seek the same Creator. I have been harshly criticized for this, but I have always been taught that the Sacred Hoop of All the Nations will never be repaired if exclusivism and denial are made the rule. I respect that there are those who sincerely disagree with me on this point, but I note that such great elders as Grandfather Tachcha Hushté (Lame Deer) held the same view I do. As one Grandfather I knew often said, "I care about the contents of your heart, not the contents of your pedigree." Before the Bureau of Indian Affairs made blood quantum an issue, leading to the current situation, in which many tribal governments use it as a criterion for enrollment, it was not an issue among the traditional peoples. As a friend said to me of those who would deny to mixed-bloods and non-Natives any right to walk the Red Road, "G-d help them if the White Buffalo Calf Woman should ever come back looking for the Pipe she gave the people. She'd probably tell them the same thing she told them in the first place: 'You people have lost the ways of respect.'" He is right. She gave to us the most sacred prayer of all, "*Mitaquye oyashin!*", which means "All my relations!"—not just those I approve of.

These are *wakan* ceremonies, and they are polluted when drugs or alcohol are involved, when money is required, when behavior is not impeccable. Moreover, since these are *wakan* ceremonies, their sacred power can be diluted by overuse, just as overuse of spices or healing herbs or medicines dilutes the intrinsic sacred power within them. When *washichu* indiscriminately and frequently hold sweat lodges, the very frequency tends to dissipate the sacred power for those who genuinely carry the ceremony.

I learned the dangers of overusing the sacred ceremonies when, at two different continent-wide gatherings of traditional peoples, I saw respected ceremonial leaders pour water for (lead) three or four traditional *Inipi* ceremonies in the same day. One, a highly respected Grandfather, poured for several very hot sweats in a gigantic lodge that held upwards of forty people. He had to be carried out of it after the last one, and his health declined after that day. The other, a man my age, was barely able to walk afterwards, half-crawling up the hill sometime after midnight to collapse in his tent. In both cases, it was as if they had taken too much powerful herbal medicine: the effects had gone beyond sacred into potentially dangerous.

Among traditional peoples worldwide, the philosophy is, as one Grandmother put it to me: "Let everything you do be a ceremony. Let just the making of your bed in the morning be a ceremony, in this way to mark an ending and a beginning, giving meaning to the day." Among observant Muslims and Orthodox Jews there are traditional prayers for just about every act of each day—beginning with getting out of bed. The teaching is that *everything* we do is, or should be, a little ceremony. Even such things as urinating and defecating, for instance, are sacred acts if done respectfully, participating in the cycle of life. Within all the ordinary, *washte* events of daily life, the *wakan* is there—as Kabalistic Jews and Sufis know—and it is good for us to remember and respect this presence.

Ceremonies, if they are properly done, extend well beyond the period in which they ostensibly occur. In the before time, they are felt in our long walk of approach and our prayerful preparations; in the after time they are felt in the effect we take with us back into our lives and the world around us. Native American elders know that the real ceremony begins when the ritual ends: the real ceremony is life itself, and how you live it. One thing ceremonies are supposed to do is bring the *wakan* (sacred) into the *washte*.

Sunwise and moonwise are the two ways things go in nature. Sunwise is known as clockwise in the dominant culture, and moonwise is known as counterclockwise or anticlockwise. These pairs of terms are actually equivalent, since the clock, especially in its original twenty-four hour sundial version, follows the movement of the Sun. Sunwise is the circle of the Red Road, while moonwise is the circle of the Blue Road. It is important to do all things in balance. When we smudge in the way I was taught the sacred smoke of the sage is moved around the person both sunwise and moonwise, to recognize the fact that every person has both *washte* and *wakan*, male and female within.

Most of the ceremonies are done in a sunwise manner, such as the Sun Dance, in which the sacred dancers move around the Sun Pole in a sunwise direction, and the Sun Lodge, in which everything also is done sunwise, even when, after the ceremony proper, the women enter the lodge. Other ceremonies, such as the Moon Lodge, are done in a moonwise manner, even when, after the ceremony proper, the men enter the lodge.

Even sunwise ceremonies are done in a moonwise way at certain times and for certain reasons. These include the Sacred Pipe Ceremony, the Sacred Stone People's Lodge, and the Talking Stick. When men smoke the Sacred Pipe alone, or when men and women smoke it together (though not all nations do the latter), it is passed sunwise, and each person turns it sunwise. When men keep the Sacred Stone People's Lodge alone, or when men and women keep it together (though, again, not all nations do the latter), people enter and exit sunwise, and prayers are said going around the circle sunwise. When women keep the Sacred Stone People's Lodge by themselves, it is customary for everyone and everything to proceed moonwise; when women smoke the Sacred Moon Pipe or talk with the Sacred Moon Talking Stick, it is passed and turned moonwise. (The only Moon Pipe I have been allowed to see is made not of red pipestone, but of materials that represent the Grandmothers to the North: a white stone with a stem made from white pine, criss-crossed with white sage.)

I know some nations keep the practice that, when people are in mourning, men or mixed groups will also keep such ceremonies moonwise. Moreover, I am told that groups of *heyoka* (sacred clowns) keep such ceremonies moonwise simply because they do everything backwards. And, finally, there are times when the moonwise direction is followed because of a particular need to seek the *wakan*. When the Sacred Stone People's Lodge is turned around so the door is pointed toward the West, and the people are huddled together inside the lodge to the East, the place of new beginnings, then the *wakan* powers are particularly likely to enter into the ceremony. The ceremony can also be done in the deepest part of the night, at the New Moon, and/or at midwinter, in order to move more boldly into the regions of darkness-like-death where great dreams and visions may be found. I do not recommend these particular ways of seeking the *wakan* except for the most dire of reasons, however, and not without the guidance of a very wise medicine man or woman.

Since women in their moontime are in that *wakan*, the elders of some nations teach that they are not safely brought into the sunwise ceremonies just as you wouldn't put large quantities of a powerful *wakan* herb into your supper. This is not a misogynistic attitude, but great respect for the sacred power that is in Woman. (Still, I suspect that this separation of the genders is at least partly influenced by mainstream society's misogyny or perhaps reflects an evasive maneuver to deal with their assumption that the old ceremonies were evil and sinful. If only one gender went into the lodge at a time, it could presumably be argued that sexuality was not the reason why they came out again naked and hot and sweaty.) When the women of these nations are in their moontime, they stay separate from the men. The women can enter into their sacred powerful prophetic spirit in the Moon Lodge, and the men also, in a sense, have their "moon," tending the children and making the meals, while themselves going into the Sun Lodge.

When the traditional people lived together in communities yet undisrupted by the ways of the dominant culture, women commonly had their moon at the same time. Women still today often find this happens if they live together (like sisters growing up, or women in a dormitory or convent). This being the case, the chief or ceremonialist would schedule ceremonies accordingly. A ceremony where women needed to be present would not be held during the moontime. When the men held a ceremony while the women were on their moon, the men would know the women were in the Moon Lodge, praying for and supporting the men in their own sacred work.

Even though I am a man, one Grandmother taught me a little about the moon traditions, which I have gathered are today largely lost. The lodge is constructed of blankets on a sapling framework, a little like the Sacred Stone People's Lodge, but much more ovoid in shape, more like a womb. The entrance is to the South. It has an opening in the center of the roof, and a small fire is lit underneath. The women come in moonwise and sit around the center. The door is closed. The Moon Pipe is passed moonwise. A Grandmother sits in the place of honor to the North and offers the Pipe to the Four Grandmothers (going moonwise), after which certain ancient songs are sung. The women are naked in the lodge, allowing their menstrual blood to drain out of their bodies right into Grandmother Earth, or alternatively they spread out their long skirts and put their womanhood directly against the Earth (before the Black Robes came, of course, women didn't wear underwear beneath their skirts). The most powerful part of the ceremony comes when the fire burns down and the Full Moon shines directly into the roof opening. I recall the Grandmother using the Biblical phrase that they "wrought miracles." I am pretty sure she meant healing took place. The ceremony went all night during the first night of the Full Moon.

Most of the time in traditional tribal society, women (like men) are basically *washte*. The women (*winyan*) are both *Wi* (which in this context refers to the Moon [*Hanhepi Wi* or *Hanwi* (Orb of the Night)]) and Rock (*Inyan*; the first thing created in the Beginning), the bedrock of the community, around which everything revolves. But, at the moontime, they are *wakan*: every one of them is *Woman*, specifically, the Beautiful Woman, Sky Woman, Changing Woman, and all her aspects throughout the world—among them, Kuan-Yin, Isis, Danu and Inanna. Some of them are Woman as the Maiden, others as the Mother and the Grandmothers as the Crone. As Manx Starfire, a Wild Witch High Priestess, puts it, these three represent the Past, the Present and the Future—the Circle of Life, the Circle of Time.

Although at this time men had to take over the ordinary women's chores, they were glad the women were not around with all their dangerous power, and moreover glad for the wisdom, the guidance, the power that came later as a result of this ceremony. Similarly, a man who inadvertently came within sight of the Moon Lodge would avert his eyes even if it were not currently in use and stay well away from it—out of respect for the powerful woman medicine there.

Yet, at dawn after the last night of the Full Moon (which can go two or three nights), men might be invited into the lodge. They would be brought in naked and blindfolded, or at least with their eyes screwed shut and out of fear and respect very unwilling even to take a peek. Shaking with fear, they were enjoined to absolute silence during the ceremony and enjoined from ever afterward speaking about their experiences in the lodge. Moreover, they had to submit without resistance to whatever the women did to them, but with the under-standing that this was sacred medicine—healing, holy and whole. But, *whatever* the men experienced, they later on looked at any and every woman and wondered if it was she who had given them such powerful medicine, realizing that *every* woman is sacred and should be treated with the greatest respect. They remembered that the Beautiful Woman said, *"Toksha ake wa chin yanktin ktelo"* (I will see you again), and her promise was fulfilled in every woman they met.

I have also heard a very little about the Sun Lodge, a similar ceremony for men. The lodge comes in various forms; among the Hodenasaunee the medi-cine societies would have their sacred lodges, for instance. And I have heard that the women were likewise welcomed in at its conclusion, to complete the circle—naked and eyes covered, to accept whatever medicine was given them.

Today, it is not easy to keep these ceremonies. Even when enough is known to carry them out, there is not always a large enough self-sustaining commu-nity. Further, the dominant culture's mores make such ceremonies largely unacceptable. Still, there is a basic human need for men sometimes to congre-gate without women, and women without men—but, having lost the gender-based ceremonies and traditions, they have occasionally forced the Sacred Stone People's Lodge to take on this responsibility. This, I believe, is at least in part why some traditional peoples have taken to the practice of not welcoming women on their moon into the Sacred Talking Stick or Sacred Pipe ceremonies or the Sacred Stone People's Lodge. The lodge, however, represents *all* of life, and—except in special circumstances—both women and men should be wel-come to take part, so the Circle of Life is complete.

I would offer this advice to those who keep the practice of excluding men-struating (or all) women from certain ceremonies: if, for example, the Talking Stick is to be passed, then, *before* the council begins, women on their moon should be reminded to share their thoughts with someone who will attend council. If a woman is on her moon and her people's ways prevent her from participating in the Sacred Stone People's Lodge or sharing the Sacred Pipe, she can still be there in spirit, praying with and for the people in ceremony.

Other elders teach that a woman on her moon *can* be made welcome in certain of the sunwise ceremonies, for instance the Sacred Stone People's Lodge. Even in this case, the welcome is extended with considerable care because bringing a woman on her moon into the lodge is equivalent to bringing in a dynamo of the *wakan*. It is likely to attract particularly *wakan* spirits in a way similar to doing the ceremony moonwise or having the opening face the West. In this understanding, a woman on her moon should sit to the West, in the elder's seat in the lodge, and allow her blood to drain right into Grandmother. Her prayers and visions are given great respect because of the considerable power she invokes at this time.

Welcoming in a woman on her moon is possible because moontime and the Sacred Stone People's Lodge are both earth ceremonies and purification ceremonies. They are connected to the Earth, and our sweat, like blood, pours out into the Earth on which we sit, and the healing energy of the Earth (as Grandfather Luther Standing Bear taught) then nourishes and heals us. However, it is still not advisable for women on their moon to partake of the Sacred Pipe because that is a Sky ceremony. If you are in doubt about how things are to be done, ask the ceremonial leader.

In sum, we all, women and men, need to honor both ways of walking the Sacred Hoop, sunwise and moonwise, Red Road and Blue Road, in everything we do.

I'm now going to talk about some of our ceremonies, at least the way in which I am familiar with them. Please do not take my descriptions and try to do these ceremonies yourself. My descriptions will no more make you into a qualified ceremonial leader than reading a book about, say, the seven sacraments of Christianity will turn you into an ordained priest or minister. Like any other spiritual tradition, the Red Road cannot be learned from books, even from incredibly wise books like *Black Elk Speaks*, *The Sacred Pipe*, or *Lame Deer: Seeker of Visions*. I hope you will seek the actual experience of these traditional ceremonies with someone well and traditionally trained in them. What you experience may indeed differ from my description, but the inner spirit will be, of course, the same.

My purpose is not to provide detailed descriptions of ceremonies but to open up for you the spiritual philosophy *behind* them. I will limit myself to talking about a few ceremonies, and describe them only to the degree necessary to share something with you that, so far as I know, has not been written about before, or not extensively.

Ceremonies are customarily and ideally done as a group, not individually. Of course, sometimes I find I am the only one there to enter into the Sacred Stone People's Lodge. If that is how it is, that is how it is. The joining together of a number of people makes the Sacred Hoop more concrete, more visceral. It's like the difference between beating the Council Drum by myself versus joining with several others to do so. The unity of our beaters swinging up and down, the unity of our voices, evokes a considerable power, an indescribable magic that is not as fully evident when it is just me alone.

It is customary to follow the traditional way of the ceremonial leader, without challenging or "suggesting" things be done another way. We still commonly follow a traditional order to participating in ceremonies. When people enter the dance circle or get on line to fill their plates with food, the elders are first, followed by pregnant women and women with children, then the other women and the men, with the warriors last.

Grandfather Black Elk taught that there are seven great ceremonies of the Lakota, variations of which are known throughout Turtle Island (North America):

> *Hanblecheyapi*: sitting alone within a sacred circle, fasting and praying, seeking a sacred vision, while others, especially elders, pray in support of the individual in a kind of "base camp"; associated with the West.
>
> *Hokshichankiya*: caring for the souls of those who have died; associated with the North.
>
> *Tatanka Lowanpi*: the women's puberty ritual; associated with the East.
>
> *Wiwanyag Wachipi*: the Sacred Sun Dance; associated with the South.
>
> *Inipi*: the Sacred Stone People's Lodge, purification of the body and soul, establishment of brother/sister relationships, and seeking of visions; associated with the Zenith.
>
> *Hunkapi*: making strangers or enemies into family; associated with the Nadir.
>
> *Chanunpah Wakan*: While Grandfather Black Elk told Joseph Epes Brown that a certain ball game was the seventh great ceremony, I believe that this was intentional misdirection, and that the Sacred Pipe Ceremony itself is the seventh of the ceremonies, the ceremony that is

present in all the others and binds them together. It is associated with the Seventh Direction, in which we travel in visions, dreams and when we die.

There are other important ceremonies too, such as the naming ceremony, the Grandmother ceremony, the wedding ceremony, the Moon Lodge and Sun Lodge. I will talk about several of these ceremonies later on.

First, in preparation for any ceremony, we smudge. Traditional peoples smudge before entering sacred circles, such as the dance circle at community dances, the circle at council meetings when the Talking Stick is passed, and pretty much all of our ceremonies. It is not uncommon for people to be smudged when they are welcomed into someone's home and to begin the circle of the day by smudging. Just as we were born clean and whole, so we want to enter into a ceremony or dance clean and whole. If we were not cleansed, we would risk spoiling the sacred story of life (as represented by the dance, council or ceremony). If we were not cleansed, it would have as detrimental an effect as someone continually interrupting a storyteller, or trying to dance in a field filled with trash.

Smudging normally takes place on the periphery of the sacred circle, at the eastern entrance, the place of beginnings where the ceremony of the day commences with the new Sun. This may be, for instance, at the entrance to a home, a dance circle, a medicine wheel, a council or sacred grounds for a traditional ceremony. If for example the ceremony is the Sacred Stone People's Lodge, this entrance is beyond the sacred fire. (In exceptional situations, such as women or *heyoka* meeting or ceremonializing alone, or when there's particular need to seek the *wakan*, smudging is done at the entrance to the west or south.)

The smudging ceremony is only effective if we do it with great care and attentiveness. Whether you are smudging yourself or being smudged by someone else, be silent and prayerful. Normal (*washte*) conversations should cease; there should be no idle chitchat. Think of the place where you are being smudged as a borderline encircling a sacred space. As if we were going through a customs station—and, indeed, we are entering a different country, the Spirit World—we have to "declare" what we are carrying, and leave behind anything that would bring *sicha*, unbalance, into the sacred space.

This keeping of silence continues within the sacred circle: each person should continue to avoid *washte* chatting, only talking when necessary about practical considerations of preparing for the ceremony or dance or talking circle. Once one is within the sacred circle it would be disrespectful to leave for any reason until the council or ceremony or dance is completed; even if one has to urinate one should not leave, but find an unobtrusive spot that is still within the sacred circle.

As I have mentioned, children and elders are always considered particularly sacred because of their closeness to Spirit. For this reason, children and elders are not as fully bound by the customs within the sacred circle as adults are. It is not necessary for children to smudge before entering, though it is good for them to start learning how to become spiritually cleansed. It is not necessary for them to be quiet or to remain within the circle if they don't want to, and they should never be chastised for just being children. Elders are not usually exempt from smudging; indeed, they seem to welcome the purifying smoke, and bathe in it even more fully than the adults do. Like children, elders, being so close to Spirit, may at any time speak, even interrupting a ceremony, if they are so directed by Spirit.

There are many different ways of smudging. Some people use loose sage placed in a bowl or shell, or on a stone. Others prefer to use sage sticks. Some people use sage and cedar or other combinations mixed together. It is very common to use a feather fan or a wing to direct the smoke, but people often use just their hands. The smudging ceremony begins by establishing the entire sacred circle, walking along its periphery in a sunwise manner (or moonwise, in the exceptional circumstances I've mentioned), waving the smoke with a feather fan or wing. Then each person already within the sacred circle is smudged, as is each individual arriving to enter the now-established circle.

If someone is at the entrance ready to smudge you, it is customary to acknowledge the person silently, for example, with a nod. Should you be carrying sacred articles such as Sacred Pipe or Drum, you may hold them forward to be smudged on all sides. Then you may either hold your arms up and out a bit so you can be thoroughly smudged, or you may want to draw the smoke in to your face and hair as if you were lifting water up with your hands to wash yourself. People may be clothed for smudging, but it goes "deeper down" into their spirits within their robes (bodies) if they are naked.

I was taught to begin smudging by moving the smoke in a sunwise circle around the person's (or my own) face, and then sunwise around the body. Both feet should be lifted (first left then right, going sunwise) so we are pure and clean where we are in contact with our Mother Earth. Then the person being smudged turns around sunwise, or the smudger walks sunwise around to the individual's backside, so the latter can be smudged in a moonwise circle around the back of the head and then moonwise around the body. In this way, we honor the masculine and feminine components within the individual. It is customary for the individual doing the smudging to touch the person on the shoulder with the wing or smudge fan or fingertips to let the person know when the smudging of one's backside has been completed.

You can smudge yourself, and that is fine when no one else is available. It takes a little practice to learn to smudge yourself thoroughly. Sage often is added to a ceremonial fire, in which case the wind may distribute the smoke through the whole area, smudging everyone and everything. Just the smell of sage smoke has a powerful effect on me, putting me in a calm, prayerful state almost immediately.

One beautiful autumn day I was up on a ceremonial hill in Vermont. There were no other two-leggeds nearby, but around me were "all my relations," and they were all dancing. Monarch butterflies, though soon they would close the circle on their little lives, were dancing in great circles through the wide grassy field below the Sacred Stone People's Lodge. Leaves painted with the same colors as the butterflies spiraled slowly among these winged people in the circling breeze. A couple of deer danced up in the high field of moss and flat rocks where people would go for the *Hanblecheyapi*, the Vision Crying ceremony. High above me in the Sky, birds wheeled around each other in their own dance, reminding me of the vision that gave me my name. With all these brothers and sisters dancing all around me, I could not remain still. I danced too.

Dancing is essential and central to life. All living things, all our relations, dance. Gnats dance about in swarms. Snowflakes dance and spin as they travel from Grandfather Sky to Grandmother Earth. Horses dance in fields. Whales and dolphins dance amidst the waves. The waves dance in to the ocean shore. Rocks dance, though we two-leggeds rarely have the patience needed to see their stately passages. The flames of the fire dance among the sparks. The tall grasses dance in rippling lines as the wind combs its way through them. The clouds dance together on their celestial journey. The stars dance slowly through the year in a great circle around the Pole Star, while Grandmother Moon dances through her phases and Grandfather Sun dances from the South in winter to the North in summer. Dancing is a speaking in the First Language, the language of spirit to spirit, mediated through the various kinds of robes (bodies) the spirits wear.

Grandfather Hehaka Sapa (Black Elk) saw in a vision the entire universe dancing to the song of the stallion in the Sky: the leaves in the trees, the grass, the waters in the streams and rivers, the four-leggeds, the two-leggeds, and the wingeds. When everything else is dancing, we surely can see that dancing is not merely an entertaining activity, but a sacred and vital one necessary to life. Dancing is not something we do only because we feel like it, but something we should be doing all the time, even if without fully realizing it!

Some dances are ceremonies celebrating birth. Watch robins dancing with ecstasy in the air around the nest when their babies break forth from their eggs. Watch young otters playing together. When my children were infants, often I cradled them in my arms and danced with them. How close I felt to them; how much love there was in those precious moments!

Some dances are ceremonies of mating: birds, squirrels, humans and many other creatures dance to attract the attention of the other sex. And when the mating dance is over and two living beings make love, that too is a dance and a very sacred one. We two-leggeds have our mating dances too; one traditional Native American way is with the women in one circle facing out and dancing moonwise, and the men in a circle around them facing in and dancing sunwise.

Some dances are simply for love. A friend of mine once watched wolves dancing together in the moonlight, and sensed the love for each other that prompted their silent sacred pavane. Humans too dance for love. Dancing it I think is so much better than saying it. I remember once, a long time ago, when I was embracing someone I loved very dearly. As we embraced, our bodies began to swing together within the circle of our arms, first sunwise then moonwise. Not a word was said. None was needed.

Some dances are ceremonies of warring or hunting. You may have seen two bucks fighting over a doe by engaging in a stately but dangerous dance of rearing and goring with their antlers. Or you may have seen the solitary dance of an eagle on the thermals as it watches the Earth below for game. The traditional two-legged peoples also have war dances and hunting dances. In essence these dances are to prepare them spiritually for warring or hunting by harmonizing their spirits with what they are about to do, through prayer in the form of dance. Humans may dance as part of a fist fight or in battle, or to attract the deer (or whatever they plan to hunt) by moving their spirit closer to that of the four-legged.

Some dances are ceremonies of death. Many living creatures dance as death approaches, like the monarch butterflies and falling leaves I was watching in the field on the hill, and it used to be that the traditional peoples had songs and dances that were expressed only when they were about to die.

Some dances are ceremonies of mourning. I once saw a mother bear whose child had been killed by hunters, clearly overcome by grief, dancing around her baby, coming up to it and poking it, then dancing away when it did not respond. I have been told that elephants and magpies, too, dance their sorrow in the face of death.

And some dances are medicine dances—there are dances, for instance, that can only be done out in the midst of fierce storms, or during a rain, or in a dark field beneath the full Moon, or in the midst of swirling snow, for instance—dances that can only be done with and for the particular spirits who come out at these *wakan* moments.

For the traditional peoples, dancing is not an entertainment you sit and watch others do, but wholly participatory. Even the Grandmothers and Grandfathers who can hardly walk any more will often get up and join in, or at least sing or drum or clap their hands. Everyone is shapeshifted through the ceremony of dancing.

While I have mentioned many different purposes for dances, I want to remind you that ultimately all these purposes are interrelated—they are work, they are play, and they are sacred ceremonies.

There are two kinds of dances traditional to Native Americans: social dances and solitary dances. Social dances often accompany such important occasions as births, coming of age ceremonies, weddings and deaths. It is customary for men and women dancing together or men alone to dance in a sunwise circle, and for women dancing alone to move in a moonwise circle. Certain social dances are "honor dances," in which case there is a traditional order to who enters the dance circle first. Some social dances are to get acquainted with the other gender, or for hunting or warring, as I mentioned. Some are very sacred, such as the Sun Dance or the Ghost Dance.

The social dances are always centered around the drum. The deep voice of the council drum, surrounded by several people beating on it in unison and singing a traditional chant, calls us so authoritatively that we simply cannot sit idly! The circle of the drum surrounded by the circle of drummers is a microcosm of the circle of dancers, and both are a microcosm of the Sacred Hoop, the circle of all living things, the circle of life from birth to death. When the people first begin to strike the drum it takes a while before they synchronize the rhythm. After that, we who are seated around the council drum find that the beat continues of its own accord, the beaters dancing in our hands, energized by bouncing off the rawhide, and the song emerges of its own accord not from several throats but from the drum itself.

It is the same way with those who join in the circle of the dance. The story of the dance is a microcosm of the story of life itself. I suspect many of you, like me, sometimes feel shy about joining the dance circle. I feel at first self-conscious because my arthritis makes me move rather clumsily, at least until my joints warm up. As the rhythmic movements take over our bodies, and our logical minds cease from worrying and controlling, the flow of the dance begins to stream through us. You have to let go, and not think logically about it. In dancing, if you remain self-conscious, you can't do it well. As we dance in sacred time (*wakan* time), not ordinary time (*washte* time), we lose ourselves (or find our sacred selves!). For a while we break through and out of mundane existence into the sacred realm. Slowly as we feel the dance build, our bodies begin to tire, as the dance enters its elderly time. When the dance ends, even though our bodies are now still and it feels good to rest, we still feel the dance flowing inside us, ready to flow into a new dance. And, sometime later, the drummers begin to beat that great council drum again, and we are reborn into a new life, a new ceremony, a new dance.

Then there are the solitary dances. One kind is used to tell a story. Sometimes a storytelling dance is a traditional dance acting out an old story, and sometimes it is the dancer dancing out a sacred vision or dream she or he has had. In either case the dance is not a *representation* of the story, vision, or dream, but is in its own right a sacred experience.

Another kind of solitary dance is for prayer, or, you might say, for sacred magic. Examples include the Rain Dance, the Eagle Dance, and the *Ononharoia*, the Naked Dance kept by the Hodenasaunee (Iroquois Confederacy) at the New Year, as a sacred *heyoka* way of celebrating new beginnings. Some dances, like the hoop dance, though often thought to be traditional are not; they were invented relatively recently to please general audiences.

Even if there is no formal occasion, and no other human beings to dance with you, don't let that keep you from dancing! From feeling Grandfather's light on your bare skin and Grandmother's breast beneath your naked feet, breathing in the air and feeling your oneness with all your relations as they, too, dance with you!

In his essay "Circles," Ralph Waldo Emerson speaks of circles within circles, and how each circle, as an adumbration of the infinite, is the same Circle. Medicine Wheels have been found in ancient locations throughout the world: are not the installations at Stonehenge and Avebury Medicine Wheels too?

For Native Americans, the Medicine Wheel is a way to be conscious of the many circles that are one Circle. Its genius is that, while in physical reality we are always at the center of the Sacred Hoop, the horizon, at the Medicine Wheel we can actually move away from the center to the horizon, from *washte* "here" to *wakan* "there," to meditate on or seek certain sacred powers. We can sit and pray, say, at the East when we are expecting the birth of a child, or our life to change and be reborn. To the Medicine Wheel we traditionally come for weddings, birth-namings, Buffalo Sings, and death ceremonies. At one ceremonial ground in Connecticut there was a large Medicine Wheel, constructed by Native Americans we cannot know how many years ago. Oftentimes people have smaller Wheels of their own—one Tsalagi (Cherokee) woman I knew had painted one on a circular woven mat, on which she placed small stones from a medicine bag.

To make a Medicine Wheel, first be sure the place is the right place. Ask the Grandmothers and Grandfathers in prayer. Stand in the place and offer tobacco to the sacred directions. Going sunwise, you should smudge the location with sage and sweetgrass. When the place is ready, place a large stone (or two stones, one on top of the other) where the center is to be, with a pinch of tobacco placed underneath. Then place another large stone (or two stones) to the West, above another tobacco offering. Walk back to the center, and follow the same procedure for the North, East and South stones. Many people like to fill in the rest of the circle with smaller stones, and/or mark the "spokes" with smaller stones. This is not necessary, but is fine. Listen to your teaching spirits.

After all this has been completed, again smudge the circle (walking sunwise) with sage, and offer tobacco to the sacred directions and leave the tobacco at each circle-stone, beginning with the West. Finish with the center stone. At each stone, you should offer prayers to the Grandmothers and Grandfathers of that particular sacred direction. If you know a traditional song, like the Four Directions Song, that is good to sing. This completes the formation of the Medicine Wheel proper.

For ceremonies, it is often customary to mark the four cardinal directions with medicine sticks, decorated with the colors or emblems of the sacred directions. These vary from nation to nation, even individual to individual within the same nation, but the way in which I was taught was thus: We denote the West with black or blue. The North, the Grandmother Direction, we decorate with white. The East we honor with yellow. The South we honor with red. Such medicine sticks are commonly placed for weddings, Buffalo Sings, and other such ceremonies. Medicine sticks are no more necessary than any other physical symbol, but they help us to remember and honor the sacred space and all the sacred beings that we invite to join us. It is interesting to me that identically decorated medicine sticks are used as part of the ancient Bön religion of Tibet, to honor the Lord of the Soil.

The Medicine Wheel, as the world in microcosm, is a teacher. It helps us to learn and respect our connections in the Great Wheel, the *Changleshka Wakan* of the Universe, bringing the entire Universe down to a scale that we can more easily comprehend. In it we see all the Seven Directions at a glance, and can find more easily our place within them. We learn to see the entire Universe about us as the spiritual Medicine Wheel of which our little Medicine Wheel (like the physical pipe in relation to the Spirit Pipe) is but a reflection in physical form—a robe.

The Vision Crying Ceremony is known by various names, and is kept in various ways. The Lakota call it *Hanblecheyapi*, which literally means, more or less, "Vision-during-the-Night (Dream) which They are Crying For." I will be describing the way I was taught it by Tsalagi (Cherokee) elders who in part were trained in the Lakota manner.

The ceremony is often kept by youths, both male and female, as they enter into their teen or young adult years. It is also kept by adults who feel a need for sacred guidance or strength, for example when they are on the verge of a very important decision or task.

One prepares for the ceremony, if one has not done it before, by learning about it from one's teacher. If one has not made a Sacred Drum, one's teacher will probably have one do this. One will probably also prepare a medicine bundle with the four sacred herbs. One may do some preparatory work ahead of time at the place where the ceremony will transpire, such as setting stones to make a medicine wheel.

In the days before, it is a good idea to familiarize oneself with the place that one's teacher affirms is the correct site. Usually such a site is at the top of a high hill or mountain, but I know of one person who kept the ceremony in the deepest room of a series of caves. Among some nations, the ceremony is done in a pit. In any case it must be far from the human realm, to avoid distraction and safety concerns. (These days, hunters can be a more significant concern even than wild animals.) This place is *wakan*: it is not an easy or comfortable place to be in, but difficult and unwelcoming to humans.

When the time comes for the ceremony, one prepares oneself by undergoing the first two rounds of the Sacred Stone People's Lodge Ceremony. It is customary, if this is the individual's first Vision Crying ceremony, that one's teacher pour water (leads the Sacred Stone People's Lodge ceremony), and that the individual who is going to do the vision crying sit in the "honor seat," farthest from the entrance. It is acceptable to have close friends and supporters come into the lodge too.

Following these first two rounds, the person, without dressing again, is silently escorted by the teacher (and the supporters if any) up to within sight of the sacred place. One brings the Sacred Drum and sacred herbs, and the Sacred Pipe if one carries it. It is not uncommon to take water, but never food. In the old days it was traditional to take a buffalo robe to keep warm at night, but these days people most often take a blanket or two. Once the place is within sight, the person walks the rest of the way alone. Once the person is within the stone circle, the escort party leaves silently.

The person then sets about making four sacred altars to the Four Directions. They need be no more than small piles of stones, but may be elaborate—hung with shields, for instance. The four altars are smudged and purified and given tobacco gifts. The person now remains within this circle day and night.

In the morning, one offers dawn prayers. At sunset, one offers evening prayers. In the way I was taught, a small fire is allowed from time to time in order to make tobacco offerings; certainly its warmth is welcome as well. At dawn and sunset this is especially appropriate. At other times one may drum and chant or pray or simply remain silent. One should be aware of the constant presence of people on the ceremonial ground where the lodge is, keeping one in their prayers and keeping a lookout to make sure one is not in any danger, though from a distance sufficient to avoid disturbing the individual or the spirits.

One remains awake and aware as much as possible. The person will feel her or his body slowly cleansing itself as the digestive system gradually shuts down. There is a period, after a couple days, during which one can get very itchy, and/or have diarrhea. This is normal. The mind and soul will also go through a cleansing. One seeks to work through the various "temptations" that come, as both Jesus and Gautama Buddha did. It may be the desire for a comfortable bed, or for human interaction and entertainment, or even the temptation to make up a vision and stop sitting up in this uncomfortable, inhospitable, inhuman place.

Different nations have different traditional lengths to this ceremony, but in the way I was given, one is in the place for no less than three days and two nights and no more than four days and three nights. One may or may not have a vision, and of course it does not have to be anything earth-shattering. And there is no shame if one does not receive a vision.

When one has had a sacred vision, or when the time for being in the sacred place has come to an end, one goes back down to the Sacred Stone People's Lodge. With the same people (if any) with whom one did the first two rounds, one now does the last two rounds. It is appropriate during the third round, which represents the age of "now" and "adulthood," to describe what happened up in the holy place, and during the fourth round, which represents the future, for any interpretation that seems appropriate to be offered by one's teacher and/or trusted supporters, and perhaps for the person to be given a traditional name. As appropriate, any messages from the Grandfathers and Grandmothers are passed on to the right individuals or to all the people.

There are many ways weddings are celebrated among the traditional peoples. Among a number of nations, there was no wedding ceremony *per se*, since it was understood that two people fell in love by the will and blessing of the Creator. So, as one Onodowahgah (Seneca) elder has told me, elders just offer blessings: "Now that you are married, I ask for blessings on you both." Among other nations, there have been traditional wedding ceremonies, but these are not understood as *making* a couple married, but as *publicly confirming* their relationship. The Jewish concept of covenant—a constant choosing to give oneself wholly to another, demanding nothing in return—expresses well the nature of the relationship. Native American couples do not chattel each other in a contractual set of mutual demands, but free each other, content in merely seeking the other's happiness.

I was taught the following way to perform wedding ceremonies:

Before the wedding, I talk with the groom and bride, to make sure they are ready, and to discuss the wedding ceremony with them, so they fully understand it. If the two people aren't already committed to each other, they have no business at a wedding ceremony. Given this fact, it might seem unnecessary to hold the ceremony at all, but it serves as a "reality check," in the same way the physical representation of the Spirit Pipe is helpful, to remind us to stay true to the "inner ceremony" of commitment, honor and respect.

Usually there is purification in the Sacred Stone People's Lodge before the wedding (traditionally a "two rounder" instead of the usual four-part ceremony), so they are emptied of impurities, filled with the good *nagipi* and made ready for the future.

For the wedding itself, I prefer it to be at a Medicine Wheel. I stand inside the Wheel, facing East. Behind me, on the center stone, is a buffalo skull altar, with sage in its eyeholes, the Sacred Pipe prepared, and other sacred things. The people gather outside the Medicine Wheel, leaving an opening to the East. Then the men bring out the groom, coming sunwise around to the entrance, and the women bring out the bride, coming moonwise around to the entrance. Usually the Sacred Drum is singing while they come toward the Medicine Wheel; oftentimes a Sacred Flute plays too. The couple comes into the Wheel, leaving their escorts behind to close the gap in the circle, and stand before me.

First I smudge them carefully, and bless them with eagle feathers. Then I ask them their intentions, with four questions. Then I lift the Sacred Pipe, offer it in the sacred way, and share it with the two of them. (A wedding done "before the Pipe" is indissoluble; if the couple choose not [yet] to commit to that, it is done without sharing the Sacred Pipe.) Following that, I bind their wrists together with red ribbon (or red string or thread, if that's all we can find) to represent the joining of their two bloods/families, and then I put a star blanket over their shoulders to represent their giving shelter to each other. I talk to them and the people about what these sacred things mean.

After that I sing a traditional song, while they walk sunwise around the Medicine Wheel, to greet everyone just outside it. They leave the Wheel when they come around to the entrance again. After that we have lots of dancing, Sacred Giveaway and food!

There are many traditions when someone dies. One thing I was taught is to make a medicine bundle. This may contain sacred things or personal mementos associated with the deceased. Everybody is smudged, and the bundle is also smudged, very carefully. A medicine song may be sung while the bundle is passed around the circle moonwise, with everybody silently saying good-bye. Later, the elder or elders take the bundle to a sacred place somewhere in the wilderness, where it is secreted away, to be taken by the *nagipi* (spirits) whenever they choose to do so.

Variations of the Sacred Stone People's Lodge Ceremony (or *Inipi* in Lakota) are found in most of the Northern Hemisphere, including Scandinavia, Siberia and Japan, as well as in parts of South America and Africa. As the *Kalevala* shows, the *sauna* was originally done as a spiritual practice; Finns still call the steam *loyly* (from *lil*, "soul"), meaning "spirit" and "life." They switch themselves with soft branches to stimulate the skin, just as Native Americans often do with sage or willow, as well as Jews with eucalyptus in the *shvitzbad;* they finish with cold water or snow, as the peoples of this continent and others do as well. Muslims still enjoy "Turkish baths," in Kyoto the *mushiburo* survives, in South America one finds the *temascal* done in an adobe hut. An honored Grebo elder told me about a similar ritual practiced in his West African homeland.

Now, first, to talk a little about the sacred meaning and purpose of this ceremony, as it was taught to me. Like the Sacred Pipe, the materials that make up the Sacred Stone People's Lodge itself represent the whole universe in both time (the Circle of Life) and space (the Sacred Hoop). In Lakota, the lodge itself is called *onikarë* (which I believe is related to the verb *oniya* or *niya*, to "breathe") or *initi* (literally, house [*tipi*] of breath/spirit [*ini*]). I've already told you that the lodge may be referred to as *keya*, "turtle," to help us remember Turtle Island. In these and other ways, all of life is invoked.

In front of the entrance is the spirit trail, which connects the lodge to *Unchi* (Grandmother), called in English the Sacred Mound. These are connected because we are connected to the Earth. *Unchi* appears to be only a little pile of soil, but the elders and the spirits see it as a huge mountain that reaches all the way into the Sacred Realm, in which the Creator is found. Beyond the Sacred Mound is the *Peta Owankeshne* ("Fire That Never Goes Out"), a physical fire representing the one Spirit Fire eternally ablaze in the Spirit World. The Sacred Fire represents Grandfather, who is beyond the Sky or Heaven. As Pete Catches points out, the white ashes represent the hoary head of "Old Man." The spirit trail does not extend to the *Peta* because we do not (yet) walk the Sky path.

The door of the lodge normally faces East, the source of light and life (except in the circumstances I have previously explained), calling to mind the fact that the lodge is often seen as a womb. The darkness within represents ignorance, which we must dispel by opening the "single eye of the heart" (*chantë ishta*): we learn to see those who are in the lodge with us, both two-leggeds and spirits, with other senses than the five outer senses. The entrance is small, like the vagina; down it we must crawl to enter this world. For this reason, and because the lodge is womb-shaped, it is sometimes called *tezi*, or "uterus." When we go outside into the light again, blinded by the light outside like a newborn child; we are literally "enlightened" by the Spirit World.

At the same time, the lodge is seen as representative of the body. In this understanding, the saplings are the bones, the blankets are the skin, the glowing hot rocks in the center are the heart, and we are the life-essence. The moment when we enter it is the first breath of life inhaled, and the four ages of the ceremony represent the four stages of life, to the last breath of life exhaled. All elements of human life are implicitly present, and the ceremony is the entire story of life from birth to death. When we crawl out again, it is death out of this world, and at the same time our spiritual rebirth into the world of the Grandfathers and Grandmothers, the Spirit World.

Or we can think of the lodge as the body of Earth Herself, overarched by the sapling-and-blanket structure representing the Sky Above, just as the trees arch over us in the forest, and of our moving through the entrance as a symbolic act of sacred sexuality, entering the inner sanctum of her sacred warm moist darkness, and coming out again, emptied and spent but feeling wonderful.

At the same time, we can think of our reemergence from the lodge after the ceremony as emergence *into* the Earth Herself. As I've already intimated to you, the traditional stories most often tell of "the people" coming to this Earth from another world, even from a series of worlds—and doing so by passing through a small hole like the entrance to the lodge and emerging into this world. This is a common feature in the sacred stories of the Hopi, Kiowa, Hodenasaunee (Iroquois Confederacy), Anishinabeg (Ojibweh or Chippewah), Lakota and others. So we too, emerging from the lodge, are the First Humans, and what we say and do sets the pattern for future generations—so let us set good patterns.

The lodge is as well a kind of spiritual vehicle that transports us in both time and space around the Circle of Life and the Sacred Hoop of All the Nations. The ceremony includes brief openings of the entrance to let in the light of the Four Ages of the universe and of the individual life. We who are inside represent not merely all of humanity, but, indeed, all living beings. In fact, I've sometimes had other kinds of wild creatures enter into the lodge during the ceremony, and often spirit beings as well. We sincerely believe that what we do, even though unnoticed by the world, has a significant powerful and positive effect on the world. People always feel euphoric and buoyant afterwards, filled with love and light. The ceremony is also health-giving and helps us stay balanced within.

The heat and steam represent the visible breath of the Creator, equivalent to the smoke, the visible breath, issuing from one's mouth during prayer with the Sacred Pipe. In the high humidity inside, the participants also exhale visible breath, and their very bodies exude water vapor as sweat steams off them. This is why we must speak and be truth inside the lodge (and indeed at all times). Once when I was younger I confess I was not, and my mouth froze so that I could not speak. A few minutes later I was able to speak again. Never before or since has this happened to me, and I can only conclude that spirits did this.

I was told that one of my teachers took a Vietnam War veteran into the lodge, to help the man work through his deeply repressed anger. During the ceremony, his anger came bursting forth in a screaming rage. The vet told me later that, without thinking, he balled up his fist and swung it at our medicine man friend. He felt a hand grab his wrist, forestalling the blow, and hold it still with a great strength the vet could not break—until the anger slowly dissipated. After the ceremony, he asked the medicine man how he was able to see the punch coming in the dark and grab his wrist in time. The medicine man replied, "I didn't." Again, it was clearly the spirits.

The dome of the lodge is like the upper half of a sphere, which is completed by the Earth below us. At the center of a globe representing the entire universe, we sit in a circle representing the Sacred Hoop of All the Nations. At the center of the circle is the pit in which the red-hot Grandfathers will be placed, representing the navel of the universe, where the Creator dwells in greatest power. The ceremony is, in part, meant to establish oneness: what we do we do not for selfish reasons, but for the Circle of Life. The fire outside represents G-d as Father (*Atë* in Lakota), as represented by the Sun. The Sacred Mound just outside the entrance, the lodge entrance and the lodge itself represent the motherness of G-d, as personified by the Moon. The Sacred Mound is connected to the lodge by the spirit trail, which represents the fact that we walk upon our Mother, Iotsitsisen, the Woman who Fell from the Sky. We always walk along the spirit trail, and never step across it—that is, we never cross between the Sacred Mound and the entrance to the lodge, but keep the mound to our right, going sunwise around it and straight along the path into or out of the lodge—to represent our walking along the Red Road of life. A Buffalo Altar, that is, a decorated skull, or else a pipe rack made from sticks, is put on the Sacred Mound.

There are variations among different nations and water pourers. The Anishinabeg, for example, do not have a door, but construct the lodge right around them. When they leave, they lift the whole structure right up and throw it in the direction of the setting Sun! The Pawnee have the rock pit right near the door. Some nations practice "dry sweats," in which no water is placed on the hot rocks. Very small lodges, for an individual, have four saplings, those for a small group have twelve, and larger ones usually have multiples of twelve.

Often people ask me what the purpose is of this ceremony. Properly speaking, the purpose of this or any ceremony is to take us away from purposiveness altogether, out of the comfort and the bustle of ordinary *washte* society, not to do but simply to be, as Zen teaches, and allow the full force of the *wakan* to flow through us. In this way, the ceremony enables us to purify ourselves in body, mind and soul, bringing physical and spiritual health by purging away *sicha* impurities. Often people may come only once to the lodge and think they've taken care of their impurities, though truly one cannot cleanse oneself spiritually just once and never have to do it again! If we regularly empty ourselves in the lodge by letting the full force of the *wakan* flow through us, it is far easier to pay attention to Spirit.

Many years ago someone of European ancestry came to the lodge who had allowed herself to become dangerously "constipated" in her spirit. She was not only retaining her own emotions, but taking in other people's feelings—their anger, their sorrow, and so on—to the degree that she had become unable to vent them or even to discern, let alone express, what *her own* feelings were. She realized she needed to purge all this, but even in the lodge she had trouble letting it all out. Toward the height of the ceremony, she suddenly exclaimed in her frustration, "I can't even let myself sweat!" I reached over and touched her, and was surprised that, unlike the rest of us, her skin was cold and dry, even clammy. With her permission, I gave her some healing, and eventually she was not only sweating profusely, but weeping with abandon, crying and crying all the *sicha* out of her. After the ceremony she expressed her gratitude, but I advised her that this was not a once-and-for-all matter, but somehow—in whatever way worked for her—she needed to cleanse her spirit on a regular basis.

Once we are purified of the dross, the *sicha* within us, we are better able to reestablish and reharmonize our relationships with our own selves, with each other, with the world and with the Creator. The flow of the *wakan* also helps us to open the single eye of our heart (*chantë ishta*), to see and understand more with Spirit, and to be open to G-d's voice. It also gives us an opportunity to receive visions that teach, admonish and guide us.

Here are some suggestions if you are about to participate in the Sacred Stone People's Lodge for the first time. It is very good practice to fast before for at least a few hours, so your bodily energies are focused on the ceremony, not on digesting a belly stuffed with food. But, if you cannot, don't. The same people excepted by Muslims during Ramadan may be excepted from fasting here: diabetics, those in poor health, pregnant or nursing mothers, the elderly and children. If you must eat, at least eat only lightly and healthily (no junk food). Often folks will bring healthy food to share after the ceremony. In any case, it is very important to drink lots of water before and after the ceremony. If you can, bathe yourself and say some preparatory prayers before coming, so you've already removed some of the physical and spiritual dross in advance of your spiritual work in the lodge. When you come, wear old clothes. If you have a cold or similar malady, be sure to come (as long as you can get there safely), because the ceremony is very curative and preventive of colds and the like. If you have chronic heart or respiratory problems, you might want to check with your physician.

Let me describe the way I usually go about the ceremony, but bear in mind that this is just to serve as an example.

People often like to bring a personal item (such as a wedding ring, photograph, manuscript, etc.) to place on the Sacred Mound to be blessed, or a rock that "speaks" to them (as long as it as it doesn't explode when heated, like quartz, or crumble, like granite). The rock is a gift to G-d in thanks for the Sacred Stone People's Lodge ceremony.

If the lodge is being built on the day you come, please bring any of these you have: a saw or hatchet and as many old blankets as you can scrounge up, because there are never enough to cover the framework to create complete darkness inside.

As participants enter the sacred area, we are smudged. Within that area we maintain quiet and respect for all. We then locate prayerfully the exact building site, and smudge the entire area to prepare it and us. Then some of us will locate saplings, cutting them down only with hand tools. Others will dig the pit and prepare the Sacred Mound. Still others will gather stones and wood. All of these things are done prayerfully, asking permission of the sapling or stone. It is traditional and proper to leave a tobacco gift when asking, whether or not we take it, on the North side of the sapling or stone. Shortly we will get the *Peta Owankeshne* (Sacred Fire) started, with prayers and sacred herbs, then situate the saplings, first putting tobacco and other herbs in the holes, and tie their tops together to make the frame, cover the frame with blankets, and other finishing touches. Then we will move into the ceremony proper.

The ceremony may be kept at any time of the day or night. At dawn, it can bring the motherly gift of new beginnings. During the day, when the Sun is at its height in the South, it can bring the fatherly gift of protection. As the Sun sets in the West, it can bring the grandfatherly gift of wisdom. And during the night, especially during the New Moon or at midwinter, the ceremony can bring the grandmotherly gift from the North—the most powerful medicine, which comes from the Spirit World that we enter into after death and come from when we are born. I was taught that, done in the deep of the night, especially Midwinter Night, the ceremony can seek this powerful medicine even more strongly with the doorway opening to the West if a woman is the water pourer, and if everything is accomplished moonwise, in a mirror image of how I will shortly describe things. Midwinter Night especially is a night associated with closeness to the Spirit World. (But I must warn you again, the *wakan* is nothing to be trifled with! Do not do this unless you or someone with you is thoroughly trained in the traditional ways!)

Some only keep the ceremony at night, not realizing that this is only "traditional" because their more recent ancestors did so to avoid being caught by the missionaries or police or soldiers when traditional ceremonies were illegal. Far better for us proudly to hold it during the day, when that is appropriate, to honor those who kept it alive in secret so they could pass the ceremony on down to us. And doing it *only* at night can have risky consequences by unintentionally calling up the wild spirits in greater abundance or of a different kind than was actually sought. Another danger is to make the ceremony too familiar and routine, in effect wearing a *washte* path in the night; the night should remain a trackless *wakan* wilderness of Spirit so that when people really do need to seek the *wakan*, they can find it.

The ceremony begins with the lighting of the Sacred Fire, done with prayers and sacred herbs. In the old days, of course, lighting a fire was a difficult procedure. Nowadays we do it with, as one elder calls it, "the Sacred Bic." Nevertheless, it should be done in a spiritual way, not thoughtlessly, not as we might light a fire in the woodstove at home, as an ordinary chore. It is good to say a prayer like the following, which I have been told came from Larry Kibby, a member of the Wiyot Nation from Nevada. He has said it is good to share this with all the lodges so the Sacred Hoop will be mended, and all the people will become one as the Creator wants:

> *As we enter into the Circle of the Sacred Lodge, we send life to all who do the same. The power of times gone by shall be with us and these things that are meant to be shall be. It is true what our Elders have taught us, that the songs of our Ancestors are upon the Four Sacred Winds, the Seasons of Life, and these songs of life and death awaken our hearts, souls and minds. The wisdom, knowledge and understanding that we share is for our youth who shall follow our paths, and the unity we establish in this most Sacred Way will indeed make the Circle stronger. Through life we live as our Ancestors who have gone before us, whose blood does cover this, Our Mother Earth.*

The rocks are heated in the fire for a couple of hours until they are white-hot. Meanwhile we gather wood and prepare the area and the sacred things. Often we tell stories, such as the story of the White Buffalo Calf Woman and the gift of the Sacred Pipe. If we converse, it is quiet, spiritual talk only, allowing others to prepare themselves inwardly. We may also have some drumming and singing. Or we may just have a good sacred silence. When the time comes for the ceremony proper, I enter the lodge first, alone and naked. I offer some traditional chants, and burn sage or *kinnik-kinnik* (a leaf-and-bark mixture) as incense smoke, to purify the lodge, the Pipe and myself.

When I come out again, we gather naked around the Sacred Fire. Nakedness means birth (this is a birth ritual), our equality with all life in G-d's eyes and our willingness to respect each other as brothers and sisters—as is also the case with corresponding ceremonies in other traditions, such as the *Mikvah* of Judaism, the ways of Digambara Jaina, and the Left-Handed Tantric ceremonies of Vajrayana Buddhism. "Why do you worry about clothing?" Jesus once asked. "Consider the lilies of the field, how they grow; they neither toil nor spin, yet I say that even Solomon in all his glory was not clothed like one of these." As Jesus taught, we need no more adornment than the beauty G-d clothed us in, certainly not the *washte* artifice of human manufacture.

Removing our clothes also symbolically represents the shedding of societal conventions and prescriptive laws of *washte* society, leaving exposed the sacred chaos of the *wakan* wilderness. By removing our clothes we put aside our social status and peer groups, commonly represented by the clothes we wear, and literally strip to our essential and universal humanness. As Shel Silverstein once put it in a poem, whether we're tall or short, fat or thin, dark or light, young or old, we all look alike when we "turn out the light," when we are in the darkness of the lodge.

By this act our bodies become sacred (*wakan*) themselves, part of the sacred place-time. Removing our bodies' robes is evocative of removing our bodies themselves, the robes of outer appearance that cloak our spirits, revealing our own sacred spirit *within* these robes and perceiving the same sacred spirit within the robes of others. We have, in effect, shapeshifted, as individuals and as a sacred community, into the most sacred form: spirit form. Spirit is, spirits are, always around us, but in ceremony we move closer to them, we attend more deliberately to them, in ourselves and others.

Just as we don't take the *washte* rules of society into the *wakan* ceremony, so too we don't take the *wakan* indiscriminately back into *washte* society. Thus, the power of neither the *washte* nor the *wakan* is diluted by intermixing it with the other. Whatever happens during the ceremony is therefore never discussed back in society as a part of ordinary conversation. Yes, *wakan* visions and experiences are meant to be shared, but the sharing is only to happen where, when, and with those with whom it is appropriate to do so.

The sacred ceremony is a stripping away of our individual selves, a sacred shapeshifting that re-places them within the Sacred Hoop. In the darkness of the lodge we don't see our own or each other's bodies but, if we look with *chantë ishta*, the eye of the heart, we see rather ourselves and each other as spirits. It goes even beyond that to the extinguishing of the "little I" as Buddhism teaches, and recognizing instead the oneness of all life within "the Great I Am" spoken of by Judaism, Christianity and Islam. It is the highest and greatest magic of all: the shapeshifting of the many into the One.

I remember once, many years ago, when a devout Muslim woman came to the Sacred Stone People's Lodge, even though by her tradition's laws of '*awrah* women must be very modest, and nakedness in the presence of someone other than one's spouse is not normally accepted. The *hadith* about '*awrah*—which are not found in the Qur'an and hence, she knew, are not ultimately binding— are properly intended to protect people, women especially, from being looked at with arrogating greed by others. But she knew that there was no need for such protection at this sacred ceremony since she knew those in the ceremony are considered one's family, since she knew people walking the Red Road are likewise enjoined to constant respect.

In explaining how then she could participate, this woman told me that the wearing of the *hijab*, the traditional headscarf, is an outward sign of an inner spiritual commitment. Modesty, she said, comes from within: one can be immodest even with one's body entirely hidden, and honorable even when entirely unclothed. Without the spiritual commitment, she said, the mere physical act of wearing the *hijab* or the rest of a traditional Muslim woman's clothing is pointless, but, with the commitment, wearing these things becomes a sacred act. Since this ceremony was for her likewise a sacred act and a spiritual commitment, wearing the physical *hijab* or a long, shapeless dress was not necessary in her view, because her inner spiritual commitment, her spiritual *hijab*, remained in effect. And the Indian tradition of looking respectfully at beauty was likewise no issue for her because this, too, represented a spiritual commitment, on our part. To me, her beliefs were identical to the teaching of the Spirit Pipe that the physical pipe we carry is meaningless unless we honor the Spirit Pipe. Her courage and her sharing of her very self and her vibrant faith with the rest of us was spiritually powerful and deeply moving.

Some people today avoid nakedness, although this "tradition" was originally adopted solely to avoid attracting trouble after the newcomers arrived. Some traditional people perform the ceremony today with men wearing breechclouts or towels around their waists, and women wearing sweat dresses, but it is much harder to sweat freely and be fully purified when one is even partially clothed, to say nothing of how physically uncomfortable it can feel. Clothing, moreover, dulls the power of the *wakan*, especially manufactured clothing, which carries the *sicha* of the machinery that made it and the synthetics from which it is made, and of the workers in distant countries who make these garments for pitiful wages. The elders taught me not to be afraid to return to how the ceremony was originally, and nakedness is a very important and powerful spiritual tool. I myself feel more a part of the natural world around me. The magic flows through my entire self (coming in the breeze and sunlight from Grandfather Sky, and up through my unshod feet from Grandmother Earth), out through the power of touch. If you have ever swum naked in a pool in the wilderness, you will have some idea of what I mean.

After we gather around the Sacred Fire, the Sacred Pipe, having been prepared ahead of time by the ceremonial leader, is now lit, and passed sunwise around the circle. As each person receives it, the first puff of smoke is offered to G-d. Don't inhale the smoke; take it in your mouth, then release it to the Heavens as sacred breath, carrying your spirit and your prayer. As you expel a second puff, you can use your hands to move it around your body as a purification. It is then placed against the Buffalo Altar so G-d can keep smoking it.

The water pourer enters the lodge first and goes sunwise all the way around and sits next to the entrance. Then the others enter the lodge, going sunwise along the spirit trail (never across it). As you enter, be sure to say "*Mitaquye oyashin!*" or the English equivalent, "All my relations!" After each person crawls through the entrance, she or he continues sunwise around the pit in the center, finding a place next to the person before. Any elder enters in the middle, in order to wind up sitting to the West, in the honor seat. The water pourer's assistant enters last, winding up on the other side of the entrance. Anyone new to the ceremony, or particularly afraid, or in need of healing, is encouraged to sit next to the water pourer or the assistant.

It is very helpful to have one or two people remain outside: a firekeeper to keep the fire going and the rocks hot, and a doorkeeper who hands in ceremonial things when they are needed; when not otherwise occupied, they pray with and for the people inside the lodge. Great honor is given to those who take this responsibility, since they are giving up the opportunity to enter into the lodge. One traditional way they are honored is that some of the ceremonial water in the lodge is shared with them, usually during the Third Age. When no one is available to take this responsibility, the people inside the lodge share it—one or two of them going out between ages to care for the fire and bring in more rocks.

Once everyone is inside, seven rocks are sent in by the firekeeper and blessed by the assistant with sacred herbs. The firekeeper always says "*Mitaquye oyashin!*" as the rocks pass through the doorway, and the water pourer or the assistant responds in kind. It is traditional to say this phrase, or its equivalent in English, when anything or anyone passes in or out through the lodge door. This is a proper ceremonial greeting and farewell to the spirits of the lodge, but, when it comes to the hot rocks, the phrase also warns people to take care so they aren't burned, and the people inside, by responding likewise, signify that they are prepared and watchful. As each rock enters, the pourer adjusts them into the proper position with sacred deer antlers, to the four lateral directions, two corners, and the center to signify the Seven Directions, and the assistant puts some sacred herbs on them, and the people in the lodge traditionally offer their welcome and thanks to these Grandfathers.

When all of the seven rocks are in, the water pourer blesses the spirit trail with sweetgrass that is passed through the door by the doorkeeper. "*Mitaquye oyashin!*" is said by the doorkeeper and the assistant; the sweetgrass passes sunwise from hand to hand around the lodge to the doorkeeper. Everything else that is passed in is likewise passed around the circle. The sweetgrass is held against the rocks until it is smoking, and is batted against the spirit trail, after which it is passed out to the doorkeeper again, with the same words, and the doorkeeper bats the rest of the spirit trail up to the Sacred Mound. After the spirit trail is blessed, the door is closed. It is now pitch dark and warm inside. You will hear the hot hissing rocks. As your eyes adjust to the darkness, you will see them glowing, and the shimmering heat will flicker and flow—I urge you to look closely into the red glow, red like blood, and see if you see the images of the dreams and visions these Grandfather Rocks have had over the millennia.

Presently the water pourer will begin to put water on the rocks. Some pourers use dippers; I prefer to use my bare hands; yes, it can be scalding for my hands to be above those rocks, but it is a gift I can give to the spirits and the Creator. The water makes a *wakan* storm of steam and water vapor.

During the First Age, we go sunwise around the circle, introducing ourselves to the Grandfathers and Grandmothers, and to the *nagipi* and medicine animals who are present with us. We introduce ourselves using our sacred medicine names if we have one, rather than our common names. The assistant begins the prayers, and each person prays in turn, going sunwise around to the water pourer. There are certain traditional prayers during this first round: thanking the Creator for these sacred elements—the rocks, the fire, the water, the darkness, the steam, the trees, the spirits. I always make a point of thanking our ancestors in this sacred tradition, who kept this ceremony alive through the century beginning in the 1870s when it was illegal, often risking arrest or lynching to do so. As one elder, a descendant of Cornplanter, taught me: "The Creator says: 'I don't want you to honor me, but to show gratitude for the things that I have given you.' So, in the sweat lodge, we are sure we say, 'Thank you for honoring the people who have passed over before us.'"

At the conclusion of this age, and the next two ages, the door is opened, letting in air. More rocks are sent in each time. Each age has its sacred meaning, which the water pourer should make clear. The first round corresponds with the East, the mothers, infancy and adolescence, the color yellow, the coming of the spirits. The second round corresponds with the South, the fathers, adulthood, the color red, the seeking of protection. The third round corresponds with the West, the Grandfathers, old age, the color black or deep blue, the offering of prayers. And the fourth round corresponds with the North, the grandmothers, the time between death and rebirth, and purification. During the Fourth Age vast change and renewal may be sought, through the *Wakinyan Wakan*, the Thunder Beings, if people need it.

During each age, there are also traditional songs that may be sung. A number of the medicine songs that I sing myself, and have heard others sing, are comprised largely or entirely "nonsense syllables" such as *hey, ho, hey-ya*, and so on. The descendant of Cornplanter gave me such examples as: *oyé oyé oyé*...and *owajinë owajinë owajinë*....Another Onodowahgah elder gave me to carry old songs with these simple words: *Wani ho, wani ho*...and *ashawë ashawë ashawë*....(I have never seen any of these chants written out; the foregoing are my own poor attempts at transcription.)

The words of the traditional songs are not "nonsense syllables" but words in the First Language. They have meaning just as do the cry of the eagle, the growl of the bear, the snapped bowstring of the bullfrog, even if they do not "translate" in a dictionary sense into logical phrases. And they do have meaning for the other beings—the ancient ones and the spirits to whom we sing them. If we listen with our spirits rather than our rational minds, we may catch something of the meaning behind these ancient sounds.

To put modern words to these ancient songs, or just to burden them with "translations," is to put words between us and the deeper sacred meaning, even to confuse and distort it—which may possibly even be dangerous, if the spirits hear new messages that they do not like. Therefore, as my Zen Master, Seung Sahn, taught me, don't let the desire for a rational translation get in the way.

Other traditional songs have words in modern Native American languages, and a few are now even sung in English—but, whether you understand them or not, don't concentrate on the meaning with your rational mind, since the intellectual quest gets between you and the sacred experience itself. Rather, just join in the singing and let the song speak for itself as an entity in its own right. Whether a song is ancient or relatively recent in its origins, it is not "owned" by anyone or any nation, and certainly not copyrighted! In fact, it is an honor if a song that originated among one nation is picked up and carried by another nation. Songs are still best learned orally—even if that widens the range of variations—rather than from transcriptions or recordings.

The Second Age, or round, is also done in "formal round"—with prayers progressing sunwise around the circle, beginning with the assistant and concluding with the water pourer. But the last two are done "open round," which means whenever Spirit moves someone to share something, they share it. In the last two ages people pray, as they wish, silently or aloud, for themselves or others, or chant, or invoke names of friends whom they are concerned for or who could not attend the ceremony. You should feel free to share from your own religious tradition or spiritual path. You should feel free to say or do whatever Spirit moves you to share; this is a time to let the *wakan* flow freely as it wishes. You can neither say nor do the wrong thing, as long what you do is done in goodness, respect, truth and love.

During the Third Age, healing may be given, by the spirits or the human participants who are present. During this age, the bucket of water is passed around, so everyone can refresh her- or himself. This water, which is the blood of the Earth from having gone through the ceremony, is particularly powerful: *mni wakan* or sacred water.

Bear in mind that whatever is said, is done, or happens within the lodge is *wakan*. People may say or do things of an intensely personal nature. Even when we think we are speaking or acting in a deliberate manner, it still is Spirit moving us. Years ago, an elderly woman who attended the lodge was partly blind and almost deaf, which rendered her particularly sensitive to Spirit. So, if unexpectedly she spoke or acted, the rest of us remained quiet and fully *attended* to what Spirit moved her to share.

This is not a survival ceremony, or a contest to see who is the most macho. I've attended lodges where it seems the water pourer wants to impress everyone with how hot he (it's always a "he") can make it. It should be hot, but not dangerously so. Between ages, water will be passed, which you can take from for drinking or wetting your face, hair and chest. If someone is chanting or praying or moved by Spirit to do something, do not interrupt; if it is something you can join in on, then by all means, do. Follow the directions or example of the water pourer. Do not be surprised if you find yourself "seeing things" or "hearing things," or even "feeling things"—the sensation of beings our minds say are not there, for instance. A common experience is to see bright lights fluttering around like fireflies or comets. These are signs of the presence of the *nagipi*, the spirits. But do not be disappointed if you do *not* have such experiences; it is not unworthiness on your part, but simply that the spirits choose otherwise.

Some people hold ceremonies that are not at all traditional but are still very good. Once, for example, I was invited, even though I am male, to a women-only ultra-feminist sweat. I found that, though it was not in the least done in the traditional way of the original peoples of this continent, nor were they pretending to do it in that way, it was very sacred.

There are others, however, who—even though they may keep the ceremony in an ostensibly traditional way—invite people into the lodge because they have paid the right price, not because they have the right spirit. The ceremony is made easy to allow people to participate who have not been prepared for it. The truth, however, is that these ceremonies are difficult because there must be balances, which means we do not receive sacred gifts unless we give of ourselves first.

Traditionally, if you go through the Sacred Stone People's Ceremony with someone, you are forever afterwards part of that person's family, and you are obliged to treat that person accordingly just as if you had taken a most solemn oath. But when strangers go together through the ceremony, they are in effect making a promise of sacred bonding that they will never keep. In short, they are lying to each other, the Grandfathers and Grandmothers and to the Great Mystery.

At the lodge where I pour, it is appropriate and traditional to give the water pourer a small tobacco gift, but it is not necessary. If anyone who participates wants to give something monetary, I suggest that he or she offer the gift to a worthy organization. This is all I ask for in return: be good to each other as sisters and brothers. Be good to all life.

If a water pourer talks about money (unless you feel it is legitimate, such as to help pay for the wood), or has a legal medical liability form for you to sign, or if you feel Spirit warning you to stay away, then stay away. That person may be just fine for others, but that doesn't mean she or he is fine for you. Keep in mind that this is a *sacred ceremony*, and you don't want to enter into such a powerful ceremony with just anybody. There are many people I love, honor and respect, but it still wouldn't be advisable for us to go into the lodge together, simply because they and I walk the Red Road in such different ways. As water pourer, it is my responsibility to listen carefully to Spirit, and ensure that the people who enter the lodge where I pour are persons who will trust and respect the others enough to be one with them when the outer *washte* robe of society drops away—persons who will be truly covenantal with each other.

My suggestion to you is that you avoid going into the lodge with people you will never have anything more to do with. You should at least know the water pourer, and the water pourer should make sure beforehand that you have ample opportunity to become acquainted with everyone else. And you should be made to feel welcome to come again—since properly and ideally those who sweat together form a small spiritual community.

Sometimes people who are new to the Sacred Stone People's Lodge will be afraid of passing out from the intense heat and humidity or from claustrophobia. You may have trouble breathing at first. Don't panic, and don't pant. You shouldn't fight the steam and the heat but flow with it. Just relax and be peaceful. If it's still difficult to breathe, put your face down and smell the cool, sweet, moist Earth. Some people stick a finger under the lodge's framework behind them to feel the outside air. Remember, the door will be briefly opened four times, letting in cool air. Also, the water dipper is often passed around so you can get a drink, or pour it over your head. If you really can't stand it, say "All my relations!" and the door will be opened. Go outside (just exit going sunwise), get a few breaths and come back in the next time the lodge is opened between ages. Still, while there are things you can do to prevent fainting, don't be afraid of passing out—it doesn't happen as often as you think. But if you do pass out, that is wonderful—it means the spirits want to talk with you! It may come as a surprise that even old medicine men and women, who have been keeping the sweat lodge for many years, pass out too, and in fact are glad to do so! Indeed, this is ceremony is meant to *help* us break down the barriers and enter into the visionary state.

Fear is not an enemy but a friend. It is only when we avoid or repress fear that it becomes problematic. I tell people not to fight fear but to follow it, and learn what it is rooted in within themselves and what it wants to teach them. I tell them fear is like the ballast in a ship, or the tail on a kite: it keeps us from floating away out of balance.

I've also known people who aren't in the least nonplussed by the ceremony. Steam? Darkness? Squeezed naked in a tiny little hut out in the wilderness? No problem, they say. They are like the first boy who encountered the sacred woman: they fail to recognize the *wakan* before them and make it all *washte*. But those who give little, who risk little, receive little in return. It is extremely rare that such individuals have any significant spiritual experience—though I have sometimes seen the spirits really do a number on these people, and come to them in a powerful way that *does* scare them back to their senses.

And I've known people who want to enter the lodge, but never do because their fear is stronger than their desire; they are like the second boy.

Precious indeed are those few courageous souls, of whatever ancestry, who are filled with debilitating fear but approach the *wakan* anyway! When these individuals come to a sacred ceremony for the first time, they may be almost panicked as they prepare to participate in the Sacred Stone People's Lodge. All through the ceremony, I hear them struggling to breathe, their teeth chattering despite the heat. But what they're feeling is okay, I tell them; it means they are serious about this ceremony and that they respect the sacredness, the *wakan*, just as they should. After all, they're in the lodge! They should feel proud of the courage they have shown.

One never should lose that nervousness entirely, the first time or the hundredth time one enters the lodge. The gift of courage, walking with our fears, leads to great spiritual gifts in return. Christians might think of Jesus, who prayed, "Would that this cup [of death] could be taken away from me!" He was afraid, but he went ahead anyway.

This ceremony is not an endurance test. We are not supposed to grit our teeth and *withstand* the darkness and heat, to fight to defend our individual selves against them as if they were an enemy. We are invited to *welcome* these *wakan* forces as wise friends, and let them teach us as they wish.

As the ceremony progresses, you will sweat profusely. When you think you've sweated every drop inside yourself, the water pourer will make more steam and you'll sweat some more. This is all to the good. It purges your body of impurities, and your spirit too. You're never so clean as after the Sacred Stone People's Lodge ceremony, because you're cleaned from deep inside your pores right out, and your soul is cleaned too. It is traditional to use your hands to scrape sweat off your skin and flick it onto the hot rocks. This is a way to share with others since it creates more steam.

The door is opened four times, representing the Four Ages of the universe and of the individual. Some water pourers I have known have the doorkeeper send in the Sacred Pipe to be shared around the circle when the door opens for the fourth and last time. When it has been around the circle, the doorkeeper receives it again and smokes the remaining tobacco down to ash before putting the Pipe carefully on the Sacred Mound once again. Then everyone leaves the lodge.

As I carry the ceremony, just before the door opens for the fourth and final time, any remaining water is poured on the rocks, creating chaotic conditions like those to come at the end of the world's Fourth Age, and, in the last burst of steam the door is opened and we leave the lodge, going out sunwise—the first person in (the water pourer) is the first person out. Outside, there's often a lot of embracing, for we have been through a powerful experience together. Then we cleanse ourselves in a nearby stream or lake. (Though I have heard that the Diné [Navajo] people sometimes use sand.) If no water is available, water is brought in jugs. Then we dry off by the Sacred Fire (you can use a towel if you need to, but

I think air-drying is much healthier). We break our fast with some simple, healthy food people bring. We definitely drink water, because we come out thirsty!

After the ceremony, be sure to thank your water pourer, doorkeeper and firekeeper. (It is traditional to give them a bit of tobacco wrapped in red cloth.) Don't be in a hurry to leave, but stay with your sacred family as long as you can. And be sure to help clean up the ceremonial place. And be sure to drink lots of liquids after you get home!

I remember once, down in Georgia—where I'm called not Distant Eagle but Diss Neagle—when some Tsalagi (Cherokee) folks asked me, "Do y'all really go in the lodge in the winter? How can you stand the cold?" The implication was that we Northerners are pretty strange folk. And they aren't the only ones who have seemed amazed that people would voluntarily expose their bodies to the raw power of winter. My answer is invariably that I love keeping the Sacred Stone People's Lodge ceremony in the winter, because the contrast between cold and hot is deliciously invigorating.

Winter is an especially powerful time to hold this ceremony—it is the time between lives, between summers. It is the time when our breaths rise visibly up to the Creator. It is the time of short days and long nights, when we are closer to the world of dreams and visions. When we get undressed before entering the lodge and feel the cold wind for a few moments on our bare skin, we feel the power of Nature with an intensity to which we are unaccustomed. This, I believe, is a *wakan* experience—a powerful, sacred, even risky experience—in which, by giving something of ourselves (giving up our warm clothing), we become open to receiving sacred gifts. Certainly we can, for these moments just before entering the lodge, manage to let Grandmother breathe upon us with her wintry breath! We must remember that, even (and perhaps especially) in the winter, Grandmother loves us.

(A bit of advice: when you undress, roll your clothes up inside your jacket or coat, and they will stay reasonably dry for when you put them on again later.)

Then, when we have gone inside the lodge, still feeling the shock of the cold, we sit with our bare cold skin touching the bare cold skin of Mother Earth, and realize with our whole bodies that the sacred Grandfather Rocks, glowing with the deep red of life itself, are vital to us. Slowly but surely the rocks and the steam warm us up and we find ourselves, incongruously, naked outdoors in the winter and yet sweating profusely.

Coming out of the warm lodge in the winter and standing naked in the snowy world, cold and hot at the same time, I say a silent prayer of thanks to those Grandfather Rocks, who have warmed me so thoroughly in body and spirit that, although I feel the cold, it is easily bearable. Truly those Grandfathers give us a sacred gift of strength and courage!

When we come out we wash off the sweat, which contains the *sicha* impurities that were within our bodies and spirits. If the nearby stream or lake hasn't frozen over yet, we go in the water, no matter how cold it is. If it is frozen over, we use snow; if that is not available, we use water we have brought with us, though this only as a last resort, because it loses its healing and spiritually cleansing powers once it's put in containers. It is essential, no matter what the season, to resist the temptation to just dry our sweat by the fire and get dressed. We clean away the *sicha* in the sweat first—and only then dry and warm up our bodies by the fire before getting dressed.

In the winter, a good, well-trained firekeeper will keep track of the clothes of those inside, and be ready to put them under shelter or keep them by the fire, if the need arises, so they stay dry and maybe warm too. When we kept the ceremony once during a subzero day, the firekeeper and doorkeeper surprised us when we came back from rinsing ourselves off in the stream, wrapping each person as she or he came back to the fire in blankets that had been warmed up by the fire. Those blankets felt wonderful!

At a winter lodge, it is not unusual or inappropriate, when undressing for the ceremony, to keep one's boots on over one's bare feet, or wrap up in a towel, and then take them off just before coming in. Similarly, it is not wrong or uncommon to rinse the sweat off and dry off with a towel right after leaving the lodge, and get dressed as quickly as possible. I think it is preferable, though, to walk on the snow in your bare feet and with your skin entirely exposed to Grandmother, both before and after the ceremony, and to let the *Peta Owankeshne* (Sacred Fire) dry you off after you've rinsed. It's really not as painful as you may think to walk naked and barefoot on snow for a minute or two. One Grandfather taught me that the mind, our *fear* of the cold, is more the problem than the cold itself. But, if we take the *wakan* risk of opening to a new experience, we will know Grandmother's love in a powerful new way.

The embraces that may be shared within the lodge, or after we leave it at the end of the Fourth Age, are especially wonderful and precious during the winter. We realize through this ceremony how utterly we need and cherish each other, and how utterly we rely on the presence of the ancestors and medicine spirits.

The Sacred Giveaway is an ancient tradition among all the Native American nations with whom I have any familiarity. The Giveaway is done in various ways, but usually in my experience a big blanket is spread out on the ground, and things are put on it. These things are usually handmade and *washte:* healing oils, carvings, sage sticks, skin pouches or woven pouches and so on. These days I often see purchased items on the blanket too, but these should be inexpensive useful items, too. I may be old-fashioned, but I think handmade or hand-gathered articles are better, whether or not the givers made or gathered them—in fact, something's that been through many hands can bring a lot of honor with it.

People are invited to come to the blanket in the same order that people get on line to eat at community meals: grandmothers and grandfathers, veterans, pregnant women, women with little children, other women, older children, and men last. As each group comes forward, every person reaches down to the blanket and takes something. It is impolite to look around and consider carefully what to take, or to take something and then put it down because you want something else more; that is greedy, *washichu.* Instead, just let Spirit guide you, and let your fingers just go instantly to whatever you are led by Spirit to take. Make your choice quickly and step back so others can come forward.

Make sure that your children know that one should not exclaim, brag or complain about the gift one received, but just be quietly grateful. If you think you picked up the "wrong thing," think again; perhaps Spirit is telling you something about your needs. If truly you do not need it, then perhaps you can give it away at the next Giveaway.

The Sacred Giveaway often accompanies social ceremonies such as infant namings, Buffalo Sings, weddings and burials. Where it is common in the dominant society to give gifts to *the central participants* at such events, it is common among Native Americans for people (and/or their family) to give gifts to *everyone else.* The Sacred Giveaway often follows these events because the family wants to express its thanks to the community for being there and giving its blessing, support and prayers. At the same time, at rites of passage, when a person is moving on to a new stage in life, one does not want to be held back by one's possessions: one's generosity is in recognition that there are "greater gifts than these."

If a person receives unexpected abundance, a Giveaway commonly follows. I heard of a Lakota man who won the lottery; within a couple of days he had given away all of the money to members of his nation, since it was his conviction that this money was the result of *their* good fortune as a people, not *his* good fortune as an individual. Gambling has long been traditional, for example wagering on a game of snowsnake or lacrosse. I might lose a precious object this time, but that will inspire me to improve my skills and win it back next time. Unlike casinos, friendly gambling like this is another way to fairly and freely exchange property.

The term "Giveaway"—*otuhan* in Lakota—usually refers to the general kind of sharing described above. But, under certain circumstances, Sacred Giveaway is from one individual to another. If one person has, let's say, a very nice loom, but is not a very good weaver, that person is likely to give it to someone else who *is* a good weaver. If an adolescent has performed a brave or difficult deed, an elder may give her or him a weapon. Since carrying a weapon is a high responsibility, the elder is saying, "I recognize you for your maturity." Individual-to-individual Giveaway is more likely to be of a *wakan* nature, like the giving of the Sacred Pipe. I've already mentioned the tradition of the tobacco gift. This, too, is a particular kind of Giveaway: it is given to a specific person, animal, plant or spirit in response to a specific gift to you.

When we hold on to things too long, they start to possess us; or, more accurately, *wanagi sicha* (unbalanced souls) trick us into becoming greedy or envious. The Black Robes—despite their teaching that worldly possessions are to be eschewed (*sic transit gloria mundi* [thus passes worldly glory])—and the American government were determined to stamp out the Sacred Giveaway because, when people possess things, they are more easily made subject to the laws of property. When we let go of things, especially of things that we greatly appreciate, we cleanse our spirits. As one elder taught me, "Walk lightly upon this Earth." He meant that, if we are carrying a large burden of possessions on our backs through life, we are walking with heavy footsteps, and cannot adjust our course easily—and also can more easily cause harm to ourselves or others.

The Sacred Giveaway "tunes up" one's relationships—that is, it keeps them well-maintained—and helps us to know that it's not how much you *get* but how much you *give* that truly provides real, lasting happiness. As spiritual traditions teach worldwide, giving to others is, in a way, giving to the Creator. Lord Krishna teaches in the Bhagavad-Gita: "Anyone who offers to me in devotion a leaf, a flower, a fruit or just a cup of water, I accept it because it was offered with love from a pure heart." Jesus says almost the same thing: "Whoever gives even a cup of cold water to any of these little ones in the name of a disciple...will not lose his [or her] reward." Likewise, for faithful Jews and Muslims, even those who are poor themselves, it is a strict requirement to give to the unfortunate.

You remember the elder's warning that "with gifts you make slaves." The Sacred Giveaway isn't giving, actually, but sharing. One gives whether or not one has an overabundance because one knows and assumes that one will receive from others—the traditional peoples (not only humans but all the nations in the Sacred Hoop) axiomatically know that the right way to live is to share.

The Sacred Giveaway is, symbolically, an act of courage. Sometimes it has been hard for me to put down on the blanket something I cherish, something into which I put a lot of effort to make it beautiful and useful, or something given to me by someone I love, or something I have appreciated for years. As I put it down, I do not know who will pick it up. It may be picked up by someone I love or someone I know little or not at all, or someone I dislike or who dislikes me. I may see it some day in a stranger's hands; I must, then, treat this person with respect. (This book is, in this sense, a Sacred Giveaway on my part.) Similarly, as I pick up something, I don't know who put it down: is its giver someone I love or someone I don't get along with? Since I do not know, it might be *anyone* in the community, and so I am motivated to treat *everyone* in the community with respect.

It is our responsibility to share. We share whatever we don't need in order to survive; that is, we don't share to the point that we endanger our own survival. Likewise, we give, but we should not close ourselves off from others' gifts to us. With this we maintain balance.

In our most sacred ceremonies, the highest form of Sacred Giveaway occurs: the giving away of our very selves. This is a *wakan* form of giving, because, ultimately, it is most difficult to give out of the depths of our very selves. In the Sacred Stone People's Lodge we give up our sweat and prayers and the comforts and protections we put around our bodies. In the Vision Crying Ceremony (*Hanblecheyapi*) we give up sleep and food and human society. In the Sun Dance Ceremony (*Wiwanyag Wachipi*) we give pieces of our flesh. In all of these we are giving to all living things and to the Creator. This kind of giving is not contractual, in which one gives only if one is sure to be given something of at least equal value in return, but covenantal, in which one gives and *trusts* that balances will be maintained. In this sense, all of our relationships are forms of Sacred Giveaway—we give of ourselves to foster the well-being of all of our relations.

The traditional peoples believe that the wild plants and wild creatures choose, willingly, to give their robes of physicality to us, who lack the natural protections of fur, so that we may live. In the traditional stories, it is often affirmed that, though they die for us, they yet live. If, occasionally, a wild creature hunts and kills a two-legged, we give that life willingly and gladly, so that *that* nation may also live, and we affirm that, though we die for them, we yet live. Kahlil Gibran said, "It is when you give of yourself that you truly give."

There's an old Lakota story in which a young man, grieving for his dying mother, offers the Great Mystery all sorts of gifts—the Sacred Pipe, tobacco, his best horse. Eventually he realizes his mother is giving her very life to the One who created it, and he can do no less. When he offers his very self in prayer, the Great Mystery answers that this is acceptable, and that he should give his life by teaching the children likewise to be giving to others, keep the spiritual ways alive, and be patient, respectful and honorable with all.

Sexuality is, of course, a very *wakan* form of Sacred Giveaway, since it is truly a gift right out of ourselves. The mutuality of sexuality is a perfect balance of exchanged giving. As William Blake sang in "An Ancient Proverb":

> *What is it men in women do require*
> *The lineaments of Gratified Desire*
> *What is it women do in men require*
> *The lineaments of Gratified Desire*

While what I said above—that we don't share to the point of endangering our own survival—is true most of the time, we do very rarely see examples of the most *wakan* kind of Sacred Giveaway of all, and that is the giving away of one's life for the sake of another or for all. Death, no matter after how few or many years it comes, is the ultimate and final thing that each of us can and *will* give away. This is why we should honor the great souls who, in their lives and in their deaths especially, have taught us how to give generously for the sake of all: Crazy Horse, Spotted Tail, Tecumseh, Roman Nose, Sitting Bull, Chief Joseph, Big Foot and many others far too numerous to mention here—as well as the great souls of other nations. Jesus said, "Greater love no one has than this: that one lay down one's life for one's friends," and kept his word, willingly dying on something like the Sun Dance pole for the sake of everyone else. And we think of those whose names are not at all celebrated or even remembered—mothers who died saving their children's lives, soldiers who died bringing their fellows or civilians to safety, doctors and nurses and medicine men and women who strove to save lives at risk of losing their own. All such brave spirits should be remembered, even if we do not know their names, since from their examples we find the courage ourselves to make our last Sacred Giveaway a truly good one.

X

Healing

Healing is a very important matter, as the need is very great for healing for individuals, peoples and the whole of Grandmother Earth. Healing is not something we do as individuals. Those who try to heal using their own personal energies will, at the very least, wind up draining themselves of vitality, feeling very tired or even nauseated, and any healing they manage to accomplish is unlikely to have a lasting effect. At worst, they could do themselves, those they are trying to heal, and possibly both a lot of harm. And those who falsely pretend to heal will most certainly do themselves and others much harm.

Healing, rather, is something done in harmony with the flow of life, with the cleansing ways of Grandmother Earth. If you do healing in this way, it will not tire you, at least not much, and it will always be effective.

You should never force healing on another person. The person should want to be healed, and should realize that she or he has to work *with* you in the healing process, and not leave it up to you alone. The person should also realize that any healing is provisional, so she or he must take responsibility to stay cleansed and whole thereafter, or else come back to you or another good healer. It should be remembered that some things are not deficiencies, but just nature. An elder I know who is a great orator says his tendency to stammer is a gift that early in life taught him the power of words and encouraged him to learn to enunciate clearly and effectively. And, as Manx Starfire teaches, if the person is dying, healing will do no lasting good; in fact, it could make death come more slowly and, hence, with greater difficulty. When a person is dying, only palliative healing is appropriate, such as giving herbs that help ease pain.

It is also very important to make sure, before you try to heal someone, that you are in good shape yourself. If you are not in good shape, take care of yourself *first*, before you take care of others. Regularly cleanse your body and spirit with the Sacred Stone People's Lodge and/or the Sacred Pipe, and, if you have any need for healing yourself, set a good example and go to a good traditional sacred healer. Also, if you have any *sicha*, any emotional "imbalances" such as anger, guilt or fear, you should get these issues resolved *first*, before you try to heal someone, especially if they concern the person who comes to you for healing. If you don't take care of yourself *first*, you will probably be, at best, ineffective as a healer and at worst you can even pass on some of your own inner concerns to the person who comes to you.

Healing is sacred activity. Always begin your healing work (whether you are the healer or the one being healed) with prayer. I strongly recommend a careful and thorough smudging, of both healer and patient, with sage. In smudging, be sure to cleanse the whole body, including parts often overlooked, like the bottoms of the feet. Throughout the healing ceremony, be sure to keep a sense of spirituality and a connectedness with Grandmother Earth.

Blue Eagle (Luc Bourgault) stresses three important rules for healers to observe: unconditional love, nonattachment and clear intention. Unconditional love must be there, even if the person to be healed is a stranger. Nonattachment means a placidity within and not having any imbalances of shame, sorrow, desire, anger, and so on with the person. Clear intention means to know exactly what healing is needed and to focus entirely on that.

A good healer knows he or she cannot heal everybody; there has to be a good "connection" between the healer and the person being healed. They don't necessarily have to be friends, or even to know each other at all, but there should be a bond, a trust between them. It is good for the person being healed to give something—not a "price" and certainly not money, but a tobacco gift of some sort given freely and gladly, and not out of a sense that "a gift must be given." It could even take the form of an embrace—or, as the Bible and the Bhagavad-Gità both say, even a leaf or a cup of cold water.

There are many ways of healing, and many of them are quite effective. The fact that they differ from each other means nothing. If it works, it works. Like all of our ceremonies, there are just different traditions. It is important to remember that the actions or words or whatever the healer uses are just a means, not an end. They serve as a way of connecting to Grandmother Earth and Grandfather Sky, from whom all healing comes. The words or actions are just a reminder, a reality check, to help us connect. The method of healing reminds us of our connectedness to the Sacred

Hoop, and that, once the connection is again complete and strong, we will be healthy. The healer's words and actions are the outer representation of the real healing work, which is done through Spirit. The actions and words are not as important as doing what one does with a good heart, so the true work of healing may be done well.

All traditional peoples around the world recognize the medicinal effects of water—good, clean, flowing water. Flowing water—or, as it's called in the Bible, "living water"— is especially healing. Flowing waters, as I have told you before, are *wakan,* while water kept in a container is not. Native Americans have also long recognized the powerful healing effects of mineral springs, such as several that come to my mind not far from where I live, in the Catskills and the Adirondacks.

Years ago when I was camping high up in the Rocky Mountains, the temperature was hovering around freezing in the early mornings. I would go down to the stream and wash myself in the frigid waters. They were fast-running and invigorating, and the cold was as powerfully able to pull me out of the *washte* and into the *wakan* as even the hot breath within the Sacred Stone People's Lodge. After coming out again, I would walk naked back up the hill to my camp, where I would sit, uncontrollably shivering, but feeling vitally alive, whole and healthy and holy (the same word in German—*heil, heilig*), as the rising Sun slowly warmed me up again. One wonderful morning, as I was gradually thawing out, a hummingbird appeared and hovered so close to me that I could feel the gentle wind of its wings on my cold, damp skin. Experiences like this are truly healing. Just thinking about it is healing me at this moment!

One can have a person lie down and drop cool drops of water along her or his spine. Crystals, like water, can have the same healing effect. (Water is technically a liquid crystal; consider snowflakes and ice, which are six-pointed crystals just as is quartz, just as is Turtle Island, with its four limbs, head and tail.) The Tsalagi (Cherokee) go into a river wearing white clothes, which they let float downstream, after which they lave water seven times over themselves in a healing and purification ceremony. One can also take off one's clothes and walk beneath a waterfall, a cleansing summer rain or a winter snowfall to be purified as well. And water is, of course, central to the Sacred Stone People's Lodge—not only the water brought into the lodge for pouring onto the Grandfather Rocks, which is often passed around the circle so everyone can partake of its healing properties, but also the ceremonial laving in a stream or pond after the participants leave the lodge.

I will tell you a little bit about how I was taught to heal by a wise Kanien'kéha:ka (Mohawk) Grandmother. I am not telling you this so you will blindly imitate my outer actions and words (which would be foolish and possibly dangerous), any more than you would read about a surgeon's technique and put a scalpel into your friend, but rather so I can give an example of one good way of healing, and so I can talk about healing in general.

I begin by thoroughly smudging myself first, then the person needing healing. I also pray very carefully, offering tobacco to the Grandfathers and the Grandmothers, asking them to help me. Then I have the person lie down. Best is outdoors, right on Grandmother Earth. Grandfather Luther Standing Bear always taught that his people always knew to go to Grandmother Earth and sit or lie right down on her when they felt unwell, and she would heal them. "That is why," he wrote, "the old Indian still sits upon the Earth instead of propping himself up and away from its life-giving forces. For him, to sit or lie upon the ground is to be able to think more deeply and to feel more keenly; he can see more clearly into the mysteries of life and come closer in kinship to other lives about him." Take off your sandals, as the Creator advised Moses, for this Earth upon which you stand is holy; indeed, take off everything and lie naked upon this Earth, and let it heal you. But, if outdoors is not possible, then healing is best done on the lowest level of the house or building, closest to the Earth.

I prefer to do healing with the person wearing as little as he or she is comfortable wearing, preferably nothing at all, because it helps my fingers to "see" what's wrong (*sicha*) within. Nakedness also helps the person, in a psychological sense, to feel open to healing; it symbolizes letting down all the psychic walls that one generally keeps up, especially when one is unwell, to defend oneself.

In order to help us keep a sense of sacredness, I will often put sacred stones, or other objects I am not going to name here, around the person in a circle. This is, in effect, integrating the individual's body into a Medicine Wheel. Remember that these things, while sacred in themselves, serve as a kind of "reality check" to help us keep our spirits in sacredness. I may also sing healing songs or use the Sacred Rattle or healing feathers, or other sacred objects. The next thing I do is to take a "reading" of the person. First, I always ask if the person has any particular problems I'm not aware of already, or any areas that are in particular need. Then, I start at the head, very carefully moving my hands down the whole length of the person, going extremely slowly, close to the individual but not quite touching. Throughout the process of healing my eyes are almost constantly closed, so my fingers can "see" better without being distracted by things in the environment. As I do this I am always very aware of warm and cold areas. They feel to my fingers like the warm and cold spots you go through when swimming in a lake. The best I can do is to tell you my fingers "see" them with I think the same sense that "sees" the glow of the humans and other beings in the Sacred Stone People's Lodge. Whatever the nature of this sense, it is definitely something quite palpable.

These warm and cold spots are very important. The warm spots are *washte* and "friendly." The cold spots are *wakan* and "unfriendly." In the way of healing that I do, the healing comes through removing blockages, so the *washte* and *wakan*, the "friendly" and "unfriendly" forces, can flow freely through the person's body and spirit. I have met a Taoist healer whose healing teaching and method are amazingly similar; he spoke, respectively, of *yang* and *yin* blockages and forces.

Let's say the person has some kind of localized ailment. I usually find there's an overabundance of *washte* or *wakan* around the ailment, and a lack of one of these elsewhere. There's no general principle of which I'm aware, though I'm sure the truly great traditional healers I have known did at least intuitively understand the principles involved. However, this is not necessary; all you need to do is find what you find, and go from there.

What I do then depends on the need. Sometimes I do a kind of gentle massage of the area, starting on the heart side of the cold spots and the side away from the heart from the warm spots, in order to break the blockage, like knocking down a dam of rocks so a stream can flow freely. Sometimes I find a spot that feels like a hole to me (even like a vacuum pulling my fingers in), and I press harder on that spot, rather like acupressure. Sometimes I draw the warm over to the cold, or the cold over to the warm, by sweeping with my hands just above the person's skin. I've gathered that this is similar to Reiki techniques.

Sometimes there will be areas that are filled with *sicha*, spiritual (or even physical) poison. This *sicha* I draw out carefully and throw away, so Grandmother Earth can cleanse it in her own good way. I do this with my right hand, which is my removing hand, since I am left-handed. If you are right-handed, your left hand is most likely your removing hand. It may take some experimentation for you to confirm this for sure. Sometimes, with serious *sicha*, I have to suck it out and spit it away. It is extremely important to remember not to absorb the *sicha* within the person into yourself when you heal, any more than you should (or can) heal your own spiritual imbalances. Once these poisons are removed, you can use your other hand to put healing and goodness in in their place. Being left-handed, I find *wakan* healing energy flows sunwise out of my left hand, so I must be careful to ensure that it heals and doesn't cause more harm. Those who are right-handed will likely have *washte* energy flow moonwise from their right hand, and they will find that it takes more effort to heal, but the healing that flows from them is less likely to cause harm.

Be prepared for this *sicha.* Once I was healing a woman and, when I touched a spot on her back that was particularly cold to my "reading," she started babbling about being abused by her father and uncle when she was little, weeping uncontrollably. It turned out that she had been so angry and ashamed and irrationally guilty about all this that she had repressed it, and had told no one, not even her mother or husband, about it. I removed the *sicha* with my right hand and tossed it away, and then let the woman weep in my arms. Later, she talked with her husband about her memory, and he continued to help the healing process.

As this ceremony of healing progresses, I feel a tingling in my hands, provided I am doing it correctly and letting the sacred forces flow through me, not relying on my own individual energies. If I use the latter, I quickly feel numbness in my hands, then drained, and I often develop a headache. In recent years I have been exploring this "tingling" aspect of healing. Remembering how one of my teachers healed using a powerful radiant heat coming from his hands—a heat so intense that he could light a fire with it—I have been working on drawing the energy that nourishes this heat from Earth and Heaven.

Oftentimes, just simple touch is itself healing. I remember once when a healer put her giving hand on my knee, which had been wracked with pain, and just gently stroked it. After several minutes she took her hand away, and my knee felt wonderful—and stayed free from pain for months. I asked her later, "What did you *do*?" She replied, "Oh, your knee just needed some love." This kind of healing any sincerely caring person can do, as suggested by the teachings of Blue Eagle (Luc Bourgault). It's the giving of unconditional love. It's *grokking*, in the Martian language of Heinlein's *Stranger in a Strange Land.* It's the kind of healing used by Jesus, as well as by myriad saints and bodhisattvas. If touch heals, don't go on to other healing medicines—do not squander the *wakan.* But, if more is needed, be prepared to provide it.

Healing is a ceremony. It's *wakan.* So don't be surprised if the *wakan* manifests itself in unexpected ways. It clearly was when the woman released her past pain. Also, sometimes people get aroused or even have orgasms while they're being massaged or healed. As I told you before when I talked about the sharing of pleasurable (*washte*) touch, that's nothing to be embarrassed about, since the *wakan* comes and goes as it wishes, not as we wish. Years ago, I was healing a heterosexual male friend, and he got an erection. He became upset and ashamed, and was terribly worried I would think he was gay and attracted to me. I reminded him first that there's nothing to be ashamed of if one *is* gay or lesbian, but still I knew he wasn't gay. Then I assured him that his arousal didn't bother me and shouldn't bother him; arousal doesn't always relate to sexuality; in fact, it's more frequently associated with sensuality. Men often get erections while they're asleep or when they wake up, when they're exercising or swimming, when they're angry or scared, and of course when they're enjoying a massage or receiving healing. Likewise for women, their womanhood often opens its petals and fully blossoms under the sunlight and rain of pleasurable or healing touch. Wise healers and wise patients (or friends sharing the pleasure of mutual touch) won't be bothered by this, but rather welcome it as a good sign that the recipient is relaxing and feeling better. Wise healers won't avoid any portion of the robe (body) as demanded by social laws, but rather heal or caress the arousal as much as any other part of the body; no more and no less. Making a detour with your hands around the so-called erogenous zones leaves the healing work unfinished, and has the discomforting quality of ignoring the obvious, a kind of negative note in an otherwise joyful experience. There is a significant difference between this *washte* sensual touching and the deliberately *wakan* sexual touching that is entirely another kind of ceremony. During a massage or healing the person may have an orgasm not as a goal, but as a consequence of the healing process. Just as the patient has muscular twitches or shivers spasmodically or weeps or yawns or farts, an orgasm can occur to release the sickness, tension, pain or sorrow within.

After the healing session, the person and I may share the Sacred Pipe, as there is so much good healing in it, and pray carefully with it. I always encourage the person to keep doing good things that will promote and protect healing, and to be sure to stay cleansed inside and out (especially by entering the Sacred Stone People's Lodge).

I cannot emphasize enough that healing is sacred, and must be done with respect given to the Grandfathers and Grandmothers, the Earth and her children, and, certainly, to yourself and the person being healed. Always be sure that the person being healed is comfortable and peaceful and understands the ceremony. I find repugnant the actions of those who are so intrusive as to force healing on others, or who use healing as a way of dominating or extorting from them. On the other hand, if done carefully and well, the healing you bring to others from Grandmother Earth and Grandfather Sky will also bring healing for you as well.

These are the basics, in the way I was taught. I don't think it's right to give more here, because you need to develop your own method, and what works for me isn't necessarily what's going to work for you. Besides, you could get in over your head and not be able to cope with it. Please, if a person comes to you for healing and you don't feel entirely capable of dealing with it, or if that bond of trust isn't there, refer the person to an experienced traditional medicine healer, or to a medical doctor if that's appropriate. Every individual should master at least basic healing skills. But don't overstep your own abilities, or you run risks for yourself and the other person. I am not a highly experienced and capable healer myself, so I never hesitate to refer the individual to someone else.

The healing techniques of the dominant culture are primarily curative, not preventive. That is to say, most people refuse to take full responsibility for the welfare of their own selves (body and spirit), polluting themselves and each other physically and spiritually, neglecting the good things (nutrients and activities) that could nurture them, and then, only after their health falls apart, do they seek out a doctor or healer—long after they could have found much healing in clean air, pure water, fresh food and a good night's sleep.

The healing techniques of the traditional peoples of this continent (and traditional peoples worldwide) emphasize prevention over curing. That is to say, traditional peoples always take full responsibility for the welfare of their own selves (body and spirit), regularly cleansing themselves physically and spiritually, and making sure they have the good things (nutrients and activities) that nurture them, and they regularly seek the wisdom and touch of a healer, not waiting until their health falls apart. One of my great-grandmothers lived to be well over a century old. She slowed down a bit in her last few years, but she still had great teeth, bones, eyesight and not a speck of cancer or heart disease or any other serious illnesses. Yet, today, even older Native Americans—whose bodies are especially susceptible to rich diets and sedentary lives—often succumb to cancer or diabetes. It was so heartbreaking to watch one respected Grandfather lose first one leg, then the other, then his life, to diabetes.

To name but one important element to good health, the time when we sleep is ideally so incredibly sacred and restorative; few modern people realize this. In the dark regions just beyond the twilight of near-sleep, one travels among sacred beings; there one is taught and nourished in spirit. Sleep is also a time when our natural walls, our defenses against the waking world, are largely down. It is also a time when the Creator intends us to express love in sacred and beautiful ways. For all of these reasons, it is vital to share our sleeping time with the right person or persons, and not with any people who are not right for us or who mean us no good. It is also good to sleep beneath blankets woven of traditional materials in old patterns, or beneath furs— imagine the dreams of Bear you might have if you sleep beneath his robe! It is good, moreover, to smudge before going to sleep, and/or to smudge when facing the new day. Sleep, in other words, is like a ceremony —indeed, it *is* a ceremony, so it must be approached in a respectful manner, such that its essential *wakan* nature is undisturbed.

It's also important regularly to cleanse ourselves not only in the body, but also in the soul. Bathing or showering is fine, but far better is the traditional Tsalagi (Cherokee) cleansing ceremony done in a river, or the Sacred Stone People's Lodge ceremony. I remember one elder recommending that someone overloaded with spiritual "gunk" dig a hole and scream all the emotion into it, and then fill it in. That's not bad, but it must not be done repeatedly in the same place, just as a Sacred Stone People's Lodge must be moved from time to time so the *washte* impurities we've sweated out of our bodies and souls don't make the land too *sicha*. A friend told me how a woman she knows was told by a tree that she had buried too much of her emotional pain beneath it, and that it was time for her to go somewhere else.

Traditional peoples who keep their souls clean, on the other hand, can go even several days without washing, and still not smell. They wear clothing that is looser and made of natural materials, designed to be more open to the air— letting in the healing breath of Grandfather. They smudge often as well. They maintain good relationships within and with others, since sour relationships can cause bodily odors and illnesses. Cleansing our spirits is like cleansing our bodies: elimination of spiritual or bodily wastes, returning them back to the Earth, helps us to stay clean and healthy.

Occasionally someone comes for a healing, and I or another healer will work terribly hard to get the person healthy again, and tell the person what to do to *keep* herself or himself healthy—but the person gets lazy after a few days or weeks, and then eventually comes back a total wreck again. How much better it would be if the person did the things needed to remain healthy, or at least sought healing on a regular basis, so not so much would have to be done so often to restore health.

So the wisdom of our Grandfathers and Grandmothers advises you to drink plenty of *clean* water, preferably flowing right from Mother Earth herself, and eat good food (without chemicals), breathe lots of fresh air (not near cities, not air-conditioned or kept stale inside tightly insulated buildings) and breathe it deeply, filling your lungs rather than just breathing into the top portions. Make sure you get sufficient sleep. Keep your bodily habits (sleep, elimination, work, rest) to a regular *washte* routine. Pray over your food and water, and especially over all medicines you take yourself or give to others, and offer some of every-thing to the Four Directions and all your relations. Take walks. Spend as much time as you can in sunlight, out of doors, with animals and plants. Tell stories. Sing songs. Play with children. Laugh, cry, embrace. Keep your body clean. Keep your spirit clean. Avoid junk foods, avoid junk reading materials, avoid junk television, avoid being around agitated or hateful or greedy people. You are what you eat—and read and watch and do. You are what you think about; you create your own environment with your thoughts and expectations.

What we eat regularly should be mostly *washte*: easy on the digestion, full of healthy nutrients. We should gather foods within our own Medicine Wheel, indigenous to where we live, and appropriate for the season we are in. Food should be cooked slowly and lightly so the nutrients are preserved. Likewise, we should eat slowly and drink slowly. As the Zen masters teach, "Chew your liquids and drink your foods." And, after we have finished, we should sit for a while and digest before we get on to other activities. Remember that all foods, even the most *washte*, have something of the *wakan* in them, which is to say they too are medicines that affect our well-being. There are those who say that only certain compounds are psychotropic drugs. But experience tells us that "hot" spices and vegetables and many seasoning herbs, for instance, which contain more of the medicinal, even slightly poisonous *wakan* properties than more predominantly *washte* foods, can pull us momentarily into an extraordi-nary state of being. The ozone-tinged air after a thunderstorm is a good healer. The rain that falls from lightning clouds is filled with electricity, with energy. A cup of water straight from a natural spring is not only good medicine; it will affect our mood—calming and relaxing us.

Conversely, some of the medicines that have been misused to the point that they have been branded as illegal, such as marijuana and peyote, can be pow-erful healers and spirit teachers. Coffee, chocolate and tobacco, too, would be controlled if their producers and distributors weren't such a major force in the modern economy. Marijuana and peyote shouldn't be rendered *washte* from overuse or misuse, of course. But, used sparingly, marijuana is good for treating stomach ailments and glaucoma, and both medicines, used strictly under the tutelage of an experienced medicine person, can help one find one's way to the Spirit World.

This understanding of the nature of food is similar to the macrobiotic diet, in which the *washte* is equivalent to *yang* and the *wakan* is equivalent to the *yin*. For most healthy people, a proper balance is about five parts *yang* food to one part *yin* food, though they would do well to eat more *yin* in the winter and more *yang* in the summer. *Yin* foods include alkalis, those with sodium (salt) in them, and cereals. *Yang* foods include acids, those with potassium in them, and sweet foods, including fruits. Entertainments like television and popular music are *yang*. People who have too much *yang* suffer from nervousness, aggressiveness, difficulty sleeping, and frequent sexual desire that is hard to satisfy. The best cure is to spend time alone and in silence—to meditate or take a walk alone out in nature, especially at night, in the winter and near water or in woods. People who have too much *yin* suffer from difficulty concentrating, overtiredness, inobservant behavior and diminished sexual drive. The best cure is to spend time in close interaction with friends or lovers, in order to evoke the *yang* (*washte*)—to jog together, to hold a party, to hug and kiss, to trade massages, to play an athletic game, to dance or act in a play, to join in yoga or karate or *t'ai chi ch'uan*—or to do something outrageously, irrationally delightful yet sacred. And, yes, it is possible to have too much or too little of both yang and yin.

We must remember to be sparing in the ingestion of things that are more predominantly *wakan*, lest we diminish their powerful healing effect over time. Through frequent use of them over time, our bodies become tolerant to them, such that the threshold of dosage is higher in order to make them effective— a path becomes worn through the trackless forest, and the *wakan* medicine becomes *washte*. Sugar, salt, chocolate and spices are *wakan*. If we use a lot of salt with our food, for instance, and keep adding more because we can no longer taste it, we gradually ruin our health. Alcohol, too, is *wakan*, and should be consumed with great care. Tobacco is *wakan* as well, and should be smoked in a prayerful way and not as a habit or a tension reliever.

When we do need to take medicines, we must remember that they are not problem solvers. They simply make it easier to find the solution. If one takes a medicine (be it a doctor's medicine or a traditional, natural curative) over a period of time, the medication will slowly lose its effectiveness and even become increasingly a part of the problem. For instance, antibiotics over time depress the immune system and lead not only to more infection, but infection that is immune to those antibiotics and all chemically similar compounds. Likewise, antidepressants often become increasingly addictive at the same rate that they lose their effectiveness.

The medicines dispensed in the dominant culture tend to depress symptoms (such as fever) rather than deal with the causative concern, but eventually their effectiveness is diminished, and then the fever can return. Traditional medicines are often homeopathic. For instance certain herbs, being *wakan*, actually cause a fever in a healthy person; in a feverish person, they intensify the fever, forcing the body to seek balance naturally, so that the fever breaks instead of spiking again. This induced high fever also kills the bacteria or virus, since the body becomes inhospitable for the pathogens, being too hot. White blood cells also work better with heat.

It is essential to exercise—not just by walking or doing chores, but even in small ways. Stretch your limbs before going to sleep and after awakening, so your muscles relax properly. Exercise your facial muscles; I often do this by making funny faces for children. Stand on tiptoe. And, when you eliminate, clench your sphincter muscles a few times so they stay strong and healthy into your old age. Do the same thing with your pubococcyx muscle when you urinate—especially if you are a woman!—so it, too, stays strong and healthy.

Remember this: our outer world and our inner world reflect each other. If your outer world is filled with unhealthy, unpleasant, unhappy people, it will be harder for you to keep yourself healthy, pleasant and happy. If you live in a highly toxic area, such as a city, or with highly toxic family dynamics, you will have a harder time keeping yourself clean. If you find being in such a situation unavoidable, make it a point to begin and end each day with sacred prayers to the Seven Directions, and smudging yourself with sage (for cleansing) and cedar (for protection). If you have it available, be sure to enter the Sacred Stone People's Lodge as often as you can.

Remember also that it is the nature of the spirit to create its own environment. If you are at peace within, you will be more likely to find your environment peaceful—or less unpeaceful if it is not peaceful. If your spirit rages within, there will be more likely raging in your outer environment. This is not to say your environment will *automatically* be wonderful if you are at peace within, but, if you are at peace within, the vicissitudes of life will have less transitory or lasting effect on you. I once knew a medicine man who lived in a shabby apartment in a rundown section of a big city, and had a family beset with many issues, and yet he lived a long, happy, healthy life. And I have been in houses that cost several millions of dollars, but, though I saw plenty of food and clothes and expensive antiques, there was no love or peace to be found therein. It is very apt, what is written in the Jewish Bible: "Beware a fatted ox, and hatred and strife with it."

And—as you remember you are connected to your environment— remember also that one way to avoid getting sick is, when you are in a stressful situation, to draw upon the energy that comes from the sacred natural world around you. Don't just rely on your personal energy. Remember you are like a tree. Feel your feet-roots go deep into Mother Earth, tapping into the sacred energy she harbors. Feel your arm-branches go up into Father Sky, tapping into the sacred energy he collects. Use this energy, rather than your personal energy, and you will not feel as drained, sick, tense, or dissociated after dealing with difficult times.

When you heal (or when you yourself have an ailment) remember that illness is *not* a part of the definition of who this person is. In the dominant culture people are identified with their diseases. One person is an AIDS victim, another has cancer, another suffers from Alzheimer's disease. In the sacred ways of our traditional ancestors, however, the diseases are unwanted presences that we cleanse out of the person.

For more serious illnesses, I prefer to take the person into the Sacred Stone People's Lodge for healing. During the ceremony, spirits can come, sometimes using my hands to draw the illness out and sometimes my mouth to suck it out, and sometimes working directly. I make sure the person drinks plenty of the *mni wakan*, the sacred water that has been inside the lodge. If the illness is very serious, during the Fourth Age I may sing a very sacred and powerful song that calls to the Thunder Beings. They may or may not come; there is no guarantee, because they are *heyoka*. But if they come they bring healing, for they are very *wakan* (sacred and powerful, but dangerous).

It must be remembered that many kinds of what the dominant culture calls mental illness are considered sacred gifts in the tribal culture. Modern society puts its *heyoka* away in hospitals and drugs them, but the traditional peoples realize they have a powerful gift, and respect them. Modern society thinks you're crazy if you talk with people who aren't there, but the traditionals know this is a vital connection to the spirits and the Grandfathers and Grandmothers who have gone before us.

Similarly, many conditions are considered illnesses by the dominant culture but are not so considered by our tribal people. Being born with "mental deficiencies" or "physical deficiencies," for instance, is among the traditional peoples not a lesser kind of humanity, but rather a different individual nature.

Traditional healers do not graduate from academies; they do not receive a certificate to hang on the wall. They must, however, be effective, or sick individuals will simply go to other healers who are. All a healer can do is evoke the sacred power that flows through him or her, through you and me and all of us. This cannot be learned in a book or classroom. There is only the sacred forces that are flowing through the universe, including us, in every moment.

In the today's society, experts are specialists, and one has to go to the right one in order to get treated. People go to different experts for spiritual guidance, for physical healing and for learning history and culture. But in the Native American culture these functions are not separate but closely intertwined, and one is likely to go to the same person for several such needs. This is because the dominate culture tends to divide all aspects of life into discrete parts: it doesn't see the individual so much as it sees an aggregation of mind, body and spirit. For the traditional peoples, teaching, healing and spirituality are one, because the individual is one. This is why the term "medicine man" or "medicine woman" is not equivalent merely to the English term "physician," but also to "ceremonialist" and "cultural teacher." As a matter of fact, "medicine man" or "medicine woman" comes from *homme médécin* or *femme médécine* in French, and the French word *médécin*, like the German word *heil*, is more than just equivalent to the English word "healthy"; it carries also the meaning of "whole" (in the sense of "physically sound") and "holy." In fact, all three modern English words go back to the same Anglo-Saxon root word.

If you understand that, then you can see why some plants are among the most sacred and, at the same time, among the most medicinally useful. Are they medicinal because they are sacred, or are they sacred because they are medicinal? The answer to both of these questions is "yes." Medicines, such as herbs, can indeed be very helpful in preventing illness and promoting healing, but by themselves their efficacity is limited. In most cases when someone goes to a medicine person for healing and healing is not accomplished, it is not the failure of the medicine or the medicine person, but the failure of the individual to seek help promptly enough or to do the other things that ensure the success of the traditional medicine.

It is only in the whole context of living one's life in a way completely committed to one path, in this case to walking the Red Road, that the traditional medicines *really* do the best they can. Just as the several paddlers in a Haida canoe need to pull in harmony with each other, so in your life you should do all things in accordance with one tradition. If you pick and choose from different traditions, or only use parts of one tradition and do not bother with the rest, you will only wind up with several paddles pulling you in different directions and getting nowhere.

If you learn about the sacred plants and use them in sacred ways when it's appropriate, their medicinal properties will help you in preventive ways. Sage, for instance, is a very good healing medicine, but if you just smudge regularly with sage or drink sage tea occasionally, or just stop and pay attention to some sage you may be walking by (smelling it, listening to its spiritual voice), you minimize the likelihood that you will need it in its curative role. (On the other hand, if you don't need the healing properties of sage, or another medicine, don't use it. Thus you won't diminish its *wakan*, healing, effect by making it too familiar, too *washte*.)

When someone comes for healing, a central tenet adhered to by all traditional medicine persons I have ever known is that it is vital to consider the illness in the context of the individual's whole life. Where modern physicians look for causes, traditional medicine people look for reasons. If you complain of laryngitis or a headache to a physician, the latter will look for a physical cause, but a medicine person will find not a single physical cause but a reason, perhaps physical and perhaps nonphysical, or a complex of reasons, some physical and some nonphysical, in the context of your whole life. This is not to say you have to tell your life's story to a medicine person; they are, in my experience, universally quite able to see the whole context of your ailment, the whole of your life, without your telling them a thing—because their awareness is strong.

In the traditional cultures we realize that life is contextual, and things are connected in other ways besides simple chains of cause and effect. Three people might come to the same medicine person, for instance, all suffering from laryngitis. The medicine person might tell the first person there is something he needs to say but is afraid to, and his body is exhibiting the fear. The second person might be told she has been saying something she shouldn't, and her body is exhibiting more wisdom than her conscious mind, in forcing her to be quiet. The medicine person might tell the third person to remember his body is something sacred he carries, so he must remember to dress it more warmly when going out in the winter. The "prescription" in these situations might be herbs, healing with hands, ceremony, advice or some combination of these according to the technique of the particular medicine person and the need of the individual.

If the same three people went to a typical modern physician, the latter would, in all three cases, do a throat culture and prescribe an antibiotic. The antibiotic might counteract the *cause* of each person's laryngitis, but it will have no effect on the *reason* for it. Thus all three individuals likely will come down with laryngitis again, and return to the doctor for increasingly ineffective treatments, as the bacteria become more and more resistant to the antibiotics, and the bank account empties.

Most physicians in the dominant culture do not want you to think you can find healing anywhere except through the medical establishment. In this way the physician is no different from all the other specialists in the dominant culture, including the religious professionals, in seeking to preserve a monopoly, to keep a grip on the property (the customer) that is theirs. There are laws forbidding people from "practicing medicine without a license." Not only do the professionals keep a monopoly, but also, by not going to the root of the problem, they keep the person coming back and back again, constantly paying more money.

The fact is that you are your own most important healer. You should try to remain very aware of yourself, body, mind and spirit, and do the good things that maintain health, realizing that your self is a sacred trust you carry. More than that, you should be aware that everything you need for living well is within the Sacred Hoop, within the horizon around you. Everything around us is good for healing, such as my family's traditional "switchel," a hot mixture variably made of cider, apple vinegar, honey and lemon juice that is good for colds or sore throat. So why should we pay a lot of money so we can have processed pills prescribed for us, pills which for the most part had their origins in natural substances but have their natural goodness processed out of them?

Given the way people are destroying the environment, there is a increasing rate of incidence of diseases like cancer, AIDS and heart disease. All the hatred and greed being generated is coalescing around the pollution in the air and water, and taking the form of nasty little insects, unhealthful weeds, air pollution, dust and virulent pathogens. It used to be there were no truly evil, no truly worthless species, but that may no longer be so. Mosquitoes, fleas, ticks, weeds, bacteria and viruses all have their place in the ecosystem, but *sicha* thoughts and actions have caused them to become especially nasty, even to mutate and multiply into new forms that actually harm the ecosystem—and massive chemical efforts to exterminate them only make these noxious new species ever stronger. Zen Master Seung Sahn, who himself died as this book was nearing completion, once said to me that, because of the massive human population explosion, there aren't enough human souls to be reincarnated, and the souls of four-leggeds and insects are now often given human form. I have been taught that all these things were prophesied as part of the ending of the Fourth Age. Given these facts, there are some diseases which I would encourage the individual to see a modern physician about, though I would try to ensure that the person still received as much contextual care, traditional medicine, as possible.

If you wish to learn about what herbs and other healing remedies to use for what illness, I encourage you to go to a qualified herbalist or medicine person; failing that, there are several fine books on the subject. My favorite is *Back to Eden*, by Jethro Kloss. Since healing is a *wakan* phenomenon, cultivated herbs will never be as powerful healers as those found in the wild. And processed pills are as different from the living healing plants from which they are made as a pail of water is from the flowing stream: their livingness has been cut off, the livingness from which much of their power is derived. For that reason I encourage you to be observant as you walk about on Mother Earth, and see how bountifully she provides for your sustenance and health.

As you do, bear in mind what Skaniadariyo (Handsome Lake) taught: "Let this be your ceremony when you wish to employ the medicine in a plant: First offer tobacco (sprinkling a little on the glowing embers of a fire). Then tell the plant in gentle words what you desire of it and pluck it from the roots. It is said in the Upper World that it is not right to take a plant for medicine without first talking to it." An elder I know advises that, when gathering medicine, we should never take the first of that plant we see, but only every fourth, thus allowing three for future generations.

Most people these days live in their heads. They think of their bodies as possessions rather than as an aspect of themselves fully as sacred as any other, and so they ignore what their bodies have learned. But when I give healing to people, I almost always find their bodies remember a great deal that their heads do not know or recall, but that unfortunately their heads don't pay attention to what their bodies are telling them. Sometimes while doing healing I will touch this or that spot on a person, and the person bursts into tears, or suddenly—as in the example I gave you a little while ago—starts talking about a traumatic event from years before! And sometimes just an embrace, or sucking the *sicha* out of the place that hurts, will enable a person at last to hear what the body is telling him or her.

All of this has led me to realize the truth of something which several elders have taught me, and that is that the mind is not located solely inside the skull, but throughout one's body. When we see a rock suddenly flying toward us, we don't waste time calculating approximate trajectories and deciding how to move to avoid a collision, we just duck! In the same way, all the experiences we have ever had are fully remembered by our bodies. Once as I was giving healing to someone, I gently massaged her lower back. I noticed a flinch, and asked if there was pain there. "No," she replied, but in the same moment she began to weep, as the once-abused woman had also done, and had memory flood into her thoughts—she started talking about a long-forgotten memory of her father kicking her in that very spot. Her head had forgotten the blow, but her body still remembered it. A friend of mine told me that a Maya elder taught her: "We need to use all our bodies to remember everything. The physical, mental, emotional and spiritual bodies are needed. Without desire, wonder and curiosity there is no intention to remember. Without study there is no understanding."

The thing is, humans, like all animals, are ultimately descended from plants. Scientists document this fact by pointing out the fact that animal hemoglobin is biochemically similar in structure to plant chlorophyll. Perhaps our ancestral plants were only one-celled plankton in the primordial soup of Mother Earth when she was but a little girl, but the fact remains that we have something of a "root" in our makeup. Certainly the *medulla oblongata* and spinal cord are the "root" of our brain. Though zoologists may say there is no evolutionary connection, I think most animals still have in their spines a sense of the stem and in their tails a sense of the root of their plant ancestors. For any animal who has one, the tail represents the past, pointing back toward where it has come from, just as the root reminds the plant of the seed from which it came. Every plant knows its root past, and every animal knows its tail past. But humans, having lost their tails, forget their past all too easily.

All too often we do not listen to our bodies, even when they are fairly screaming to be heard, until they eventually give up, and minor ailments give way to major illnesses. All too often we do not listen to our Mother Earth, who is screaming to be heard by way of unusual weather and natural disasters, who wants us to realize how much we are cutting and hurting her; eventually she like our bodies will give up, and there will come a time of cataclysmic disasters.

Our bodies remember, even though we have lost the tail of memory. And Mother Earth remembers, even though we do not listen. I believe in the truth of what Grandfather Luther Standing Bear taught: that we should stay close to our Mother, we should sit upon the skin of our Mother, and listen to our bodies and her body talking with each other and remembering together. Our spiritual tail can go deep into our Mother when we sit. She can then heal us, and our sitting will help heal her too. Remembering together the wisdom that she and we hold in her and our bodies, we will begin to grow wise.

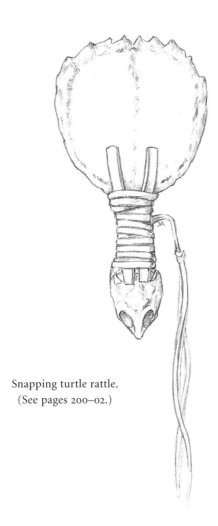

Snapping turtle rattle.
(See pages 200–02.)

XI

Dreams & Visions

I<small>T WAS</small> C<small>HUANG-TSE WHO DREAMED</small> that he was a butterfly, and then awoke to wonder if now a butterfly was dreaming it was Chuang-tse. And Empedocles dreamed that he was a butterfly who died on Mount Ætna, casting itself into the Sacred Fire. I had a similar dream that I sometimes tell as a story:

I dreamed that I was a moth. I was a moth flying with many moths, stroking the heavy night air with our fragile rose-petal wings. We knew no concepts. We were moths unaware. Ours was a dream of light, of a day we never found. It was by night that we sought light ceaselessly, with every fiber of our being. A streetlamp, a campfire or phosphorescent rock, all were to me, to us, perfect joy. For when we found a source of light, no matter how small or lowly, we saw uncountable images of perfection in our multifaceted eyes. One candle became a thousand, a mere lighted match was myriad loveliness, a streetlamp shadowed by shifting tree boughs broke into unnumbered coruscations in our patterned eyes.

How can I tell you what it was like? For us there was no life but in light. There was only light, and into light we would go, gladly embracing the fires of Heaven. It was not death, but sacrifice, a holy act, to burn in the celestial fires of light. We would flutter so gladly in closeknit circles around a flame, not a flame to us but rather a door to Heaven, and we would circle round, in every sweeping arc drawing closer, then soaring away again to prolong the delicious agony—we dipped in, then out, watching the pattering drops of light fall like rain on the windows of our eyes.

The dream culminated in a darkest night. We flew through perfect darkness, weary and lost—on and on we flew, seeking light, hungry for light, and never finding. And then the clouds cleared away, revealing a Sky filled with stars and a full Moon. I did not know who this was who so suddenly filled my eyes with light, and I did not care. I and my sisters and my brothers flew upwards, straining mightily with our fragile wings, through currents of air ebbing thinner and thinner, until we rode the atmosphere, balanced on its brink like leaves trembling on water, still seeking to climb higher, but unable.

What we did then I cannot recall. We may have remained there atop the world until we died and floated down like snowflakes. Perhaps we shed our wings and flew into the depths of infinite space, among the shining stars and planets. Or then again I wonder whether the morning caught us there, unprotected by the gauzy envelope of atmosphere, and we burned in the first rays of the Sun to reach around the curving Earth.

I cannot answer your questions. I am awake now, and know fully well that I, like you, am human. You and I are meant to walk the Earth, to carry a burden of self-awareness, and only to seek goals within our grasp. But sometimes at night the moth in me awakens, and I dream of a terrible goal, a wrathful joy, a door to Heaven to fling myself upon, to die in the impossible glow of a celestial light.

In modern American culture, dreams are largely ignored, except by psychologists and artists, who cut their way through whole forests of chaotic material for those rare nuggets of some potential aesthetic or analytical value in the waking world—just as loggers and environmentalists value physical forests only for their commercial or aesthetic value. Most people so devalue their dreams that they almost always immediately forget them upon awakening, and some believe they rarely if ever dream. Only a small minority pay attention to their dreams, let alone take them seriously.

Among traditional peoples worldwide, dreams are universally and fully respected. But the respect attached to them is not in how they can be exploited in one's waking life, but in the *very dreams themselves*. The dominant culture sees dreams at best as secular raw material that is occasionally useful, while the traditional culture sees them as sacred, to be respected, to be left as they are.

From the very beginning of one's life a traditional person is encouraged to live a full and rich dream-life. Anthropologist Elisabeth Tooker notes that among the Northern Algonquians mothers ask their children every morning whether they dreamed during the night; by doing this, they teach their children to pay attention to their dreams. Behind this is a general philosophy of paying attention to Spirit, so that Spirit will provide accurate and helpful guidance.

This Algonquian teaching points to the fact that anyone—even in the dominant culture—can learn how to remember dreams better. To remember dreams better, you could smudge yourself before you go to sleep, just as you would before any *wakan* ceremony (which sleep is, as a time of spirit-travel) to cleanse away the spiritual impurities of the day, or just set a little sage to burning so your bedroom is filled with the good smell. Remind yourself, as you compose yourself for sleep, that you will remember your dreams. As soon as you awaken, if briefly during the night or in the morning, write down or tell someone anything you remember—even if it's just a phrase, an action or a color. Don't put this off; the act of putting what you remember into words "fixes" it in the memory; otherwise, the dreams dissipate like dew in the bright sun of the morning.

Visions, like dreams, are also common to all cultures. At any time, particularly in unexpected moments, one may have an experience that does not fit into the structures of common experience or the expectations of reason—that is to say, the *washte*. There is no difference between vision and dream other than that we are awake for the one and asleep for the other—in fact, the same root word, *ble*, is used in Lakota for both. To have a vision is to enter into the same sacred world in which dreams come to us, but to do it while we are awake.

Even though the dominant culture militates against accepting the existence of visions, I believe that more than a few people, if they were honest, would concede that they have had such experiences. Morton Kelsey reports a psychological experiment in England that showed that ten percent of the nineteen thousand people involved in it were willing to admit that they had had visions. One can assume that the percentage would have been even higher if everyone who had had visions had been willing to report this fact.

I remember talking with a respected professional of European ancestry who had insisted for years, both personally and publicly, that visions were either the product of overheated imagination or fabrications of self-aggrandizement or the intention to deceive. He saw dreams as nothing more than random memories related to his waking life. But he confided to me after years of such rhetoric that he, too, had had such an experience, but he still could not bring himself to talk about it. I could see how deeply he was moved by it, and wondered at the depth of his campaign against such experiences. It is my guess that this experience somehow severely frightened him or shamed him.

Another friend of European heritage once told me about her experience dreaming while taking a crosstown bus. She was perfectly awake, but dreamed she was having a conversation with someone very wise and dearly loved by her. The conversation gave her profound insights into a problem that was currently troubling her. Moments later she "snapped out of it," and found herself alone on a bus full of strangers. Briefly she was tempted to think of the experience as mere fantasy, simply because it had not happened in "reality." But the longer she thought about it, the more strongly she realized that this experience, whatever its nature, contained within it the solution to her problem. When we talked about it, we agreed that the question whether it was a "real" experience was irrelevant, since, "real" or not, it had given her the answers she needed. Intuitively, she was following exactly the path traditional people follow when they have been given a dream or a vision: that the experience be shared, listened to and lived by. Such an experience is understood among traditional peoples the world over as a flow that one can enter into from time to time— just like the waters of the river.

The common understanding in traditional culture is that such a gift of sacred seeing is to be shared. There is no question on this matter. It is not necessarily to be shared with just *anyone*, but, still, it must be shared. The gift is understood as given by the Creator, or indirectly by the Creator through one's ancestors or the good spirits that accompany, guide and protect one. If this is a gift from the Creator, then it would be an affront to hold back from one's people what has been given. Hoarding sacred things is in a sense, stealing, and can result in dangerous consequences: the individual is too small and fragile a chalice to hold such sacred nectar. One does not "own" one's dream. Such a gift is given not *to* a person, but *through* a person, to be shared as widely or to as few people as the spirits dictate. The individual is just the means, the vehicle, by which this precious gift is given to the community. While it may seem immensely personal, as might be the case with life-changing dreams, the community still benefits from the fruits of that bettered life. If, for example, one receives a dream or vision that "ordains" one as a healer, all the people benefit from the healing power which the individual is now capable of mediating.

As in traditional cultures worldwide, it is virtually impossible for a Native American to become a medicine man or woman without having received a powerful dream or vision that not only "ordains" the person to such a calling, but, in itself, literally bestows the sacred powers through which the person works. However, the mere experiencing of the sacred seeing is not in itself sufficient. The holy experience itself "conceives" the sacred powers in the individual, but it is in the *sharing* of the experience that the sacred powers are actually brought to birth. (Remember the four stages of life that I told you about before; these two are equivalent to *sichun* and *tun*). The beginning of the sharing is in seeking out an elder for interpretation. It is then shared repeatedly as a teaching and as a story that bestows meaning. It is shared with one's children or grandchildren, and the healer or medicine person shares it as a part of her or his sacred activities. (That is equivalent to the third stage, *ni*). Eventually, the vision becomes integrated into the cultural heritage (this being the fourth and final stage, *nagi*).

My own teachers repeatedly told the stories of the sacred experiences that empowered and "ordained" them as holiness persons. When I was in my early teens and learning from my first teacher of the traditional tribal ways, I often grew frustrated to hear this or that story again and again. Today, I desperately miss that teacher, who has long since dropped his robe, and would be overjoyed to hear him tell it again. For I have learned that it is *not* "the same story over and over again," but, rather, a sacred act.

Jews tell the story of the Exodus every time they gather for the Seder, Christians tell the story of Jesus's Last Supper every time they celebrate the Eucharist, Muslims tell during Ramadan the story of the Angel Gabriel coming to the Prophet Muhammed, on whom let there be peace, Buddhists tell the story of Gautama Buddha struggling with the forces of Maya (delusion) as he sat beneath the Bodhi Tree. None of the faithful complains about hearing "the same story yet again," knowing at least intuitively that the *telling of the sacred story itself* is a holy ritual that opens up the secular (*washte*) to the presence of the sacred (*wakan*). Every time a woman or man tells her or his own central story, it is a similar evocation of the presence of the sacred.

Someone tells a story, thinking back to the bright shining days of youth.

When I was hardly more than a child, I went alone at my teacher's instructions to a lonely place at the top of a high hill in the midst of a forest. Still buzzing from the Sacred Stone People's Ceremony he and I had undergone together to gain strength for the ordeal, I settled down naked inside a circle consisting of a sacred number of stones. All I had with me was a drum and a Sacred Pipe, and a sleeping bag to keep me warm at night. I remained awake as much as I could, singing old songs or praying aloud, or simply being silent and watchful.

This was not an easy thing for me, what I was about to do. Having been brought up in a reasonably typical post-World War II suburban set-

ting, I found myself frequently assailed by the "demons" of comfortable life. My stomach begged me to put a fast-food burger into it. My eyes yearned to watch television. My ears ached to hear a human voice, my body to feel some simple human contact. It was all I could do to keep myself from leaving the place. "You could be back home eating a nice hot meal and watching a sitcom!" a voice within me kept telling me. At times also I was assailed by pride and fear: a hope that I would receive a great vision, and fear that I would not. And at this point I'd only been up there for an hour or two!

But this was just the beginning. I don't mean to compare myself to them—but, just as Gautama Buddha was himself attacked, tempted, by the forces of Maya and Jesus Christ in the wilderness by the same nonbeing under the name of the Hinderer, Satan, so now I was besieged by all these desires as they welled up from within me. There were visions of hamburgers dancing in front of me, visions of televisions, visions of soft beds, visions of my friends mocking me. I now believe none of these desires was intrinsic to my nature, but, rather, that they are all a part of our cultural conditioning. We believe we cannot live happy lives unless we satisfy these beasts of desire, because we have been trained so to believe since our infancy. And, when we do not have access to them, by necessity or choice, there is a common first stage of feeling ennui, nervousness and frustrated desire, followed by a second stage of surprised peace. "This is amazing!" we tell ourselves after a while: "I can get along without television!"

And finally came the most difficult temptation of all—the temptation to go down the hill and just say to Grandfather, who I knew was waiting patiently, "I have had my vision!" and describe to him some likely-sounding experience. Somehow, thanks to powers far greater than I, I managed to stay within the circle.

It took a long time of sitting and crying out to the Great Mystery for strength before the gunk blocking my spiritual eyesight was cleared away. I personally believe it was not by my doing that I was cleansed, but by the power of a loving Spirit, the Spirit of all things. Still, at last I felt peace beginning to well up in my heart: peace and love, and a wonderful inner quietude. Suddenly the wilderness around me was not a chaos, but a warm loving place filled with stories and love. It accepted me the moment I, in this way, accepted it. My eyeglasses were beside me, on the rock, and my nearsighted eyes could not see very far. So, instead of relying on sight,

I began to hear the stories being told all around me: the stories the trees were telling in their own holy, windblown language, the stories of the little creatures, the ants and spiders, as they went about their business on the moss- and lichen-covered rocks all around me and sometimes over me as well. The story of the Sun as it etched its track across the Sky and the shadows shifted and grew. The story that I knew I was telling all of them as well. It was a beautiful and perfect moment that I will always cherish.

Words cannot describe what happened in that moment. The best they can do is to be like a finger pointing the Moon out to someone who is blind. But let me try to point, as best as I can. In that moment I was not in the least thinking about why I was there, or what I had come desiring to experience. In that moment I was not looking at things and immediately dividing myself from them and them from each other by naming them, but just participating with them in perfect unsundered reality. In that moment I had no wishes, no thoughts, no fears; I simply was. In that perfect moment there was not even any "I." There was just...what Grandfather called Skan, *the Spirit that unites all things. I had, for a moment at least, or perhaps an eternity, a respite from the continual attacks on my psyche by the forces of Maya and Satan, and was literally one with all things.*

In this sacred shining moment I happened to look up. Directly over my head my eyes just happened to fix on a tiny dot in the midst of the Heavens, even though under normal circumstances my eyes would not have been able to find it without my eyeglasses. I could not have told you what kind it was, but I knew it was a bird. It was so small that I know I could never have found it with my myopic vision except, as I did, by accident. And I knew that, if I looked away from it for even a moment, it would be lost to my sight. So I stared at it for the longest time, my eyes streaming with the tears of strained vision, hardly daring to blink. Despite the distance, it felt close to me somehow, united by this arrow of vision flying out from my eyes. And it never moved from the location that it had taken right over my head but so far away.

It is very difficult for me to explain what I felt. The main problem in describing this moment is that there still was not a sense of "I" and "bird," but just of love, of a bond, of a kind of exchange. It was like rain, a life-giving rain was coming down from this distant creature. It was more than like love; it was *love.*

Slowly dusk spread her veil across the Sky, and I knew that evening would soon shroud this speck of life from my eyes. In the same moment that I contemplated this fact, something happened that is almost impossible to explain. For years I hesitated to tell about this part, afraid people would think I am strange. But I have slowly, over the years, become more comfortable with telling it, for several reasons. You know that experiences like this are meant to be shared, even if it is difficult to do so. I also share it because it encourages others to share their own stories: this Western culture, so afraid of such experiences, is not going to get healthy if we hide the medicine. And, finally, I share it because it is the first story for me, the one that bears me into the world, that gives me my name, that shapes me, that makes possible all the other stories. No matter what other visions and stories have been shared with me since, this one remains special for me.

So. In that holy moment at the fragile edge between day and night, between Sky and Earth, between two-legged above and two-legged below, there was no thought of "vision." There simply was this: For just a moment, a moment that felt and still feels like an eternity, I left my body. For just a moment I found myself in the Sky, riding the waves atop the ocean of darkening air, in the last high rays of the setting Sun, stroking the atmosphere with strong wings, and looking down a at a tiny dot on the Earth far below. For just a moment there was this absolute, utter, perfect, beautiful and sacred oneness between young human and young eagle. Around me was the Sky, the blue fields in which the angels, the ogligle wakan, *dance. But I was perfectly alone, and the pain of the loneliness was my medicine. I am not sure, but I believe I uttered a single cry into this Heaven all around me, a single word spoken by neither the eagle nor the human but by both as one, the Word that called light into being; a cry that was the song of the universe itself. "A sacred voice is calling you! All over the Sky a sacred voice is calling!"*

Tears streaming down my face, I went down the hill to my teacher, with no doubt that I had been given my vision. He already had the sacred fire going; he was already heating the rocks for the Sacred Stone People's Lodge—and I realized how good it was that I hadn't succumbed to the temptation of giving him a false vision!—for he had known in his sacred inner sight that I had received my vision. In the closing ceremony he confirmed for me my name.

The adult telling this story has long since realized that, in reflecting on it, in telling it again and again, there is a certain powerful dialectical tension: at the same time the human and the eagle are so close and yet so far apart. The bird, in its being right over the child's head, felt, and still feels, very near. Yet the distance between it, in its home in *Atë Makpiyah* (Father Sky), and the child in its home on *Maka Ina* (Mother Earth), gives a strong sense of warning, that one must strive to keep that connectedness to the spiritual ways, lest one become lost on the Earth.

I have often in the years since felt the presence of this same medicine man, including many times while I was writing down what you are reading. It is of great and sacred import to me that the Creator has in the past few years brought into my life one of this man's relatives, himself an extremely wise elder, who has read this manuscript and has significantly bettered it by sharing generously of his own wisdom.

Many examples of empowering sacred seeing abound in Native American storytelling, and in the traditions of traditional people worldwide. The vision of Black Elk, received when he was nine years old, became the central experience that shaped his whole life as a medicine man. In the vision each of the Six Grandfathers gave him a significant sacred gift to be used for healing and teaching. He was then shown signs of the future: the spoiling and poisoning of the Earth by the "blue man" (the *washichu* of whatever ancestry who violate the Earth), followed by a time of war, disease and starvation. But, with the defeat of the blue man, another man, a red man, would arise, and all peoples, the red people, the yellow people, the black people and the white people, would join their sacred hoops together into the great Circle of Life surrounding the Flowering Tree, beneath which all the children of all the nations would find shelter. It was made clear that, in the future, the Native American people—and all people of whatever ancestry who carry the traditional ways—will be instrumental in spreading the ways of peace and understanding.

When Grandfather Black Elk was young, he was scared to tell his vision, afraid he would be disbelieved, or have trouble putting it into words. As a result he became sick, and remained so until he shared the story through a medicine man with all the people. Learn from him. If you are so honored by the spirits or the ancestors, I recommend that you share your vision with an elder. Or at least share it with your sisters and brothers, with your local traditional community or other sacred fellowship. Share it humbly and respectfully. Ask them for their guidance and help in understanding it and acting on it. And be sure to give thanks and tobacco to the ancestors for giving you this gift. Never should you use your dream or vision as a way of gaining power or respect. If you carry the Sacred Pipe, it would be best to sit on Mother Earth and pray with the Sacred Pipe, asking for help in framing your dream or vision into words, and to be sure to whom you should speak about it.

I have seen people go astray from the Red Road by sharing their very sacred, very true visions and dreams too widely to the wrong people, and for the wrong reasons. Like anything *wakan*, dreams must not be shared too often or paths of familiarity are beaten down through them, and they become *washte*. The Diné (Navajo) wisely teach that we shouldn't talk too widely, let alone boast, when the spirits send us dreams and visions to help us, because they may think that we don't need their help any more.

Among the traditional peoples, after a person has received such a gift of a sacred seeing, an elder, a wise teacher, helps the person to interpret the dream or vision. It is important that this be an elder, as elders are, by virtue of their age and wisdom, familiar and comfortable with the ways of the Creator, and closer to the spirit and soul of the ancestors. When the person comes to the elder after having received a vision, a gift of tobacco will be given, to keep a sense of balance and harmony, and the individual will describe the experience to the elder. This exchange may take place informally, in the elder's abode, or more formally, in the context of a sacred ritual such as the Sacred Stone People's Lodge ceremony. The traditional elder will consider the experience real and meaningful *on its own terms*, and wholly applicable to whatever situation may be at hand.

The sacred experience may be shared with the community in several ways. One way is through its being danced or acted out. I've read the descriptions of Jesuit priests who in 1656 observed the New Year ceremonies of the Iroquois Confederacy, the *Ononharoia* ("Turning the Brain Upside-Down"), in which, despite the extremely cold winter, men, women and children ran naked through the streets, some acting out their dreams—forbidden to use words to do so—and others tried to guess and join in acting out the dreams others had dreamed. Often it would be a dream that something was given by one person to another: an object, a teaching, a sexual encounter, almost anything. The custom barely survives to this day in the "Naked Dance," though significantly tamed from what it used to be. An Onodowahgah (Seneca) elder descended from Cornplanter told me also of "Worry Night," which no longer survives, during which people would sit together through the night of the new year, until dawn began to break, telling each other their dreams.

Another Jesuit, Père Paul Ragéneau, adumbrated modern psychology when he said of a similar tribe in 1648 that: "In addition to the desires that we generally have that are free—or, at least, voluntary in us—which arise from a previous knowledge of some goodness that we imagine to exist in the thing desired, the Huron believe that our souls have other desires, which are, as it were, inborn and concealed.... Now they believe that our soul makes these natural desires known by means of dreams, which are its language. Accordingly, when these desires are accomplished, it is satisfied; but, on the contrary, if it be not granted what it desires, it becomes angry, and not only does not give its body the good and the happiness that it wished to procure for it, but often it also revolts against the body, causing various diseases, and even death."

The acting or dancing out of a dream or vision is not to be seen as a necessarily inadequate attempt to represent it in waking life. This action is as sacred in its own right as the sacred experience itself. Its presentation to the people is viewed as an essential outcome or extension of the sacred experience, just as the fruit is the outcome of the seed. The sacred experience came to the people from the sacred realm, and in its being portrayed before all creation it is in a certain sense returned to the sacred realm. Vision leads to portrayal, and portrayal leads to ceremony. And in ceremony visions are born. So the cycle continues.

I have tried to follow this tradition in my own creative work. Almost all of my novels and plays, and several poems, short stories and even songs are the careful reconstruction of dreams or visions. Once I even had the opportunity to play on stage, in a play based on a dream, the part of the "character" who was my dream-self, and it was literally a visionary experience to be awake yet in that dream—indeed, a very Hodenasaunee thing to do! Others in the cast also told me they felt themselves to be in a dream, or in a sacred ceremony.

Storytelling is central to traditional cultures worldwide. It is stories—and the visions and dreams behind them—that gather the people of a nation together and give them a common identity. Dreams and visions are an important resource for such peoples, perhaps the most important, and the way their sacred power is saved and utilized is through the telling and retelling of stories.

In Shakespeare's play *King Henry IV*, Glendower brags, "I can call spirits from the vasty deep." To which Hotspur mockingly replies:

Why, so can I, or so can any man;
But will they come when you do call for them?

The traditional peoples believe strongly in the reality of the spirits and the medicine animals, and in the continuing guidance of our ancestors who have died. They believe that these presences love us and watch over us. But we don't get something for nothing. If they are going to help us, then we must honor them. We must give them tobacco gifts, pray for them and thank them.

The first step in learning to listen to Spirit, to having true visions and dreams, is to empty yourself. I find I hear Spirit surprisingly well when I just stop thinking and let my mind become still and clear, like the surface of a pool. If you see a deer drinking from a forest pool, you go absolutely still, hardly daring to breathe, your senses fully focused on this lovely sight, but hushing your presence lest it sense a "noisy spirit" and bolt away. Once my mind ceases all activity, I hear Spirit speaking to me, in pure nonverbal concepts—the original analogical, intuitive, orectic First Language that all creatures spoke in the beginning but that humans have since largely forgotten. After years of practice, I'm pretty good at this, and can do it almost any time at will. It's a good thing to practice, the stilling of the mind, letting go of all thoughts; Zen Buddhism offers some good techniques for learning to do this well. I find it also is vital to practice regularly some ceremony of spiritual purification, such as entering the Sacred Stone People's Lodge. Above, all we must not yearn for Spirit to speak to us, or fear that it will, for this yearning and fearing is the very kind of thinking that occludes the voice of Spirit, but rather let go of all emotion, and just be still within, letting Spirit come as Spirit may.

One old Grandfather confided in me that he had never had a vision (in the general sense of a message from the *nagipi*) in his whole life. I knew another Grandfather who had them often, and who spoke with feeling about the great burden and pain they bring, because you *can't* control them, yet you must act on them. Still, lots of people have the impression that it's really great to have visions, and that it's a cinch that you'll have lots of visions if you just do this ceremony or that ritual or whatever. This is not so. The most we can do is to join in the ceremony or dance the dance, and simply be open to Spirit without fear or desire.

We must be very honest and clear with the Grandfathers and Grandmothers, with the medicine animals and the *nagipi* (spirits). If we pretend to visions we didn't really have, or misuse the visions we truly are given, they will eventually not come to us any more. To be truthful with them and about what they give us is a way of saying thanks and giving them tobacco.

Although G-d, whom many traditional peoples call the Great Mystery, is present everywhere and in every moment, it seems to me presumptuous to take that omnipresence for granted. When people expect you to come to a meeting, don't you prefer to be asked first if it's all right with you? What if you were occupied elsewhere, and they went ahead and had the meeting anyway, and talked about you, and gave you work to do, even though you weren't there to participate in the discussions? Or if you actually were there as they met, but they ignored you and never asked you to speak, but just kept talking about you just as if you weren't there? Well, how much more we need to afford proper courtesy to the Great Mystery!

A few years ago I received a newsletter from a local band of Native Americans. In it was an article saying that some members of the band would be undertaking Hanblecheyapi, the Vision Crying ceremony. Something about the wording concerned me. There seemed an expectation that the spirits would of course be there, as if they could be invoked as easily as light from a lamp.

I remember once years ago, when we had everything ready for the Sacred Stone People's Lodge ceremony, and Grandfather arrived and said there wasn't going to be a ceremony that day, because the spirits had told him they weren't coming. Several people simply reacted with disappointment; only a few under-stood—and understood the teaching implicit in this turn of events.

A friend who was learning from my first teacher went up for his Vision Crying ceremony, and eventually came back in shame because he had not received a vision. But Grandfather said there was no shame. He should be proud, Grandfather said, because the spirits needed more time to get ready for his vision. When, months later, my friend went through the ceremony, he had a wonderful vision. It was worth the wait, and had received the gift of learning to be patient.

We must never forget that we can do nothing sacred without the spirits' help.

A traditional person customarily sleeps lightly, so that she or he, as necessary, can move quickly either way across the metataxis between waking and sleeping. This is because there is *wakan* on both sides of that spiritual border.

One may need to awaken occasionally during a long, cold winter's night to stoke the fire or kiss one's beloved or tend an infant or a sick or elderly relative. At the very least one must remain subconsciously vigilant for wild creatures or stormy weather or enemy two-leggeds, by using the extended awareness I've told you about. A traditional's home isn't climate controlled; one's bed is not very soft, and one's blanket is not made of comfy synthetics. Thus, one is not wooed by extreme comfort into wandering far into the Spirit World. Sleeping lightly is the same moderation practiced in all things; like keeping the fire one tends through the night just the right size so it can be easily kept going yet easily put out if need be. This twilight area, the metataxis, around the border between sleeping and waking is called the middle road by the Atisokanak people, according to John Boatman—the road between the Atisokanak World (Spirit World) and the Now World.

But there's a deeper reason for usually going only a short way along the pathless path of the Seventh Direction, staying close to the twilight regions and not straying far into the darkness-like-death—and this is to show respect for the extremely *wakan* spirits, the nightmare beings who bring the great visions and dreams. These beings are so alien to us that we cannot accurately perceive them when they are right in front of us, and our minds cannot even begin to conceive of them. There are times when traditional people do approach them— that is to say, do enter into deep sleep, do walk the pathless path of the Seventh Direction to its incomprehensible destination, but these times are only sought out ceremonially, after preparation, and only with the deepest respect.

When traditionals go to sleep, they sleep beneath blankets woven in a traditional pattern of natural materials or beneath the warm furry robes of wild creatures. They smudge before lying down and leaving their own robes behind and entering into the Spirit World. Since they are surrounded by the natural world during the day, and since they are lying beneath the robes of wise beings during the night, they are far more likely to dream of sacred, wise, natural beings and events.

Traditional peoples know that the dreams one encounters walking in the twilight regions near waking reality almost always provide wisdom or teaching of value for the individual to carry back into waking reality. Even if the importance or meaning of the dream seems clear (for example, showing where hunters can find the deer congregating), it's still a good idea to consult with an elder about it. Yet, even staying close to the twilight regions, one may sometimes have a dream that is not clear in meaning but is remarkably rich in import—foreboding or especially promising. That is because sometimes the spirit-beings responsible for the great visions and dreams pass through the metataxis, the gray area between sleeping and waking, and into the *washte*, leaving a residue of powerful medicine behind in human society. Indeed, some dreams are *clearly* to be shared directly with the people; one should certainly discuss this with an elder, then share it (at the elder's direction). And don't go trotting from elder to elder until you get the interpretation you like; only go to a second elder if the first one tells you to do so. As one Grandfather teaches, you can't say, "I don't like that vision; gimme another."

Use your best judgment and listen to Spirit when you choose which elder to approach. Some elders are more expert on one thing as opposed to another. I prefer to talk with a certain Grandmother when I dream about some things, or a particular Grandfather when I dream about others. Even when your recollection of a dream is vague or incomplete, if you feel it is important, do talk with an elder. The elder may have the wisdom to understand it, even though it is imperfectly remembered.

And, of course, there are ceremonies—like the *Yuwipi* of the Lakota or the Shaking Tent of the Anishinabeg, for instance—in which the individual goes deeply into the dark lands, where these strange spirit-beings dwell, in order to bring back powerful visions or sacred powers for the people. The *wakan* darkness inside the Sacred Stone People's Lodge (as well as the *wakan* of the wilderness without, especially if the ceremony is held at night or in the winter) is also equivalent to this darkness-like-death, and there, too, we may encounter the visions and dreams that come from these incomprehensible spirit-beings. Moreover, the traditional person can deliberately choose to set her or his spiritual feet down the pathless path of the Seventh Direction in dreams, into the darkness-like-death even while composing him- or herself for sleep. But this must only be done by those who have been thoroughly trained by an elder in these matters.

The Now World, the "ordinary" world, is closer to the deepest regions of the Spirit World, to the darkness-like-death, at midwinter than at midsummer, at autumnal equinox than vernal equinox, at midnight than midday, at the New Moon than the Full Moon. In the winter and during the night, when most people are born and die, we are very near the Spirit World, the *Bardō*, from which we all have come from and to which we shall all return. When awake in the night we are consciously walking-in-spirit in a region where usually we walk in our sleep, and we are more likely then to come upon visions.

If we do see something that may be a vision, we must not assume that it is a vision for us the observer, let alone only for us. It may be for other individuals too, or just for them and not for us at all. In any case, we must not be so presumptuous as to assume we are wise enough to know the meaning, or that there is a message for us. If we are at least seeking wisdom, trying to move forward on our path, then perhaps we may be blessed with a vision. Even then, don't assume everything will be quickly made clear. I have had elders tell me that sometimes it was many, many years before they even began to understand a sacred experience. Grandfather Black Elk pondered his whole life the great vision he was given when he was about nine. I have no understanding whatsoever of some visions I have had.

How do we distinguish a "vision" from an ordinary experience? We cannot ever know for sure. It is relatively "normal," for example, to see the spoor of a bear or even the bear itself in the distance while you are walking through the forest. A bear once entered the camp where my son and I were sleeping in the deep Catskills, just looking and sniffing around in the moonlight. My son, then thirteen, watched with shining eyes—this was wonderful, almost dreamlike, but still a reasonably "normal" sight. But it is relatively unusual to see, as I also have, a bear circling sunwise around your campsite late at night, just at the edge of the firelight, speaking once from each direction, and then disappearing from sight altogether. When the wild, *wakan* beings behave *abnormally*, when they leave their otherworldly domains and enter the human realm—when, for example, a golden eagle flies down and hovers on madly beating wings right in front of our faces, as one did once in front of my daughter and me—that is surely a *wakan* event and, moreover, one that may well have meaning for us.

The metataxis—where the *wakan* verges on the *washte*—is the "very border of strangeness," as Wallace Stegner calls it. When, of its own unpredictable will, the *wakan* crosses the line and enters into the *washte*, then great visions may come. We know this to be so, for visions seem more common at those times when *wakan* and *washte* overlap to some degree—at the twilight times between day and night; at the verge between summer and winter; in the moment of birth and the moment of death; between Full and New Moon.

Arthur Rimbaud envisions this state in his prose poem "Villes": *Toutes les légendes évoluent et les élans se ruent dans les bourgs. Le paradis des orages s'effondre. Les sauvages dansent sans cesse le fête de la nuit....* (All the legends evolve and the elk surge into the cities. The paradise of storms dies down. The savages dance unceasingly the festival of the night....)

But, remember, many people go through their lives yearning for a vision, and are fortunate if they have even one. Other people have visions so often that they yearn for a life free from constantly being torn out of the mundane and thrust into the sacred realm. Either way, we cannot know what is ahead of us. I, for instance, may have a vision tomorrow, and I may never have one again. I do not know, which is how it always is with the *wakan*, and so all I can do is pray to the Creator, through the spirits and the Grandfathers and Grandmothers, and be open and listening constantly with what is called *chantë ishta* (literally, "heart-eye") in case they choose to give me a vision. Only they know if I am going to have a vision.

If we decide in our own minds, "I am never going to have a vision," or "I insist on having a vision," we make it harder to have the vision that the Grandmothers and Grandfathers may want to bring to us. It's like telling yourself, "I could never learn to play the piano" or "I insist on learning to play the piano." If you tell yourself either, it becomes that much more difficult to learn to play the piano. Rather, *chantë ishta*, seeing with the heart, is learning to be quiet within and not make presumptions, so the vision, if there is to be one, may come to us. Gautama Buddha taught well that desire (including anti-desire, or fear) blocks us from progress. Zen Buddhism in particular teaches us how to be quiet within so the delicate *wakan* presence of a vision, like the sighting of a rare bird or of an albino deer, such as I once saw in Vermont, is not chased off by our loud desires or fears.

Some years ago, a set of parents talked with me about their young child, who had told them that she was talking with spirits. The parents were understandably quite concerned about this. If the spirits were real, how could the parents be sure, despite the child's insistence, that the spirits were benign? If the spirits were figments of her imagination, could the child have some kind of emotional problem that needed therapeutic attention? In either case, should their response be minimal (and run the risk of letting a bad situation worsen) or maximal (and run the risk of either scaring the child with their fear or giving the child a means of manipulating them)?

I first reminded them of the traditional people's understanding of ontology: "What is real-for-us is what is real." In other words, if this child believes these spirits exist, then they exist. Just because others have not encountered them does not mean they do not exist; I would be equally foolish to tell you your cousin in Peoria (for example) doesn't exist just because I haven't met him or even been to Peoria. We adults would do wrong to tell the child, "These spirits don't exist," when she knows perfectly well that they do. We would then appear to her to be lying, or foolish and mistaken; in either case, we would undermine our own trustworthiness in the child's eyes. Or the child would believe us, but we would have undermined her confidence in her own spiritual perception, or even destroyed the child's ability to perceive Spirit.

If she is intentionally making up this story about talking with spirits (for attention, to stave off boredom or whatever), I said, then they do not exist. She (like all children) should be taught as a part of growing up to be truthful in all things, including about the spirits. As long as she believed the spirits were really talking with her, I told her parents, her statements should be taken seriously. William Blake, the great visionary poet and painter of the early nineteenth century, told people how he talked with spirits all the time. He was considered insane by many who knew him. Yet the illustrations and poems these spirits helped him create are among the most powerful and beautiful in history. Like the Native American elders he had heard of and honored in his writings, he never doubted the existence of these spirits.

I do believe in the existence of spirits, the *nagipi*. I believe they are around us all the time. I have heard their voices and felt them touch me. I carry two chants that were taught by spirits. For many years I carried a *wotai* (sacred stone) that was given to me by spirits and was eventually taken back. Is this a matter of my imagination? I consider that a foolish question. All I can tell you is that these spirits are real-for-me. Whether or not you accept their reality is your concern.

I believe that spirits are just like human beings in that they are neither good nor bad by nature, but sometimes do what subjectively seem to us to be good things, and sometimes bad things. A few do good all the time and some do bad all the time, but that is coincidence, since the actions of most vary somewhere in between. Those who can be relied on to do good all the time are *washte*; they like us and try to help us. Those who do things that are discomforting to us are *wakan*; they don't like us, and they can hurt us (just as wild [*wakan*] animals and poisonous plants can), but they still can be powerful medicine. The ones who usually do good will tell you they are good, and the ones who can hurt us, being unpredictable (*wakan*), may also tell you they are good, so it is up to the individual to be very aware and discriminating. As with human beings, we must learn to discern with the eye of our heart (*chantë ishta*).

I believe that morality is something associated with being in the body. Being in the body is what leads to *sicha*, imbalance, when we injure, rape, steal from, or kill others, directly or indirectly. Spirits, not being in bodies, are essentially amoral, not subject to *washte* cultural standards regarding behavior. On the other hand, being spirits, they cannot harm us unless, at least subconsciously, we give them permission to do so. In other words, if we *believe* they can hurt us, they *can* hurt us, since the traditional ontology tells us that our believing anything makes it real. All spirits, whether they tend only to do good or not, can try to manipulate us, so we must always be attentive, ready to accept guidance and protection, and resist the dangers—just as we would be careful when approached by a bear in the woods.

I concluded what I had to say to the parents of this child by saying that they needed to teach her that it is important not only to know how to care for and protect ourselves physically, but to care for and protect ourselves spiritually. Just as (for example) we resist unwanted sexual attention, so should we resist unwanted spiritual attention. What I said to them I say to you: it is foolish (and potentially dangerous) to be afraid of the spirits, and even more foolish (and potentially dangerous) not to believe in their existence. It is best to accept their existence, but to be discerning, to keep oneself physically and spiritually clean and protected, and to listen to the spirits as we should listen to other beings, for whatever teaching, guidance and protection they may offer us, but cautiously.

Imagination is the intuition of the spirit within, and we should not be afraid to set it free. For Spirit comes to us on the paths of imagination. Very often we think we see things, hear voices, smell things, that we often tell ourselves "aren't there." I've been in the woods and have been sure I smelled the scent of a female spirit. Or sometimes I've heard voices, or seen forms at the edges of my sight. The dominant culture would say this is just my imagination. But I didn't choose to imagine anything; even as I considered the possibility that I was imagining it, I was still absolutely sure that I was smelling the sweet savor of that female spirit, or overhearing or glimpsing things. If it was imagination, then it was an unexpected, unpremeditated and pointless exercise of imagination. In other words, while we do sometimes actively choose to use our imaginations, sometimes imagination (call it what you will) chooses to use us—to be unexpected, *wakan*. That's Spirit. In either case, if we believe it, it becomes real-for-us. In the case of what we imagine, we must be careful still to behave honorably, just as we would in ordinary, *washte* experience.

XII

Breaking the Cycle of Life

Here is a story one Grandmother shared with me about the coming of the *washichu*:

> *It was a hard winter. One night, a ghostlike figure was seen creeping around in the woods near the store of meats. Some people followed this figure at a distance. It was white and it almost glowed in the dark. They saw the figure circling their store of food and finally, the figure went in. It stayed in there only a very short time and then ran out and into the woods with a small bundle under its arm. When the people went to see what it had taken, they found that it had taken a bundle of fat. They wondered at this apparition and called it the* washichu.

The word *washichu* must not be misconstrued as a term for the European invaders, even if it is often applied to them. Properly, the Lakota term for the person of European ancestry is *wichasha ska* (white man) or *winyan ska* (white woman). The word *washichu* is composed of *washin* (the "n" is up in the nose, as in French), which means "fat," and *ichu*, which means "to take." So *washichu* literally means "to take the fat." When the soldiers delivered provisions to the Lakota, Dakota and Nakota, the people left behind on the wagons all the salt pork, which they found detestable. Later, the soldiers would take it to feed themselves—hence "fat takers." One Grandfather spoke about this in terms of taking the fat of the land. He also referred to the fact that many greedy people have become overweight through overeating or neglect of their health, while his own people were starving. The word refers to the attitude of arrogation, of greed, of taking without giving back. A person of any ancestry, including Native American, can be *washichu*. Because such individuals are so common among people of the dominant culture and because the dominant culture often promotes such behavior, it appears that *washichu* and these people are one and the same. But they are not; some traditoinal people are *washichu* and some modern people are not *washichu.*

While my understanding of the Lakota language is limited, there seems to me to be a very serious sacred pun here, since *sichun* (the "n" up in the nose again) refers to the sacred power of a thing that can do medicine, what is called *potens* in Latin. So, if the prefix "*wa-*" (which means something that or someone who is or does something) is added—*washichun*—you have the word for medicine bundle: literally, something that is in potential a source of sacred medicine power. The pun, according to one old medicine man, refers to the fact that the invaders had all sorts of power (steam-powered locomotives and earthmoving equipment, alcohol and gunpowder), and this power was sufficient to steal two continents. The traditional peoples watched in horror as these newcomers built bridges and dug tunnels for their railroads, killed the buffalo by shooting from moving trains, and tore the ancient hills apart in their search for gold and later coal, petroleum, natural gas and uranium. And this *sichun*, potential-power, used for evil purposes, brings us back to the first meaning I gave to you: "to take the fat."

There is another kind of sacred pun. The word is close to *sicha*, which suggests "out of balance" in the sense of very wrong or unnatural. With the prefix "*wa-*" added, *wa-sicha*, the word refers to someone or something that is or acts out of balance.

The dominant culture typically changes nature to fit to humanity's desires, though there are a good many individuals who care about this Earth and seek to protect it. They are battling the powerful combined forces of the military-industrial-governmental complex, which sees nature as a chaos, a "howling wilderness" that human beings are to "subdue" and "have dominion over" (as the King James Version translates the Hebrew in Genesis). So the *washichu* complex knocks down hills to make room for superhighways, turns night into day with bright lights, and lives without experiencing animals—other than pets—except as plastic-wrapped slices of meat in the grocery store or as miserable creatures in zoos. This complex not only defines some portions of the Earth, some animals and plants and even some humans as worthless, as garbage, but *creates* incredible amounts of garbage—some of it virulently poisonous.

Traditional peoples typically maintain balance by changing humanity's desires to fit with nature. Nature teaches the traditional person how to live. Humans don't consider themselves the "crown of creation," but consider animals and plants, rocks and spirits to be the elder and wiser members of their own family. Nothing is wasted, and what little "garbage" is unneeded is prayerfully and gratefully given back to nature, where it can be appreciated by other creatures, including scavengers, insects and bacteria.

The tools of a tribal culture work with nature, not against it, and hence are relatively less visible. It is harder to perceive a shovel than a bulldozer, a stone chipping tool than a jackhammer. While modern tools are single in their use, having only one cloak of identity, traditional tools have a multiplicity of uses, which is to say they are shapeshifters. Some are *completely* invisible: Native people determine time and season and predict the weather by natural and celestial events, by the behavior of plants and animals, not by clocks and calendars and satellite imagery. Often members of the dominant culture are amazed at how accurately a traditional person can judge time simply by looking at the position of the Sun or the direction shadows lie in, or predict the weather by observing the birds.

Modern science seeks to know everything and to make everything predictable, reducing all of existence to an inexorably *washte* set of laws. Its goal, as Gregory Cajete points out, is to predict and control, unlike the traditional goal, which is to seek meaning and understanding. Modern science seeks to dispel the unknown, the *wakan*. Although Nature is ultimately unknowable, this science seeks to know it, to make it regular and predictable and answerable to the bidding of humanity. The dominant culture has a very complex technology, and that's fine when it's used for good and not for destructive purposes, but its abysmal ignorance of natural, magical ways is equally great. It limits all things, including human individuals, to a single nature. It turns the wild creatures into packaged food or else it exterminates them, it turns the wild plants into pills, it turns humans into economic slaves. It forces all things to wear only one cloak of identity, rather than allowing all beings to carry an infinity of cloaks and shapeshift at will.

Unfortunately, even Native Americans often become *washichu* in this way. That is what was wrong with the complex chart one Lakota gave me, which supposedly explained the nature of the Four Directions: it reduced sacred wisdom to a single, logical, discursive, scientific set of facts, a commodity. And Native Americans become *washichu* when they overuse or misuse the sacred ways—when they visit the Spirit World out of mere curiosity, when they become invisible or do magical work to impress the gullible. Every real medicine man or woman has visited the Spirit World at least once, one medicine man taught; in fact, being able to get there is a requirement that proves one is a medicine person. But, he added, these things are done sparingly, only for the best of reasons. Otherwise, he warned, one might become permanently invisible or wind up stuck in the Spirit World away from one's body (with the doctors convinced one is in a coma). Another elder I knew said such misuse of these medicines wastes the powerful energy of the *wakan* and, by frequent use, wears down a path and makes it *washte*, easy, predictable and convenient. The Bible, too, warns against showy and too-frequent miracle-working.

Western culture is only interested in something if it has value. The rain forests of Brazil and New Guinea are being destroyed because the lumber is most valuable when pulped for paper products and the land has more pecuniary value when it's farmed. Some people are saying the forests should not be cut down because they may be contain cures for cancer or AIDS, or because there is æsthetic pleasure to be derived from them, or because they are the "lungs of the planet." There is truth in all these statements, but each states a value for human use. The traditional peoples who live in the rain forests, such as the Yanomamö, the Waorani and the Orinoco, simply see their environment as their sacred home. For them, there need be no more reason for preserving the rain forests than that. But there is an even deeper reason—the fact that they exist. The Creator made them. That should be reason enough to let them be.

Tellingly, modern people speak of conquering a mountain, such as Everest, while—as I have heard a Tibetan elder say—traditional people are likelier to speak of *befriending* the mountain, and to call it by its proper name, either its Tibetan name of Chomolangma (Goddess Mother of the Snows) or its Nepali name of Sagarmatha (Mother of the Universe).

Remnants of the traditional ways are still found in Western culture. For example, one sometimes sees parents taking their young children into the woods so they learn its "language" and learn to love and respect it. However, since most people in Western societies have little access to nature and the culture does not practice respect for nature, their ancient ancestors' tradition of respect has increasingly died out.

Although there is a similar respect for and love of nature and the natural life in early European history—still barely surviving in Paganism—Western people seem more eager to take on Native American spirituality. They sometimes so want to become or to take advantage of medicine men or women that some genuine elders I know got coöpted by the people around them and turned into cash cows. One lent his name to Tarot-like cards based on Native American spirituality—obviously trying to market the product to people interested in either—even though there's no historical connection between the Eurasian Tarot and the spiritual traditions of his nation. A genuine medicine man (or his users, actually) created a pseudo-tribe, put his name on books he didn't write, and even advertised a "shamanism course," for instance, giving people a certificate for a fee—and even offering to throw in the medicine bundle (*washichun!*) for free! Such foolishness is potentially dangerous; there are no shortcuts.

However, so much of the dominant culture is attracted to excesses of this kind. Books, mostly spurious, trade on the interest in Native American spirituality by inventing "revelations" out of whole cloth. Several come to mind for their works set in a highly questionable Native American context. Though the content of what such writers offer is, usually, reasonably harmless, the harm is in the arrogation of the cloak of these sacred traditions, and the chipping away at fragile traditions trying to survive not as disparate ideas but in their full culural matrix in a worldwide flood of European-American *washte* civilization.

The *washichu* way, in whatever culture it infects, is to take as much as possible, whether one needs all of it or not, even if the taking destroys another culture. The traditional way is to take respectfully no more than is needed, give thanks, and return what isn't needed. The Zen master Dogen Zengi once chastised a young monk for taking a bucketful of water from a stream and then pouring out on the bank the water he didn't need. Even in small ways, waste not.

If nature is ultimately unknowable, so too is the human soul. When we say a person is predictable, we have dehumanized that person. The dominant culture seeks to make people as predictable as computers. But, while computers are predictable, people by their very nature are not. By the time we think we have fully understood someone, she or he has changed. Truly to love someone is to say, "I can never fully know you, but I love you anyway." So, because there is no room for mystery in science, there also is no room for love. Love is reduced by science to hormonal reactions.

I had a vivid dream a few years ago (which I've since turned into a stage play) of a future in which modern civilization has completely stamped out the last vestiges of love and sexuality along with the last wildernesses, replacing it with the laboratory conception of various grades of mass-produced workers. An underground movement is trying to keep the *wakan* of love, sexuality and spirituality alive; the dream and the play revolve around two people of this underground movement spending their last night in prison before being executed for their "crimes" in the morning. This is not fiction, I believe. Unfortunately, it could happen in just this way; for a long time the dehumanization of human closeness has been moving in this direction. Certainly for centuries, until relatively recently, most Europeans and European-descended peoples thought of sexuality—or even pleasurable human touch—as evil, and partook of it furtively, often with a sense of guilt.

When the Christian teachings came to this continent, through the Black Robes, some Native American individuals and communities accepted the view that the body and its pleasures and desires are evil and to be eschewed. They became as emotionally stunted and sexually constipated as these priests, avoiding pleasure of touch of self or other. This view has been reinforced ever since by the rather simplistic, repressive version of Christianity found on most reservations.

Previous to the arrival of Christianity, touch was welcome among the traditional peoples simply because it was pleasant and harmed no one, and could even be therapeutic. Many records suggest, however, that early European visitors took this open-minded view as a golden opportunity to have sex with as many Native women as possible. In many cases, the Native people were as welcoming and willing to share in this matter as they were in others, such as food and shelter. But quickly they learned that these new arrivals did not share their ethics, and that they saw sexuality as something to be taken, by trickery and often violently, without any sensual play first, just as they were taking the land and its wild inhabitants, brutally and without warning. Moreover, these new arrivals had no idea how to prevent unwanted pregnancy by avoiding lovemaking at ovulation times, or how to use certain herbs as natural abortifacients. They cared not at all that they spread terrible venereal diseases. These uncivilized (as they appeared to Natives—dirty, smelly, noisy, uncouth, violent) newcomers seemed to have no idea of the sacredness of sexuality, but rather saw it as a *washte* possession to be taken by right of force.

More recently, many Europeans, and individuals of Native American ancestry who separate themselves from the traditional culture with its overlay of Christian repressiveness, have joined the cultural swing to the other extreme, embracing all too literally the dictum of taking all the pleasure you can grasp. But this extreme is ultimately just as empty as demanding avoidance of the evil of human closeness, for it too reduces physical interaction to a *washte* commodity.

I use the word "spirituality" in contrast to the word "religion." "Spirituality" refers to something we all possess, an innate need to seek a connection with Spirit beyond the self. It does not require rules or doctrines or rituals or even a deity or deities. "Religion," however, suggests the organized religions that entered Turtle Island with the European conquerors. It comes from the Latin *religare*, "to bind up" or "to bind together." These are all too often secular organizations, even businesses, determined to bind up their adherents the way a spider binds up its prey for future meals (no offense to spiders intended). As businesses, they "milk" their adherents to accumulate the money and willing workers needed to continue to expand their empire. Meanwhile, to justify this enslavement of adherents and to guarantee their continued expansion, they name an enemy and exaggerate its threat. They become like a monster that devours to satisfy its appetite, which then grows bigger from having devoured so much, in turn making it even hungrier than it was before. They are infested with rules and commonly discourage free thinking, not to mention any direct connection between the individual and Spirit. They try to preserve a monopoly over spiritual matters, saying you will never attain the sacred except through them. They say they are setting you free, but they are in fact limiting your freedom of choice and inculcating in you a love for staying in a comfortable womb and never growing up and accepting responsibility for yourself. Like grass lawns, they keep their adherents from ever growing up; like dairy cows, they keep their adherents at peak production. As one elder taught, each of us truly has a choice in our words and actions, and, though the *washichu* would wrest it away from us, we must recognize that we *do* have that freedom-and-responsibility, and assiduously practice using it properly and well.

According to the great Jesuit teacher Father Bernard Lonergan, the shrine of spirituality is in each of us; the atheist may declare it empty and the agnostic may not have looked deeply into it, but the shrine is still there. There are those adherents to the Western religions who are deeply, genuinely spiritual, but their spirituality is often found and cultivated *despite* the organized religions they are a part of, and they often must struggle to avoid being chastized, psychologically beaten into submission or rooted out by the organization.

Organized religion, when it becomes a business, tends to dull and trivialize the *wakan*, finding ways to make it comfortable and expedient so people are rarely truly spiritually challenged, essentially making the *wakan washte*. Religion often tends to give people reason to feel good about their lives as they are, to jus-tify their failure to change their self-centered ways. Religion tends to "inoculate" its adherents with a dead virus of *wakan* spirituality that shields them from experiencing the living presence of the holy. In the various organized religions one can indeed find pockets of true spirituality, though they are usually frowned upon by the religious organizations, and have to be kept quiet and remain hidden lest they be stamped out. The only tradition I know that fully and openly affirms the spirit of the individual in community, that uninhibitedly allows the full flow of the sacred (*wakan*) unimpeded by societal rules (*washte*), is that of the traditional peoples, in this continent and throughout the world.

For example, while confession and absolution is part of the cycle of shame and guilt that pervades Western culture, the traditional people understand this sacred activity as rather a positive act of community spiritual cleansing, not unlike cleaning out the longhouse. Among the Hodenasaunee, it was essential that at the closing of the old year every individual, beginning with the Faithkeepers, publicly confess her or his wrongdoing while holding up a string of white wampum, the color representing peace and (restored) purity. A lock of hair from each person's head was burned in seeking of forgiveness. The ashes from every hearth were raked out by two Faithkeepers called "Our Uncles the Big Heads," a term referring to minds that had been touched, disturbed, by the *wakan* (the sacred).

At the New Year itself, the Black Robes were fascinated yet shocked to see the Hodenasaunee doing a sacred ritual I mentioned before called the Naked Dance through the snow-covered streets between the longhouses, and to see anyone who had had a dream go from house to house, silently acting it out, and seeing if anyone could correctly guess the nature of the dream. A particu-larly powerful or troubling dream would be acted out by all the people, as what concerned one concerned all. Thus, by paying attention to dreams—to fears and angers and desires that had not yet reached the conscious, volitional mind, and thus could not be confessed while holding white wampum—the Hodenasaunee continued to empty themselves of *sicha*.

Finally, as the New Year traditions drew to a close, the Condolence would be (and, fortunately, is still) said as an act of—not absolution quite, but of reestablishing unity with all that is. In this beautiful litany the leader thanks, one by one, every living thing in creation—plants, animals, Sun, Moon, Stars, the Earth, and, finally, the Creator—with the community response to each, "And now our minds are one."

In the dominant culture art and nature are often spoken of as if they were opposites. The question is often asked, for instance, "Does art imitate nature or does nature imitate art?" Art is seen as deliberate activity to create beauty, and nature as random events in which humans can occasionally discern beauty—but that the beauty is "in the eye of the beholder," in the act of ascribing beauty to nature, not in nature itself.

Among the traditional peoples, art and nature are seen as closely akin, if not identical. The Creator is seen as the maker of all things and all things—as we learn from the story of the White Buffalo Calf Woman—are both *washte* and *wakan*: beautiful and sacred. Because we are creatures of the Earth, just the same as all other creatures of the Earth, the things we do create beauty just as is the case with other creatures.

Of course, humans now make many things that destroy beauty, such as implements of mass destruction, earthmoving equipment, propaganda and synthetic poisons. These things are not natural; they are neither *washte* nor *wakan*, though they commonly pretend they are—they have a "terrible beauty," as the poet Yeats put it—the terrible beauty of massive urban ghettos with imperialistic skyscrapers rising above them, the terrible beauty of Big Brother's beatific face in Orwell's nightmare novel *1984* (or the earlier and even more frightening *We*, by Yevgeny Zamyatin), the terrible beauty of the gas chamber and mushroom cloud. Rather, they are *sicha*, out of balance, and striving to tip the rest of the world into imbalance.

But let us be fair. All cultures, including the Native American, have done things that are *sicha*, for instance the forced stampeding of buffalo herds over a cliff, or the torturing or enslavement of war captives— though the torture of enemy warriors was often understood as a way of respecting them, since they would gain great honor by stoically withstanding the pain, and the slaves were often ultimately adopted by their captors (as many tribes did this, new blood was circulated in the gene pool). Still, it is my opinion that there is far more *sicha* in the dominant culture than any other—to the point that it is destroying minority cultures in its mass production of *sicha*.

In modern society people create things for the value they produce. Whether it is a symphony or a widget, it is made so that its maker may receive value in return. The symphony and the widget both are assigned a monetary value. It is therefore possible to determine the comparative value of making a widget and composing a symphony. Besides the monetary value, people create things for personal satisfaction. The maker of the widget and the composer of the symphony both want to feel pride in what they make, and want to be praised and appreciated for making it.

In Native American culture, like tribal cultures worldwide, people create things out of utility. When a Diné (Navajo) woman weaves a blanket, the blanket is meant to keep people warm at night, not to be displayed on a wall. It pains traditional Native Americans to see a perfectly good blanket displayed in some rich *washichu*'s parlor, to see a sacred mask put in a museum, to see beaded moccasins preserved unworn on a shelf. Yet, even in museums, the power of *wakan* things sometimes still can flow. A friend told me about the Sacred Pipe on display at the State University of New York at New Paltz, presented to the school in honor of Adam Nordwall for his efforts at Alcatraz in the early 1970s, efforts that ultimately led to the Indian Religious Rights Act, signed into law amazingly enough during the Nixon administration. Even entrapped, that Sacred Pipe is still doing medicine. The original wampum made by the Kanien'kéha:ka (Mohawk) when they first saw Europeans and the Two-Row Wampum they made to record their treaty agreement between the Europeans (long since broken by the latter) are put away under tight security —but, somehow, their sacred medicine continues to be felt.

In modern society artists create their art at least in part to be appreciated: the symphonist and the lug nut maker both want recognition for making what they make. Both would like it if their *particular* creations were eternal. Both would like to be remembered forever as the creator of that particular work. In that culture, great artistic works remain forever fixed—out of the fear of change that is related to the fear of death. So Bach's works are commonly presented note-for-note as they have been since his death, and Shakespeare's plays are offered using upper-class British accents (even though linguistic historians tell us that actually the British accent of Shakespeare's day was closer to the Southern American accent!) and wearing doublets and pantaloons. But I have seen a traditional Japanese *Nōh* production of *Othello*, and planned a presentation of *A Midsummer Night's Dream* in which the stage represented the magical forest and the fairies were nude, and mundane Athens and the fully clothed Athenians were located in the wings and proscenium. Versions like these, as well as such films as *Forbidden Planet* and *Ran*, help to keep Shakespeare's genius alive; they help us to experience it fresh and new.

In the Native American culture the self-conscious artist whose ego feeds on the acclaim of others, the artist who creates, as Picasso said, "*l'art pour l'art*" (art for art's own sake), is not to be found. At least traditionally, there are no artists *per se*—no people whose specialty is making works primarily to evoke aesthetic pleasure. Rather, every person in the nation is able, to at least some degree, to make things that one needs, and the art is simply a part of the nature of the things. They may vary from artist to artist, but the designs and techniques really belong to the *people*, and not to the individual.

To me it is a sad thing to see that traditional Native Americans (and people of other traditional nations worldwide) are being economically forced, simply in order for their crafts to survive, to become *artists, for art's sake*, to make things not so they may be used, but to put a value on them and take money for them. I see more and more Native carvers and weavers, painters and dancers presenting their works to customers or audiences of people who do not really understand what they are seeing or purchasing. The works are often "glitzed up" in a way meant to appeal to these money-wielding people—they are less traditional, less *wakan*, and more *washte*—more beautiful, so they will look good on a shelf or a stage.

Sadder yet, these "artisans" rarely receive the major portion of the final sale price of their works, but are exploited by the brokers who sell the works to wealthy collectors. Money has destroyed the spirit of traditional cultures worldwide with far greater effectiveness than the weapons of earlier centuries. When I talked with an importer of Asian tribal art, I mentioned that when the objects are made just to appeal to Western collectors, the tribal traditions die out. He told me, with a shrug: Too bad—such is the way of the world and the way of the international market. His lack of concern was shocking and appalling to me. He was doubtless counting on these pieces gaining in value once they were produced no more, and remaining on display like the artifacts Hitler planned to put in his "museum to a dead race."

The saddest thing of all is when those who carry the sacred ways of traditional peoples sell these as "crafts" too. I have seen genuine medicine men and women accept money for entrance into the sacred ceremonies, or lend their respected names to books by charlatans, or record the most sacred songs, or put the most sacred dances on stage. One may argue that this selling of the traditional ways is necessary, or else they will not survive but go the way of the Ainu traditions and so many others. Whether or not this is so, it still pains me to see utility and beauty, the *washte* and *wakan*, separated in this way. If beauty and usefulness are meant to be found together, then it is my view that it is better to let the traditional ways go than to allow these two, the *wakan* and *washte*, to be separated, to allow traditionally made things to be "preserved" in a way that only sits them on a shelf or puts them before an audience. Better to let them go than to assign to them a certain pecuniary value. The latter seems *sicha* to me.

What is natural? What is unnatural? This is a matter of some controversy. There are those who say Native Americans should never use materials that are unnatural, as that is not traditional, or because they carry a wrong spirit. I have seen many people who sincerely walk the traditional way (not to mention "wannabes") criticize each other for using "unnatural" materials.

This kind of discussion often takes place regarding aspects of the Sacred Stone People's Lodge ceremony. There are those, for example, who say no plastic should be used to cover the lodge, yet in a day when skins are much harder to come by and we must use blankets—most of which these days have synthetic fibers in them. Others say metal pitchforks should not be used to carry in the rocks, but rather the more traditional forked stick. I myself have lovingly kidded one honored Grandfather because there are strips of wall-to-wall carpeting on the floor of his lodge.

Someone once wisely pointed out to me that, actually, *everything* is natural, because everything we use (except the occasional meteorite or Moon rock) is from *Maka Ina*, Mother Earth. This is true. Even styrofoam and polyethylene, Astroturf and fluorocarbons, are made from materials that come directly from the Earth herself. He also noted that we ourselves are a part of *Maka Ina*, and so what we do is of necessity also natural. Just as the fabrications of other creatures, such as birds' nests and coral reefs, are a part of nature because their makers are a part of nature, this argument suggests that the human creature too *a priori* creates natural things.

I think the problem is that we humans, the youngest and most foolish of creatures, sometimes forget how to walk in harmony with the rest of creation. So some of the ways we do things hurt the rest of creation, and often ourselves as well. Plastics, pesticides, polychlorinated biphenyls, nuclear waste and fluorocarbons, for example, are all "natural" by the definition that in their original state they or their raw materials came from the Earth herself. But I hope no one questions that each one of them poses a huge threat to life on Earth. In this latter sense they are not merely natural or unnatural, they are *counter*-natural. Certain combinations of materials, or certain preparations of them, lose their connectedness to the Earth, thereby becoming *sicha* (wrong, out of balance).

As I have already said, the traditional peoples' way seeks more that we bend to Nature's will than that we bend Nature to our will. Certainly the dominant culture tends more toward the latter. It lives almost entirely divorced from Nature, with powerful lights that turn night into day and push away the nourishing light of the Moon and Stars, energy-hungry systems that turn away the cold of winter and the heat of summer, plastic grass, skyscrapers, and so on. Air conditioning, for example, pushes heat out of houses and buildings and automobiles—collectively, a great deal of heat is displaced on a hot summer day, becoming an unnatural burden on the natural world and the wild animals and plants who live in it, as well as the poor humans who cannot afford climate control. In the same way, we can see some of the materials that the dominant society creates flout the ways of nature—into this category fall nuclear waste, many hydrocarbon products, many war materials, genetic manipulations, and mutated viruses.

I think the key factor is permanence and impermanence. Biodegradability, if you will. The materials that are most injurious to Mother Earth and the proper way to live are those that take a very long time to "die," to break down into simple natural materials again; these compounds go on virtually forever in a horrible kind of everlasting life. The twentieth and twenty-first century's electronic records and its books printed on high-acid paper may not last another hundred years, but the poisonous wastes that began to collect in the eighteenth century will outlast those of any other age.

Native Americans traditionally have used materials that extend the useful life of an object, but not to the point of this horrible everlasting pseudo-life. This is the difference between eternity and everlastingness. Everlastingness is sought in avoiding change, while eternity is found in allowing the Circle of Life to flow at its proper rate. This is why traditional preservatives are always entirely natural substances. It was expected that a Sacred Pipe or a Sacred Drum or an eagle feather would some day become unusable; when that day came, it was disposed of in a sacred way to release its spirit. But, in order to extend the useful life of an object, preservatives would be used, just as individuals take care of their bodies so they last a normal lifetime. Let us take as an example shellac, which can be used to preserve wood. Being natural (in the

sense of being found and not concocted) and not able to extend existence forever, it is not injurious to Nature.

It might be said that it is the very impermanence of things that gives them
a certain beauty. There is nothing about which this is more true than our lives.
It is the inevitability of death that lends our lives beauty. The dominant society
seeks to extend youth and life indefinitely, often at the expense of dignity. As a
woman ages, she "seals her beauty in" with makeup and surgery, holding on to
what should flow naturally, like *wakan* flowing water. When individuals die,
they are enbalmed and placed in hermetically sealed coffins and vaults, so they
cannot continue to take part in the Circle of Life. On the other hand, it pains
Native Americans to see their ancestors' bodies and their ancestors' sacred
things permanently preserved and displayed in museums for this reason: the
Circle of Life is thereby broken. Traditional peoples do not seek to extend life
artificially. When a body has become overworn and tattered from long use,
then it is time to let it go to be cleansed by the *wakan* forces, while our soul
seeks out and enters into a new lodge, a new body.

It is a recognized fact that our spirits and bodies return to the Creator: our
spirits to *Atë Makpiyah* and our bodies to *Maka Ina*. Some day, perhaps, just
as rain falls from the Sky (like sperm) to bring forth fruit from the Earth, our
spirits may return from the stars to unite with new bodies, and we will live
again; such is the teaching of the Flowering Tree. But the fact is, we are
"biodegradable;" we take part in the cycle of life. That is to say, we two-
leggeds are, and should always seek to be, *natural*, and not seek to extend in
an unnatural way the sacred circle of life and death.

Years ago, I visited the Pacific Northwest to meet with some traditional
Tsalagi (Cherokee) people there. While in that region I saw many things that
were powerful teachers. I saw hills denuded of the forests of gigantic trees
that had once stood proud and tall, and covered instead with human constructions. Along the Columbia River I saw where those trees had gone: onto
barges piled high with huge piles of logs stripped of their branches—entire
forests waiting to be shipped to Japan. And this was but one day's load! I
mourned to think of all the forests being killed, all the decades these trees
had been growing into the Sky, their leaves rustling quietly in the breeze,
giving a home to the woodland creatures, all gone in a day. I could not help
but think of the famous words of Chief Sealth, who walked those hills for the

last time one hundred and forty years before I did, words spoken at a time when his people were being forced out of this sacred land. He spoke with righteous anger and sorrow of the ways of the newcomers, which even then were destroying the sacred land for the sake of shopping malls and residential developments and factories.

However during the same visit I saw something more heartening. Already, by the time of my visit, the effects of the eruption of Mount Saint Helens—or, in the language of Sealth's people, *Louwala-Clough*, Smoking Mountain—the fertile deposits of ash that had been spread over all the countryside, wiping out homes trees, and fields, were giving rise to new growth. These forests destroyed by nature, unlike those destroyed by humanity, were coming back. So appropriate, as the story of this mountain teaches us:

> *Wy'east and Klickitat, two sons of Sahale, the Creator, both fell in love with a beautiful woman named Loowit. She would not choose between them, and, since each brother wanted her for himself, they fought over her. Their raging battle buried villages and destroyed forests. It caused earthquakes, even destroying the Bridge of the G-ds that had once spanned the great river (the Columbia). Wy'east was especially fierce, hurtling hot rocks at Klickitat, sending rivers of liquid fire at him, and filling fertile valleys with rock. Sahale was angry, and smote down all three lovers, putting up a high mountain where each fell. Loowit's mountain, Louwala-Clough, is beautiful like the woman it honors, a symmetrical cone of perfect white. Wy'east (Mount Hood) still holds up his head in hubristic pride, but Klickitat (Mount Adams)—who wept to see his beloved buried in snow, now bows his head in sorrow as he looks out at her forever.*

Almost every summer, it seems, forest fires rage out of control in various parts of North America, Turtle Island, and human beings struggle to put them out. It may seem strange to you, but, while I mourn the cutting of the forests, I rarely mourn for the trees and other living things consumed by natural fires. I only mourn for them when the fires are started by human stupidity, such as a carelessly extinguished campfire or a flung cigarette butt. Why do I feel this way? Because, while it is unbalanced (*sicha*) to take whole forests of trees in the prime of their life, it is simply a part of the Circle of Life when a forest filled with elderly trees and dead, decaying trees, is cleansed by the power of the *wakan* (the lightning, *wakangli*) to make room for new growth. In fact, in some lands, the traditional peoples did set fire to forests or grasslands every now and then to foster new growth.

It is a difficult thought—like you, I certainly wouldn't want my house to burn in a forest fire (though, if you and I lived as simply, as lightly on the Earth, as the traditional peoples once did, this would not be so much of a concern)—but we do have to recognize that forest fires are part of a natural cycle, at least when they are started by lightning as opposed to a match or cigarette. They are part of the Earth's way of renewing herself. When forests have a lot of older, hence more flammable trees, and a lot of aggregated dead wood, leaves and needles beneath them, they are more likely to burn. When forests age like that, it is harder for them to support new growth through the choking blanket of detritus from yesteryear on the ground and the impervious canopy of interlacing branches above, and there is also less food for many other forms of life. However, after the trees burn, the healing spirits soon bring green shoots out of the ground, just as they were doing through the volcanic ash when I was in the Northwest. With these forest fires, and also floods and other so-called disasters, the Earth tries to heal herself—just as a body fights off infections with fevers and chills.

Which teaches us this truth: that Nature constantly seeks to live. Nature, the Earth our Mother, as a single whole entity, Γαια (*Gaia*), is herself living, and wants to continue to live and bear children as much as any female creature, if not more. This is why, when left to herself, we see Nature constantly reasserting her right and will to live. This is why stones come up every spring into fields and gardens. That is why ice makes cracks in all the asphalt and cement, so in the spring we find grass coming up through the highways. This is why abandoned buildings and roads are slowly overcome by the work of winter and termites and vines. Indeed, if humans did not constantly work to prevent it, Nature would within a few years reclaim the land suffocating beneath the buildings and highways, and fill it with her living children again. Unless, of course, industrial poisons or nuclear radiation so thoroughly destroy the Earth that nothing can live any longer.

Often humanity forgets its status as a child of Nature like any other of her children; instead it has the temerity to struggle with its mother. How right Chief Sealth was to decry the dominant culture for forgetting that the lakes and rivers, the deer and buffalo, are our own elder sisters and brothers, and the Earth herself is our mother! He said a century and a half ago that the newcomers' cities stink of pollution—and, today, the stink is far more fetid, and dangerous, than it was in his day. Bodies and cities stink with the stink of living death that no perfume can mask. So bad is the pollution that cancer is rampant and Mother Earth has grown sick in many places—species of plants and animals are dying out every day, and others are exploding in population. Summers are getting hotter, winters are unusually mild or marked by snows in unlikely places; wet areas are often abnormally dry, and dry areas wet; robins are appearing in the far North among the Inuit, who have no word in their language for them, and the Antarctic ice shelf is melting—clearly, Mother Earth is growing sick, feverish, and yet still people pay little heed to her health.

Like the people back in the time of the two brothers, like the first of those brothers who saw the White Buffalo Calf Woman, members of modern society see our Mother Earth as something to be raped for their own pleasure. Much of humanity, Nature's youngest child, tries to make Nature into its own child, creating a "nature" eviscerated of her sacred power. They forget the teachings of their own sacred books—the Bible mentions the first sin, the murder of Abel by Cain, as a sin against Mother Earth because the blood of Abel, her child, was spilled onto her body, and his blood cried out from the soil, the body of his mother.

People now pride themselves on their parks of tame trees and mown grass, in which the only animals are dogs looking for a place to poop, which then by law their attendant humans must scoop up. Homeowners pride themselves on their lawns kept green and lush, and their swimming pools kept antiseptic, through the use of powerful and dangerous poisons. City residents rarely feel real soil beneath their feet, or see trees grow except in cultivated plots and pots. Nor do they often breathe air free from toxins, or escape the constant background noise of radios and automobiles and planes to hear the beautiful silence—silence that is anything but empty!—of the natural world. I ask you, is it not good to walk in a forest of Nature's making, to breathe clean air and to swim in a stream or a lake pure enough that you could drink from it, in water that moves and breathes as a living entity? This joyful experience is fast disappearing.

Those in control of civilization try to make the natural world *washte* by stopping the Circle of Life, stopping the passage of time. They try to manage Nature, to improve on Nature, to keep everything just at the point that is considered most beneficial to the newcomer culture's way of living. Forests are maintained at the point of highest lumber yield. Rivers are straightened and cleared of sandbars and strangled behind dams, until inevitably destructive floods occur which never happened when the river flowed naturally. Tomato vines are made to be incessantly fecund, without ever being given a rest; ways are even being perfected to grow vegetables under constant light without using any soil at all. Dairy cattle are unnaturally maintained at peak milk production. Parks and golf courses have nice green lawns, whatever the environmental cost in fertilizer and weed killer and water during droughts, and the grass is never allowed to grow to maturity. Millions of acres of fertile land (not only the forests and tallgrass prairies of Turtle Island, but also the precious rain forests of South America, Africa and New Guinea) are set to growing grain, but instead of giving that grain to starving multitudes in poor nations, it is fed to beef cattle destined for fast food restaurants in the wealthiest countries. At the same time, factories spew unnatural chemicals into the environment, in other countries when not legally permitted to do so in this country, though factory owners have lately won some rollbacks of U.S. environmental laws.

Meanwhile, individuals ruin their bodies with cholesterol, dextrose sugars, alcohol and nicotene, and people reproduce themselves at exponentially increasing rates. The governments of the world do nearly nothing to stop these horrors, which are the very epitome of *washichu* ("fat stealer"). Night is turned into day, winter into summer, until time is all the same—the *wakan* kind of time, the spirit-oriented καιρος (*kairos*) is pushed away, leaving only the *washte* kind of time, the production-oriented χρονος (*chronos*)—and people lose their psychological moorings. Where traditional peoples sometimes deprive themselves of sleep in order to seek the *wakan*, modern people find themselves unable to sleep; but their insomnia is but one of a plethora of psycho-physical illnesses. Haruki Murakami observes that Edison's lightbulb dispelled the outer darkness and Freud's and Jung's researches the inner darkness, but that "the darkness in our hearts remains, [which] creates a deep contradiction or confusion within us."

The more the *wakan* tries to reassert itself, the more it is pushed away, into tighter and tighter corners of what wildernesses are left, concentrating it into small nodes of such intensity that the merest mistake causes it to erupt powerfully. A moment of inattention or stupidity by one driver on a fast highway whose mind is on a phone conversation, and dozens die in the accident that follows; a nuclear technician or an oil tanker captain makes a mistake and thousands of fish and birds die; a careless driver flicks a cigarette butt out the car window and hundreds of homes burn in a forest fire; a powerful country ignores the anger in a poor nation until it finally erupts in violence that brings the death of thousands of innocent civilians.

A forest is valued by some for the lumber, and by others for its aesthetically pleasing vistas. Both groups, those who see nature as a resource to be exploited and those who see nature as a resource to be preserved—loggers and environmentalists, for example—often violently oppose each other. But both seek to preserve the trees unnaturally, at the "peak forest" stage, trying to arrest time. However, both loggers and environmentalists fail to realize their common mistake of assigning value to nature. Whether the forest is valued for its lumber or its vistas, the dominant culture is still valuing it as a *washte* commodity. Both groups make the mistake of seeing humanity as apart from nature rather than a part of nature, of uniquely having the role of deciding the value of nature.

Traditional peoples also see the forest as *washte* to an extent, as providing useful materials (wood to build with and to burn, edible animals and plants, and so on), and as beautiful. But, unlike environmentalists or loggers, they mostly see it as *wakan*, to be treated with humble respect. And traditional peoples do not use the forest's *washte* without first seeking permission from its *wakan*.

Traditional peoples know that there are mysterious spirits in the forests, in the deserts, in the open prairies—and so they are careful not to disturb these *wakan* presences in their own realm. They enter these sacred places respectfully and quietly. But modern people cut down the forests and settle the wildernesses, displacing these spirits. What havoc comes from this, as these mighty spirits are displaced, to roam the world releasing their powerful magic without a proper context, or to die, taking their powerful magic out of this world.

These people try to stop the Circle of Life out of their fear of change, probably trying subconsciously to forestall the inevitability of death. Newcomers fear their own deaths as individuals, little realizing that there is no life without change, and that death is part of a circle, and that even humanity as a whole must recognize its own eventual extinction, for there is nothing to say we too will not some day go the way of the dinosaur. People can erect great monuments and enbalm their dead to prevent natural decay. But, despite all the efforts of the *washichu* to stop it, the Circle of Life and Death will still turn. And a bigger circle continues to turn: eventually the Earth our Mother will shake off the deadness that humans have burdened her with, just as a forest burns with lightning to rid itself of the deadwood. And, virtually unbeknownst to us, other yet greater wheels are turning: some day, the Earth Herself will cease to exist, and, in an even greater cycle of time, the entire Universe will cease to exist, to be supplanted by other Universes—to say nothing of the Universes all about us in other dimensions and even within atoms. Perhaps we would acquire a greater respect for our own world if we were to learn, as William Blake did,

> To see a World in a Grain of Sand
> And a Heaven in a Wild Flower,
> Hold Infinity in the Palm of your Hand
> And Eternity in an Hour

or if we heard a tiny world hidden in a dandelion, as did Horton the elephant in Dr. Seuss's profound story, *Horton Hears a Who*.

There is only a certain amount of human change and intervention our Mother Earth will stand. Like other creatures with massive constructions (coral reefs, the huge dwellings termites build in Africa), humanity is allowed a certain degree of latitude to control and manipulate the environment, in order to make its *washte* home on Mother Earth. But no creature is allowed to exceed the limits she has established to ensure that all living things, and she herself, will continue to live. Mother Earth is growing angry and impatient with the huge weight of the dead things of human manufacture being placed upon her skin, things that stop the Circle of Life and kill her children. In the future, she will shake off all these human creations, and Nature will stand up again, naked and beautiful. And humanity will either learn to live in harmony with her, and live on only what she is willing to share of the bounty in her breasts, or humanity will perish.

Modern people sleep more deeply than traditional peoples every night as a matter of custom, and yet, ironically, they sleep more fitfully, hence their sleep is less satisfying and less spiritually enriching. Their homes are safe and ordered, their beds are warm and comfortable; there is nothing to keep them from going deep into the dream world—and so they do, thrashing blindly, some with minds blunted by alcohol or sleeping pills, unaware of how to manage their travels in the Seventh Direction, often stumbling quite far into the darkness-like-death, even into the deep mysterious lands where the incomprehensible spirits of the great *wakan* dreams and visions dwell. They waste these encounters since they forget their dreams, or remember them only as nightmares; moreover, since they are unprepared for and unprotected from these spirits, the spirits do whatever they will, and these dreamers' waking reality is as a result itself often nightmarish. By their blundering, aimless presence, they make it harder for those who *do* know how to travel in these lands and what to do there, by causing these incomprehensible beings to move even deeper into those lands, out of reach of all but the most intrepid of medicine people (if any are left), or to be less trusting when dreaming human souls come near them and take offense at the least provocation. If these individuals have around them the reek of alcohol and drugs, of exploitation and hypocrisy, if their souls are dead or dying, stinking of spiritual filth and decay, the beings who live in the Spirit World are going to stay well away—or come at them angrily in an attempt to get these foul, repugnant invaders out of their realm!

Since the Industrial Revolution, members of the dominant culture have been filling the Spirit World with *washichu* constructs. As these people enter into that world in their dreams and dream of their own things and events, as they invade this sacred realm, which they call virtual reality, with their Internet, they are actually beginning to do to the Spirit World what they have already done to this world, the Now World. Their Internet is filling the Spirit World with huge mountains of data, and with "spam," advertisements for larger penises and breasts and invitations to go further into debt, as well as infecting it with new species of "virus." And they fill the Spirit World with the insanity of their dreams, which, like movies, are often replete with big scary cities, inhuman factories, pollution, war, vampires and other nightmare beings, explosions, abnormal passage of time and constant noise. Their psychologists may say the things and events they dream of are merely figments of their imaginations or an expression of deep-seated dissociation and the like, that they do not exist—but they do! All these nightmares exist in many parts of the planet in this Now World—and now they're filling in the deep forests and still lakes of the Spirit World with similar if not worse horrors—with the worst imaginable *sicha*, and perhaps the even more terrifying *sicha,* that which is *unimaginable.* And all this is causing the mighty beings deep within that world to get very, very angry. Some day, they will reassert their stewardship of this domain, and their coming will be more fearsome than anything of which the human mind can conceive—as I have dramatized in two of my novels, themselves based on dreams that were given to me: *A Stitch in Time* and *Undr.*

This invasion of the Spirit World is, furthermore, confusing the natural patterns and borderlines that connect it with the Now World. Not only is the Spirit World being filled with horrible new constructs, but the Spirit World is vomiting some of these back into the Now World. Spirit people have always occasionally entered into the Now World, but always for some high sacred purpose. Nowadays, between anger at what's happening to them and their Spirit

World and the very fact of their forcible displacement by irruptions of *sicha* constructs in their world, they are coming into the Now World much more often—and often angrily. Has not the Now World grown more nightmarish and dangerous?

I personally believe human beings are by nature good, like all living creatures, though it seems I'm unusual in that assessment. Yet I also believe that there is a kind of cultural "cancer" of evil, greed, arrogation, nastiness and ethical corruption that is spreading throughout the world. It is not intrinsic to human nature, but it is profoundly and perhaps permanently changing it. Personally, I believe it happened to begin in Europe, though it could have begun anywhere; in fact, I have known people of European ancestry who have courageously sought, with some success, to cure themselves of it, though they like anyone these days must strive constantly not to fall into the same sickness all over again! Yes, there is much in European culture to celebrate—music, science, literature, art, architecture—but, at the same time, there is much to mourn in how the Europeans and their cultural descendants have ravaged the world.

This social cancer of arrogation has recently achieved its greatest growth, however, not in Europe but in this continent, from which it is currently spreading worldwide, fast as wildfire. A Grebo elder I knew told me how crime, rape, prostitution, usury and so on were utterly unknown in West Africa until his people got exposed, through well-meaning but misguided Westerners who believed their culture was superior, to European-American culture. I heard once how, in the "post-colonial period," well-meaning Peace Corps workers dug a well for a nomadic nation in a desert region of North Africa. With water now plentifully available, the *Badawi* (Bedouins) left behind their nomadic way, a way carefully attuned to the seasons so their flocks would never over-graze one area, and instead settled around the well. But within a few years the well went dry, and they had no choice but to move their flocks again—but they had lost the old knowledge of attuning themselves to the land around them, and their flocks died and they starved.

The dominant Europeans and Americans have exported their religion and capitalist economy and democratic politics, insisting that these are the finest and fairest. But this is only a chimaera. Democracy, supposedly the most impartial of governments, leads to a tyranny of the majority (or more often a tyranny of those who manipulate and control the electorate) and the subjugation of minorities (or more often the disenfranchised true majority). Capitalism, as the name suggests, is a system in which those who have the capital are able to use that capital to leverage more capital. We must not forget that, in this system, when someone wins, someone loses as well. It is the poor who lose—not only in the developed countries, but the less-developed countries as a whole. In the developed countries, the rich get richer, while the poor wind up ever further in debt to creditors and government, working ever harder while falling ever farther behind in their payments. The national debts of most poor countries exceed their gross national product, and they have no funds to feed their hungry or heal their sick, yet their military grow ever larger and their corrupt leaders get ever richer. Put democracy and capitalism together and you have the rich and powerful buying control over the halls of political power.

The traditional way is true freedom for each individual to live, and worship or not, as she or he sees fit, but to be deeply aware of how much she or he is dependent on all life for survival, and to be thankful—which is the heart of true worship. It is an economy based on sharing: when one has more than one needs, one gladly shares it with others. It is a "government" (in the loosest sense of that word) based not on majority rule but on consensus—a consensus that is not reached until the last remaining individual is "of one mind" with everyone else (to quote the Condolence, the great prayer of the Hodenasaunee [Iroquois Confederacy]).

I've had so many Native American elders tell me that they mourn the fact that most young Indians can't be bothered to learn the old ways, but just want to get a good job and make money. Reservations are all too often the last place where one can find the traditional ways surviving, because either there is so much poverty and crime, drug abuse and alcoholism, or there is so much greed and politics coming from the casinos and the BIA-recognized pseudo-governments. I have seen with my own eyes as one reservation, desperately poor but at least respecting its traditional ways, changed into a multimillion-dollar mini-empire that is just as *washichu* as the worst of mercantile interests. Worse yet, this rez, despite its apparent wealth, is actually enslaved to the organized crime bosses who now run it, squeezing it (and those who come to it) for all the wealth they can get. I have seen how *nouveaux riches* Indians, unfamiliar with having all this money, don't know how to handle it, and lose it to drink and drugs or other foolishness—just as their ancestors lost the house and plot of land they were given under the resettlement acts when the newcomers forcibly took their traditional lands away from them. I have seen other rezzes struggle to resist eating the forbidden casino fruit, while they slowly suffer all the ravages found in a Third World nation. As a result, in neither kind of rez is much being done to carry on the traditional ways.

Fortunately there are some few reservations—particularly in the West and Southwest, because they were warned in the nineteenth century by what was happening in the East—that have managed to hold on to their traditional ways. Although subjected to the same demands of the national government and the same pressures of the national economy, the Pueblo, for instance, have historically found ways to "get around" such attacks. They accepted Roman Catholicism but blended it into the traditional spirituality, as traditional nations in Guatemala and Colombia magnificently did as well. In 1680 the Pueblo gave the Spaniards the choice of leaving their land or dying, and they have ever since with the same strength maintained much of their culture. They have casinos, but, unlike other nations, they are spending the proceeds to strengthen the community, thus the gambling is closer to the fair exchange of goods in the Sacred Giveaway.

Though today so few people seem willing to learn what little they can of the traditions and pass it on, this work is essential: since this continent signif- icantly fostered the spread of the *washichu* cancer, Turtle Island owes the world much work toward healing the effects of the disease.

Onoda'gega (Onondaga) Faithkeeper Oren Lyons once said, "Times change, but principles don't. Times change, but lands do not. Times change, but our culture and our language remain the same. And that's what you have to keep intact. It's not what you wear—it's what's in your heart." Alfonso Ortiz likewise said, "One is not born a Tewa, but rather one is made a Tewa. Once made, one has to work hard continuously throughout one's life to remain a Tewa." Just as Percy Lomaquahu said, "We strive to be Hopi. We call ourselves Hopi because maybe one or two of us will become Hopi. Each person must look into their heart and make changes so that you may become Hopi when you reach your destination."

The *washichu* are threatened by nature, which they see as chaos, as an enemy to be conquered. The *washichu* are also threatened by the "chaos" within the human being. The most powerful *washichu* seek to repress the desires of those under their sway, to eradicate their imaginations, their dreams, and all that makes persons unique as individuals, and mold them into a uni- form pattern, subject to the laws and conventions of the culture or subculture. The *washichu* teaching is that human desires and imagination are evil except when they conform to socially promoted norms—and otherwise should be repressed. When individuals act on them they are censured or imprisoned or put on drugs. Or, sometimes, more subtly, the powerful lavish attention and praise on the artist who dares to be starkly truthful, which has the effect of making the artist's *wakan* outrageousness once again safely *washte*.

In short, the *washichu* see order and chaos as antipathetic opposites. Gibbs's Theorem suggests that, according to the free energy equation, the entropy in the universe is constantly increasing, because of the lost energy in each energy transfer or reaction. This means order is constantly slipping into disorder. Machines break down. Grass grows through the cracks in the pavement. People get sick, get old and die. Aware of this tendency, the *washichu* see order as good and chaos as evil. But, without massive infusions of effort on the part of humanity, chaos will eventually destroy all order in the universe. The *washichu* must therefore bend mind and will to creating and maintaining order. They must be constantly vigilant for outbreaks of chaos, and constantly prepared to exert energy to impose the desired good of *washte* order, first to overcome and then to keep subdued the evil of chaos, the *wakan*. Humanity must be like the Western religions' understanding of G-d and force chaos to assume order.

The Native American peoples, like traditional peoples worldwide, do not see nature as either order or chaos, as either *washte* or *wakan*, but as a complex and ever-fluid interplay of both. The traditional view is a recognition that human beings are an integral *part* of nature, also a dynamic interaction of *washte* and *wakan*, no more or less important than any other creatures, and certainly not free to impose on nature an order that breaks natural cycles.

Order and chaos are not seen by the traditional peoples as antipathetic opposites, as good versus evil. Rather, they are seen as complements that move in harmony with each other. Order is what is *washte*, what is regular, expectable, comfortable, dependable. Chaos is what is *wakan*, what is unexpected, unpredictable, dangerous, uncontrollable. There is order and chaos in every thing and every event. Order and chaos always succeed each other: nothing is forever; everything is evanescent.

Let us take as an example the tradition of sand painting kept by some traditional peoples in the Southwest, in Tibet and Australia and perhaps other places as well. The artist can spend quite a long time seeking sands of different colors and textures, or coloring the sands him- or herself, and then carefully sifting the diverse sands through her or his fist or a tiny funnel to create the painting. Clearly such paintings are *washte* in that they are the result of human order imposed on nature, but they are also *wakan* in that what is represented in such paintings is usually sacred stories and sacred beings. The very fragility and impermanence of these paintings clearly augments the sense of *wakan* in them. Eventually the *wakan* manifests itself—the sand painting is ritually destroyed.

The *washichu* seek order (*washte*) at the expense of chaos (*wakan*) by taking things (as raw materials) out of the context of nature and/or by destroying nature itself. But the *wakan*—like a butterfly put in a jar, to borrow an image of Manx Starfire's—will not live thus for long; it only lives if it's free to flow, like wind, like water. The Native American peoples, like other traditional peoples, seek to maintain in what they do an integral connection to nature: once the connection to nature is lost, there is *sicha* (imbalance).

The sands used in a sand painting are painstakingly arranged into living stories. So *gagosa*, the "false faces" of the Hodenasaunee, are delicately carved while still part of the living basswood tree, and continue to be fed and talked to, treated as living beings. So the Sacred Pipe is considered alive and treated as such; so it is turned to all the directions such that all living things can partake of it. So the Sacred Stone People's Lodge and the Sacred Drum are skin or blankets stretched on wood and inhabited by Spirit. When any of these things are put on display in a museum, when any of the sacred ceremonies or dances are put on display before an audience, they have been removed from their natural context. To do so is to impose order on chaos, to stop the natural flow of the *wakan*. We must remember always to let both order and chaos flow as they will.

The M'sing, or Masked Spirit
of the Lenape.
(See pages 202–04.)

XIII

What Is To Come

It is winter now as I complete this book. Snow fell through last night, and now this morning the Catskill Mountains are wrapped in a cocoon of white. The world around me is silent and still. The stream near my house is frozen; the voice of the water that has spoken to me since last spring is hushed. The eagles who I heard singing last summer are gone. The flowers who gave me a vision of Morning Breeze have long since faded and dropped their glory; now their heads are bowed toward the snow, their knees broken in prayer. I have not been up the steep forested hill to the ceremonial ground, yet I can visualize the Sacred Stone People's Lodge under a white mantle, with no footprints near it except for those of a few wild creatures and perhaps a spirit or two.

But I know spring will soon be here. Life will come again, renewing the world around me. The stream will burst its mantle and talk to me again. The eagles will return to the high trees, circling in the heavens overhead. The primroses will lift their faces up to the dawn again. The lodge, like the bear, will come forth from hibernation. And up on the ceremonial hill I will unexpectedly be given a wonderful sacred gift. The Circle of Life will turn and turn again. Always winter and summer, death and life, follow each other in their dance of beauty and harmony and peace.

The number of years in my life has nearly doubled during the time that it has taken me to write this book. I am moving into my Grandfather years, whether I feel ready for that awesome responsibility or not. Being an elder, a Grandfather or Grandmother, is not a matter of having children who are parents, or having a certain number of years, or having gray hair and wrinkles. It is a matter of truly learning humility. It is my humble but sacred responsibility, as I grow old, to be worthy of the responsibilities that come therewith.

Unlike most people, I actually look forward to growing old. I find it fascinating sometimes to look at my lean hands and all the old scars on them, and remember the soft pudgy little fingers that once were there, or look at the lines in my face, the gray in my hair, or into the deep roots of the wisdom I carry, into the peace and love within my heart. No, I don't look forward to even more aches and pains than I have now, to more frequent spottiness in my memory, to greater difficulty seeing and hearing, but when we give goodness or accept difficulty without complaint, we receive abundantly. So I look forward to the greater understanding, the breadth of perspective, the scope of time, the lightness of psychological burdens that will come in my last years. This lodge my spirit prays in is slowly getting rent and tattered. After not that many more winters it will be time to let this lodge, this robe, go. But spring will return. The eagles will return, and the morning flowers—and me. There is no death, only a change of worlds. My only fear is of dying before I complete the tasks the Creator has given me to do and learn the lessons the Creator expects me to learn.

Many times I've been in the presence of people breathing their last breaths. I've been with a very young woman dying of massive trauma and blood loss after an auto accident, her blood pouring through my helpless hands. I've been with a poet more than a century old, whose body seemed every day lighter and lighter until her soul just floated away leaving almost nothing behind. And I've been with all kinds of people within this spectrum, with all kinds of reactions to the sure knowledge that they were dying. Some, as in Dylan Thomas's poem, raged against the dying of the light, and others—not all of them old—went gentle into that good night, accepting the coming of death with equanimity. Never have I seen this peaceful acceptance of death more clearly than among traditional peoples; not only Native Americans, but also, in my experience, Zen Buddhists, Native Africans and Taoists.

Wise are those who know they do not "own" their loved ones who have left the body, who know the individual life is *wakan*, and must be allowed to move on along the sacred path when the time comes. Skaniadariyo (Handsome Lake) taught: "Our grief adds to the sorrows of the dead. . . . Ten days shall be the time for mourning and when our friends depart (the soul leaving the Earth on the tenth day) we must lay grief aside. . . . You can journey with the dead only as far as the grave." Traditionally, the Speaker of the Longhouse gave the deceased ten days to make the pilgrimage to the next world; at the end of that time, a sacred meal including "ghost bread" (now called frybread), left to strengthen the deceased on her or his way, was eaten by a relative. Just so, the spirits of the dead enter into us, sustaining and nourishing us.

If anything, for these people death is not a "dying of the light" to rage against, but a joyful entering into the light. I remember one medicine woman, for instance, slowly dying of cancer in her poor little home in northern Vermont, but still filled with jubilant love for everyone who came to say good-bye. She died as she lived, teaching us, showing us by example, how to do it right and well. I remember the last time I left her, looking from the door back at a shrunken, sickened body that hardly gave shape to the blankets, one hand raised in a feeble farewell. I could already see the light around her, preparing to take her to the Spirit World.

Death is the ultimate shapeshifting: dropping our outer robe and revealing our truest nature as spirit. In the traditional stories, death is always a shapeshifting: after being killed by the hunter, the wild being returns home and puts on a new robe, a new body. (Oddly enough, the old Bugs Bunny cartoons, in which the four-legged characters always come back in a perfect body after being violently killed, are correct on this point.) With the exception of a few particularly wise sages, such the lamas of Bön and Vajrayana, we humans have virtually lost this shapeshifting magic; unlike our elder brothers and sisters, when we die we do not simply put on a new robe, a new body, and continue this present life. Still, all the ancient stories tell us that death is not a finality, but a change of robes—a change of worlds, as Chief Sealth put it. As in the Law of the Conservation of Matter and Energy, as in the scientific theories of Theravada Buddhism, there is no ending, only change. As Igjugarjuk, the great Inuit *angakoq*, or medicine man, told Knud Rasmussen, "No life once given can ever be lost or destroyed."

Anyone who has truly looked at the river after it drops its robe of the sheltering, guiding hills and reaches the ocean understands the nature of death. The river is still there, but merged with all the other rivers in the infinite expanse of the ocean. So too each individual, when she or he dies, merges with all of the ancestors. Anyone who has looked with thoughtful eyes from the peak of a high mountain or the top of a cliff, or into the darkness-like-death far inside the dreamlands—or who has been on the very edge of death itself—understands that death is no ending at all, but truly a change of worlds. At the summit, Mother Earth and Father Sky are especially close in a way they usually are only at the unreachable horizon. At the summit, the ordinary *washte* laws of existence are rolled back—and the very laws of time and space, the basic immutable laws of the Circle of Life and Death itself, are more plainly seen.

From traditional nation to nation, there are variations in how these matters are understood. Some say the owl is a harbinger of death; others say the crow or the raven. Some say if you dream of a deceased relative it means you or someone close to you is about to die; others say, no, the relative is doing what "those who have gone before" customarily do—teaching, guiding, protecting, admonishing the living. But, among all these different beliefs, none teaches, so far as I ever discovered, that death is a final ending.

The way I understand death from my teachers is that, when we die, we remain close to our nation, our people, our loved ones. And we guide, protect, admonish and instruct them. Being closer to the Creator, we carry their prayers to the Great Mystery. Sometimes we come back, either temporarily or permanently, and speak to those living here through animals, visions or dreams. It is not uncommon for the living to sense the presence of those who have "dropped their robe" in dreams, during ceremonies or even at unexpected moments. Many people offer a bit of food and drink from their meal to their ancestors. I have often myself seen, heard and felt the presence of those who have gone before, especially in the lodge. And it is universal for the living to tell their children and grandchildren about them, and even to talk directly to them. Centuries past, elders used to show the young where certain ancestors were buried, or the depressions in the earth where their lodges had been. I remember the happy day when I took my children to meet many of their ancestors in old graveyards in northern New York, some of whom are among those to whom this book is dedicated.

My teachers said that, when the last living person who remembers us alive dies, then we "die a second death" and join the "cloud of witnesses," the shining presence of Grandfathers and Grandmothers without name and individuation, who have gone on before. Later yet, there is a third death when there is no one left who remembers the name by which we were known in life, when no longer is it given voice; then we grow toward oneness with the Creator.

Beyond the Red Road of *washte* and the Blue Road of *wakan*, there are the White Road to the Spirit World taken by those who are not to be reborn (seen in the form of the Galaxy and the Aurora Borealis) and the Yellow Road that leads to rebirth (represented by the Daystar and the morning Sun). Some say the Stars are the campfires of those who now walk the White Road to the Spirit World. According to the Lakota medicine man Napa (Finger), the spirit (*sichun*) of an individual takes the spirit trail (the band of the

Galaxy across the night Sky) to the Spirit World, and the individual's ghost (*wanagi*) goes among the stars—but, whenever a baby is born, *Skan* takes one of these ghosts from among the stars and gives it to the child. So when we look at a newborn life, we see in the tiny, wrinkled face something of the features of the old, wrinkled face we have long loved—a soul who has returned. Therefore, when we keep the tradition of thinking of the seventh generation to come, we realize—as do the Hindus, Jains, Buddhists and Taoists—that the people of that generation may well some day be *us*, as well as those whom we love most. "There never was a time when you and I did not exist," Lord Krishna says to Arjuna in the Bhagavad-Gità, "nor will there be a future in which we shall cease to be."

I remember with delight camping in Maine with my children, when they were young, and watching a lunar eclipse from our pup tent. We also went into the cabin from time to time through the same night to watch live photographs of the rings and moons of Saturn coming back from a passing spacecraft on the little television I had brought just for this purpose. Some day, very likely, space ships will carry us past the Moon and even Mars, to the planets of this and other stellar systems. When traditional people go out there—as the medicine people do often and as we all will do when we die—we should think of it as returning home. Though we love this Earth our Mother, we also love the Sky, our Father—and, when we die, we will spend time walking the White Road with our Father and Grandfather; indeed, with all our elders.

Astronomers, to their credit, often have a sense of awe, akin to a sense of the *wakan*, when they look at distant stars and planets, galaxies and nebulæ. But, unfortunately, if modern people ride their fiery space ships to other planets, they will not have a sense of coming home and meeting relatives, but of "conquering" the universe as they have already "conquered" all the continents of Earth. I have often heard the story that a Diné (Navajo) medicine man was asked to record his greetings on a spacecraft about to be sent into interstellar space. A Native American scientist laughed when he heard the words, telling his superiors that they meant: "Watch out for these people. They will take your land, too. They bring death." The story has been deemed an urban legend, but no matter; the peoples of other planets do not need to be warned—just as the elders of this continent knew the Hoop-breaker was coming, these elder ones of other worlds likewise know already.

Modern culture indeed does bring death, but ironically the people are uncomfortable with the subject of death. People rarely get to see death coming and rarely even see dead bodies. So there is a gruesome fascination with death: people enjoy watching movies that are filled with depictions of bloody violence, and they slow down and stare as they drive by a traffic accident.

In one of my novels, *A Mirror Filled with Light*, the poet Sappho says of modern people:

> *Without the desire to die, nothing dies: no thought, no hope, no memory, ever perishes in their brains. The desire to die is the desire to change. So it is that their senses are choked with plenty, and jaded beyond reason. Their memories, their minds, are full to bursting; their thoughts are a dark and heavy burden they must bear day and night. They are weighted down fast by themselves—the loneliness of an overfull life.*

In other words, if you don't know how to die, you don't know how to live.

In traditional cultures, death is a familiar presence—sacred (*wakan*) and sometimes frightening, but never gruesome. Just as in the longhouse children grow quickly used to observing people sexually involved, so too they are accustomed to seeing people dying. They know the sight, the sound, the scent of death. And they know well how the individual prepares for death, and how the community as well prepares for the event. I have previously referred you to the elucidation of this offered by Evan Zuesse, in his book *Ritual Cosmos*: young children stand at the outer periphery, as it were, of the traditional death ceremonies, but, as they progress through life, they move closer and closer to the center, until the time of their own death comes, when they can look out and see all those circles of life around them, as the people now carry out for them the proper ceremonies.

Traditional ceremonies prepare us for death: they are death-in-microcosm, *petits morts*, as it is put in French. And sexuality, illness, even walking and breathing, can help us in small ways to become familiar with death. When we leave our physical bodies and travel the Seventh Direction in sleeping or visioning, we sometimes walk far into the mysterious regions in which we will walk even more deeply when there is no body drawing us back to waking reality. Those approaching death have no worries, no responsibilities tying them to this world. Thus, far from something to be afraid of, entering into the world beyond is a matter for rejoicing and celebration.

Traditional people think of death like a Sacred Stone People's Lodge that has fallen apart and is no longer usable. When a lodge is first built, it is tight, it is solid; it seals out the outer world and keeps the steam within efficiently, but it has little Spirit. As it ages, and the seasons and storms act on it, blankets blow and slip around and rip, or the saplings shift or even break, we have to repair the lodge to make it tight again—but it has great Spirit in it. Our bodies, as they age, need to be healed increasingly often, but our spirits grow ever wiser. But eventually the lodge is no longer functional: the blankets get too tattered, the saplings start to sink down. When that time comes, and the spot has become too much *washte*, it is time to move on. A healer knows not to try to heal someone who is coming toward death. We let this lodge, this body go—"drop our robe"—and move on to a new lodge, a new body.

Death is part of living. Being *wakan*, it comes in its own time. In fact, individuals in traditional societies often know when their time of dying has come. A great elder rose from sleep and looked at the morning sun for what he knew was the last time, before a battle with the European invaders that he knew he would not live through. He said, "Behold, it is a good day to die." However, forcibly making death happen out of its time, as in murder or suicide, is *sicha* (out of balance). Those who die in this way, it is generally believed, remain behind as ghosts until the time comes when they would have naturally died, and only then do they move on to the Spirit World. Stories told about love ending in tragedy or revengeful ghosts clearly show the belief that death is meant to come in its proper time. When it does, it is a good and beautiful thing. We sing our songs, and we go on to the goodness that awaits.

The traditional tribal cultures see time as a set of concentric circles—heartbeat, breath, day, lunar month, year, lifetime, "age"—such that, while they can come back to the same point in one circle, for instance, the morning point in the day circle, they are at different points on some or all of the other circles. In each of these circles there is a part that is *washte* and a part that is *wakan*. Systole, daytime, Full Moon, summer, young adulthood: all of these times are *washte*. Diastole, nighttime, New Moon, winter, old age and death: all of these times are *wakan*.

In preparing for the future, the traditional person is conscious of these circles. In the morning and afternoon one prepares for the night. In summer and autumn one prepares for the winter that lies ahead. In adulthood one prepares for old age and death. When more than one of these circles is in the *washte* time, it is particularly good to work: during the days of high summer one can better find food or make things, given the bright clear light available for several hours. When more than one of these circles is in the *wakan* time, it is particularly good to rest (in the Jewish sense of spiritual rest, שבבת [Shabbat]): during the night at the New Moon in deep winter, for instance, one cannot do anything in the long hours of darkness but sleep and dream, tell stories or simply be quiet as if in death.

The way of the traditional tribal people is to know where one is in these sacred circles and go forward with preparations appropriate to the current turning of the circles. In this way the traditionals learn sacred wisdom from the natural world.

Let me tell you a story that teaches us about this.

A hunter went off into the forest, determined to catch a deer. As he walked quietly in the forest, a rabbit went by. But he let the rabbit go, because he was hunting for deer. Later on, a wild turkey went by. But he let the wild turkey go, because he was hunting for deer. Later yet, a moose went by. But he let the moose go, because he was hunting for deer. As it does, the sun circled around the Red Road of the Sky, and came to its setting. The man returned home in the deepening darkness with nothing to show for his day of hunting, because he was hunting for deer.

So it is the traditional peoples' way always to be prepared: not to set goals, but just to work with the world around us. If we can't tan hides because it's raining, it is a good day for catching fish, or perhaps just staying inside and mending fishnets. We recognize the wisdom in the weather and let it determine what we *should* be doing. The wisdom of our ancestors helps us to know how to listen to the world, and how to prepare.

The traditionals see past and future as together in a circle. Because of their understanding of the nature of time, they are better equipped to know what is going to happen in the future. Of course, events foreseen with "sight" don't always happen exactly as we expect. Sometimes sight comes to me in the form of direct messages, which I hear inwardly and pass on to the right person or persons. And often sight is like flying high over a temporal landscape (which, as Eagle, is what I do), and seeing the various possibilities like paths branching. What I then do is use common sense and tell people what is the likeliest future event. But I can be wrong; circumstances can change. The simple fact of telling a person what one sees can itself change the contours of the future; the person may choose differently because of my words.

But there are others—wise women and men—who see far better than I what lies in the spiritual directions commonly called the future and past. The elders are not bound in one space or time, but by way of shapeshifting can at will talk, or even travel, through all the dimensions of space or time. Jesus and William Blake both spoke with the elders of other times: the one with Moses and Elijah, the other with Isaiah and Ezekiel. In the same way, just as the elders of this land knew about and expected the coming of the Long White Bones Man, the elders of the future and the elders of distant worlds are aware, forewarned and prepared. And of this I am utterly sure: the traditional ways will return. Yes, the Long White Bones Man, the *washichu*, will have his day, for so the story runs. He may destroy this planet with his greed, his weapons and his diseases, however this physical world, this universe, is but a robe that the Creator wears, just as the body is a robe our spirits wear. There is an infinity of robes. Thus, there will be no death, just a change of worlds.

The *washichu*'s day will pass. It will go away again like a passing storm. The smoke will dissipate, leaving only a small mound of putrefying ashes. And, once the wreckage is cleared up, the birds will sing again, the flowers will reopen their blossoms, the world will return, renewed, and the traditional, true way, the way of the Circle of Life, will welcome us all back in. We will have completed the Circle of Life and come home not to death but to a new world.

Some years ago, I had been praying for a long time that something would happen in my personal life. I had had several dreams that clearly said it was going to happen. Other people, including my own daughter, had had similar dreams. I even had the firm assurance of medicine men and women with "sight" that it was going to happen. But, because it was beginning to appear that there was less and less chance of it happening, I began to have doubts that it would *ever* happen. I began to disbelieve the clear messages I had received.

At the same time, it was being made clear to me—through dreams, visions and the teachings of my elders—what is going to happen to Mother Earth and all her children in the near future. I began to think that what I was hoping for in my personal life was so minor in comparison to the changes coming to the world. This too led me to disbelieve the clear messages that what I hoped for so much would happen some day.

But then one day, in the Sacred Stone People's Lodge, the spirits gave me the following message: "We have given you a clear vision of what is to come.

Who are you to say what part of the vision is more important than another? Something that may seem insignificant to you may be utterly crucial to the unfolding of what is to come. Every part of the vision is as important as every other part! Therefore, the part of the vision that you think has to do only with your personal life is also vitally important. You cannot know what important things will never happen if that part of the vision is not fulfilled! And, if you start doubting parts of the vision you have been given, even the apparently insignificant ones that seem to apply only to your personal life, the doubt will start spreading like a cancer, and you will wind up doubting the whole thing!" So the spirits spoke to me, and insisted that I must believe every part of the vision.

What I had done, in fact, was to start thinking like a *washichu*. I had begun to assign a hierarchy of values to parts of the vision. I had begun to pick and choose what parts of the whole vision I wanted to believe. I had labeled some parts of the vision as "higher," since they affected all people, and other parts as "lesser," since they affected only one or a few people.

I must continue to struggle with *washichu* habits that I (like anyone who tries to walk the Red Road in the midst of a largely *washichu* culture) must always seek to eradicate.

"The first factor in the revolution of consciousness is the mystic death of the ego—the death of negative thinking, negative personalities. We must purify the soul of the inner enemies." Thus teaches Willaru Huayta, born Quechua and become Inca.

What I have been taught is that you must live the way of the Red Road *all* the time, not just when it suits you. Everything we do is part of how we walk the Red Road: every step we take is a sacred act, a walk in which we tread the dust of our ancestors and, sown in that sacred dust, the seeds of our descendants. For now we who try to walk the Red Road are forced also to take our place in a culture that forces us to work at demeaning jobs, to pay taxes and bills, to get licenses and so on. This may, for now, be unavoidable. But as is taught by the Two-Minded Generation Prophecy, which I will relate to you presently, we cannot continue indefinitely trying to ride in the traditional peoples' canoe and the newcomers' boat at the same time.

The sacred traditions that I have been talking about with you belong to no individual, and to no one people. They belong to the Creator, to the Spirits, to the Ancestors and to the Earth and all her children. To say "These are *our* ceremonies and we forbid you access to them" is an offense to the Creator who made us all, who taught us these ceremonies by sending the Daughter of the Sky that arches over all living beings, and who told us that all four colors, Yellow, Red, Black and White, have their place in the Sacred Hoop of All the Nations.

Here is a prayer of the Anishinabeg: "Grandfather, look at our brokenness. We know that in all Creation, only humanity has strayed from the Red Road. We know that we are the ones who are divided, and that we are the ones who must come back together to walk on the Red Road. Grandfather, Holy One, teach us love, compassion, and honor so that we may heal the Earth and heal each other."

Long ago, Inktome, Spider, the trickster, the bringer of bad news, came to camp after camp of the people with the same message: "I have heard from the Seashell Nation that a new man is coming. He is a trickster, like me. He is not very wise, but he is very clever. He has long, long legs, and he will run over you. I will now reveal his name; he is Hu-hanska-ska, *the Long White Bones Man. But the best name for him is* Washichu, *because he will steal all the land, all the food, all the animals, steal even the Sky, the rivers and the lakes."*

Most of the people laughed to hear such nonsense. How could anyone steal all the wild animals? How could anyone steal the Sky? But some of them asked, "Why is he coming? We don't want him here!"

"He will come whether or not you want him to," Spider replied. "He is a new kind of man. He will offer you many gifts that will seem good, but will destroy you if you accept them. He will try to tame you like animals. He will give you new insulting names. He will take your sacred land and your spirit away. He will replace your religion with another. He will bring you four things: sickness, hate, prejudice, mercilessness.

"He will say the land is not sacred, that the Creator is not really G-d. You will have to work hard to hold on to your ways, and you must remember to listen to the animals and plants when you have forgotten your own way, your own soul."

Listening to Spider as he spoke, more and more of the people began to take his warning seriously. "How will we know when he is going to come?" one of them asked.

"The buffalo will all be killed, or go on to the Sacred Land," he answered.

Many of them laughed to hear Spider say these things. And, though some did take him seriously, they forgot what Spider said as the years went by and life went on as usual.

But, one day, two sisters were gathering chokecherries for wojapi, *when they saw a strange man, with hair on his white face, wearing strange clothes, and carrying a metal stick that made a loud noise. They ran away. Like the two brothers who encountered the White Buffalo Calf Woman, their testimony was not taken seriously. But, in time, more people saw this strange individual, or two or three together like him. Then more of them started coming, in great waves like the ocean tide. They built fences. They put up telegraph wires. They constructed a railroad. They brought rifles. They took all the land. They built villages, then big, smelly, noisy, smoky cities and factories.*

Their cavalry came and gave the people a choice between living on a reservation or being killed. The sacred buffalo were slaughtered from moving trains, the eagles were shot down out of the Sky. The people's women were raped, the men were put into virtual slavery, the children were carted off to mission schools and forced to deny their heritage, the old ones were left to starve to death. Rivers ran red as blood.

Then one day a young woman, rising up early and walking through the dawn mist, looked across Medicine Creek, near Mount Scott, and saw dimly through the fog as the last wild buffalo herd went by, appearing to her as if in a spirit dream. The buffalo leader walked straight toward Mount Scott, and behind him followed the few cows and young bulls who still survived. As the young woman watched, the face of the mountain opened up. Beyond the opening she saw a world green and fresh, as she remembered her grandmothers and grandfathers saying it had been in this world before the coming of the washichu. *The Sky was wide and open, the wind was fresh and clean, the rivers ran clear, not red. The wild plums were in blossom, and the slopes were covered with flowers. Into this world of beauty the buffalo walked, never to be seen again.*

It began early in the history of contact between the two cultures; the Vikings, Columbus, Pizarro, Hudson and many others. Even colonist Conrad Weiser, who was unusually sympathetic toward the Native Americans, being an adopted Kanien'kéha:ka (Mohawk), still sought power and advantage. The story is told that one day in the early 1700s Weiser was walking with his friend, Chief Onkiswathetamy (Shikellamy), who was a naturalized Onyota'a:ka (Oneida), having been born a French Canadian. They happened to be on the Susquehanna Road, an Indian trail in what is now Pennsylvania, near a certain river island that

Weiser coveted for its potential strategic value. Onkiswathetamy said, "I have had a dream. In the dream you gave me a new rifle." Weiser, understanding the importance of dreams, immediately handed Onkiswathetamy his rifle. Then Weiser said, "I, too, have had a dream. I dreamed that you gave me this island in the river." Onkiswathetamy, for his part, told his friend that the island was his. "But," he added, "I will never dream with you again."

In the mid-nineteenth century, Aseenewub of the Red Lake Anishinabeg repeated a prophecy his great-grandfather had received from the Master of Life: "At some time there shall come among you a stranger, speaking a language you do not understand. He will try to buy the land from you, but do not sell it; keep it for an inheritance to your children." Aseenewub surely remembered this prophecy when he witnessed the United States government forces surrounding the elders of his people with weapons and threatening to hang them if they did not sign a treaty ceding all rights to their land.

Crazy Horse said:

> *We did not ask you white men to come here. The Great Mystery gave us this country as a home. You had yours. We did not interfere with you. The Great Mystery gave us plenty of land to live on and buffalo, deer, antelope and other game. But you have come here, you are taking my land from me, you are killing off our game, so it hard for us to give. Now you tell us to work for a living, but the Great Mystery did not make us to work, but to live by hunting. You white men can work if you want to. We did not interfere with you, and again you say, "Why do you not become civilized?" We do not want your civilization! We would live as our fathers did, and their fathers before them.*

Often, the invaders got the Native peoples to do their dirty work for them, which they did—out of fear and desperation. We must never forget that the Kanien'kéha:ka (Mohawk) themselves betrayed several of their fellow nations, including the Shawnee, the Huron and the Abenaki, in a desperate but ultimately fruitless attempt to save themselves. We must never forget that, when Native warriors defeated European armies, the captives were often and unnecessarily put through considerable torture. Yet it must also be recalled that the Native Americans were forced to fight like Europeans, against Europeans or their fellow Natives, realizing all the while that they were doomed, unable to save their land and their people, their homes and families, from destruction.

Here is what the Arapaho Ghost Dancers sang as they rode to their death:

> *My children, when at first I liked the whites,*
> *My children, when at first I liked the whites,*
> *I gave them fruits,*
> *I gave them fruits.*
> *Father, have pity on me,*
> *Father, have pity on me;*
> *I am crying for thirst,*
> *I am crying for thirst;*
> *All is gone.*
> *I have nothing to eat.*

I have talked with elderly Tsalagi (Cherokee) who remembered their own ancestors describing the Trail of Tears. I have heard similarly living recollections of Wounded Knee and Big Horn. The Shoshone remember to this day exactly how the invader soldiers made it clear they had no choice but to sign the so-called Treaty of Ruby Valley—so these invaders could get gold delivered through Shoshone land from the West to the East, to pay for their Civil War. They shot a hostage in front of the chiefs, cut up the body and cooked the pieces in a pot of water, and then forced the chiefs to eat their dead brother.

Lest we forget, the evil of betrayal and brokenness and greed is still going on today. Consider the massive effort in recent years to plunder Hopi and Diné (Navajo) land for its vast reserves of coal, natural gas, uranium and oil, or the chicanery behind plans to build an extensive complex of hydroelectric facilities in both the James Bay region and in eastern Québec, which would destroy the fragile ecology, especially the caribou range, and the traditional bush culture of the Nehiyawok (Cree) and the Innu (Montagnais).

Only a few miles' walk from my home is a waterfall, where long ago Preuwamakan, Sachem of Atharhackton, the last great leader of the Waronawonka (Munsee) people, had his home. On May 29, 1660, when he was in his nineties, he was fishing at the confluence of what are now called the Esopus Creek and the Wallkill River. Dutchmen brutally murdered him with his own hatchet so they could steal his canoe and use it to bring some members of their militia across the water. His last words, however, I am sure were not the string of invectives they later claimed he had issued, clearly in a feeble attempt to excuse their crime. The accusation attests not only to their ignorance of his language but their utter inability to perceive before them not a nearly defenseless old savage but one of the greatest and wisest of human beings then alive. His culture, which did not even have "swear words," greatly honored the art of eloquent oratory, particularly in a supreme sachem and chief, and especially in the last moments of one's life, when what one said was always remembered and was often strongly visionary.

It is ironic that the murderers got lost after crossing the river—and were guided to safety by Preuwamakan's son. Later, his people secretly carried their beloved sachem's body up into the hills behind my home and buried it in a sacred spot. His death was mourned as far away as the places now called Manhattan and Long Island. Sadly, this great soul today is, at best, a footnote in history. His name survives phonetically garbled into English as "Preymaker," and the stream going over the falls near where his home was is still called Preymaker's Creek today. However, the name "Preuwamakan" is probably a faulty transliteration (there was no "r" sound in his language) of *Peemo-ahk'n*, a very sacred word indeed—the term in his native tongue for the Sacred Stone People's Lodge!

Only seven years before Preuwamakan's death, the Waronawonka and the Dutch agreed to peace terms ratified in the form of a wampum belt still carefully preserved by Ulster County in New York, even though the beads were hardly strung together when the senseless murder of this old sachem and other equally violent acts broke the treaty and sent the beads of amity flying. Sometimes, when I see or hear things late at night in the woods behind my home, I wonder. I am sure his spirit still walks these hills, smoking his pipe, and fishes in the Stony Creek near my house or down along the Esopus. A traditional friend of mine who knows well the spirit of Preuwamakan says rightly that what he and all the ancestor spirits who fill this Earth want is to be *acknowledged* and *respected*, as still present with us. What he, and they, want are the same things they wanted when they walked this Earth: for the Sacred Hoop of All the Nations to be whole, for the Circle of Life to turn freely.

In his old age, Hehaka Sapa (Black Elk) described to John Neihardt the great vision of his youth. As recorded in *Black Elk Speaks* and confirmed in the more accurate *The Sixth Grandfather,* he described how at one point "I saw that the sacred hoop of my people was one of many hoops that made one circle, wide as daylight and as starlight, and in the center grew one mighty flowering tree to shelter all the children of one mother and one father. And," he concluded, echoing G-d's reflection upon completing Heaven and Earth in the Bible, with which he was quite familiar, "I saw that it was holy."

However, Neihardt tells us the old man now looked back on his youthful vision with eyes that could not forget the destruction of his people:

> *I can still see the butchered women and children lying heaped and scattered all along the crooked gulch as plain as when I saw them with eyes still young. And I can see that something else died there in the bloody mud, and was buried in the blizzard. A people's dream died there. It was a beautiful dream. And I, to whom so great a vision was given in my youth—you see me now a pitiful old man who has done nothing, for the nation's hoop is broken and scattered. There is no center any longer, and the sacred tree is dead.*

If Grandfather Black Elk actually said that, and it appears doubtful, then I will boldly say he was wrong. But it is more likely that Neihardt, who was a fine poet, echoed, perhaps consciously, the line "the center cannot hold" from Yeats's famous poem about the end of a civilization, "The Second Coming"—and thus, in his wish to write an emotionally satisfying conclusion, misrepresented Grandfather's wisdom. One cannot blame Neihardt, who loved the Native people and watched with great sorrow their destruction at the hands of his own people. But I believe *Tunkashila*, Grandfather, did not say this, since he knew fully well that there is no death but rather a change of worlds and that, while the power of armies is one thing, there are other far greater powers that this mighty culture is unaware of and cannot control.

Modern people say spirits do not exist or that, even if they do, they are powerless over their machines. But nothing could be further from the truth. For the land and the spirits of the land abide. And they are very powerful *(lela wakan)*, and they are waiting for the right time to act. Indeed, the more they seem to be vanquished, the more powerful—and the more angry—they are becoming. As these powerful spirits are packed into smaller and smaller spaces, as the wilderness and the traditional people's land are more tightly squeezed by the corporate and governmental *washichu*, as the Internet and the *sicha* dreaming of modern people destroy ever more of the Spirit World, as ever fewer people seek to appease these spirits, the more concentrated becomes their energy. Chief Sealth warned in 1854, "At night, when the streets of your cities and villages are silent and you think them deserted, they will throng with the returning hosts that once filled and still love this beautiful land. The white man will never be alone; the dead are not powerless. 'Dead,' did I say? There is no death; only a change of worlds."

When Grandfather Black Elk spoke of his great vision, he did not tell everything. "Even now," he said, "I know that more was shown to me than I can tell." So, while he told of Six Grandfathers, I believe firmly that there was a Seventh Grandfather, even though he did not mention one. The Six Grandfathers represent the six directions: the four compass directions, plus zenith and nadir. The Seventh Grandfather represents the seventh direction, the sacred direction represented by the Center, the direction in which we travel whenever we drop our robe, be it in dream, in vision or at the end of this physical life.

The time has come to talk about the teaching of the Seventh Grandfather. The Earth itself, the entire universe, is Spirit, and she carries as does every individual being the potential of wearing an infinity of different robes. Granted, the dominant culture has forced living beings and the Earth herself into a singleness of identity, but the Earth still carries her infinite power. The change of worlds—the change of cloak—will happen. The Earth, the Great Below and the Great Above, is but a robe for the Creator Spirit. The *washichu* can harm this robe, and even kill it, and they can even affect the Spirit World to a great degree, but they cannot harm the spirits who dwell in it, or the Creator him/herself. With the destruction of this physical Earth nearly complete and the destruction of the Spirit World, which they call virtual reality, well under way, it is soon time for the Creator to act. The Beautiful One promised she would come again when the people needed her most, and the time of the fulfillment of her promise is almost upon us. Aionwantha (Hiawatha) likewise promised to return should his Constitution not last as long as the Earth. And the Earth will shuck off this damaged robe, this ruined land, this soiled Sky, these polluted waters, this mangled Spirit World. The Earth will drop this robe, this enforced singleness of identity with which she and her children have seemingly been enslaved, and She will be set free once again. The world that abides beneath and beyond the superhighways and shopping malls and factories will reassert herself. The sacred beings—the Dragons, the Thunder Beings, the Little People—will return.

"The world will be consumed in fire," William Blake wrote, and, when it is,

> ...*the whole creation will be consumed, and appear infinite, and holy whereas it now appears finite & corrupt. This will come to pass by an improvement of sensual enjoyment. But first the notion that man has a*

body distinct from his soul, is to be expunged...by...melting apparent surfaces away, and displaying the infinite which was hid.

In other words, when the new world reveals herself, we too can and will return to our true nature, if we choose the traditional canoe instead of the washichu boat and shuck off all the shackles that the washichu have burdened us with. When the καιρος (*kairos*), the sacred time, comes, we will if we choose let go of the single-identity cloak of slavery to secular powers and embrace instead our shapeshifting nature and the infinity of our original sacred identity.

According to elders of many nations, including the Apache, Hopi, Lakota, Tsalagi, and Onodowahgah (Seneca), we are coming to the end of the final age. There are similar prophecies in Ezekiel and Zechariah in the Jewish Bible, and in the Revelation to John of Patmos at the end of the New Testament, as well as those told in the Qur'an and other sacred traditions. According to a Vajrayana (Tibetan Buddhist) prophecy, the time of Maïtreya Buddha, the last Buddha, will come when horses run on iron rails and the teaching of Buddha reaches the land of the Red Men.

The Hopi prophecies (written on tablets and hidden in a sacred cave within a mountain) speak of a time when great roads pass like rivers through the land, when people talk to each other through cobwebs (telephone systems), when people travel along roads in the sky, when wars have been fought by armies under the symbol of the bent cross (though sacred to many Native nations, the Nazis bent the swastika the opposite way, turning the Circle of Life into the Circle of Death) and the rising Sun, when people visit the Moon and tamper with the Stars. The end is near, the prophecies say, when the House of Mica in the Lands to the East where world leaders meet to resolve issues and settle disputes ignores three times the message of peace and harmony with Nature (as the United Nations has done) and a "gourd of ashes" is dropped upon the Earth (nuclear war). Soon after that, all land and life could be destroyed—it could happen to this world, just as it happened in a senseless war that engulfed the planet that once swung between Mars and Jupiter—unless human beings remember first how to live in peace with each other and in harmony with Nature.

Elders have told me this future is all but unavoidable—but that that's not necessarily a bad thing. And that, in fact, it might be a bad idea (or at the least wasted effort) to try to stop it from happening. Just as we are taught not to try to heal someone whose time to die has come but only use palliative medicines to make their passing as comfortable as possible, we should do what we can to provide comfort and safety for all nations. We may need to let the *washichu* descend into nuclear war. It will be devastating and many people will unfortunately die (though remember there is no death, only a change of worlds, so they will yet live), but, as in homeopathic medicine, the *débâcle* will cleanse the Earth of all chemical, mental and spiritual pollution. Mainstream modern culture may already be terminally ill; it may already be impossible to change the direction of this juggernaut enough to avoid annihilation, but its worst effects might yet be blunted somewhat. We can prepare for the time that will follow this nuclear winter, so that the teachings of the traditional ways, the descriptive law of how humans properly live, will still be remembered and taught and followed. That is why I must write this book.

The Hodenasaunee (Iroquois) remember the meaning of the Two-Row Wampum—both the agreement it represents with European newcomers, and a famous prophecy, the Two-Minded Generation Prophecy, associated with it. The English word "wampum" comes from *wampompeag* in Narragansett, meaning "white strings." The Kanien'kéha:ka (Mohawk) word is *anakoha*. Contrary to popular belief, wampum is not the Native American equivalent to money. Wampum does have value, however that value is not pecuniary but spiritual. Properly speaking, wampum is *wakan*, which is to say those who carry wampum carry it in a sacred way, remembering what it means. Wampum belts serve as reminders of particular aspects of sacred spiritual teaching. One might say that wampum is a spiritual record of the traditional people. Wampum represents words in the First Language—the language in which every word is the Λογος (*Logos*), an incantation revealing the sacred presence, the language in which it is recognized that all beings have a fluidity of outer form.

There have already been one hundred and forty-four Tadodahos, spiritual leaders of the Hodenasaunee, since the establishment of the Great Law of Peace— exactly twelve times twelve, a very sacred number squared. This is the time spoken of in prophecies, when the Hodenasaunee will be threatened not only by the forces without, the government and the dominant culture, but by greed and dissension within. Now more than ever the traditional peoples must listen to the teachings of the Peacemaker and Handsome Lake, remember their ways and stand in solidarity with each other and all good people who live lives touched by the grace of humility, dignity and respect.

One of the most important things taught to us is recorded in the *Gaswentah* (literally, the River [of Life]), also called the *Tekeni Teiohate* (literally, the Two

Parallel Paths), and known in English as the Two-Row Wampum of the Hodenasaunee. It represents a treaty that was agreed to in 1613 by the Dutch and Hodenasaunee peoples. This wampum specifically describes, in the First Language, how the Hodenasaunee understood the agreement. It shows two parallel rows of purple beads on a field of white beads. These two long lines parallel each other but never touch. They represent a boat and a canoe traveling side by side, but not close, down the same river. The two lines are identical, neither taking precedence or wielding power over the other. The agreement is: "You stay in your vessel on the river and we'll stay in ours." The two peoples agree with this wampum to live side by side in peace and friendship, never interfering with each other. The white background appears as three bands, which represent Peace, Friendship and Forever. This was the agreement, intended to last, so it was said, "for as long as the grass grows and water flows and the Sun shines." The Hodenasaunee still believe in this agreement and hold to their side of the bargain. Like all the hundreds of other treaties made between the Native Americans and the European invaders, it was broken by the latter.

Associated with the wampum, however, is a prophecy that the seventh generation to follow would be known as the Two-Minded Generation. By the time of this generation, the prophecy says, the two cultures will have become so muddled together that the people will have no choice but to try to satisfy the requirements of the dominant culture, and yet also, as much as possible, to live in the traditional sacred ways—often surreptitiously, lest they be ostracized or worse. These people will be, as it were, trying to navigate the river with one foot in the boat and the other foot in the canoe. At the best of times, this would be difficult to do. But during the course of this generation, the prophecy says, there will come a time of great change. When this time comes, these two-minded people must decide whether to stay with the boat or the canoe. On that day a great wind will blow across the river, and the water will become choppy and treacherous. Storms will come, there will be earthquakes and rapids in the river, hurricanes and tornadoes. Try as they may to keep their balance, those who are stretched between the canoe and the boat will fall into the water and drown. Those who are in one vessel or the other will be likelier to survive. This generation will also be, it has been said, the last to live in a way contrary to the teaching of the *Gaswentah*, the Two-Row Wampum.

This Two-Minded Generation, it is us. You and me. It was our parents and grandparents, and it is even more our children and grandchildren. More and more with each succeeding generation since the coming of the Europeans, those who walk the Red Road have also had to walk the mainstream American road. Let's face it, painful though the truth is. Though we all try hard to be traditional in the ways of our people, whichever people they are, though we try to be good to the Earth and the Sky and our fellow living beings, we cannot do it all the time. We are forced to work at a job, we have to pay income tax, we must carry identification. We, more than any preceding generation, have been sucked into the dangers of the *washichu* way. Many of us have turned our heritage into a hobby — something we squeeze into our few hours free from working for the master. Or selling the traditional crafts to the idly curious. Or dressing up in ridiculously over-fancy Native American "costumes" with numbers on our backs to dance at pow-wows. Whether we like it or not, whether we can help it or not, we too are guilty of breaking the spirit of the *Gaswentah* treaty.

It has also been said that the Two-Minded Generation will be the final one to have known the last of the Old Ones, the last of the traditionally raised and trained Grandfathers and Grandmothers. So many elders have dropped their robes in the past few years, and most still alive are very old and often in extremely poor health. I am sure you mourn, as I do, the incredible repository of wisdom that is lost every time one of these elders passes over. Even as I make the final edits to this book, my friend the novelist André Norton has died; she was part Indian by ancestry but fully wise in the heritage, as her stories reflect. Though some try to gather up the crumbs of this wisdom to pass them on to the seventh generation, I am all too painfully aware that it is still so little compared to what is being lost. What I carry is, truly, just a tiny bit of wisdom compared to the great repositories within elders I have known. Yet what if these few crumbs I have gathered together are lost because I didn't share them? No crumb is too small. Like what Spirit said about the prophecy given to me, it is *all* important. From even one leaf, one word, a forest of wisdom can be recovered.

People often mistakenly think that the Two-Row Wampum Prophecy foretells a day when only the Red people will survive and go on. Since all nations are a part of the Sacred Hoop, as is clear in the fact that all four colors are a part of it, there will be people of all four races who will go on. This was the vision of great elders like Hehaka Sapa (Black Elk) and others, and I am sure it is a true vision. But the Two-Minded Generation will drown as surely as the *washichu*, the greedy individuals of all ancestries — unless they choose carefully between the canoe and the boat. That too is a true vision.

My suggestion to you is this: if you cannot completely live in the way of some particular traditional people — not only tribal but also Pagan, Taoist,

Jewish, Muslim, Zoroastrian, Hindu, Buddhist, then at least keep your weight on the foot in the canoe (the traditional way), and be light on the foot in the boat (the way of jobs and bills and taxes). Follow the traditions of your people, whoever they are, as much and as carefully as you can, and try not to get too heavily involved in *washichu* ways—greed, destructiveness, imbalance.

Washichu may be a cultural disease most common among people of European ancestry, but the original ways of European ancestors are healthy and good, and individuals are not bound or fated by ancestry to a certain path—they can still choose the path they walk. And be ready, when the time comes, to get to a safe sacred place.

One last story, told to me by a Tsalagi (Cherokee) elder:

A boy decided he was going to trick the elders and show how foolish they could be. So he captured a baby bird and held it tightly cupped between his hands. His plan was to go in to the elders and say, "There is a bird in my hands. Is it alive or is it dead?" If they said "alive," he would quickly crush the tiny bird between his palms and show them the dead creature. If they said "dead," he would open his hands and show it to them unharmed.

So the boy went in to the elders and said to them, "There is a bird in my hands. Is it alive or is it dead?"

And the elders looked at him and replied, "It is as you choose."

The future will be as we choose. That's what the ancestors tell the present generation. Like the two brothers, humanity today must decide whether to possess the world as *washte*, or run away from it as *wakan*, or bring to all people the message that it is both, and love and respect the World and all Her children.

The generations to follow us will be unlike us, the Two-Minded Generation. They will not be stretched between two boats in the River of Life. They will know who they are. They will learn from us what the last of the Old Ones taught, but they will not make the terrible mistakes in life so many of us have made, to our shame. They will not say one religion or ancestry is better than another. They will not blindly insist on one or another way of doing things. Rather, they will live fully as traditional people, in complete harmony with each other and all living beings.

How can this be? Because they will see the dawning of the new world. They will follow the four-leggeds to safety when the time comes. And they will live in Grandmother Earth following her renewal.

Perhaps you say, "Not in my lifetime." But, as for me, I want to see this day come. I want to see the Sacred Hoop of All the Nations come together again, whole and perfect. Whenever we say "Not in my lifetime," just that very thought pushes the day farther away—or, to put it another way, the very thought makes it harder for us to see it when the day does come. We make our own reality: if we believe or fear it won't come, it won't come, or at least not for us or not as quickly. But, if we yearn for it to come and do our part to help it come, it will come more quickly.

Ironically, the Two-Minded Generation is the most vital link, and yet the weakest link. We are the ones to pass on the precious wisdom from the seven generations past in the West through the darkness of the North and on to the seven generations to come in the East, and yet we are the ones most confused and tired by trying to stand in two vessels, the ones most polluted by the *washichu* way. It is for us to pass on the best of the past in the teachings of the Old Ones, but it is for us to let die with ourselves the worst of the past, lest the broken, unbalanced *washichu* side of our natures plant a seed of *sicha* in the world to come.

These New Ones will live in a world I may never fully see, though I greatly desire to see it. Yet I can see that world now, reflected in their eyes. In their lifetime, sooner than we dare expect, the long-prophesied changes will come. In their lifetime Grandmother Earth will be renewed, and they shall live in the Promised Land. The old medicine men and women say that at the end of this age, the Fourth Age, *Wohpe*, the Falling Star, the White Buffalo Calf Woman, the Corn Woman, the Sky Woman, will come again. Though many express hope whenever a white buffalo calf is born in captivity on someone's farm (does no one see the irony?), it is actually the falling star, the Great Meteor that will presage her coming. She will not come from any of the six physical directions, but from the Seventh Direction, the direction of Spirit, from the Seventh Grandfather! And, when she comes, the world will shake off the *washichu* constructs—just as an animal shakes off irritating insects to be rid of them. The entire Earth, so filled with *sicha* now, will be *wakan* again. The forests and the grasslands will reappear. Good people (of whatever ancestry) will survive. The sacred mountain will open, and the buffalo will lead the good ones through to a sacred beautiful land, the land where *Wohpe*, who brought us the Sacred Pipe, awaits.

And what should we do in the meanwhile, as we prepare for the difficult times coming? We should learn the traditional ways and practice them, as best we can. We should scatter them, like good seed on good earth, among souls who will nourish them. We should carry them with care, gathering them up and preserving them, as for a long winter, bearing in mind the seventh generation to come, the Earth and all living things.

The Talmud of Judaism teaches (in *Yalkut Shim'oni*): "G-d formed Adam of dust from *all over* the world: yellow clay and white sand, black loam and red soil, so that the Earth can declare to no race or color of humanity that they do not belong here, that this soil is not their home." In the Acts of the Apostles, Peter the disciple of Jesus declares, "I truly know that G-d pays no attention to your face [i.e., race], but in every nation those who fear G-d and do what is right are acceptable to G-d." The Prophet Muhammed, on whom let there be peace, is remembered for standing in respect one day as a funeral went by; according to the *Hadith*, when his disciples asked if he realized the deceased was a Jew, he replied, "Was he not a living spirit?" Lord Krishna says to Arjuna in the Bhagavad-Gità, "Many are the paths of humanity, but they all in the end come to me." The Creator created us all, and not only humans, but all living things.

As Leon Shenandoah, the incredibly wise late Tadodaho Chief of the Hodenasaunee, taught, "Every human being has a sacred duty to protect the welfare of our Mother Earth, from whom all life comes....We must abide by the Natural Law or be victim of its ultimate reality. We must stand together, the four sacred colors of man as the one family that we are in the interest of peace."

Just this morning I picked up a huge old turtle trying to cross a country road and brought him to safety down near the Esopus Creek. He reminded me that we are all responsible for the safety of Turtle Island and all her children. I managed to halt a couple of impatient drivers who otherwise would have crushed this elder without a thought. However, turtles live long lives—not just for decades, but possibly even centuries. If not this wise one himself, then surely one of his ancestors walked the same path he was taking today on a day when the great sachem Preuwamakan was fishing nearby in the Esopus.

As I carried him to safety, I felt this elder's weight deeply. I felt his powerful rear limbs thrusting into my stomach. My nostrils expanded with the overwhelming scent of earth and marshy water coming from this aged one. I saw the rich black of the sky-shaped carapace, the mighty foreclaws, the sharp, intelligent eyes looking back at me. I saw dried mud on his shell and thought of the Kanien'kéha:ka (Mohawk) story of mud spread on the primæval

Turtle's shell for the first woman, Iotsitsisen, to live upon. I felt deeply the truth that we humans are but the youngest and most foolish of the Earth's children, yet we are no less obliged to ensure her survival. As I was carrying this elder to safety, I was conscious of being given a great gift of wisdom to carry as well. As I come to the end of the thirteenth and last chapter of this book, the thirteenth plate on the turtle's shell, the thirteenth moon in the shell of the sky, I am particularly conscious of the weight I carry. I place it, like the great turtle, safely on the Earth. Caring for every living being, and carrying the sacred wisdom, is my responsibility in every moment. And yours too.

The Creator demands truth within our heart so that truth flows naturally through all our words and actions. The Creator doesn't demand perfection—which is an impossible goal—but simply a sincere and assiduous walking-forward on the path. Becoming part of a church or sangha or synagogue or masjid or ashram or gurdwara, or even going to a Sacred Stone People's Lodge, isn't the point. Go into the lodge or not, as you wish; it's just a ceremony like any other. None of these things is really important.

What *is* important is to remember what the ancient turtle taught me, that not only does the Earth carry us, but each of us carries the Earth.

What *is* important is being truthful, honorable, and good in your mind, soul and body—being moderate in all things, including moderation, keeping your promises, and burying all weapons, physical and verbal, beneath the Tree of Peace.

What *is* important is being an optimist: believing that the world will be at peace, with each soul loving all other souls, even if some souls have gotten a little confused on this point.

What *is* important is showing respect to all beings—being accepting of differences, and being generous in the act of giving and forgiving, neither taking without permission nor taking without giving back, and never giving without accepting what is generously offered in balance. "Love your neighbor as yourself."

What *is* important is walking with the flow of creation, and not twisting nature to our own needs.

What *is* important is the way of the Sacred Pipe, in whatever spirituality we honor that way, which is simply to pray not for ourselves alone but with and for all living beings—to pray honestly and simply and directly, and keep the promises we make in prayer. Always to say "please" to our sister and brother creatures and always to say "thank you" to the Creator.

What *is* important is not to be possessive, even of our very selves, but to give ourselves to others, to shapeshift, to take on the new robe of sacred identity we all carry within us. To be courageous, to walk through our fear of the unknown, and into the sacred new world that awaits.

These are the things that the Creator asks of us. Do these things and you are no longer a "stranger in a strange land"; you are at home!—a child of this Earth our Mother, a child of this Sky our Father. His daughter, the Sky Woman, the Beautiful Woman, is coming soon. Aionwantha is coming soon as well. The Sacred Hoop of All the Nations can be mended. It must be mended. It *will* be mended. We human beings and every member of every nation must and will take our place in it, and help all others to do the same.

Know the Creator's love is with you, for the Creator makes you new in every moment, and in every moment gives you a chance to make better choices. Know that likewise the Creator's love is with all living things, so we should all love each other.

My gratitude remains with you for your listening to me all this while. My prayer is that you will put this book down now, and turn from learning to doing, and never rest until the sacred vision comes true. The path begins within your heart and soul and flows from that wellspring out into the Earth, beginning right beneath your feet. Anywhere you walk, the path is before you. It is a pathless path, and it will lead you directly into the *wakan*, and the sacred new world that awaits. Walk it with a brave heart.

This is how I have been taught, and this is all that I have been taught. I have nothing else to say. I thank the Creator and the spirits, the Grandfathers and the Grandmothers for all the beautiful miracles in my life. I ask them to forgive me for my stupidity and foolishness and selfishness, and to accept my small voice and my words and my very life as my gift—the only gift that is truly mine to give. I pray that these words may help in some small way to bring the Circle of Life back together as one.

Hau, mitaquye oyashin!
Nia:wen skenno ko:wa!

Afterword

Hᴇʀᴇ ɪs ᴀ sᴛᴏʀʏ told by the spirit people:

In the long ago, it was very dark at night, even darker than it is now. The animal nations met together to discuss what to do. After much conversation they decided to lift the reflection of the Moon from the still pool in the middle of the forest, so they could each carry a little bit of it around with them.

When the night of the Full Moon came, each of the animal nations sent an emissary, one by one, out into the waters. Several sky dwellers— Eagle, Hawk, nimble-footed Owl—tried to pick up the shining disc, but when they approached the water's surface, their shadows blotted out the moon's reflection. Wise old Fish himself made several attempts, but he was not able to reach the surface from his watery home. The Spirit Beings floated as a group across the water, but even together their nature was too insubstantial to raise the shining silvery shield of the Moon. Some land dwellers also tried—Bear, wily Coyote, even agile Raccoon—but all of them, no matter how gently they moved forward, broke through the waters and sent out little waves that shattered and splintered the shining light. Not one was able even to come near the radiant image on the waters before it was obliterated by their approach.

Only Grandmother Spider was left. She stepped out carefully onto the surface of the pool, causing not even the slightest ripple, seeming hardly to touch the surface with her delicate tiny feet. Watching as she approached, the other creatures were scarcely breathing, amazed to see the face of the Moon in the water remaining whole. Then they saw the silhouette of Spider step carefully onto the Moon's reflection, just as if she were walking on the Moon herself—just as they had seen the Eagle or the Owl sometimes soar in front of the Moon's face, way up in the Sky.

Once Grandmother Spider reached her destination, she wove a delicate web, put the light of the Moon in it and brought it back to land with her. Once on the shore, she placed a little bit of this light into the eyes of every creature to help them find their way through the darkness. But, even

after her web was empty, some Moonlight still clung to its delicate strands.
This is why, to this day, spiderwebs shine at night with the dewy radiance
of the Moon, even when She is not in the heavens above.

There are many words in this book, but I humbly pray that my words step as lightly across the waters as did Grandmother Spider. Too often these days, words insist on drawing attention to themselves rather than quietly pointing the way toward eternal, wordless truth and falling into silence in the face of that truth. In today's society we tend to overuse words the same way we do herbs and spices—to the point that the magic in the words is squandered and bereft of its full *wakan* power. People are drowning in a sea of words: political speeches, trashy novels, junk mail, the constant chatter of radio and television, and now spam e-mail, each trying to outshout the others. Shakespeare said rightly of all this coercive clamor for our attention that:

> *...it is a tale*
> *Told by an idiot, full of sound and fury,*
> *Signifying nothing.*

In his novel *House Made of Dawn*, N. Scott Momaday mentions how in one of the most sacred stories of Christianity, the Word, the Λογος (*Logos*), calls all things into creation. He goes on to prophesy that people will also perish by the Word. He may well be right; in grotesque parody of the sacred act of the Λογος (*Logos*), some people use words to create falsehood and to destroy goodness. As Daniel Boorstin brilliantly said in *The Image*, the art most acclaimed today is not truth-telling but spinning beautiful lies that are easy and comforting to believe and that successfully distract us from the painful truths we would rather ignore. Politicians, clergy and advertisers alike bombard the people with cynical duplicity, repeating the same words over and over until the people give up the fight to maintain the truth and settle for the lie. Powerful word merchants turn language into mere noise with but one level of meaning (and sometimes no genuine meaning at all), with the purpose of effecting control over a population. In varying contexts, they replace poetry with precision, meaning with value, story with affidavit, and loving covenant with mistrustful contract. Words are also used to judge and condemn—to decide the fate of the powerless in the operating room, the council room, the war room and the courtroom.

I do not want this book to be turned out as one more piece of noise, one more whine screaming for the attention of a jaded public. It is my intention that the words in this book walk delicately across the water of truth, as delicately as did Grandmother Spider, and fall to silence in the face of the Sacred. It is also my intention to honor the silence itself.

People today all too often see silence and speech as opposites, while the traditional peoples worldwide know that these are not opposites—that silence includes the Word and that the Word is a form of silence. That is why there is meaning in silence, as the elder taught us when he held the Sacred Talking Stick without saying a word. That is why there are moments of thrilling silence in stories, why the night is silent, why the wilderness is silent. Those who keep the traditional ways know that spoken words can carry a little glint of moonlight—a tiny sliver of the silent Word, the exhaled breath, the divine Name of G-d spoken in the beginning that echoes still in everything that exists.

Let us reclaim the Sacred, which is most powerfully present not in human words or society, but in the wilderness and in the natural rhythms of life. When Jesus spoke of faith the size of a mustard seed, there were mustard bushes growing nearby. When he spoke of sheep and shepherds, the hills around him were dotted with them. When he spoke of the fields being white with the harvest, they were. When the early Christians baptized, they did so in natural, wild settings, going naked and vulnerable into the roaring cataract of water. Most modern Christians, however, are familiar with mustard as only a yellow conglomeration of artificial ingredients inside a squirt bottle, with sheep as only in pretty pictures accompanying a nursery rhyme or as depressed creatures at petting zoos, of baptism as tapwater in a basin or at best a convenient artificial pool behind the communion table. It is no wonder that these people see the wilderness not as the very wellspring of their and every faith, but as an impediment, a chaos to be subdued.

Instead, we should walk with care in the wilderness, listening to the silent Word being spoken all around us. If possible, we should walk barefoot, like Moses, or with our feet clad in moccasins so we can feel the earth beneath our feet; we would be less likely to snap twigs as we walk and make harsh noise with our footsteps. We should wear as little as possible, avoiding modern constricting artificial garments that are as asphyxiating and sense-blinding as the whalebone corsets and vests of old. If we let our hair grow long and hang free, it, like the whiskers of the catamount and mountain lion, can help us sense better everything around us—the living beings and the spirits—increasing our extended awareness and enabling us to see in all directions, even with our eyes shut. And we should realize that the natural world is a sacred text written by the Creator in the First Language. We should take care not to brush away spiderwebs, which are words in that language. We should watch the movement of birds and fish, and read the footprints of deer in soft ground, and see how all natural events form letters and words in that original tongue.

When we enter the wilderness, we must do so with care and respect, mindful that what is *washte* to us is *wakan* or *sicha* to much of the natural world, and what is *washte* in nature is *wakan* to us. For example, within a bear's cave, the odor of Bear, which is the very aroma of "home" to the cave's resident, signifies *washte* for the bear. For us the same odor is the overpowering scent of the *wakan*. Thus we enter only with permission, humility and respect, and only if we must. The same is true in an eagle's eyrie, a spider's web, a snake's hole, a fish's dark cave, a ghost's haunt and so on. We know, by the intense sensation of Other, that we are in the presence of the *wakan*. These creatures are to us *wakan*, which in this context means they do not want to have anything to do with us. They do not want us anywhere near their homes—and, indeed, for the most part they show us the same respect. We rarely, if ever, see them enter our cities or our houses, which to them are filled with the stench of human habitation and likewise for them are *wakan* and therefore off-limits. They stay away except in rare instances of dire desperation, warning, or abject captivity—or when forced out of their own homes by natural or human-made disasters .

We should remember that the First Language allows no lies. Human languages have different words for the entity in the tree that appears first as an owl and then as a clump of leaves, because these languages concentrate on outer, physical reality. But in the First Language, which concentrates on essential nature not outer differences, the entity in the tree is described with one word—a word that fully describes the entity in all its infinity of potential robes—indeed, this word *is* the entity.

The Word is the truth. Traditional cultures understand this concept instinctively, while newcomers seem to require labels, which tend to separate persons from direct experience of the objects so labelled. In the same manner, they seek to separate body and spirit. The *washichu* are the victims of this separation: normally death separates the soul from the body, but these people are already divided. As a result, they are unable fully to integrate spirit and body as the Creator had intended. Thus, too, they are unable to shapechange. Even familiar shapechanging, such as the bodily changes during sexual activity or reproduction, necessitates some degree of spirit-body integration. One cannot will arousal or pregnancy or gestation; in fact, these states typically happen unexpectedly, as is the way with the *wakan*. With the spirit and body fully integrated, one realizes that one is not a discrete entity—not, as John Donne said, an "Iland entire of itselfe"—but ultimately united body and soul with all one's fellow beings, united with the circle of life.

In the *Hadith*, Abu Huraira tells a story told by the Prophet Muhammed:

> *A man walking along a deserted road found himself very thirsty. When he found a well, he climbed down and drank and then came back up again. Near the entrance to the well he found a dog panting and almost eating soil out of thirst. The man thought, "This dog must be just as thirsty as I was." So he went down into the well again, filled his shoe with water, climbed back up again and gave it to the dog. G-d was thankful to the man and forgave him all his sins.*

According to Abu Huraira, the Prophet's hearers then asked him, "O Messenger of G-d, do we get a reward, then, even for helping animals?" And the Prophet replied, "There is a reward in helping any living creature."

Expressing this point another way, let us never forget Preuwamakan's warning to his own murderers: "Like you, your descendants will lose themselves in their own greed and prejudice, and destroy what they most need." Remember the irony, these murderers became lost right after killing the old man and forced his son to guide them to safety. The cultural descendants of these criminals still murder today—sometimes with a swift stroke but more often with the weight of greed and a culture of prejudice—those who carry Spirit.

And remember this too: It is the newcomers who came to this continent and said, "The earth belongs to us." Traditional peoples worldwide say, rather, "We belong to the Earth." How can we quarrel about ownership over a Mother Earth who is very much alive? How can we hurt and destroy our own family, her children? We cannot if we are reasonable. And we must not if we, and all Her children, are to continue into future generations. I pray that, when my body is given back to my Mother the Earth and my soul soars among the stars, I will have become what the Creator intended me to become, and I will have done all that I can do to place sacred light in the eyes of my brothers and sisters.

Acknowledgments

MOST OF THE STORIES HEREIN have been told before; some of them in fact are very old, and I have done my best to relate them in a way reminiscent of a storyteller speaking aloud. A few of the stories I am the first one to tell, at least the first still wearing a robe (body).

Personal conversations from years ago are reconstructed from memory, and identifiable details about individuals have been avoided to protect their privacy.

The title of this book was given through a dream that came to me in 1996.

With humble appreciation of their great kindness I would like to list those who critically read the manuscript at various stages of completion, in many cases offering profound thoughts, which I have gratefully and respectfully included. They include, alphabetically, Jody Abbott (Munsee); Aziz Ahsan, J. D.; Saba Ali; my daughter-by-honor Woman of the Wind (Odessa Arceri, Apache-Cherokee); my sister-by-honor Brightstar (Joyce Keeler, Diné); Elga and Bill Brown; Rabbi Jonathan Case; Donna Coane (Mohawk-Blackfoot); Trudi DeCicco (Lakota); Airy Dixon (Tutelo-Saponi); Doug George-Kanentiio (Mohawk); Tim Giago (Lakota); my daughter-by-honor Shammara Humphrey (Cherokee); Mona Keebler; Tom Lake; the Rev. Nickolas M. Miles (Powhatan); Moof (Dog Nation); my brother-by-honor Otter (Doug Lister); Rebecca Rothbaum; Sings-Alone (C. W. Duncan, Ph.D., Cherokee); Prof. Harvey Sprung; my sister-by-honor Karen Stortz (Cherokee); the Rev. Alfred R. Twyman, Jr.; Gabriel Wasserman; and Henrietta Wise (of an unknown Native American ancestry).

Considerable gratitude also goes to Harmon Houghton and Marcia Keegan of Clear Light Publishers for their joyful and deeply spiritual nature, their sincere and indefatigable lifelong commitment to doing what they can for this Earth, and their strong desire to present this book as it should be presented. Thanks also to Sara Held and Carol O'Shea of Clear Light for their sensitive, supportive work editing the manuscript. Deep gratefulness to Jody Abbott for beautiful and powerful drawings that proceeded directly from Spirit through her generous heart and wise soul onto the paper on which she drew—and to her magnificent husband Fred Steuding for proudly bearing the amount of time she had to devote to these renderings. And, most of all, to everyone with whom I live, of both two and four legs, for not complaining (much) when my nose was once again buried in writing instead of attending to them, and especially to the Beloved One who is by my side in this walk on the Circle of Life.

Selected Bibliography

The following texts were either consulted during the writing of this book or are prominently quoted from or referred to herein:

Black Elk. *Black Elk Speaks.* As told through John G. Neihardt. Lincoln: University of Nebraska Press, 1979. Reprint of first edition, 1932.

_____. *The Sacred Pipe.* Recorded by Joseph Epes Brown. Norman: University of Oklahoma Press, 1953.

_____. *The Sixth Grandfather: Black Elk's Teachings Given to John G. Neihardt.* Edited by Raymond J. DeMallie. Lincoln: University of Nebraska Press, 1984.

Boatman, John. *My Elders Taught Me: Aspects of Western Great Lakes American Indian Philosophy.* Lanham, Maryland: University Press of America, 1992.

Bourgault, Luc (Aigle Bleu). *L'héritage sacré des peuples amérindiens: La spiritualité autochthone.* Boucherville, Québec: Mortagne, 1985.

_____. *Le cristal en thérapie: L'humain et le règne minéral dans la tradition amérindienne.* Laval, Québec: Guy Saint-Jean, 1992.

Brown, Joseph Epes. *The Spiritual Legacy of the American Indian.* New York: Crossroad, 1982.

Cajete, Gregory. *Native Science: Natural Laws of Interdependence.* Santa Fe: Clear Light, 2000. An impressive essay comparing Native American and Western scientific philosophies and methods.

Catches, Sr., Pete S. *Sacred Fireplace (Oceti Wakan).* Santa Fe: Clear Light, 1999.

Cogan, Priscilla. *Winona's Web: A Novel of Discovery.* Hopkinton, Mass.: Two Canoes Press, 1996.

_____. *Compass of the Heart: A Novel of Discovery.* New York: Simon & Schuster, 1998.

_____. *Crack at Dusk: Crook of Dawn: A Novel of Discovery.* Hopkinton, Mass.: Two Canoes Press, 2000.

Deloria, Jr., Vine. *God is Red.* New York: Grosset & Dunlap, 1973.

Eastman, Charles A. (Ohiyesa). *The Soul of the Indian: An Interpretation.* Lincoln: University of Nebraska Press, 1995. Reprint of Boston: Houghton Mifflin, 1911.

George-Kanentiio, Doug. *Iroquois Culture & Commentary.* Santa Fe: Clear Light, 2000. A magnificent introduction to the heritage of the Hodenasaunee.

Lame Deer (John Fire) and Richard Erdoes. *Lame Deer: Seeker of Visions.* New York: Washington Square Press, 1994.

Martin, Calvin Luther. *The Way of the Human Being.* New York and London: Yale University Press, 1999. An autobiographical meditation on the traditional peoples' understanding of place, time, story and spirituality.

Morton, Edward D. *To Touch the Wind: An Introduction to Native American Philosophy and Beliefs.* Dubuque: Kendall/Hunt, 1988.

Nabokov, Peter. *A Forest of Time: American Indian Ways of History*. Cambridge: Cambridge University Press, 2002. Brilliantly contrasts not only how Euro-Americans and Native Americans record history, but how they understand it.

Pritchard, Evan. *No Word for Time*. Tulsa: Council Oak, 1997, revised edition 2001. Traditional Algonquian teaching.

Rolling Thunder. *Rolling Thunder Speaks: A Message for Turtle Island*. Edited by Carmen Sun Rising Pope. Santa Fe: Clear Light, 1999.

Sandoz, Mari. *These Were the Sioux*. Lincoln: University of Nebraska Press, 1985.

Seung Sahn. *Dropping Ashes on the Buddha*. Edited by Stephen Mitchell. New York: Grove, 1976. Teachings of my Zen Master, Seung Sahn.

Sings-Alone, Grandfather Duncan. *Sprinting Backwards to God*. Hopkinton, Mass.: Two Canoes Press, 2000.

Standing Bear, Luther. *My People, the Sioux*. Lincoln: University of Nebraska Press, 1975. Reprint of Boston: Houghton Mifflin, 1928.

Starfire, Manx. *Wild Ways: The Path to Wild Magick*. An as-yet-unpublished book about Wild Magick and our connections to the Earth, often closely paralleling Native American teaching.

Tedlock, Dennis and Barbara, eds. *Teachings from the American Earth: Indian Religion and Philosophy*. New York: Liveright, 1979.

Tooker, Elisabeth, ed. *Native North American Spirituality of the Eastern Woodlands*. New York: Paulist Press, 1979.

Underhill, Ruth M. *Red Man's Religion: Beliefs and Practices of the Indians North of Mexico*. Chicago: University of Chicago Press, 1965. Some useful ethnology somewhat marred by social Darwinist analyses.

Walker, James R. *Lakota Belief and Ritual*. Edited by. Raymond J. DeMallie and Elaine A. Jahner. Lincoln: University of Nebraska Press, 1980.

Weltfish, Gene. *The Lost Universe: Pawnee Life and Culture*. Lincoln: University of Nebraska Press, 1965.

Whorf, Benjamin Lee. *Language, Thought, and Reality*. Boston: MIT Press, 1956. A significant anthropological text that compares the Native way of expressing thought to that of the newcomers.

Young, William A. *Quest for Harmony: Native American Spiritual Traditions*. New York: Seven Bridges, 2002.

Zuesse, Evan. *Ritual Cosmos: The Sanctification of Life in African Religions*. Athens, Ohio: Ohio University Press, 1979. Provides some useful ways for considering traditional tribal spirituality.

Index

About the Illustrations

WHEN DISTANT EAGLE ASKED if I might be interested in illustrating this book, I was working on a drawing of the wampum belt given in 1658 to Peter Stuyvesant, Governor of the New Netherlands, by the sachems of the Waronawonka (Munsee) Nation at Atharacton, now Kingston, New York. The belt was a "present" to Stuyvesant, to bind the covenant of peace between the natives and the newcomers. It was, and still is, a physical symbol of that covenant.

I was moved to realize that, at the same time as I was drawing the wampum belt, Distant Eagle was writing about it. Now that I have read and twice reread the book, I realize how much it is kin to what I have sought to do. Most of the time, when I am asked to illustrate a book, I read it and draw what I think the author is trying to say. But the unfolding of this book has been similar to the art of drawing—Distant Eagle, in writing it, has spent time enough with sacred matters to go beneath their surface and learn their story and teaching, just as I seek to do in my art.

That is what called me to draw this belt and other sacred objects and artifacts of Turtle Island. These objects symbolically tell us something, a message from our ancestors. They also impart symbolic meanings to us, enhancing our connectedness to all other beings of our Mother Earth. I do not question the objects or images given to me to draw, but rather I pray that they may enhance this book and embody the essence of the Creator and spirit helpers who have helped me and given them to me. This is the message of *Circle of Life*, that these sacred things speak to all people.

I am thankful to the Creator for all things, including the opportunity to work with Distant Eagle, a man of humble kindness and integrity, and for the Great Mystery, whence my inspiration comes.

Anishi (I am thankful).

Jody Abbott

List of Illustrations

All line drawings by Jody Abbott

Hau, mitaquye oyashin!